All-Age Lectionary Services

Year A

All-Age Lectionary Services

Year A

Resources for all-age worship

Copyright © Scripture Union 2010

ISBN 978 1 84427 504 5

Scripture Union England and Wales

207-209 Queensway, Bletchley, Milton Keynes, MK2 2EB, England

Email: info@scriptureunion.org.uk

Website: www.scriptureunion.org.uk

Scripture Union Australia

Locked Bag 2, Central Coast Business Centre, NSW 2252

Website: www.scriptureunion.org.au

Scripture Union USA

PO Box 987, Valley Forge, PA 19482

Website: www.scriptureunion.org

British Library Cataloguing-in-Publication Data: a catalogue record of this book is available from the British Library

Printed and bound in India by Thomson Press India Ltd

Cover design: Grax Design

Internal design: Helen Jones

Typesetting: Richard Jefferson, Author and Publisher Services

Scripture Union is an international Christian charity working with churches in more than 130 countries, providing resources to bring the good news about Jesus Christ to children, young people and families and to encourage them to develop spiritually through the Bible and prayer.

As well as our network of volunteers, staff and associates who run holidays, church-based events and school Christian groups, we produce a wide range of publications and support those who use our resources through training programmes.

Foreword from the
Archbishop of York

I am delighted to have been asked to write the foreword for this new book by Scripture Union, aimed at equipping church leaders to communicate effectively the Bible to children, young people and adults in an all-age context.

Many of you will already be familiar with the *Light for the Lectionary* series and how helpful this has been for churches in enabling them to discuss interesting and challenging issues with people of all ages and worship God together. I am sure that this *All-Age Lectionary Services Year A – Resources for All-Age Worship* will be another useful tool.

Some say that young people are the leaders of tomorrow, but they are not – they are the leaders and our hope for today. This book helps recognise that young people in our churches can engage with a wide variety of important issues – if we only approach them in the right way.

All-Age Lectionary Services Year A – Resources for All-Age Worship focuses on the importance of doing the following together: studying the Scriptures, being reflective, being prayerful and being active, but most of all the need to be joyful in our faith. I hope that you will enjoy using this resource in your churches and that it will assist whole congregations of all ages to worship God together!

May the Holy Spirit help you to hear, learn, mark and be fired up as you study the Scriptures and listen to the voice of your young people.

+ Sentamu Ebor

Contents

Leading all-age worship

Leading all-age worship that is focused around the Lectionary is a privilege, as leaders introduce God to people of all ages, of various abilities, learning styles, spiritual maturity and backgrounds.

In Scripture Union, we believe that the ministry of all-age services is vitally important for the following reasons:

- children and young people benefit because they experience what it means to be part of God's new community, as everyone contributes, learns and worships together. (Children build relationships with a much wider range of people than would normally be possible in contemporary society. It is easier for them to have a go, make a mistake and try again. Their gifts and skills also help adults grow in their faith. Their opinion and wisdom matter, since God cares for us all as unique individuals. We can all know him and experience his love.)

- adults benefit as they learn from children and young people, often with a greater variety of approaches than are usually on offer. (All-age services are not an opportunity for Sunday group leaders or people with no responsibility for children to have a Sunday off. Relationships can be developed in additional ways and on different levels.)

- visitors or people on the fringe often feel more comfortable because fewer assumptions are made of them. (It should be OK to just sit and watch. Often churches offer an all-age service at festival times, welcoming to all, free from jargon and appropriate.)

- people with a variety of learning styles and abilities benefit because the interactivity and creativity in evidence in all-age worship require a variety of approaches and responses.

- the team that leads all-age services benefits because the components to a service call for a variety of gifts, encouraging people to take risks, grow in maturity and enjoy being part of a team.

- the church is making a statement about the nature of 'church' – everyone matters, all can know and belong to God, all can be included and all can contribute, whatever their age, ability or spiritual maturity. (All-age services however messy they may be are one of the most exciting opportunities for church leaders to nurture faith, from any starting point.)

All-age services could be one of three different styles of a meal. All have value but which do you find the most satisfying? Which of these styles best suits your church?

Type of meal	What motivates this choice?	How it is consumed	What's good	What's not so good	How to describe
Soup only	the cook - wants a quick, easy meal	easily digestible	satisfying on a cold day	everyone eats the same whatever their needs or preferences	everything together and comfortable
Buffet meal	the diner - eats whatever takes their fancy	at least one dish for everyone	tasty with variety	not necessarily well-balanced	join in when you want to
Three-course meal	the cook - promotes healthy eating, adventurous new dishes	eat in order: starter main course dessert	variety, guarantees nurture	hard work for the cook	balanced and nourishing long-term

- How do you make decisions about what happens in your all-age services?
  - ☐ Whatever is easiest
  - ☐ What you have always done
  - ☐ What church members want
  - ☐ What visiting parents and carers want
  - ☐ What the leadership perceives people need spiritually
  - ☐ Who is available at any one time
  - ☐ Other

- What are the good things about your all-age services?
  - ☐ They make the majority of people happy
  - ☐ Children and young people enjoy them
  - ☐ Provide choice
  - ☐ A Sunday off for Sunday group leaders
  - ☐ Encourage spiritual growth
  - ☐ Reach out to those on the fringe
  - ☐ Enable people to grow their gifts
  - ☐ Other

The service outlines in this book assume that the leaders of all-age services are committed to the spiritual growth of everyone present and that ideally every activity should be relevant to some degree for everyone. We have to be honest - this is not always possible, but that at least is the aim.

The congregation may include people with disabilities or poor eyesight, those who find reading a challenge, those with strong views on music, the very young or the outsider. In trying to include one group of people, you may connect with several others. For example, using a variety of approaches to learning, those with reading difficulties may feel catered for. As very young children worship with adults who are welcoming, trustworthy and joyful, they will be experiencing something of who God is. The Scripture Union website provides an especially wide range of options for younger children. The *Big Bible Storybook* and the *Tiddlywinks* material, both from SU, are also invaluable resources for this age group.

May God continue to bless you in this vital ministry!

Ro Willoughby
All-age editor

These service outlines were originally published by Scripture Union as the first editions of *Light for the Lectionary*. They have been fully revised with a significant amount of new material added or available online. In particular, there is more Bible engagement and the services have been updated.

What's in All-Age Lectionary Services Year A?

ACTIVITIES

Bible foundations: a guide to the issues involved in at least two of the set passages for the day plus background information.

Bible reading: suggestions for preparing and presenting the reading of the Bible to the congregation.

Bible retelling: ideas for drama, storytelling and other suggestions for alternative ways of presenting the Bible passage.

Bible talk: engaging ways to share the Bible and discover the message for today in a mixed-age congregation.

Beginning the service and **Ending the service:** a recognition of how important these are in holding a service together.

Prayer activity: creative ideas for praying in response to the message of the Bible.

Prayers of intercession: suggestions for talking with God on behalf of our world in need.

Prayer of confession: a guide not only to recognising our need of God's forgiveness, but also asking for forgiveness and cleansing.

Helpful extras: a number of additional features including **Music and song ideas**. **Game** and **Statement of faith** and download suggestions.

Notes and comments: further advice or background information on adapting the material for your purposes.

WRITERS

Andy Bell, Sarah Bingham, Jacqueline Bull, Andrew Clark, Sue Clutterham, Michael Dawson, Andy Evans, Marjory Frances, Ian Gooding, Andy Gray, John Grayston, Lizzie Green, Nick Harding, Darren Hill, Gill Hollis, Nigel Hopper, Piers Lane, Mike Law, Eric Leese, Joel Lewis, John Marshall, Tim Norwood, Amy Robinson, Sarah Rumble, Hil Sewell, Matt Stone, 'Tricia Williams, Robert Willoughby, Ruth Wills

WEBSITE

Free downloadable additional resources are available from www.scriptureunion.org.uk/lightdownloads. Other resources are also available on www.lightlive.org.

ADVENT SUNDAY

READINGS: **Romans 13:11–14; Matthew 24:36–44**
Isaiah 2:1–5; Psalm 122:1–9

Bible foundations

Aim: to encourage one another to get ready for Jesus' return

Matthew 24:36–44 could be summarised into three points: no one knows when
Jesus will return (verse 36); as a result, some people will be caught unawares (verses
37–41); disciples must always be ready (verses 42–44). Matthew then gives plenty of
examples to illustrate his points – people at the time of the flood, people getting on
with the routines of life and households when a burglar breaks in. It would suggest
that everyone should hover over the starting blocks waiting for the starter's gun.
Such an attitude would be utterly exhausting. The later verses in the chapter would
suggest that it is more a case of living normal life in a way that is pleasing to God.
(Do ensure that these dramatic verses are not presented in a way that could cause
alarm to younger children!)

Psalm 122 suggests that those living in Jerusalem should be in a state of continual
peace. Isaiah 2:1–5 points to a time in the future when Jerusalem truly will be a
place where people come to meet with God. Interestingly, the prophet calls his
hearers to live by the light of the Lord (verse 5). The theme of being routinely ready
is one that Paul takes up in Romans 13:11–14. We can see a clear call to be ready
for God to act, only knowing that the day when we will be saved is nearer now than
when we first believed (verse 11). Paul, using the concept from Isaiah, challenges
his readers to live in the light now (verse 12), as an honest and godly response to
the possibility of Christ's imminent return. The time we have this day will not be
available again and as a Christian community we should live morally as though Jesus
could return at any moment. We would not want to be found doing something that
would bring him displeasure.

Beginning the service

Welcome everyone but look excited and jumpy. For example, look at your watch or tell some of your co-leaders to hurry up and make sure things are all ready. Explain that you are waiting for an important delivery. You don't know when exactly it will arrive but it could be at any moment. That is why you are waiting in anticipation and readiness.

Bible reading

The following adapted CEV version of Romans 13:11–14 (YearA.Advent1_1) is available from www.scriptureunion.org. uk/lightdownloads. It could be read with everyone joining in with the emboldened lines. This could be accompanied by stretching arm movements as though waking up.

> You know what sort of times we live in, and so you should live properly.
> **It is time to wake up.**
>
> You know that the day when we will be saved is nearer now than when we first put our faith in the Lord. Night is almost over, and day will soon appear.
> **It is time to wake up.**
>
> We must stop behaving as people do in the dark and be ready to live in the light.
> **It is time to wake up.**
>
> So behave properly, as people do in the day. Don't go to wild parties or get drunk or be vulgar or indecent. Don't quarrel or be jealous.
> **It is time to wake up.**

> Let the Lord Jesus Christ be as near to you as the clothes you wear. Then you won't try to satisfy your selfish desires.
> Romans 13:11–14 (CEV)

The reading of Matthew 24:36–44 could also be interspersed by the phrase: **It is time to wake up.**

Bible talk

With: three volunteers; a letter; mobile phone; email printout; *Shrek 2* DVD; appropriate equipment to play a clip to the congregation (optional)

In advance ask three people to interrupt you. The first person brings you a letter, the second, if possible, texts your mobile phone (see **Notes and comments**) and the third brings you a printed-off email.

If you have the time and equipment, play a clip from *Shrek 2*. Start the DVD at the point where Shrek, Fiona and Donkey are about to set off for Happy Ever After. Play the clip until they arrive at their destination. This clip shows how Donkey didn't know how long the journey would take, but he wanted to get there and so kept asking. He was constantly anticipating a positive answer and it never came, until, all of a sudden, it did. They had arrived, and when they did, it took them by surprise.

What Jesus says about the future

Remind the congregation that you are still waiting for your delivery. (See **Beginning the service.**) You are very excited by its arrival. Talk about the things Jesus says about what will happen in the future – what it will be like when he returns, after he has died, risen and gone to heaven. We all like to know when things will happen and those who were listening were no exception, just like you as you wait for your delivery… emphasise your excitement.

Interrupted by a letter

This is the cue for your first assistant to call out and say that they have a 'letter for… [your name]'. They should bring out the letter for you to open. Thank them and let them return to their seat. Before you open the letter ask them whether this is what you have been waiting for. Build up the suspense as you prepare to open it. The letter should say something along the lines of: 'Dear [name], I expect you are really excited about your delivery, love Mum' (or someone relevant to you or the congregation). You are visibly disappointed at this not being your delivery, but it hasn't changed the fact that you are still excited as you wait. Explain that life still goes on as you wait though, so you will just go on.

What Paul says about the present

Explain that Paul's letter was written to the church in Rome. By this time Jesus had gone back to heaven and the people who had followed him and believed in him were learning how to live without him being physically present with them. They had the Holy Spirit with them and were receiving guidance in the letters they received from the apostles, like Paul. Paul is concerned that as these Christians grow in their faith, they should live as Jesus taught them (explain

the imagery of 'living in the light') and not in the way that non-Christians live. The New Testament has many letters written to churches and individuals that helped them to live as followers of Jesus. If all this was happening today you may find that they'd use mobile phones to keep in contact with each other.

Interrupted by a text message

The second volunteer should be ready to text you. The message should be something like: 'I bet you can't wait for your delivery.' Act surprised when you receive the text, asking the congregation whether this is anything to do with your delivery, and again look disappointed when it isn't. Explain that you are finding it difficult to wait and that the anticipation of this great delivery is almost too much to take.

Living in the present and the future

Explain that the Bible is clear that one day Jesus will return and make everything right. Some Christians think that this is a long way off and so don't worry too much about how they act – we can always say sorry later. Others believe that Jesus' return is the only important thing to know and so they don't worry about this world here and now. Both Jesus and Paul are clear that we should live the right way now because we don't know when Jesus will return.

Interrupted by an email

Someone brings up a printed sheet, shouting out: 'Email for [name]. I've just printed it off at the office [or wherever].' Ask whether this is about your delivery. Read the email out loud – perhaps commenting that at least it isn't spam (or junk mail): 'Hi [name].

I heard about your delivery; I bet you are prepared and ready for it?' Explain that you are ready for the delivery. You have warned those you know that it is coming, including everyone here in the church. You have been telling people how wonderful it will be, that you can't wait for it to be delivered and that you are also waiting in readiness for it, prepared but getting on with things while you wait. It would be good to leave this hanging. There is no need to over-explain the link between the passages and your illustration.

Prayer activity

Many people right now will be waiting for something to happen. They may know how long will be their wait, such as for a birthday, wedding, or Christmas. Alternatively, they may not know exactly when something will happen, but they are expecting it soon, such as a birth, a proposal of marriage, or their moving day. Or, they may have no idea how long they have to wait, such as for an operation, or a change of job.

In small groups ask people to share one thing that they are waiting for and whether they know when it will be. Then pray for one another as they wait.

Ending the service

You are still waiting for your delivery, which hasn't yet come. You know that it will arrive but you are still unsure exactly when. Until it arrives you remain excited about it and expectant. If you wish to draw out more

clearly the parallels between your 'delivery' and the promised coming of Jesus, do so now – be aware that this theme will be continued and developed in coming weeks.

End with this prayer:

Lord Jesus,
We know from the Bible that one day you will return to us.
Until you return, we ask that you will give us the strength to live your way, and 'live in the light'.
Help us to live always ready for your return.
Send us out into the world to tell others about your love.
Amen.

Helpful extras

Music and song ideas
Appropriate hymns and songs include: 'And can it be'; 'Light of the world, you stepped down into darkness'; 'O thou who camest from above'; 'Teach me to dance to the beat of your heart'; 'The Spirit lives to set us free'.

Game
Devise some quiz questions, appropriate for all ages, which require knowledge about what will or might happen in the future (suggestions are given below). This is a fun quiz and shouldn't be taken too seriously – the answers will often be based on estimates and predictions. The key message is that it is a challenge to be ready and prepared for an unknown future. Only with God's help can we be ready for the return

of Christ and 'only the Father knows' when that will be (Matthew 24:36).

Q: When is it guessed that the earth's reserves of oil will run out?
A: We don't know. We aren't sure how much oil is left. What we do know is that the more we use the quicker it will run out.

Q: According to current scientific theory, how many more years will the sun continue to burn?
A: It is estimated that in about 5 billion years the sun will become a red giant as it runs out of hydrogen to burn.

Q: According to reports in 2007, a cure for baldness will be available in how many years time?
A: By 2017.

Q: Space agencies are aiming to land the first person on our nearest planet, Mars. What is the current predicted date for this to happen?
A: It is expected that by the year 2025 the technology will be available that will enable us to send someone to Mars.

Q: When will I be 100 years old?
A: [Tailor the answer to yourself and respond to the congregation's reactions – don't be too upset at any wildly 'off' guesses!]

Notes and comments

Note that the requirement in the **Bible talk** for someone to text you during the service may prove difficult in practice. Their phone should be turned to 'silent' until the relevant moment, with the volunteer ready to text at just the right point. Alternatively, consider using another form of message, such as a bird glove puppet or soft toy to deliver a message by 'carrier pigeon'.

(Whenever you use a DVD or film clip, think about its appropriateness to the congregation; ensure that you know the certification of the film and that parents of young children are notified of what you intend to do if you have good reason to consider an 'older' film clip to be appropriate.)

If you are going to light an Advent ring during the course of Advent, make sure that you explain the significance of this. Make this a feature of each service throughout the season.

Alternative online options

Visit www.lightlive.org for additional activities for children, young people and adults.

SECOND SUNDAY OF ADVENT

READINGS: **Romans 15:4–13; Matthew 3:1–12**
Isaiah 11:1–10; Psalm 72:1–7,18,19

Bible foundations

Aim: to explore what it means to welcome Jesus

Matthew 3:1–12 and Romans 15:4–13 deal with the way people responded to the arrival of Jesus. In Matthew we meet John the Baptist, who was sent to prepare the way for Jesus. John was a challenging preacher who called people to confess their sins and turn their lives around. In his appearance, his lifestyle and his message, he shocked, challenged and inspired. Many responded by being baptised, but some found it difficult to cope with what he had to say. John told the Pharisees and Sadducees that it was not enough to have Abraham as their father; they must also produce 'fruit'.

In Romans 15, Paul speaks about the instruction, encouragement and hope to be gained from the Scriptures (which in Paul's time only included the Old Testament). There was often a conflict in the early Church between those who wanted Christians to be circumcised and those who believed that Gentiles could be accepted as they were. Paul points out that Christ's actions confirm the promises given to the patriarchs but he also lists a number of references to Gentiles being called to welcome God with praise.

Both Paul and John have a vision of the kingdom that is universal, in that it stretches beyond the Jewish nation. God's people will be known by the fruit they produce, the praises they sing and the hope they have in Christ, empowered by the Holy Spirit. John speaks of the way in which Jesus will baptise people with the Holy Spirit and with fire. Paul prays that the Romans will be empowered by the Spirit to have an abundance of hope. This ultimately is the answer to John's challenging message. We cannot save ourselves, but God can do it for us by transforming us from within. Salvation doesn't come through our ancestry, it comes from our willingness to welcome Jesus and put our trust in him.

Beginning the service

Ask the congregation if they are looking forward to Christmas. What are they looking forward to and what are they not looking forward to?

If possible play a piece of video or music associated with anticipation, such as 'One Day More' from *Les Miserables* or the opening bars of 'Football's Coming Home' by the Lightning Seeds. Talk about the way in which people look forward to a special treat if they know what to expect, but sometimes they are waiting for something where the outcome is uncertain, such as a sporting event, an election or a battle. Discuss the different emotions that people feel at these times. If appropriate, refer back to the waiting of the person who gave the **Bible talk** last week.

Ask everyone to imagine what it felt like to be living in Judea in the years before Jesus: the nation was divided, the Romans were in occupation, the rulers were corrupt and many people were poor and hungry. People knew that God had promised to send a Messiah to sort things out, but they only had a vague idea about what that would involve. How would they feel? Would they be frightened, hopeful, or both, when he arrived? This leads on to the **Bible reading** from Matthew 3:1–12.

If you are lighting an Advent ring or candle, do that at the beginning.

Bible reading

John the Baptist made a dramatic entrance onto the scene – and could make a dramatic appearance in church, shouting out his statements in Matthew 3:2, 3, and 7–12 with a narrator filling in the gaps. A suitable costume would increase the impact as he storms into church.

The Old Testament quotations in Romans 15:4–13 could be read by a different person from the reader of the other verses.

Bible talk

With: two volunteers

Make sure the two volunteers know what you expect of them. If possible, one should work in a school or in an office and one should be particularly house-proud. Ask them both to come to the front to be interviewed.

Tell the first person that a special guest is coming to visit their school or office tomorrow. If appropriate, it could be an OFSTED inspector. Ask them how they feel about this and what they would have to do to get ready. Focus on the sense of panic and the practical details that will have to be dealt with. Then tell the house-proud person that two demanding visitors will be staying with them tonight! Draw out the overwhelming sense of panic that this is likely to induce in this house-proud host!

Then ask the congregation to think about what it feels like to be a guest. Ask them to share with one another in small groups and discuss how they have been made to feel welcome or unwelcome. Allow time for feedback. It is likely that many people will refer to the way in which a welcome becomes 'real' if it is heartfelt and genuine.

Contrast this with the welcome given to VIPs, which is often superficial despite the work put in to create a big occasion.

Now discuss the way in which people responded to the coming of Jesus. Jewish people had been waiting for the Messiah, but didn't really know what to expect. The coming of the Messiah was associated with judgement, destruction and the rule of God. It was both frightening and eagerly awaited. Recap the story of John's baptism in Matthew 3. John called people to get ready by turning from their sins, but this needed to be more than a cosmetic exercise; they needed to be ready to meet God in person.

The Gentiles weren't obviously waiting for a Messiah, but Jesus came for them as well! Refer to what Paul wrote in Romans 15:8 and 9. Do we welcome Christ with joy, or are we afraid? Do we open ourselves up to him in trust, or do we keep him at arms length because we are afraid of what he will do with us?

Conclude by referring to the Holy Spirit. John baptised with water, which indicates the willingness of the people to change. Jesus baptised with the Holy Spirit, who gives us the power to change. The Holy Spirit gives us hope because he is continuing the work of Jesus in our hearts and lives.

Prayer activity

With: cards or paper with an outline picture of an hourglass (YearA.Advent2_1) available from www.scriptureunion.org.uk/lightdownloads; a supply of pens or pencils; a real hourglass (optional)

This prayer activity focuses on those who are waiting for help in our world today. Ask everyone to think about anyone in need who is waiting for something or someone. For whom is God calling members of the congregation to pray this week?

Give everyone a card or piece of paper on which is the picture of an hourglass. Explain how hourglasses have been used in the past to measure time, and still are used today in cooking or other situations. Ask people to write names or draw pictures of the people (or the person) of whom they have thought in the bottom half of the hourglass. Note that this is not a test but an act of prayer.

Then ask them to think about what these people (or this person) may need. This may be an opportunity for teaching about how God longs to meet our real needs. Comment that we can become answers to prayer. Are those in need waiting for us? Invite people to put some of their thoughts down in the top half of the hourglass. Give them time to record their thoughts in words or pictures.

Invite people to pray quietly for the people they have been thinking about. You could run a real hourglass or egg-timer during the prayers. At the end, tell the congregation that they can take their hourglass picture home to remind them to pray during the coming week.

Prayer of confession

With: a bowl, font or baptistry full of water

It's easy to dismiss the Pharisees and the Sadducees as hypocrites, but we also can confess our failings and yet do nothing to put things right. John the Baptist invited people to be baptised. It symbolised their desire to change and leave behind the things they had done that were not right for God's people to do. It was also a way of asking God for forgiveness. (If you use a font or baptistry, you may wish to make some reference to the meaning of the baptisms that take place in your church.)

Invite people to come forward to dip their hand into the water as a sign of their confession to God of their desire to change and as a sign of their hope that God will heal, forgive and bless them.

Ending the service

With: a picture of a clock showing the hands approaching midnight

Show the picture of the clock. Note that the people of Judea were waiting for the Messiah to come. Jesus was the fulfilment of this promise, but we are still waiting for his coming again. During Advent we're waiting for Christmas and we're also waiting for blessings that God has in store for us.

Divide the congregation into two halves: one to say 'tick', the other to say 'tock'. Start people off saying 'tick-tock' slowly and steadily, with regular pauses between each 'tick' and 'tock'. Ask them to keep going until you raise your hands to indicate that they should stop. While this is happening, say the following words. Allow one 'tick-tock' between each phrase. You should practise this to make sure you're happy with the rhythm.

Christ is coming	('tick... tock...')
Christ is coming	('tick... tock...')
Coming soon	('tick... tock...')
Coming soon	('tick... tock...')
Christ is coming	('tick... tock...')
Christ is coming	('tick... tock...')
Coming soon	('tick... tock...')
Coming soon	('tick... tock...')

(*Raise your hands to indicate that it is time to stop.*)
Christ is coming soon!

Finish by inviting people to think about how they might consciously welcome Jesus over the coming week. How will they be aware of his presence in their day-to-day lives?

Helpful extras

Music and song ideas
Relevant songs include: 'Make way, make way'; 'On Jordan's bank the Baptist's cry'; 'Great is the darkness'; 'Hail to the Lord's anointed'; 'Heaven shall not wait'; 'Jesus is the name we honour'; 'How lovely on the mountains'; 'God has a plan' *Bitesize Bible Songs* CD (SU), a Learn and remember verse for 1 John 4:9.

Statement of faith
The following declaration (Year A.Advent2_2) is also available from www.scriptureunion. org.uk/lightdownloads. It is based on Paul's words in Romans 15 and is intended to help the congregation relate to the reading. Paul speaks about the Gentiles (non-Jews) worshipping God as they find hope in Christ. Jews and Gentiles can rejoice together because God's purposes have been fulfilled. You could introduce the declaration by pointing out the connection with the reading

and by explaining that we will be claiming
Paul's words as true for us. The congregation
say the words in bold.

The Scriptures were written to teach and
encourage us,
so that we might have hope:
**Let us glorify God, the Father of our
Lord Jesus Christ.
Let us accept one another just as
Christ accepted us.**

Christ became a servant,
so that the promises made to God's people
might be confirmed:
**Let us glorify God for his mercy.
Let us praise him among the nations.
Let us sing the praises of his name.
Let us rejoice with all his people.**

Jesus was the one who came
to rule over the nations:
In him we have hope.

May the God of hope fill you with all joy and
peace
as you trust in him, so that you may overflow
with hope
by the power of the Holy Spirit. Amen.

Notes and comments

Many churches light Advent candles on the
four Sundays leading up to Christmas. You
may wish to link **Beginning the service**
with the lighting of the Advent candle. You
could do this by lighting two candles as you
talk about the hopes and fears of the people
in Judea.

In many churches the **Prayer of confession**
is normally used at the start of the service.
Here, it is quite appropriate to leave it
until after the readings so that it becomes
a response to, rather than a preparation
for, the Word of God. On this occasion,
this would be particularly helpful since
the activity makes direct reference to the
content of the Gospel reading.

A note of explanation for those using this
outline not from the UK: 'OFSTED' is the
government body that organises school
inspections.

Alternative online options
Visit www.lightlive.org for additional
activities for children, young people and
adults.

THIRD SUNDAY OF ADVENT

READINGS: **James 5:7–10; Matthew 11:2–11**
Isaiah 35:1–10; Psalm 146:4–10

Bible foundations

Aim: to explore how God's people wait expectantly for him

John the Baptist can seem to be rather intimidating, with his ascetic appearance and the denunciatory tone of his message. In Matthew 11:2–11, however, he also appears vulnerable. From his prison he sends his followers to seek reassurance that his life's work and commitment has not been all in vain (verses 2,3) – a very human reaction! Was he expecting someone more like himself with fiery warnings and threats? Jesus was not like that! Jesus points John and his followers to the evidence of his own preaching and miracles (verses 4–6). These fulfil a different strand of Jewish hope to the one that John may have been expecting. With great respect, Jesus recognises that John might have had other ideas of what constituted a Messiah. He also explains to the fickle crowd that, regardless of any limitations in his understanding, John was the genuine article – the greatest messenger to come before Jesus.

James addresses Christians who, unlike many of us today, resembled John in eagerly awaiting Messiah's coming – only this time as Judge. This sense of urgent expectation is common in the New Testament. It would probably surprise them that, 2,000 years later, we're still waiting! James uses a customary earthy and practical example. This time it is farmers who just have to learn to wait for things to take their course (verse 7). As in the Gospel passage (especially as it develops in Matthew 11) impatience can lead to irritable behaviour among God's people (verse 9), with tendencies to grumble and backbite. Such behaviour will actually attract God's judgement. The patience of prophets like John, we must assume, is to be an example to the rest of us (verse 10). Christ will come again in glory to judge the living and the dead. Our role is to wait patiently and behave appropriately.

Beginning the service

Plan to delay the start of the service, without letting anyone else know of your intention! Everything should proceed as normal until such time as the congregation would expect you (or a fellow leader) to stand up at the front to formally begin the service. At that point, you should be nowhere to be seen! This gives everyone a genuine experience of expectant waiting at the outset of the service. There may well be bemusement and awkward silence, but don't be tempted to appear too quickly - you don't want everyone thinking that they haven't really had to wait after all. When you eventually appear, ask people of different ages how it felt to be waiting for your arrival. Did they like waiting? Did waiting make them feel uneasy? What were they expecting might happen?

Introduce the aim of the service and then clearly state that someone will receive a gift later on in the service, but everyone will have to wait to find out who that will be and what their gift is. You could make reference to the waiting that took place two weeks earlier.

Bible reading

Visual language is used in Matthew 11:2–11. A group of people could mime the different images as the passage is read.

James 5:7–10 is a series of personal instructions. The verses could be broken into short sound-bites, delivered by a couple of readers.

Bible talk

With: flip chart and marker pen; a box that advertises clearly (preferably with photography) what product is inside – with an entirely different product sealed inside

Experiences of waiting

Refer to **Beginning the service** for suggestions of occasions in life when we have to wait. Invite responses from people of all ages. You could write them up on a flip chart. Once you have a good sized list, go back over it, inviting people to say whether that particular waiting experience is a positive or negative one. For example, waiting for a birthday present to arrive might be deemed positive due to the excitement involved; on the other hand, waiting for a bus in the rain might be viewed more negatively.

Remind everyone that you began the service by promising that one person would receive a gift later on. Bring out your prepared gift, making sure that the packaging is clearly displayed, creating a sense of expectancy. Select someone whom you know will be eager to receive what they think is in the package (a child, for example, if the package describes the contents as being a game, an adult cook if it suggests some kind of kitchen appliance!) Choose your gift carefully to avoid the sense of this being a nasty practical joke. Make reference to the waiting that's been involved as you present the gift, but ask the recipient to wait for a few moments before opening it.

God's people in waiting

Talk about how, in the time of Jesus, God's people had been waiting for centuries for a person they called the Messiah. This was someone whom God had promised would come to establish his kingdom on earth and help his people. John the Baptist was one of those waiting for the Messiah. At first he believed Jesus was the promised Messiah but, as the Gospel reading indicates, he later began to have his doubts. It seems that Jesus didn't quite match John's expectations of the Messiah. John wondered whether he and the rest of God's people might have to keep waiting for God to act. (You could talk about the frustration that they might have felt about this and draw a link with James 5, with the warning against the damaging behaviour that can result from the frustration of waiting.)

Expectations in waiting

Now your chosen person can open their gift in front of the rest of the congregation. Watch their face as they realise that the content is entirely different from that which the packaging had led them to expect! Talk about how expectations are generated and how we feel when our expectations aren't met. You should emphasise, however, that in this case the expectation of a gift was met; it just didn't look much like what everyone thought it would.

Draw a parallel between this and Jesus' reassuring response to the question that John sent through his disciples. Jesus describes the nature of his ministry, knowing that John would recognise the description as fulfilling the expectations of prophecies from the past about what the Messiah would do (such as Isaiah 35:1–7). This should be enough to calm John's doubts. He may well have been expecting rather more in the way of a head-on confrontation between the Jewish Messiah and the occupying Romans, but he is invited

to reflect on the fact that, whatever it might look like to him, only the Messiah could do what Jesus is doing. He is invited to celebrate that the waiting is over and that God has acted in sending Jesus.

Conclude by saying something about the promise of the Scriptures that Christ will return and how, like James' first readers, we are waiting expectantly for that return, just like John and the Jews of his day were waiting for the Messiah. James' practical advice about the attitude in which we wait is therefore as relevant to us as it was to them.

Prayer activity

With: a variety of art and craft materials (for example, colouring pencils, paint, brushes, paper, modelling clay, pens, pencils)

This activity allows people to experience prayer as a time of 'waiting on God'. Use the materials suggested above to create different 'stations' around your meeting room (such as a place to draw, a place to paint, a place to write, a place to make models). Explain that, as well as talking to God in prayer, we can see prayer as an opportunity to listen to God. This is sometimes referred to as 'waiting on God'.

Ask everyone to close their eyes to focus on God and on the Bible readings they have heard today. What are they waiting for God to do in their life? After a few moments, invite people to move to the 'response station' that seems to be the most suited to the thoughts or pictures or memories of God's Word that have come to mind as they prayed and waited. At their chosen station they should use the materials provided to express something of what they have prayed for or thought about. Encourage people to share ideas and work together in teams if they wish, encouraging each other, particularly younger children present. Make time available for everyone to view each other's responses. If you think that it is important to provide a formal ending to the viewing time, ask everyone to stand, looking at what has been recorded, and lead them in a short prayer expressing thanks that God responds when we wait expectantly on him.

Ending the service

With: small red carpet or red rug

Talk about how a red carpet is rolled out for the annual film awards or festivals. Show any images you can find of the arrival of royal or state guests or people at Oscar ceremonies. People wait expectantly for the celebrities to arrive. This service has focused on how God's people wait expectantly for him to come to act in our lives. James addressed his letter to Christians who were waiting for Jesus to return, just as, before them, John had waited for Jesus' first appearance on earth.

Lay out the red carpet explaining that this is a symbol that you are all living as those waiting expectantly for Jesus to come and return as King. Invite younger children to come to stand on the red carpet and ask them to repeat after you: 'I am waiting for the arrival of the King.' They say that twice; then everyone joins in to say, 'We are waiting for the arrival of God's Son.'

Helpful extras

Music and song ideas

Hymns and songs relevant to the theme of waiting include: 'Great is the darkness'; 'Lord, I come to you'; 'O come, O come, Immanuel'; 'Open my eyes that I may see'.

Statement of faith

To tie in with the service theme, use the words of the beatitudes from Matthew 5:3–10 as a corporate declaration of commitment to wait expectantly on God. Before saying the words, explain their relevance to the aim of the service. The beatitudes could either be read together by everyone, or the leader could say the first line of each with the congregation responding with the second line. A variation on the latter would be for one half of the congregation to lead with the first line and the other half to respond with the second line.

The beatitudes declare blessing (or happiness) in the present for those who live knowing and expecting that God will, one day in the future, transform circumstances and fortunes. Emphasise that there is no guarantee that such people will have their expectations realised while they are alive. This links well with the Epistle reading where James addresses those who were still waiting for the return of Jesus, encouraging them to be a blessing to one another. If appropriate, introduce the concept of these blessings being given in a future reality (when God's kingdom fully comes), in order to avoid any suggestion that those who don't see them delivered in their lifetime don't see them at all.

Notes and comments

For **Beginning the service**, make your musician(s) aware of your intention to be late so they don't keep on playing to fill the awkwardness caused by your absence, which may unwittingly defeat the object of the exercise!

As an alternative **Beginning the service**, you could create a sense of expectancy by remaining silent at the front for an unusually long period of time. Alternatively, several times you could act as though you're about to say something to start the service but then not actually say it.

The **Statement of faith** could be used near the start of the service (but after **Beginning the service**), but it would probably have more resonance if used after the **Bible talk**.

In a service of Holy Communion, comment that we celebrate the Eucharist until Christ returns!

Alternative online options

Visit www.lightlive.org for additional activities for children, young people and adults.

Christmas Wrapped Up!
(978 1 85999 795)

- All-age Advent, Christmas Day and Nativity services
- Assembly outlines
- Christmas quizzes and dramas
- Songs, raps and rhymes

Everything you need to get the most out of Christmas!

For more details, visit www.scriptureunion.org.uk

More Christmas Wrapped Up!
(978 1 84427 261 7)

FOURTH SUNDAY OF ADVENT

READINGS: **Romans 1:1–7; Matthew 1:8–25**
Isaiah 7:10–16; Psalm 80:1–7,17–19

Bible foundations

Aim: to explore who Jesus is, the Christ-child

Matthew and Paul indicate who Jesus is in accordance with the expectations of
the Old Testament. Matthew explains the incarnation in mainly Old Testament
terms. His selective genealogy roots the Christ-child amongst the people of God,
and relates everything to the Old Testament with many quotations and allusions
(1:22,23; 2:5,6,14,15,17,18,23). Unlike Luke's account, Matthew's perspective is that
of Joseph, 'a righteous … son of David' (verses 19 and 20). It is Joseph who receives
the angelic visit to reassure him of God's involvement in the extraordinary, but
potentially shameful, things that are happening to him (verses 20 and 21; compare
2:13,19). The child is described in very Jewish terms, as the Christ (Hebrew
– 'Messiah'), who fulfils the hopes and aspirations of the Jewish people (verse 18).
His personal name is to be Jesus (Hebrew – 'Joshua'), which carries connotations of
salvation and new beginnings (verse 21). In fulfilment of the promise of Isaiah 7:14,
he will be called 'Immanuel', God with us (verse 23).

Paul is addressing a mixed group of Jewish and Gentile believers whom he hopes
to visit on his way to Spain (Romans 15:23,24). His message is guaranteed to strike
a chord with Jewish Christians, reassuring them that faith in Christ is consistent
with their past history and also insisting that Gentile Christians are fully part of
the people of God. Paul begins with a description of Jesus that is heavily Jewish in
flavour. He, like Matthew, makes the dynastic link back to David. Jesus is a 'son of
David' (1:3). This was his noble but frail and mortal human lineage. However, his
status is that of the powerful Son of God – declared, or confirmed, or shown to be
so (NLT, CEV, rather than 'appointed' TNIV) by the fact that God the Father raised
him from the dead. It is because of that resurrection that Jesus is recognised as
God's Messiah and as Lord over the whole universe (verse 4).

Beginning the service

With: images of Jesus' life to display - illustrations from children's books, works of art cut from magazines or downloaded from the Internet, such as from www.rejesus.co.uk

Display each of the images of Jesus in turn, pausing between each one to invite comments and feedback from people of all ages. Which ones are particularly liked or disliked, and why? Are there any that particularly resonate with people? Once all the images have been viewed, spend a few minutes exploring what the various images communicate about who Jesus is. Where possible, develop the comments offered as the images are viewed.

Review the suggestions received and comment on how these images give us ideas about who Jesus is and what he is like. Conclude by saying that it is only really as we read or listen to the message of the Bible and become inspired by it as we pray, live and work each day that we can discover who Jesus truly is. This service will help us explore what the Bible says about the Christ-child, whose birth we celebrate at Christmas.

Bible reading

You may wish to read only Matthew 1:18–25 and avoid the genealogy, which is not easy in an all-age context.

Romans 1:1–7 follows on appropriately. Ask everyone to listen out for what Paul said about Jesus' family tree and origins.

Bible talk

With: four individual large sheets of paper with the words 'Jesus', 'Messiah', 'Christ' and 'Immanuel' printed on them; further large blank sheets of paper; marker pens

What's in a name?

The **Game** will introduce the **Bible talk**. Invite four volunteers to the front. Each one holds up one of the printed sheets of paper for everyone to see. These are all names or titles given to Jesus in this week's Bible readings. Remind everyone how in the **Game**, meanings were matched to names. Explain how it is still common in many countries for parents to name their children because of the significance of the meaning of a name, and what it conveys about the person to whom it is given. This was very much the case at the time of Jesus' birth, so if we want to explore who the Christ-child really is, we need to know the meaning of the names and titles applied to him.

Jesus

Ask for suggestions as to what his name means. Those with keen memories might recall from the Gospel reading that it has something to do with saving people (Matthew 1:21). Mention that 'Jesus' is the Greek form of the Hebrew name 'Joshua', which means 'the Lord saves'. According to the angel who appeared to Joseph, this name signified that he would save his people (the Jews) from their sins. If you think it will aid memory, write 'saves' on one of the blank sheets of paper and ask a further volunteer to hold it next to the 'Jesus' sheet.

Messiah

Invite suggestions as to its meaning and what it therefore says about who Jesus is. It is a Hebrew term meaning 'Anointed One'. This may need some explaining. Talk about being 'chosen' or 'set apart' by God for a special task. Decide the extent to which you will go into detail concerning the Old Testament origins of Jewish belief in a Messiah. If you think it will help, write a succinct summary of 'Messiah' on a blank sheet of paper (for example, 'Chosen One' or 'Promised King') to be held up next to the word.

Christ

Help people understand it is the Greek word for 'Messiah', recapping what you have just said. It would be worth specifying that, like 'Messiah', 'Christ' is a title given to Jesus; it is not his surname! If you need a succinct definition of 'Christ', write out the definition you used for 'Messiah' again, and ask for it to be held up near the word 'Christ'.

Immanuel

Affirm and 'flesh out' suggestions from the congregation as to its meaning as necessary. It is a Hebrew word that means 'God with us'. Write 'God with us' on a blank sheet of paper. A volunteer can hold it up next to the 'Immanuel' sheet.

Remind everyone of where the names appeared in the Bible readings. Paul and Matthew both recognised the baby born at Bethlehem to be the specially Chosen One ('Messiah' or 'Christ') in whom God would live with his people on earth ('Immanuel') and who would save his people ('Jesus'). Conclude by commenting that both Paul and Matthew wrote because they wanted to communicate to future generations (us!) who Jesus, the Christ-child is.

Prayer activity

With: the letters of the name 'Jesus', each on different coloured card and each letter then cut into small pieces of card to form a jigsaw; felt-tip pens; sticky-tape

Distribute the pieces of coloured card and felt-tip pens. Ask people to think of one word to describe who Jesus is, or one of his characteristics, and write it on their piece of card. Everyone then finds people with a piece of card the same colour as theirs. In the groups that are formed they piece their cards together into the letter in the name 'Jesus'. Decide how much help to give people in making up their letter.

Give each group some sticky-tape to stick their pieces of card together. When all the letters have been formed, display them together in the correct order on the floor to spell 'Jesus'. People can walk around to read all the different things that have been written, or you can read out a selection of them to the congregation. Conclude with a prayer that recognises who Jesus is, including the words on the cards, and express thanks to God for coming to us in Christ.

Ending the service

Conclude with the following prayer:

Lord Jesus Christ, Son of the Father, Light for the world, this week we will see many images of you as a baby in the manger. Help us to remember that you came as a baby, but became much more – our Saviour, our Guide and our Lord, Amen.

Helpful extras

Music and song ideas

Relevant songs include: 'Hark! the herald angels sing'; 'O little town of Bethlehem'; 'Once in royal David's city'; 'Who is he in yonder stall'; 'You are the king of glory'; 'Jesus, Jesus, holy and anointed One'.

Game

With: the names of members of the congregation printed on strips of paper and the meanings of those names (sourced from a book of baby names) printed on separate strips of paper; paper; pencils

This is intended to prompt thinking about the significance of names, paving the way for thinking about the significance of the names given to Jesus and what they indicate about who he is.

Mix up the two sets of paper strips and stick them up randomly around the walls of your meeting room. Give everyone a sheet of paper and a pencil. Alternatively, divide the congregation into all-age teams and give each team a sheet of paper and a pencil. Explain that around the room are the names of members of the congregation, along with the meanings of their names. People are to match the meaning to the correct name.

After a few minutes, reveal the correct matches. Talk with two or three people about the meaning of their names. Was the meaning important to their parents? Do they consider it appropriate given their character and personality? Turn, then, to the significance of the name and titles given to Jesus, saying something about how they indicate to us who he is.

Statement of faith

With: a wide variety of musical instruments, professionally made and home-made

This novel idea for composing a congregational statement of faith relies heavily on the **Prayer activity** above. Draw attention to the 'Jesus' display made from the pieced-together coloured cards. Remind everyone that the words are an expression of what people believe about Jesus. The task now is to express some of those things musically in a sound-scape statement of faith.

Ask people to form into small groups and allocate each group a variety of instruments, along with a selection of different words describing Christ. Each group interprets these words using the instruments. For example, Jesus as 'King' could be presented with a trumpet sound; as 'Guide', with someone saying, 'This way please' followed by a shuffling of feet; as 'Saviour', with someone sounding out of breath saying, 'Where's he gone? Where's he gone?' and then 'Found him', followed by a loud cheer. Be as imaginative as you can.

When everyone is ready, declare your musical statement of faith together, with an agreed order. Alternatively, for something more structured, a leader could begin with words like 'Lord Jesus, we know who you are, you are…' and then speak out each word describing Christ, pausing for its musical interpretation.

Notes and comments

The **Bible talk** could be delivered in the form of the television game show *Call my Bluff*, with a prepared panel giving members of the congregation the opportunity to discover what the various names and titles given to Jesus mean by choosing between true and false explanations of their meaning. There is the risk that this will simply entertain the congregation or suggest that this knowledge is 'trivia'; there is something truly awe-inspiring conveyed in the names and titles given to Jesus.

For the **Prayer activity** you could select a few volunteers to collect comments from people and stick the pieces together to make a collage relating to Jesus' character and significance.

The **Game** needs to come before the **Bible talk** in this service and would make an ideal alternative to **Beginning the service**.

Alternative online options

Visit www.lightlive.org for additional activities for children, young people and adults.

To stimulate further thought on leading all-age worship, read *Top Tips on All-age worship* (SU) by Nick Harding, *Top Tips on Inspiring all kinds of learners* (SU) by Andy and Claire Saunders and *Top Tips on Prompting Prayer* (SU) by Sarah Bingham and Vicky Blyth.

CHRISTMAS DAY

(handwritten: C∂∂CH 2013)

READINGS: **Luke 2:1–20; Titus 2:11–14**
Isaiah 9:2–7; Psalm 96:1–13

Bible foundations

Aim: to declare the reality of Jesus' coming as a child

Luke is very specific as to where and when Jesus was born. The census provides a necessary explanation of how the carpenter from Nazareth came to be born in the city of David, Bethlehem, as was expected of the Messiah (verse 4). The exact circumstances of Jesus' birth is overlaid with traditional details for which neither Luke nor Matthew offer any basis – no ox, no ass, not really the filthy poverty of Christmas legend, nor endless rejection as they went from door to door. By the standards of the time it is quite a respectable birth. A manger is at least warm and comfortable. Meanwhile the first witnesses are common shepherds, who did not enjoy a high or respectable reputation, despite their ancient association with David and even with God himself. How typical this was for the Messiah, who kept the company of tax collectors and sinners and whose resurrection was first witnessed by a disorderly group of grieving women! The shepherds' excited discussion and departure is brilliantly conveyed. They become the first evangelists, sharing what they had seen with others. As the shepherds occupy themselves with joyful worship, Mary understandably ponders what has happened to her.

Paul offers advice as a friend and mentor to Titus. The concrete realities of Jesus' birth and life are paralleled by very specific expectations of lifestyle for the early believers. They are to live godly and upright lives (Titus 2:12). Motivation for this is derived from past, present and future. The past relates to the finished work of Christ in his incarnation and first Advent so that in the present Christians might be his witnessing people (verse 14). For the first Christians, however, the future Advent is always in view – the hope of Jesus' second coming in glory (verse 13).

Beginning the service

With: recordings of different sounds that indicate that something's coming – such as thunder (storm coming), train horn (train coming), mobile phone text message alert (text message coming), ambulance siren (ambulance coming)

Play the recording of the different sounds indicating that something's coming. It will have greatest impact if it is played loudly and with no introduction. Arrange the different sounds in segments of at least 30 seconds, with a short pause in between each. Talk about what the different sounds indicate and tease out the common link of 'something coming'. You've been waiting, through the season of Advent, to celebrate the coming of Christ into the world. Now the day has arrived; in your service you'll be declaring the truth that Jesus came, and also remembering that we are waiting for him to come again.

Bible reading

The reading of Luke 2:1–20 can be read as a drama script with people of all ages miming appropriate actions. Using an unusual version of the Bible would make this familiar story strikingly different. Alternatively, you could read the story from one of the *Must Know* books (see **Notes and comments**).

Titus 2:11–14 is less familiar. Introduce this by explaining that this is a summary of why Jesus came as a baby.

Bible talk

With: enough paper squares, one per person, with picture-symbols of a baby, a sword, a bowl of water and a hand (Year A.Christmas_1), available from www.scriptureunion.org.uk/lightdownloads

By focusing on the specific details included in Luke's narrative of the birth of Jesus, this **Bible talk** emphasises the earthy reality of Christ's coming. Give out the picture squares, ensuring that family groups do not all receive the same symbol, and that each picture goes to a diverse range of people. (These symbols are also used for the **Statement of faith**.)

Identify the four symbols, asking whether the pictures are the kind of images people would choose for Christmas decorations. Actually, these pictures are just right to help you tell the story of Christmas. Ask people to hold up their pictures one by one, as you draw out their relevance.

The baby
Christmas is about celebrating Jesus' birth – because he is 'God with us' and has a special identity as both God and human. Stress that this is not a made-up story. Explore the range of emotions those present must have experienced (verses 16–19).

The sword
This story took place in a territory dominated by foreign invaders – this passage starts with the actions of the Roman emperor and his military commanders (verses 1 and 2). Throughout Jesus' life, there was the possibility of violent rebellion against Rome, which might tear apart the land where he lived. Jesus' parents were warned that there would be violent sorrow ahead (verse 35).

The bowl of water

Every baby needs to be washed after birth! Emphasise that while we should not exaggerate the dirtiness of the house where Jesus was born (and there is debate about whether we can call it a 'stable'), it was certainly borrowed and crowded (verse 7).

The hand

After travelling to attend the census, Joseph and Mary were dependent on the helping hands of others: friends, family, strangers (verse 7). Similarly, the shepherds, not invited or expected, were called by God to declare who this child was (verses 15–18, 20).

Next, ask who knows how the story ends. This is not a question with a 'right' answer, so expect a number of responses. Suggestions might include the arrival of the wise men, Mary and Joseph fleeing into Egypt, people believing in Jesus as the Messiah, or Jesus' death and resurrection. Remind people that whilst all these answers have truth in them, many Christians would say that Jesus' story hasn't yet ended. One such Christian would be Paul, who, in his letter to Titus, shows that he, too, believes that Jesus' story is real, and he shows how much he wants to tell that story to other people and how much he also wants them to pass it on. He believes that Jesus will come back (Titus 2:13) and his special identity as both God and human will be known by everyone.

Use the picture-symbols again to encourage people with the promise of what Paul, along with every Christian who tells and celebrates the Christmas story, is looking forward to.

The baby

The hope and expectation of the return of Jesus is like waiting for a birth – we are looking forward to new, changed lives for those who trust in Jesus, as we give thanks that he gave himself up for us by coming into the world as a baby.

The sword

Paul says that 'wickedness' (verse 14) will end when Jesus comes back. This includes the threat of cruelty and violence that still ruin people's lives, as it did when Jesus lived.

The bowl of water

As the baby Jesus was washed clean, so we are given a promise that everyone who trusts in Jesus will be made 'pure'. All the bad things that may make us ashamed will finally be washed away.

The hand

Paul says that Jesus will make us 'eager to do what is good'. The help and charity Jesus' family received, God's care for the outcast shepherds, the mercy Jesus showed in his life and the good works his followers try to do now all point forward to the promise of a world made the way God wants it, a world in which we will really know how to help and serve others.

It may be appropriate to move straight into the **Statement of faith**, which uses material from Titus to declare this hope together.

Prayers of intercession

Ask for people to prepare a prayer connected to each of the symbols, for example: a baby – give thanks for Christ's birth and pray for any babies known to you; a sword – pray for areas of violence or conflict in the world; a bowl of water – pray for those experiencing Christmas who are in a dark place or pray that in the coming year many people in the church will discover God's power to cleanse and forgive; a hand – pray for all those who are serving others this Christmas.

After each prayer, say together the words of the angels: Peace on earth to everyone who pleases God.

Ending the service

With: a recording of John Tavener's 'A Christmas proclamation'; a recording of a crying baby

Set up your equipment and recordings in such a way that makes it easy for the recording of the crying baby to follow on a few seconds after the ending of Tavener's 'A Christmas proclamation'.

Play 'A Christmas proclamation' at sufficient volume so that the final organ blasts fill the room with a due sense of majesty and arrival. 10 seconds later, play the recording of the crying baby at a volume loud enough to be heard by everyone; it is a very effective juxtaposition with the majestic organ blasts of Tavener's music and will keenly focus the congregation on Christ's arrival in humility as they depart into the rest of Christmas Day. No further words will be necessary!

Helpful extras

Music and song ideas

Songs might include: 'It came upon the midnight clear'; 'Joy to the world'; 'Lord Jesus Christ'; 'Silent night'; 'There is a redeemer'; 'While shepherds watched'. Make sure that you sing at least one traditional carol since people who do not usually come to church may come to this service and want to sing something familiar.

Alternatively, there are a number of pieces of classical music (both ancient and modern) that were written to celebrate Christ's birth. Examples might include: 'Sound the trumpet' by Purcell, 'Gloria' by Vivaldi or 'A Christmas proclamation' by John Tavener (this particular piece is suggested for **Ending the service**).

Statement of faith

With: paper squares from the **Bible talk**; computer and data projector (optional); a copy of the **Statement of faith** (Year A. Christmas_2) available from www. scriptureunion.org.uk/lightdownloads

This statement of faith links Paul's declaration in Titus 2:13 and 14 with the pictures used to explore the Christmas story in the **Bible talk**. If you have not used the talk, outline the relevance of the symbols to both Christmas and Jesus' return. Everyone says the lines in bold text, with those holding the relevant symbol saying their line.

This is the good news that we believe:
Baby: That Jesus gave himself for us,
Sword: To rescue us from all wickedness,
Water: To make us a pure people who belong to him,
Hand: And make us eager to do good.
We are waiting and hoping for his return:

> **He is our great God and Saviour, Jesus Christ!**
>
> based on Titus 2:13,14

Notes and comments

The following order is suggested: **Bible reading; Bible talk; Statement of faith; Prayers of intercession.**

This material may be used on Christmas Eve, where the Lectionary recommends using the same readings for both Christmas Day and Christmas Eve.

Alternative retellings of the Christmas story are numerous. You could try one of the *Must Know* stories: either 'Family Politics' from *Must Know Stories* (SU), or 'Surprise, Surprise' from *The 10 Must Know Stories* (SU).

Additional Christmas all-age service outlines can be found in the *All-age Service Annual* (Volumes 1–4) (SU) and *Christmas Wrapped Up!* and *More Christmas Wrapped Up!* (both SU). See page 29 and www.scriptureunion. org.uk for more details.

> ## Alternative online options
> Visit www.lightlive.org for additional activities for children, young people and adults.

> New Year resolutions to last more than seven days with an everlasting impact! Challenge your congregation to regularly meet with God through the Bible and prayer throughout the coming year. For more details of Scripture Union prayer and Bible reading resources, visit www.scriptureunion.org.uk

FIRST SUNDAY OF CHRISTMAS

READINGS: Matthew 2:13–23; Hebrews 2:10–18
Isaiah 63:7–9; Psalm 148:1–14

Bible foundations

Aim: to declare that in Jesus, God entered our world, sharing its suffering and pain

Having declared in Hebrews 1 that Jesus is greater than the angels, now, in chapter 2, the unknown author asserts that Jesus is one of us. We are told that, like us, Jesus shares the pain and suffering of human life. But whereas human suffering can be seen as a Darwinian struggle for survival, Jesus' experience of human pain and suffering is all part of the process that enables him to be our High Priest. He has to be one of us. It could only be one of our kind who could carry out such duties. As the High Priests were part of Israel, so Jesus is part of humanity. It is because Jesus suffered that he is enabled or allowed to help us. Whilst there are good scriptural grounds for taking all our concerns and struggles to God in prayer, accepting the teaching of Hebrews would tend to suggest that a very important (and much overlooked) part of our prayer ought to be a continual 'thank you' to Jesus for knowing the pain that we go through.

In the Gospel passage, Matthew is constructing a narrative of fulfilment, interweaving the events of the birth of Christ with references to the scriptural testimony that foreshadows the incarnation. By quoting from Hosea in 2:15, Matthew portrays Jesus as a 'type' of Israel and links his infancy in Egypt with the exodus. This theme of Jesus-as-Israel recurs throughout Matthew's Gospel.

Jesus is born into a suffering world. His birth was surrounded by discomfort, disruption and upheaval, and the fact that it was swiftly followed by the massacre of the local children reminds us of the casual cruelty and brutality that can so often be humanity's 'gift' to the world God made. Into this world, he comes as Immanuel – God with us, who faces all that we have to face.

Beginning the service

Ask adults and children what presents they have received. When you have received a few examples, ask why we celebrate Christmas. When they have (hopefully) said that the reason is because Jesus came to earth as a baby, explain that Jesus would have been a normal baby – crying, gurgling, and even wetting his nappy! He was without sin, but he was fully human, and he can therefore empathise with anything that we go through.

Open the service with the following prayer (YearA.Christmas1_1) that is also available from www.scriptureunion.org.uk/lightdownloads, inviting people to respond with the emboldened phrase:

Lord Jesus, we know that you came into the world as a vulnerable baby, lived as a human and died – something that we have all done and will do.
Thank you that you know what we go through.

You lived as we do, among people who liked you and despised you, and can therefore completely understand all of the issues that we face. Large or small – they are all important to you.
Thank you that you know what we go through.

Thank you that we have an opportunity today to remember that you were fully God, and fully human.
Thank you that you know what we go through.
Amen.

Bible reading

Hebrews 2:10–18 is full of statements about what Jesus has done. Break these verses into different statements about Jesus that can be read by several people.

You may prefer to read only Matthew 2:13–15 to omit the evil violence of King Herod.

Bible talk

With: music; a PowerPoint presentation for the end of the **Bible talk**

This talk emphasises that Jesus became one of us and therefore knows what we go through in life. Begin the talk by asking the congregation what words spring to their minds when people think about Jesus. Expect answers such as 'Saviour' and 'Lord'. After a few suggestions, explain that we do not focus often on the human characteristics of Jesus, such as those shown in the **Bible readings**.

Go through Hebrews 2:10–18, pointing out the empathy that Jesus has for all his creation. Focus on words that show his humanity, such as 'suffering' and 'tempted'. Remind everyone that Jesus was left completely alone when he was on the cross – even God turned his face away. Jesus can therefore fully empathise with any difficulties that we may face, because he went through things that we will never go through ourselves. We need not fear this happening to us. We may face problems, but we will never face them alone.

Matthew 2:13–23 describes the vulnerability both of Jesus as a human being and of his family. We often hear about Jesus protecting us, which of course is true, but in this instance Jesus himself is being protected by his parents. He would have been like any other baby in that situation. Now in heaven, he is able to protect us.

Finish by playing the song 'One of us'. There are versions available by Joan Osborne, Martyn Joseph, Prince or Seal. The lyrics talk of the humanity of God ('What if God was one of us?'). As the song is playing, show a PowerPoint of a variety of faces, young and old, happy, sad, crying and laughing, as well as some current news headlines. Intersperse these with images of Jesus. It is important that the images of Jesus are interspersed with faces of ordinary people, to emphasise that Jesus truly is one of us and knows what we go through. You could have the cross as the final image.

If you do not have access to PowerPoint or sound equipment, sing or play the song 'He walked where I walk' and ask the congregation to think about the words of the song in relation to their own lives.

Prayer activity

With: materials for each 'prayer station'

Designate four areas as 'prayer stations', labelling them: 'Me'; 'My friends and family'; 'Our church and community'; 'Our world'. Using the information below, explain the prayer activities in each area and invite people to visit as many as they wish. Encourage parents and other adults to involve children in these activities.

Me
Using paper or card, prepare some 'teardrops'. Provide pens or pencils to write

with, and a large bowl. Place the bowl beside a cross, if possible. Display the following words prominently, or write them on the back of the teardrops: Jesus wept when he heard his friend Lazarus had died. Encourage people to think about any hurt or pain in their own lives that they want to tell God about. They could write this down on the teardrop if they want to, and place it in the bowl by the cross.

My friends and family
Create a number of different 'emoticons' – faces expressing different emotions, such as happy, excited, content, sad, angry and worried – on large sheets of paper and display them either spread across the floor or stuck on the wall. Provide people with small sticky notes and pens. Ask them to think of friends or family members whom they associate with these emotions, and write their names on the sticky notes to stick on to the appropriate face, asking God to be with them whatever emotion they are experiencing.

Our church and community
Display a variety of local newspapers and recent church newsletters or magazines. Invite people to look through these, and tear out any articles or headlines that they want to talk about with God. Provide a notice board or large sheet of paper where these can be stuck, using Blu-tack or drawing pins. Provide sticky notes and pens for people to add other issues for prayer for your church and community.

Our world
Draw a tree outline on a large sheet of paper and display it. Prepare a large number of

'leaves' by cutting leaf shapes out of paper. Invite people to take one or more leaves and write on them a country or international issue where they want to see God in action. Provide Blu-tack to stick the leaves to the tree. Alternatively, people could stick the leaves to a large world map.

A simpler alternative to this **Prayer activity** is suggested in **Notes and comments**.

Ending the service

Look ahead to the coming year. None of us knows what awaits us in the next 12 months, but we can be assured that Jesus will be with us every step of the way. He knows us, loves us and understands all of our situations. The congregation needs to leave the service feeling encouraged, not downcast.

Finish with a prayer in which you ask for God's blessing for the coming year, for example:

Lord Jesus, we thank you for being with us last year.
We thank you that you will never leave us or forsake us.

We thank you that you know everything about us.
Thank you for your protection and power, which will keep us safe and strong in the coming year.

Bless us as we leave this place now.
Amen.

Helpful extras

Statement of faith
This service is an ideal opportunity to make a statement of faith about who Jesus is and why he came to live as one of us. This prayer is an adaptation of Hebrews 2:10–18 from the CEV (YearA.Christmas1_2), which is also available from www.scriptureunion.org.uk/lightdownloads.

All-powerful God, we know that everything belongs to you,
and all things were created by your power.
We believe that in Jesus, you entered our world,
becoming one of us, sharing our suffering and pain,
so that we could be saved and share in your glory.
When we are made holy by Jesus, we become part of your family.
That is why you aren't ashamed to call us your children.
We are people of flesh and blood.
That is why you became one of us.
You died to destroy the devil, who had power over death.
But you also died to rescue all of us who live each day in fear of dying.
You had to be one of us,
so that you could serve as our merciful and faithful high priest
and be sacrificed for the forgiveness of our sins.
And now that you have suffered and were tempted,
you can help anyone else who is tempted.
Thank you.

Music and song ideas
Many hymns and worship songs explore the truth that Jesus became one of us, and achieved our salvation through his own

suffering. These include: 'How deep the Father's love'; 'In Christ alone'; 'I will offer up my life'; 'What a friend we have in Jesus'; 'Immanuel'; 'He walked where I walk'.

Notes and comments

If the **Prayer activity** that is suggested is not suitable, adapt it in the following way: introduce each section from the front. Give an example of things to pray for in each section and allow the congregation two to three minutes to pray, either silently or in groups. At the end of each time, conclude with the following prayer or similar:

Thank you, Lord, that you are an ever-loving, ever-understanding God, who entered into the suffering of our world. Amen.

If this service includes Holy Communion, draw attention to the fact that Jesus came to this world to suffer and die, as you recall his death and resurrection.

Alternative online options

Visit www.lightlive.org for additional activities for children, young people and adults.

Once January arrives, we begin to think about the summer. What opportunities are there for the children and young people in your church to go away on Christian summer activities and holidays, to expand their horizons and meet with Jesus? How might adults serve God by joining a mission team? For details of Scripture Union holidays and missions, visit www. scriptureunion.org.uk.

SECOND SUNDAY OF CHRISTMAS

READINGS: **Jeremiah 31:7–14; John 1:[1–9],10–18**
Psalm 147:13–21; Ephesians 1:3–14

Bible foundations

Aim: to rejoice in the promised hope of God's activity in this world – in the light of the New Year

God's people had already experienced a return from 'exile' in their deliverance from Egypt. It formed a key element of their thinking about their relationship with God. As Jeremiah looks forward to the return from exile in Babylon (which hadn't even taken place when he wrote this) he uses exalted language to leave no doubt that it is God and no one else who is behind this liberation and fresh start. There is more here than was directly fulfilled 70 or so years later. Here is a picture of God's work down through the ages in drawing together a people of his own from those who were exiled from him. His people will include the helpless and the hopeless (verse 8). No one will be excluded. No one will be so far away they cannot come back. This is the message the Church still has for the world.

John 1:10,11 is so familiar that we don't recognise how shocking it is. When children reject loving parents or when a protégé rejects a generous benefactor we are surprised and ready to condemn. Here we have creatures rejecting their creator. God's own people rejecting the Son of God. If verse 12 were an announcement of judgement it would not be surprising. But instead it's an amazing statement of grace. Those who are willing to receive (or believe) become children of God. They come back from exile and into the family. Here is a lasting hope to take joyfully into the New Year.

Psalm 147 extols the blessings of God to his people, making their or our rejection all the more culpable. In majestic language, Ephesians 1:3–14 unpacks just what it means to become children of God – we receive blessings that exceed even those that the psalmist records, including the Holy Spirit as a guarantee that we belong to God.

Beginning the service

With: Flip chart and pens or laptop and projector

What should we do with people who are naughty? Choose some sort of 'crime' with which children especially will identify, such as bullying, telling outrageous lies, or stealing. Ask for suggestions as to how people who commit this crime should be punished. Children often demand heavy punishments for even minor offences. Write the punishments up on a flip chart or use the lap top and projector.

Read Ephesians 1:7 and 8. Explain that God not only forgives us but lavishly blesses us (throws a party for us). Ask for suggestions as to how we could celebrate when someone who used to commit the crime you have chosen is really sorry and stops doing it. Right across the punishments, write the words 'forgiven and blessed'. Follow this by singing one of the songs celebrating forgiveness (see **Music and song ideas** below).

Bible reading

Use two readers or divide the congregation into two groups to read John 1:10–18 aloud.

> Voice 1: He was in the world, and though the world was made through him, the world did not recognise him. He came to that which was his own, but his own did not receive him.
> Voice 2: Yet to all who did receive him, to those who believed in his name, he gave the right to become children of God – children born not of natural descent, nor of human decision or a husband's will, but born of God.
> Voices 1 and 2: The Word became flesh and made his dwelling among us. We have seen his glory, the glory of the one and only (Son), who came from the Father, full of grace and truth.
> Voice 1: John testified concerning him. He cried out, saying, "This is he of whom I said, 'He who comes after me has surpassed me because he was before me.'"
> Voice 2: Out of his fullness we have all received grace in place of grace already given. For the law was given through Moses; grace and truth came through Jesus Christ.
> Voices 1 and 2: No one has ever seen God, but the one and only (Son) who is himself God and is in the closest relationship with the Father, has made him known.
>
> John 1:10–18 (TNIV)

After each verse in Jeremiah 31:7–14, everyone could shout out, 'Shout for joy! Sing for joy!'

Bible talk

With: a book of road maps and/or a satnav

Invite a small group of people (chosen beforehand, although they could be volunteers) to come to the front. Tell the rest of the congregation that these people have been naughty. Encourage shouts of 'boo', 'hiss' and 'shame' – in contrast to the shouts in the reading of Jeremiah 31. What shall we do with them? We'll send them away in disgrace. Send them off to the farthest corner of the room or even just outside the door.

Banished

Explain that God's people had disobeyed him over a very long period of time. Eventually God allowed them to be captured by their enemies and taken into exile in Babylon. But God never intended the exile to last for ever. He promised that after 70 years the day would come when the people would return to their own land. Call the 'exiles' back. Encourage cheering and clapping as they rejoin the congregation.

Restored

But now what? God had plans for his people. He enabled them to rebuild the walls of Jerusalem and the temple, so that they could worship God and live for him. They went through tough times (which are written about in books like Maccabees, not usually included in our Bibles). God was planning something very special for his people. We'll come back to that later.

New Year's resolutions may be a bit hackneyed, but ask some people to say what they hope to achieve during the coming year – pass exams, go on holiday, get a new job, new baby expected, etc. Remind people that God wants to be part of our plans and we need to find out God's plans for our lives.

God's plan

What about the special plan God had for his people? Ask if anyone, this Christmas or previously, has had a present they didn't really want. (You might want to bring along and show an example of an unwanted present you've received. Make sure it wasn't a gift from someone in the congregation!) Has anyone given a present and discovered that it was obvious the person receiving it didn't like it or didn't want it? What did that feel like?

If you still have a crib scene in church, direct people's attention to it, or remind people whose birth we've been celebrating over the past few days. Jesus is God's greatest gift to us. How would God feel when people said, 'I don't want Jesus!' Refer to the reading from John 1 because that is exactly what happened. God's special people, whom he loved and cared for over thousands of years, refused to accept his Son, Jesus. Read together John 1:12-13.

Produce a book of road maps or a sat nav. Talk briefly about journeys you've made where it wasn't easy to find the way. Tell any recent story in the media about people being led astray by a sat nav. (Searching for 'sat nav astray' on Google will pull up some stories.) How much better if we have someone in the passenger seat who has done the journey before and can direct us stage by stage. Refer back to the things we want to achieve during the year. To be on the right path we need to begin by welcoming Jesus into our lives and allowing him to guide us. If we refuse to accept Jesus, it's just as if we put ourselves into exile from God. But the good news is that there is always a welcome from God when we turn to him.

Prayer activity

With: a map of the world; sticky notes; pens

Give out sticky notes and pens and ask people to write on their note the names of people who are away from home (in this country or abroad). This could include family members, mission partners, or people who are serving in the armed forces. Display a large world map at the front and ask people to bring their sticky notes and put them on the area of the world where their person is. As they place it on the map, encourage them to offer a silent prayer. At the end, pray a general prayer for those away and those at home who miss them.

Prayers of intercession

With: video clip of TV news

This would be an appropriate service in which to pray for refugees who have been driven from their lands by famine, drought, war or disaster. If there is a recent example, consider using a TV news clip. Or, you could use a mission agency video to give a focus.

A prayer of reflection for all ages (Year A. Christmas2_2) is available from www.scriptureunion.org.uk/lightdownloads.

Ending the service

Decide whether you want to end the service with an affirmation of what God is doing in the world or by anticipating the help he is going to give. Ask people to talk in small groups for a few minutes:

AFFIRMATION: Share examples of ways in which you see God at work in our world. At the end of the discussion each person should have one item that they will share.

ANTICIPATION: Share examples of things coming up during this year for which God's help is specially needed. At the end of the discussion each person should have one item

that they will share.

Ask each person to keep in mind the thing they are going to share. Explain that you are going to start at the left of the front row (or wherever) and move along the rows. If you have a small congregation, each person should say, aloud, in turn (you may want to get them to stand up as they speak), one of the following sets of words.

AFFIRMATION: I thank God that he is… (whatever they are sharing)

ANTICIPATION: I thank God that he will help me to… (whatever they are sharing)

If you have a large congregation, say the initial phrase 'I thank God…' once only (or once for each row or section) with members of the congregation simply saying the thing they are sharing.

Finish by praying together:

Lord we thank you for all that you have done, all that you are doing and all that you will do in our lives, in our church and in our world. Amen.

Helpful extras

Music and song ideas

'Thou didst leave thy throne and thy kingly crown' is based on John 1.

Songs about forgiveness include: 'I get so excited Lord' (I'm forgiven); 'In Christ alone'. Songs of celebration include: 'You shall go out with joy'; 'Come on and celebrate'; 'I will sing the wondrous story'.
Songs about committing our plans to God

include: 'O Jesus, I have promised'; 'Be thou my vision'; 'I want to serve the purpose of God'; 'Spirit of the living God fall afresh on me' (either version).

Game
Who knows best quiz
Read out the following scenarios and ask who knows best in each case. Talk about the consequences of taking the wrong advice. You can add your own examples. There may well be some good examples in recent safety adverts on TV. Conclude by pointing out that God always knows what is best for us and his plans and purposes are always for our good.

A: Be very careful crossing the road and always use the crossing.
B: Let's nip across here. It's too far to walk to the crossing.

A: Danger! Don't climb this pylon.
B: I dare you to climb the pylon.

A: Nobody will know if we cheat.
B: Do your own homework by yourself.

A: I mustn't be late.
B: I'm in a 30 mph zone.

A: I can get across the crossing before the train comes.
B: Stop! Train approaching.

A: Drugs are cool.
B: Drugs screw up your life.

A: Love your neighbour as yourself.
B: Look after number one.

Notes and comments
If you have a real-life 'coming home' story within your congregation, such as a daughter or son who has been away for a long time, or sisters or brothers who have been re-united after a long time, it would be appropriate to interview them or have them tell their story.

Alternative online options
For your convenience the following activities are available from www. scriptureunion.org.uk/lightdownloads: (YearA.Christmas2_1) Group discussion on rejection; (YearA.Christmas2_2) Group reflection and prayer.
Visit www.lightlive.org for additional activities for children, young people and adults.

EPIPHANY

READINGS: **Ephesians 3:1–12; Matthew 2:1–12**
Isaiah 60:1–6; Psalm 72:[1–9],10–15

Bible foundations

Aim: to celebrate that God wants to show himself to the world, and has done so in Jesus

In Ephesians 3:1–12, Paul can 'celebrate' even though he is in prison. He celebrates the mystery that has been revealed and that the Gentiles can also now receive God's grace. It is precisely because he is an evangelist to the Gentiles that Paul is in prison.

The emphasis on God's revelation being made available to the Gentiles permeates the passage from Matthew. Straight after reading about Jesus' birth we read about Gentiles revering Jesus. The Magi were probably wise men and priests from Persia, whose work combined 'astronomical observation with astrological speculation' (Craig L Blomberg). They have a different motivation and status from modern creators of 'horoscopes' in the tabloid press. Their work would have been treated with respect in their own culture, which is shown by the seriousness of the expedition to find the new king. God has revealed himself to pagans and brought them to worship the Christ. Isaiah also predicts this in 60:1–6.

By contrast, the 'Jewish' Herod (regarded by many contemporaries to be a convert to Judaism) has little knowledge of the Messiah, turning to his aides for information. He leaps to the conclusion that any such figure is a personal threat to his power, not someone to be accepted or worshipped. Meanwhile, Jesus' claim to be the Messiah is reinforced by the reference to Micah's prophecy about Bethlehem, in Matthew 2:6. This is important as it shows that Jesus didn't just look, or act, like the Messiah, he was born in the right place – something no mere mortal could arrange.

Beginning the service

Invite everyone to call out things that they notice that are different about other people – their ages, families, backgrounds, and so on. Then ask everyone to share the peace and love of Jesus, particularly with people who are very different from themselves. Ensure children and young people are fully included. You could give people a 'greeting' to use, such as 'May the peace and love of Jesus be with you, (person's name).' Alternatively, they may just want to wish each other a happy New Year!

Bible reading

Introduce Ephesians 3:1–12 by explaining that Paul had determined to take the good news of Jesus beyond the Jews to the Gentiles (anyone who is not a Jew). Listen out for what he writes to the Ephesian Christians about Gentiles, which is what most of them would have been.

The verses from Matthew are familiar, so several people could read the parts of a narrator, the wise men, Herod and the teachers of the law.

Isaiah 60:1–6 could be read with a voice of wonder, possibly with a shimmering cymbal in the background.

Bible talk

With: three large signs, each saying one of the following: 'See', 'Know' and 'Worship' (Devise simple actions for each of those words, for example: 'See' – hands around the eyes like a pair of pretend binoculars; 'Know' (or 'Knew') – first finger of each hand pointing to the side of head; 'Worship' – hands open or raised.)

Start by explaining that the New Testament readings tell us about different people who met Jesus in very different ways, including the apostle Paul, and the wise men. Invite three volunteers of different ages to hold the signs. Each time one of the three words is used (shown in bold in the following text), they should raise the appropriate sign as high as possible to encourage the congregation to do the action that goes with that word, which you will teach them as you go along.

See

Teach the sign for 'See'. Paul was in prison. This could have made him angry, but instead he tells the readers of his letter to the Ephesians that he can **see** the plans of God for himself. He can **see** that Jesus came for all people, not only the Jewish nation. God revealed himself to his people through his Son. We need to **see** God at work today, changing the lives of people through Jesus.

The wise men were not of the Jewish faith, but they searched for Jesus because they could **see** an unexpected star in the sky. They continued to **see** the star for most of their journey from the East, and it even seemed to wait for them while they went to see King Herod. Herod (whose ancestors may well have been Jewish), was too confused and worried about the new king's threat to his power to **see** what the wise men were saying. It was the wise men who were given the great opportunity to **see** the newborn baby. What do we **see** about God's plan for all people? Do we **see** people discovering Jesus, and are we helping them?

Know

Teach the sign for 'Know' (or 'Knew'). While Paul was still in prison, he not only **saw** that God had a plan, but **knew** that he was part of it. In his letter he **knows** that he is an unimportant, ordinary person and yet by the grace of God he has been chosen to tell others. He **knows** that he will suffer for his work for God, but he doesn't mind.

The wise men studied ancient scriptures and their **knowledge** of the stars meant that they **knew** a new king was to be born. Because they **knew** this, they were willing to travel to the area where the star guided them. They had the faith to **know** they would **see** the new king, as indeed they did. Do we **know** that we, like the wise men and Paul, have a part to play in carrying out God's plan?

Worship

Teach the sign for 'Worship'. Paul **knows** God's plan, has **seen** it in action, and **worships** God. He could have given up when it was tough, but instead he is able to **worship** God, the maker and creator of all things. Read Ephesians 3:9–12 again to give examples of what God has done. Paul can **worship**, despite everything he has been through, because he can **see** God's plan and **knows** his part in it. Finally, consider the wise men once more. On their long journey, they were able to **see** the star that led them and **know** that it would lead them to a new king. But what did they do when they got there? They did what we should all do – kneel down and **worship**.

Epiphany is about things being shown or revealed to us, so that we can **see**, **know**, and **worship**. Today God wants us to **see** that he has a love for all people, to **know** that we have a part in his plan, and to learn to **worship** his Son, Jesus.

Prayer activity

With: the signs and actions from the **Bible talk**

Ask everyone to close their eyes for 30 seconds to think of work colleagues, friends at school, neighbours, and others in the community who do not know that God loves them and sent Jesus for them. Ask them to pray silently for those people, asking God to help them tell others about Jesus. Invite everyone to join in these prayers by repeating each line as it is read, using the appropriate signs used in the **Bible talk**:

Generous God, thank you that we can **see** your love in action, shown through Jesus.
(*All to repeat*)
Generous God, thank you that you want all people to **see** this love in action
(*All to repeat*)
Generous God, we pray for those we can **'see'** in our mind now.
(*All to repeat*)

Ask everyone to think of things that they **know** about God. Invite everyone to join in by repeating the lines of the prayer:

Creator God, we thank you that we **know** that you love us.
(*All to repeat*)
Creator God, we thank you that you want the whole world to **know** you and your love.
(*All to repeat*)

Creator God, we thank you that you want us to be part of your plan.
(*All to repeat*)

Remind everyone that when the wise men came to Jesus, they knelt to **worship** him. Ask everyone to get into a position for worshipping Jesus - kneeling, bowing their head or standing with raised arms. Ask them to close their eyes and picture the scene that the wise men saw. Invite everyone to join in this response:

Holy God, we **worship** you for your Son, Jesus.
(*All to repeat*)
Holy God, we thank you that you want all people to **worship** you.
(*All to repeat*)
Holy God, we **worship** Jesus now.
(*All to repeat*)

Follow this time of prayer with a suitable song of worship.

Ending the service

The wise men worshipped Jesus, and then changed their plans to avoid danger on the way home (see Matthew 2:12). Ask each person to think about one thing they wish to avoid or change as a result of worshipping Jesus and, if appropriate, to share this with someone sitting near them.

Conclude with this prayer:

Jesus, we have been here to worship you, and we are changed.
We have made a promise to ourselves to change.
We want to make that same promise to you

and ask for your help.
Be with us, Lord, and give us the strength we need, so we may be changed even more.
Amen.

Helpful extras

Music and song ideas
Use carols that relate in particular to the wise men, such as: 'We three kings'; 'Wise men, they came to look for wisdom'; 'As with gladness'. Other songs could include: 'The King is among us'; 'Majesty'; 'As I come into your presence'; 'The wise may bring their learning'; 'I just want to praise you'.

A version of 'Three kings from Persian lands afar' would support the theme.

Statement of faith
Use this simplified creed (Year A.Epiphany_1) to reiterate 'See', 'Know' and 'Worship'. It is also available from www.scriptureunion. org.uk/lightdownloads. Encourage the congregation to read it through carefully, joining in the emboldened words. Say it slowly, twice.

What do we see?
We see God the Creator at work in the world that he created.

What else do we see?
We see that people have damaged God's world and turned away from God.

What else do we see?
We see God at work in our church and our lives.

What do we know?

We know that God sent Jesus to save all people.

What else do we know?
We know that Jesus died and rose again.

What else do we know?
We know that the Holy Spirit is with us now.

Why do we worship?
We worship God the Father to give thanks for all he has done.

Why else do we worship?
We worship God's Son, Jesus, as he came to save the wise men, and all people.

Why else do we worship?
We worship God the Holy Spirit, because he gives us power to follow God's way.

Game

With: separate cards prepared with 'eyes', 'brain', 'knees', 'hands', 'heart' and 'body' written on them

Hand out the cards at random, either as people arrive, or during the service. Make sure that everyone has a card. Then read out Ephesians 3:6.

Remind the congregation that we are different from each other, but we are united in our worship of Jesus, as the Jews and Gentiles were. Ask everyone to move around to find others who have a different card from theirs. Once a 'full' body (eyes, brain, knees, hands, heart and body) has come together in a group, ask them to talk about the role their body part plays in the life of the church, such as making the place beautiful, creating sounds that help worship, praying or being practical. Then ask each person to tell other members of their group one way in which they think they give and contribute to the body of Christ.

Notes and comments

This service outline for Epiphany could be used instead of the outline for the Second Sunday of Christmas.

Epiphany is a time to celebrate the international nature of the church.

Alternative online options

Visit www.lightlive.org for additional activities for children, young people and adults. There are a large number of activities and suggestions for bringing alive the story of the wise men to younger children in the service.

THE BAPTISM OF CHRIST (also FIRST SUNDAY OF EPIPHANY)

READINGS: **Acts 10:34–43; Matthew 3:13–17**
Isaiah 42:1–9; Psalm 29:1–11

Bible foundations

Aim: to see that Jesus' baptism and miracles show that he really is the Son of God

Peter's brief but full testimony in Acts 10 about the life and work of Jesus follows the groundbreaking visit and vision concerning Cornelius. This event has completely changed the way Peter looks at things. He asserts that Jesus is the One sent by God.

Jesus' own baptism isn't about confessing sin, as the other baptisms that John carried out were, or baptism as we practise it. This baptism was about fulfilling all righteousness. This sounds very good and proper, but what exactly does that mean? 'Jesus identifies with and endorses John's ministry as divinely ordained and his message as one to be heeded' (Craig L Blomberg). Jesus is showing that what John is doing is right; it should happen and people should do as John is telling them. Jesus has already been linked with fulfilling scriptural prophecy and Israel's typology and now he is linked with 'all righteousness'. To do this Jesus will be baptised. This isn't for any sin to be removed but because it is the right thing to do. This is how the promise in Matthew 5:17 is attained, through everything about Jesus.

'Like a dove' doesn't mean that there was a real bird but some divine attribute symbolised by the bird in the Scriptures. There are two signs – audio and visual. God was into using multiple learning styles. The voice from heaven echoes Psalm 2:7 and Isaiah 42:1 to show us the divine son and the suffering servant motifs. It is also noteworthy that the whole Trinity is involved in the event.

Matthew has already shown us that Jesus is God's Son and so we shouldn't see this as simply an indwelling of the Spirit (which we can all experience), but a commissioning; Jesus' public ministry begins and God makes it clear that Jesus is his Son.

Beginning the service

Announce that you are really pleased to see X and Y and Z because… This needs to be a genuinely truthful statement. Ask people to think of things they could say about others present that makes them pleased to know them.

This service focuses upon God's pleasure in his Son, Jesus.

Bible reading

Acts 10:34–43 is Peter's pronouncement about the purpose of Jesus' life and death for all. For maximum impact, you will need to put it in the context of Peter's visit to the home of Cornelius; so tell the story, recorded in Acts 10:1–33, in a dramatic way. Emphasise that Jesus came for the Gentiles, as well as for the Jews; also add verses 44–48.

During the reading of Matthew 3:13–17, show a classical painting of Jesus' baptism and talk about how faithful the artist is to the biblical account.

Bible talk

With: six physically able volunteers

Ask the volunteers to come to the front to form giant letters, 'A', 'B' and 'C', with their bodies at the appropriate time. They need to have planned this beforehand. For instance, 'A' could be two people leaning on each other with shoulders meeting, and hands meeting in the middle.

'A' – Arrived
Jesus' journey on earth began with his birth

(which we remembered at Christmas). At Epiphany, we remember the wise men who arrived and worshipped him. Then Jesus grew from a baby to a boy, and from a boy to a man. Now Jesus has arrived at the point on his journey where he has come to the River Jordan to be baptised by his cousin, known to many as John the Baptist. Ask two volunteers to form the letter 'A'. In Acts 10, Peter talks of the message that John the Baptist gave, warning everyone to prepare for the arrival of one greater than him. Of course, that person was Jesus and now, at last, he has arrived.

'B' – Baptised
Ask two volunteers to form the letter 'B'. Imagine the conversation between John and Jesus. John didn't want to baptise Jesus because baptism was a sign of repentance – being sorry for and turning away from sin. John knew that Jesus was God, and that he had never done anything wrong, so he didn't need to be baptised! But Jesus was determined to show what should be done, and insisted that John should baptise him. He identified himself publicly with the sinners he had come to save. (Matthew 3:15 hints that the symbol of being 'washed clean' by baptism may also have been to demonstrate how Jesus would take the sins of the world and be punished instead of us when he died on the cross.)

Jesus probably went into the river, and John may have poured water on him, or Jesus may have gone fully under the water as a sign of his baptism. It was a dramatic moment, because as it took place we read that the heavens opened and the Spirit of God came down like a dove. Awesome!

'C' – Chosen

Ask two volunteers to form the letter 'C'. Invite the congregation to discuss in pairs or small mixed-age groups what they think Jesus was chosen by God to do. Get some feedback; then explain that, after Jesus had been baptised, the voice of God announced from heaven, 'This is my Son, whom I love; with him I am well pleased' (TNIV). Compare this statement with Isaiah's prophecy in Isaiah 42:1, which was fulfilled at Jesus' baptism. God the Father was delighted that his Son, in obedience, has come to fulfil his plan for the world.

Peter says in Acts 10:37 and 38 that this was the beginning of Jesus' work, because afterwards he 'went everywhere, doing good and healing'. God gave Jesus the Holy Spirit's power – Jesus was truly the Son of God.

'A', 'B' and 'C': Arrived, Baptised and Chosen. Jesus arrived at the River Jordan, was baptised, filled with the Holy Spirit, and went on to do the work he had been chosen to do. These letters are the beginning of the alphabet. This amazing event was the beginning of Jesus' earthly ministry, and the fulfilment of God's plan for his people. Continue with the **Prayer activity**.

Prayer activity

Ask three people to stand by the volunteers from the **Bible talk**, who reform their letters. Each person leads in prayer, along the following lines.

'A' – Arrived

Thank Jesus for being willing to come to earth for all people.

Thank God that we have arrived at this particular day in our lives.
Thank God for when he has helped in the tough times (*pause for personal reflection*).
Thank God for the good times and happy memories.

'B' – Baptised

Think about the humility of Jesus, being willing to be baptised.
Thank God that he sent his Holy Spirit to empower Jesus.
Thank God for our own baptism.
Thank God that he is with us, and his Holy Spirit lives in us.

'C' – Chosen

Think about all the work that Jesus went on to do.
Thank God for the ways he has used us.
Ask God to help us do things for him in the future.

Ending the service

Invite people to think about their own 'A', 'B' and 'C' as a consequence of the service. You may want to lead them in their thinking as follows:

'A' – We all arrived here. We give thanks for the journey of life that brought us to worship here today, and the things that God has done for us in the past.

'B' – We have been here. We give thanks for being able to be in God's presence, and for the work the Holy Spirit has done, is doing, and will do within us.

'C' – We continue from here. We give thanks for all the things we will be doing in this coming week, and we ask God to help us move on with him.

You could end with a suitable prayer of thanksgiving, with everyone joining in the emboldened response.

We give thanks to Jesus.
He came to earth for all people.

We give thanks to Jesus.
He went to the Jordan to meet John.

We give thanks to Jesus.
He was willing to be baptised.

We give thanks to Jesus.
He was filled with the Holy Spirit.

We give thanks to Jesus.
He is truly the Son of God.

We give thanks to Jesus.
He is with us now.

Alternatively, suggest that after the service, people share with others what it is that they value about them.

Helpful extras

Music and song ideas
The following songs may be suitable: 'Holy Spirit, come'; 'This grace is mine'; 'Jesus, name above all names'; 'Jesus, creation's voice…'; 'There is a Redeemer'; 'God's Spirit' *Bitesize Bible Songs* 2 CD (SU) is a Learn and remember verse based on 2 Timothy 1:7.

Notes and comments

This service outline is also the outline for the First Sunday of Epiphany.

Peter's realisation that God accepted Gentiles as well as Jews parallels Paul's convictions, as explored in the previous Epiphany service outline. You may wish to remind people of this.

Churches have different views about the meaning and significance of the rite of baptism, as well as the age at which people are baptised. This service is an opportunity to teach a little more about your church's practice of baptism.

You could explore Acts 10:34–43 in more detail by continuing the ABC theme further, as follows:

'A' – Arrived
'B' – Baptised
'C' – Chosen

Volunteers can make further letters with their bodies.

'D' – Doing good (verse 38)
After he had been baptised, the Bible tells us that Jesus did good wherever and whenever he could, and the results meant that many people were changed by him and turned to God.

'E' – Everywhere (verse 38)
Jesus travelled more widely than most people did at the time. He wasn't restricted by the size of the town or village, or the social consequences of going there (for example, he visited Samaria – enemy territory as far as the Jews were concerned).

'F' – Followers ('witnesses', verse 39)
As Jesus travelled, spoke and healed there were many who followed him, learning from

him and doing good to others too. Peter is a first-hand witness, but we too can tell of what Jesus has done in our lives, and what we have seen him do in the lives of others.

'G' – Good news

Jesus' words were good news to a people suffering under the Roman occupation, and wanting to be free. The good news is even greater for us, as we know that Jesus died for us.

'H' – Hope

Even though Jesus died, he came alive again. We are given hope, and we are called to share that hope with the world.

Alternative online options

Visit www.lightlive.org for additional activities for children, young people and adults.

Big Bible Storybook
(978 1 84427 228 0)

The award winning *Big Bible Storybook* brings Bible stories alive for the under fives.

Available as a book and an audio book, it is a wonderful resource to be used in all-age services.

For more details, visit www.scriptureunion.org.uk

SECOND SUNDAY OF EPIPHANY

READINGS: 1 Corinthians 1:1–9; John 1:29–42
Isaiah 49:1–7; Psalm 40:1–12

Bible foundations

Aim: to share in the excitement of those who discovered Jesus for the first time

The church at Corinth was the local expression of a universal society. In Paul's letter to them there are some strong warnings and criticisms, but all this is preceded by joy. This joy comes from God's grace at work in the lives of these 'saints'. Despite what is to come in the letter, Paul is sharing the overwhelming joy that finding salvation brings. He is committed to giving thanks to God for them (verse 4).

John the Baptist proclaims that Jesus is the Lamb of God, the Son of God, the One who calls people to repent, the One who takes away the sin of the world. This is a pretty good endorsement from the man who was known for calling others to repent and symbolically washing them clean in the Jordan. But his message and his whole role was that of a forerunner, as anticipated by the prophets.

Some have seen Andrew's assertion that Jesus is the Messiah (John 1:41) as a later theological addition to the narrative. (The main reason for this is that it is only later in the narrative that Peter confesses Jesus as the Christ.) However, as John the Baptist has previously made a strong attestation to Jesus, this need not be the case.

People enter the kingdom of God through evangelistic events, missions and courses, such as the Alpha course. But what has almost always preceded this is the invitation from someone. The growth in some youth groups is not down to a prayerful leader, or a fantastic programme, although both are vital, but is usually down to young people themselves inviting their friends along. Invitations often flow more spontaneously with the excitement of new faith.

Beginning the service

With: balloons; string; luggage labels; pens

Tie luggage labels to the balloons, and make sure that there are at least enough for every individual, couple or family. As people arrive, give out the balloons and pens, and ask them to sit and talk for a few minutes about things that make them excited. Those things should be written on the labels. Children and older people may need help with this, but it is important that everyone takes part.

After the formal beginning of the service, invite everyone in turn to bring their balloons out, and tie them to a suitable area at the front of the church. With permission, ask a selection of people to talk briefly about something that they get excited about.

Mention that when Jesus called his disciples, they had a genuine sense of excitement at being called to go with him and follow him. Encourage people to remember the things that make them excited, and allow themselves to be excited by the love that Jesus has for us.

Bible reading

John 1:29–42 could be mimed, with movement and gestures, while the story is read. Encourage those taking part to portray their decision to follow Jesus enthusiastically. You will need five people to be John the Baptist, two disciples of John (one of whom is Andrew), Jesus and Simon Peter.

Ask people to listen out for the personal warmth and enthusiasm in Paul's opening paragraph of his first letter to the Corinthian Christians in 1 Corinthians 1:1–9.

Bible talk

With: 2 actors to be interviewed about their experience of meeting Jesus

Explain that you are going to interview two people who met Jesus. The two actors should have prepared their answers to the following questions so that it sounds spontaneous.

John the Baptist
- What did you know about Jesus before you baptised him?
- Tell me what happened when you baptised Jesus.
- What did you say when you saw Jesus coming towards you (paraphrasing John 1:29–34)?

Andrew
- What did you know about Jesus while you were a follower of John the Baptist?
- What happened when you first met Jesus while you were with John?
- Why did you want to introduce your brother, Simon, to Jesus and what happened? (John 1:40–42)

In small groups ask people to think of two words to describe what John the Baptist and Andrew had said or done. Share any feedback and then ask: in what ways can we follow Jesus like Andrew?

Prayer activity

With: 3 balloons with a large luggage label attached to each, on which is written one of the following: 'New Opportunities'; 'New People'; 'New Places'

Ask three people to write, and then read

(with realistic enthusiasm), prayers that are focused on the following:

- fresh opportunities that the New Year presents to tell others about Jesus
- new people with whom to share the good news
- new places to visit to share the good news of Jesus

Include in your prayers any needs of your mission partners. Each person holds the appropriate balloon as they read their prayer. Alternatively, position the balloons in three different areas of the building and ask people to gather in groups around them to pray for new opportunities, people and places.

Ending the service

Close with the following prayer:

May God the Father be with us as we go,
May Jesus the Son lead us as we follow,
With the power of the Holy Spirit in our lives.
Amen.

Helpful extras

Music and song ideas

Songs might include: 'I, the Lord of sea and sky'; 'I want to walk with Jesus Christ'; 'Come on and celebrate'; 'My Jesus, my Saviour'; 'Oh, lead me'; 'Tell out, my soul'; 'Follow me' *Bitesize Bible Songs* CD (SU)

Game

Divide the church into two groups and ask for two volunteers to represent each group. Each in turn mimes one of the 'moods' listed below. Within 30 seconds, the group that they represent must correctly guess the

mood that they are portraying, for which they get two points. If they can't and the other group guesses correctly, the other group gets a bonus point.

Ask your volunteers to mime the following moods: happy, lost, puzzled, excited, shocked, tired, angry, and celebrating.

Talk about the possible moods and emotions that the first disciples may have felt when first called by Jesus. They would have been excited, but they may also have had doubts or fears about where it would all lead. That may be the same for us, but we know that God promises the best for those who choose to follow him.

Notes and comments

The Bible passages focus on being invited to meet Jesus, and the challenge of living a life following him. If we look at how Jesus called the disciples, we see that John the Baptist encouraged two of his followers to go to Jesus. Later, one of them, Andrew, went to fetch his brother, Simon, so that he could meet Jesus too. This service is an opportunity to encourage and motivate the congregation to invite others to meet Jesus. They need to understand that it is usually through personal invitation that people become part of a church community and may then move on to following Jesus.

You could plan a special event (such as an early 'Back to Church Sunday') for a few weeks' time, and encourage all ages to pray for their friends and to invite them personally to the event.

At the start of the New Year, introduce the various outreach opportunities that are being planned for the future, so that people can pray and get involved.

Alternative Bible talk

Paul's first letter to the Corinthians contains a great deal of excitement and encouragement, before later turning to some concerns that Paul has. 1 Corinthians 1:1–9 can be split into these three themes:

Be thankful

Paul encourages the Corinthian church by saying how much he gives thanks to God for them (verse 4). Are there people we should be really thankful to God for? Does being thankful to God mean only remembering what God does for us when we are in crisis?

Be blessed

Paul reminds the members of the church that God is continually blessing them (verse 5), even though at this stage they are still young in their faith. In our lives it is easy to feel that nothing happens and that life is tough, yet God is blessing us continually with his recreation every day. Do we look out and give thanks for the blessings God is showering upon us? Do we sometimes miss God's blessings because we get too bogged down in other things?

Be firm

After giving thanks for the people in the church, and asking them to recognise the blessings God has given them, Paul then challenges them to keep firm and faithful (verse 8). They have a duty to remain firm to the truth that they are learning, and not to be swayed by the other religions and dogmas that were prevalent in Corinth at that time. By the same token, we know the truth of Christ, and we know how we should live. We have a faithful God – how firm is our faith in return?

Alternative online options

Visit www.lightlive.org for additional activities for children, young people and adults.

Resources for Easter

Great gifts for young children in an all-age service or in a toddler group, or encourage parents to get hold of a copy, or provide children's leaders with new Easter activity ideas!

Happy Easter (978 1 94427 226 6)
The Easter story told in this little book!

My Little Yellow Book (978 1 85999 693 5)
Bible reading with under fives.

The Big Yellow Book (978 1 85999 692 8)
Bucket loads of ideas for toddlers groups and under-fives children's activities for Easter-time, in this book in the *Tiddlywinks* series.

Easter Cracked (978 1 84427 189 4)
A wide selection of Easter ideas, service and assembly outlines to use with children, young people and families.

To find out more, visit www.scriptureunion.org.uk.

THIRD SUNDAY OF EPIPHANY

READINGS: **I Corinthians 1:10–18; Matthew 4:12–23**
Isaiah 9:1–4; Psalm 27:1,4–12

Bible foundations

Aim: to discover how Jesus' call to his followers was straightforward and not complicated by divisions

Division is all too common an experience in the Church. It is the most damaging event that can happen among Christians, even though good can result. As Jesus said, a house divided can't survive (see Matthew 12:25,26).

Paul is so concerned about division that he places the divisions in Corinth at the start of his letter. As with so many differences, these are caused by trying to raise certain individuals above others; the cult of celebrity was alive and well in Corinth. Paul is having none of it, though. His message is essentially very straightforward (1 Corinthians 1:17,18). There is no point in claiming to take sides against each other or in claiming to be special because of who baptised whom. It is by placing Christ at the centre, and only this, that we can be joined with our brothers and sisters. Jesus himself was not divided. And Paul was not crucified (verse 13). His memory is extremely hazy as to whom he had baptised (verse 16).

In Matthew, we are told that John is in prison. With this news, Jesus returns to Galilee, again with the obligatory Old Testament passage (Isaiah 9:1,2) illuminating the way. Although Jesus will first preach to Israel, before becoming a light to the world, it is perhaps significant that Capernaum had a population that was about fifty per cent Gentile.

Matthew 4:17 traditionally sees the beginning of the second section of this Gospel, with the phrase 'from that time on'. We immediately see two sets of brothers called by Jesus, who abruptly decide to follow him. We read that the first two already knew Jesus (see John 1:42), but it is still important that their response is positively decisive. Jesus' call was uncomplicated and it is worth commenting that John did not insist that his disciples remained loyal only to him.

Beginning the service

You could play the **Game** as a means of introducing the theme of the service.

Alternatively, you could take a collection of digital photos of simple instructions that we see around us, such as: 'Stand clear!', 'Look right!', 'Don't touch!', 'BEWARE!' and 'Stop!' Talk about these as a means of introducing the straightforward message that Jesus preached and the simple instructions he gave. This is the theme of this service.

Bible reading

I Corinthians 1:10–18 could be read by several people. Break verses 10–16 into fragments of phrases (demonstrating division and brevity) with everyone joining together to read verses 17 and 18, the straightforwardness of the gospel. The reading below comes from the CEV and Reader I is the gentle voice of Paul while Readers 2 and 3 are the more commanding voice.

Reader I:	My dear friends, as a follower of our Lord Jesus Christ, I beg you to get along with each other.
Reader 2:	Don't take sides.
Reader 3:	Always try to agree in what you think.
Reader I:	Several people from Chloe's family have already reported to me that you keep arguing with each other. They have said that some of you claim to follow me, while others claim to follow Apollos or Peter or Christ.

Reader 2:	Has Christ been divided up?
Reader 3:	Was I nailed to a cross for you?
Reader 2:	Were you baptized in my name?
Reader I:	I thank God that I didn't baptize any of you except Crispus and Gaius. Not one of you can say that you were baptized in my name. I did baptize the family of Stephanas, but I don't remember if I baptized anyone else.
Readers 1,2,3:	Christ did not send me to baptize. He sent me to tell the good news without using big words that would make the cross of Christ lose its power. The message about the cross doesn't make any sense to lost people. But for those of us who are being saved, it is God's power at work.
	I Corinthians 1:10–18 (CEV)

Matthew 4:17–23 could be read by one person wandering around the building using a microphone, to demonstrate how Jesus travelled around, preaching and calling his disciples.

In reading Isaiah 9:1–4 make the connection with Matthew 4:14–16.

Bible talk

With: paper and pencils

This needs to follow the **Bible reading**. Divide the congregation into small groups where they are sitting. Ask each group to think of a name for their team.

Give out pencils and paper and invite each team to choose a scribe to write down their answers. (The answer to each question in the quiz below is in italics.)

Q1: When Jesus began preaching and teaching, did he go to Jerusalem, Egypt or Galilee? (*Galilee*)

Q2: Were the people in Galilee mostly Jews, mostly Gentiles (in other words, not Jews), or neither? (*Mostly Gentiles*)

Q3: Would people have been expecting Jesus to go somewhere like Galilee? (*No*)

Q4: Which prophet had said that this would happen – Isaiah, Jeremiah or Zechariah? (*Isaiah*)

Q5: What jobs did Jesus' very first disciples do - carpenters, fishermen or chefs? (*Fishermen*)

Q6: Jesus chose two sets of brothers to be his disciples. What were their names? (*Andrew and Peter/Simon; James and John* – one point for each name)

Q7: Did these disciples ask for extra time, say 'No' and then change their minds, or did they go straightaway? (*Go straightaway*)

Q8: What straightforward command did Jesus give? (*Come with me/Follow me!*)

Find out how the groups got on.

Jesus' command to 'Come with me' was straightforward and those who were to become his disciples followed him. We can make it seem a complicated thing to follow Jesus – this is not to say that it is unimportant to study the Scriptures, to explore the depths of our faith – but the good news of Jesus is essentially very simple.

In his letter to the Corinthians, Paul asks Jesus' followers not to waste time arguing and taking sides or rooting for one leader as opposed to another. He urges them to concentrate on what matters – the good news. It can be all too easy to lose track of the fact that there is only one person we should be following, and that is Jesus.

Prayers of intercession

As the Christians in Corinth were very divided, pray for unity among the different churches in your area, for the leaders and for the opportunities local churches have to work together in sharing the good news and serving the community. Conclude by holding hands and singing a song such as 'Bind us together'. If it is your custom, you could say 'the Grace' together.

Prayer of confession

Ask everyone to stand and turn away from the people near to them. Some people can face a wall or empty space, while others may need to turn at an angle so that they are not looking specifically at anyone. They could even sit down to stare at the floor. Ask everyone to close their eyes as you pray. Invite people to learn and then say the emboldened response, if they truly mean it.

Lord God, there are people whom we disagree with about all kinds of issues. (*Ask everyone to think about someone whom they have disagreed with or had a quarrel with.*)

Lord God, we are sorry and we ask for your forgiveness.

Lord God, there are people whom we have taken sides with, against other people. We may have ganged up on someone or a group of people. We may have been so sure that we were in the right. (*Ask everyone to think of someone whom they have taken sides against.*)

Lord God, we are sorry and we ask for your forgiveness.

Lord God, we have sometimes lost sight of the fact that as your people, we are united because Jesus died for us. We have forgotten just what Jesus' death means in making it possible for us to be your friends.

Lord God, we are sorry and we ask for your forgiveness.
Amen

Invite everyone to turn to look at the other people around them. Invite them to smile at others, knowing that God has forgiven you. If this service includes Holy Communion, now would be a good time to make the Peace and greet each other. If you sense that for some people this has been significant, you could give more time to allow people to settle a disagreement.

Ending the service

The service leader explains that they are going to leave the building but will call some people to come with them, to give them a sweet, a piece of fruit or a bookmark as appropriate. As they leave, they call out several people by name (of mixed ages) – 'Come with me X!' These people then follow.

A second leader then asks the remaining people how they feel to be left behind.

Assure them that they too can enjoy whatever is being shared with the others because Jesus calls us all to follow! Our challenge is to obey him! This leader then shares out the sweets.

Helpful extras
Music and song ideas
Songs that deal with following Jesus include: 'All to Jesus (I surrender all)'; 'I have decided to follow Jesus'; 'Make me a channel of your peace'. Songs that express the desire for unity and togetherness include: 'Bind us together, Lord'; 'Blessed be the tie that binds'; 'The Church's one foundation' (especially verses 1 and 2); 'Jesus is Lord, the cry'; 'Follow me' *Bitesize Bible Songs* CD (SU).

You could use an alternative musical idea for the adventurous! With a large music group, use the following musical illustration, if the musicians are given enough warning! Begin a song or piece of music with all the musicians playing at their own pace and out of time with each other. At some point in the ensuing cacophony, stop them and ask what has gone wrong. Each musician can explain their preference for how to play the song: one says that they think it is best played slow; another says that it is best played fast; another says that they prefer to start with the chorus rather than the verse, or that they were following the keyboard player, violinist or person next to them.

Ask them why they don't usually sound like this (which is because they usually agree how they are going to play the piece before they start, and they take their lead from one person, such as the worship leader, choirmaster or drummer). In a similar way, if everyone in the church just decided to do things as they liked, things would end up being just as chaotic. Just as a choir sings best when they are following their choirmaster, the church works best when they are all following Christ. It is really quite simple!

Notes and comments

Isaiah 9:1–4 speak of the people of the lands of Zebulun and Naphtali, who had been living in darkness, seeing a great light. Zebulun and Naphtali were sons of the same father, Jacob. However, they came from what we might call these days a 'non-nuclear' family. Naphtali's mother was Bilhah, who was the handmaiden of Jacob's favoured wife, Rachel. Zebulun's mother was Leah, Jacob's first wife, whom he was deceived into marrying. You can only imagine what kind of family tensions must

have been at work here – each a son of a different mother, each seeing that their own mother was not their father's favourite. Yet together, Naphtali and Zebulun were to 'see a great light'. Divisions in the family of Israel and among the subsequent tribal groups were replicated in the early Church and up to the present day among God's people.

If this service includes Holy Communion, comment on the simplicity of the symbolism and the unity to be found as you break bread and drink wine together. See, also, a suggestion for passing the peace in the **Prayer of confession**.

Alternative online options

Visit www.lightlive.org for additional activities for children, young people and adults.

FOURTH SUNDAY OF EPIPHANY

READINGS: I Kings 17:8–16; John 2:1–11
Psalm 36:5–10; I Corinthians 1:18–31

Bible foundations

Aim: to recognise God's power and authority as he comes to those who are in need

The prophet Elijah is caught in the midst of a power struggle (I Kings 17–19). On the one side there is a fertility god (a baal) and on the other, the Lord God. Ahab and his foreign wife Jezebel are representatives of baal, and Elijah is the messenger of God. The baals were thought to control the weather, the cycle of agriculture, life and fertility, and the lightning and rain. Through Elijah, however, God shows that he is the one who is in control. God controls the weather. He sends drought (17:1–7) and rain (18:41–46). God controls the availability of food. He gives bread (17:8–16). God controls life. He revives the widow's son (17:17–24). God controls lightning. He sends fire to burn up the sacrifice (18:38). Here is a series of miracles or acts of power. But on a human level in today's reading (verses 8–16) God comes to those in human need, as Elijah, the widow and her son faced starvation.

This theme is picked up in the story of the wedding in Cana. A potentially disastrous and embarrassing event was solved when Jesus stepped in, turning water in vast quantities into the very best wine possible. This was a very human situation but the presence of God made all the difference. Paul writes of this in I Corinthians 1:18–31, for the message of the cross 'doesn't make any sense to lost people but for those of us being saved, it is God's power at work' (verse 18 CEV). Jesus' disciples put their faith in him as he had showed his glory to them.

The generosity of God and his love are reflected in Psalm 36:5–10. May this service encourage people of all ages to look expectantly to God whose power is at work among those who are in need!

Beginning the service

With: a recording of, or by singing, 'Our God is an awesome God, He reigns from heaven above.'

Ask what it means to describe someone as 'awesome'. Who are the people anyone would describe as 'awesome'? Explain that the focus of the service is on our awesome God, his works of power and his miraculous deeds as he comes to those in need.

Then listen to or sing the words of 'Our God is an awesome God'. Vary the speed and volume as you sing it several times.

Bible reading

The reading from 1 Kings 17 can be read by a narrator, and three character voices (The LORD, the widow and Elijah).

Narrator:	The LORD told Elijah:
The LORD:	Go to the town of Zarephath in Sidon and live there. I've told a widow in that town to give you food.
Narrator:	When Elijah came near the town gate of Zarephath, he saw a widow gathering sticks for a fire.
Elijah:	Would you please bring me a cup of water? Would you also please bring me a piece of bread?
The widow:	(wearily) In the name of the living Lord your God, I swear that I don't have any bread. All I have is a handful of flour and a little olive oil. I'm on my way home now with these few sticks to cook

	what I have for my son and me. After that, we will starve to death.
Elijah:	Everything will be fine. Do what you said. Go home and prepare something for youself and your son. But first, please make a small piece of bread and bring it to me. The Lord God of Israel has promised that your jar of flour won't run out and your bottle of oil won't dry up before he sends rain for the crops.
Narrator:	The widow went home and did exactly what Elijah had told her. She and Elijah and her family had enough food for a long time. The Lord kept the promise that his prophet Elijah had made, and she did not run out of flour or oil.

1 Kings 17:8–16 (CEV)

The story in John 2:1–10 is well known. Try reading it in a modern version such as *The Message*.

Bible retelling

The story when Jesus turned water into wine is well told in Episode 2 of *Wastewatchers* DVD (SU). The script of that episode (YearA. Epiphany4_1), which could be read out loud as it is, is available from www.scriptureunion.org.uk/lightdownloads

Bible talk

With: a marker pen; five large signs made of card as follows: 'DO NOT ENTER!', 'NO BREAD LEFT!', 'BE AFRAID!', 'NO WINE!'

and 'PANIC!' – allow space to add the words 'DO NOT' in front of 'BE AFRAID!' and 'PANIC!' (Each sign can be placed in a different area of the worship space so that the idea of God being everywhere is being acted out during the talk.)

Each sign is dealt with in turn.

DO NOT ENTER!

At the time of Elijah, people often thought God was confined just to one place or territory. But Elijah knew that God was more than that. In today's story, God sent Elijah to a foreign country, Phoenicia, and he sent him, as his messenger, to a town called Zarephath near a city called Sidon. Elijah went to this foreign land not with a timid spirit but trusting in God. He was showing that there is no area where God cannot go! God was breaking any boundary that limited him. Break up the 'DO NOT ENTER!' sign.

Elijah trusted in God and this gave him courage. If appropriate, teach the Learn and remember verse from 2 Timothy 1:17: 'For the Spirit that God has given us does not make us timid; instead, his Spirit fills us with power, love and self-control.' To learn this as a song, see **Music and song ideas**. Stress the idea of not being timid and speak the second part boldly.

NO BREAD LEFT!

The woman and her son had almost run out of the ingredients needed to make their last loaf of bread. Drought had affected the crops. This woman expected to die. But Elijah reassured her that everything would be fine. God had promised and he keeps his word. What is more, God is all-powerful. The woman did what Elijah said and there was always enough oil and flour to make bread for the woman, her son and Elijah.

Elijah demonstrated God's power and compassion. Break up the 'NO BREAD LEFT!' sign.

BE AFRAID!

The woman was deeply fearful before she met Elijah. But she discovered that an all-powerful God who keeps his word can be trusted. She did not need to be afraid. Instead of destroying this sign because it is not true, we can change it to read 'DO NOT BE AFRAID!' That's what Elijah said to the woman in verse 13.

NO WINE!

At the wedding Jesus went to, they ran out of wine. It was a disaster for the man in charge of the wedding festivities. It could have brought shame on the family. But Jesus, who was God and therefore had power, authority and compassion too, did something to change everything. Ask what he did. Then break up the sign.

PANIC!

Several people, including the servants and Jesus' mother were panicking that they had run out of wine at the wedding. But because Jesus did something to make a difference they no longer needed to be sad. Add 'DO NOT' to the sign.

What we are left with are two signs that say what we must do if we trust in an awesome, powerful God. We do not need to be afraid and we do not need to panic. There is no place where God cannot be or go. So he is with us all the time. There is no need that he cannot meet.

Repeat the Learn and remember verse from 2 Timothy 1:7.

Prayer activity

With: a piece of paper in the shape of a water pot for everyone; pens

God works through ordinary people who trust him. Often it is in the actions that we take that God shows his power and compassion. It was through Elijah that God showed his care for the woman. God is active in ordinary situations too, such as a wedding. So how might God want to bless someone else through everyone present?

Comment that the water pot is empty. Ask everyone to draw a line where the liquid would be if the pot was full up. Then ask everyone to write or draw something that they would do to help someone this week so that their life does not feel empty. They need to think of someone who is sad, afraid, sick or alone in some way.

Then pray as follows:
Lord, we thank you that you are great and powerful. Yet you choose us to bring your love.
Help us to share what we have in love.
Help us to share our homes, our hospitality, our toys and our time.
Lord, you are great and powerful yet you choose us to bring your healing.
May we give our time to bring help to those in need and those who face a crisis in their life.

Use us, we pray, in Jesus' name. Amen.

Ending the service

Hundreds of years ago people used to look out west from Cornwall, France and Spain and all they could see were waves and the ocean. They thought there was nothing else beyond. Then in 1492 Columbus discovered America. Everything changed.

Some people look out on life and all they can see is things going wrong, emptiness, sorrow and pain. God acted in the life of the widow and everything changed. God acted to turn water into wine at the wedding and everything changed. Jesus came alive again and everything changed.

Close, as you began, by singing 'Our God is an awesome God', only now we appreciate more fully just how awesome and powerful he is. Alternatively, you could sing 'God is an awesome God' from *Light for everyone* CD, which provides a list of what Jesus did – see **Music and song ideas**.

Helpful extras

Music and song ideas

Some of the many song options include: 'Our God is an awesome God, he reigns from heaven above' (*Celtic Source Volume Two* includes a setting of this); 'God is an awesome God' *Light for everyone* CD (SU); 'All my days' (Wellspring's CD *Lord of the Ages* includes a setting of this); 'The Lord's my Shepherd'; 'Sing of the Lord's goodness' (speaks of the power wielded by God to give new life to all and 'pardon for the sinner'); 'O Lord my God'; 'You are the King of Glory';

'God's Spirit' *Bitesize Bible Songs 2* CD (SU), the Learn and remember verse for 2 Timothy 1:17.

Game
With: paper and pen

Ask everyone to get into pairs (or threes). Give each group some paper and a pen and challenge them to write or draw as many powerful things as they can think of in three minutes. It can be anything at all that is powerful. When the time is up, each group in turn tells everyone what they have on their list. As each thing is mentioned, anyone else who has written it down crosses it off their list. Which group had the longest list?

Ask the children which thing they think is the most powerful.

Statement of faith
The song 'Our God is an awesome God' is a statement of faith that recurs throughout the service.

Notes and comments
In Holy Communion, as you eat the bread and drink the wine, draw attention to the fact that in the two stories in today's service, God provided bread and wine – just as he provided his Son, whose body was broken and whose blood was poured out.

For some people the words 'power and authority' have negative connotations. This is an opportunity to present God, who holds ultimate authority, in a wholly positive light. However, be aware that for some people you may need to work hard to overcome an understanding that may be challenged by this service. Make sure that the prayer team is ready and available to pray for those in need.

In the **Bible talk** reference was made to God being everywhere and not territorially limited. In the light of this, pray for your mission partners who have certainly put this truth about God into practice by going to serve him elsewhere.

Alternative online options
Visit www.lightlive.org for additional activities for children, young people and adults.

FIFTH SUNDAY BEFORE LENT
(also known as PROPER I)

READINGS: **Matthew 5:13–20; Psalm 112:1–9**
Isaiah 58:1–9a; I Corinthians 2:1–12

Bible foundations

Aim: to explore what it means to shine as a light for God in this world

The gospel reading, taken from the 'Sermon on the Mount' in Matthew, is a popular passage, the subject of many children's or all-age talks. The image of salt and its uses, along with the power of light which is not hidden, are tangible and appear straightforward. However, when read alongside the other Bible passages the challenge to be 'salt and light' for Jesus in the world becomes more pronounced and involves action to bring about change in the lives of others. Psalm 112:4 speaks of light dawning for the upright and compassionate. Isaiah 58:6–8 challenges the hearers to care for others, 'then your light will shine like the dawning sun'.

Ghandi once said: 'The earth has enough for every man's need but not for every man's greed.' Global issues are part of everyday conversation and many non-faith organisations such as Comic Relief set out to overcome global poverty in the lives of millions of people. This is also true for God's people but with a different motivation, called to be lights in the world so all will see and praise Jesus' Father in heaven. Salvation is not achieved by good works. Jesus implies that in so doing, good works (being 'a light in the world') not only bring about change, but have an outreach dimension, leading others to the Father.

In first century Palestine, those who were outcast, sick or 'different' in any way were excluded from society thus leading them into poverty. It has been said that Jesus had a 'preferential option for the poor', choosing to spend his time with those people. To read any of the gospels in one sitting makes this quite clear in a profound way. In the gospel reading and Psalm 112, we are invited to join in this 'preferential option for the poor' and take up the challenge to live differently to be 'light for God in this world.'

Beginning the service

With: goody bags (such as party bags available from major supermarkets); contents for the bags might include - an individually wrapped piece of fair-trade chocolate, a candle, a pen, a piece of writing paper, a cut-out shape of a person, a campaign postcard; candles around the church

If possible, provide each person present with a 'goody bag' at the beginning of the service. See **Notes and comments** for further details. These items will be used throughout the service.

Welcome the congregation and explain that the service will focus on the theme of God's people being 'light in the world'. As the opening song 'Shine Jesus Shine' is sung, encourage the safe lighting of candles around the church. Light torches or lanterns as an alternative and safer option.

At the conclusion of the hymn, lead the congregation in an opening prayer including Matthew 5: 13–16.

Bible reading

In Psalm 112:1–9, three themes are identified – worship, justice and kindness. Ask three people of different ages to read. The following version from the TNIV (YearA.5Sunb4Lent_ 1) is available as a PowerPoint from www.scriptureunion.org.uk/lightdownloads.

Reader 1: (Worship)
Praise the LORD.
Blessed are those who fear the LORD,
who find great delight in his commands.

Reader 2: (Justice)
Their children will be mighty in the land;
the generation of the upright will be blessed.
Wealth and riches are in their houses,
and their righteousness endures forever.
Reader 3: (Kindness)
Even in darkness light dawns for the upright,
for those who are gracious and compassionate and righteous.
Reader 2: (Justice)
Good will come to those who are generous and lend freely,
who conduct their affairs with justice.
Reader 3: (Kindness)
Surely the righteous will never be shaken;
they will be remembered forever.
Reader 1: (Worship)
They will have no fear of bad news;
their hearts are steadfast, trusting in the LORD.
Their hearts are secure, they will have no fear;
in the end they will look in triumph on their foes.
Readers 1 and 3: (Worship and kindness)
They have scattered abroad their gifts to the poor,
their righteousness endures forever;
their horn will be lifted high in honour.
Psalm 112:1–9 (TNIV)

Explain that the three readers in this reading represented the themes which will be explored in the **Bible talk**. Read the psalm again altogether with the congregation divided into the three groups, reading from words on a screen or service sheet.

Before reading Matthew 5:13–20 ask a few people to dip their fingers into some salt.

How would they describe the taste? As verses 14–16 are read, cover up a candle in a slow dramatic way.

Bible talk

With: copies as hard copy or on PowerPoint of Psalm 112 (see **Bible reading** above) and Isaiah 58:6–8 (YearA.5Sunb4Advent_2) available from www.scriptureunion.org.uk/lightdownloads; images of musical notes, people dancing in worship, praying and singing (whatever is symbolic of your church's worship), a symbol of justice such as a lighted candle or broken chains, and a helping hand (kindness); display boards with information or a relevant DVD representing an organisation that fights for justice

Psalm 112 (especially verse 4) suggests that 'those who do right' – those who are kind, merciful and good – will be a 'light in the dark' for others (CEV) or 'Even in darkness light dawns for the upright, for those who are gracious and compassionate and righteous (TNIV). Matthew 5:13–20 encourages Jesus' disciples and followers not to do good things in secret, but to 'shine' so that others might see.

The question for everyone today is, just how can God's people 'shine' as lights in the world today? Psalm 112 provides three suggestions.

1. Worship

(*Show the worship images/symbols*) For many, worship takes the form of singing, participating in liturgical prayers or receiving communion. God loves hearing his people come together in worship; in the Old Testament God is pleased with the 'aroma'

of the sacrifice brought in worship and in the New Testament, the theme of 'aroma' continues, but in the context of being God's aroma being spread to those 'who are being saved' (2 Corinthians 2:15). The Bible also provides a challenge to those who worship. Just as without love, speaking in other languages, prophesy and faith are empty and hollow (1 Corinthians 13), Isaiah presents the challenge for a life of worship that is deeper and more costly than singing songs.

Read Isaiah 58:6–8a together. It presents suggestions as to what worship really means. As you read it aloud, encourage everyone to follow and contemplate what it might mean to them.

2. Justice

(*Show the justice images/symbols*) God is a God of justice and there are many references to this in the Bible especially the Old Testament. Psalm 112 says it is about doing right (Reader 1), being fair and honest (Reader 2) and being kind, merciful, generous and forgiving (Reader 3).

Break into small groups to talk about what it means to act justly and fairly at home, school or work.

3. Kindness

(*Show the kindness symbols*) Psalm 112 indicates that those who are kind are not troubled by their generosity and freely give to those in need. In times of recession and economic instability, financial generosity can get lost from personal discipleship. Later in Matthew 5:25–34, Jesus reminds his followers that God in heaven takes care of material needs. Paul in 2 Corinthians 9:7 reminds

Christians that 'God loves a cheerful giver.' Kindness and generosity can be offered on two levels – in personal kindness to those in need known locally and to those internationally who suffer.

To 'shine' in the world, God's people must be on the side of justice and practise kindness and generosity. Our challenge is knowing how to make this teaching real and tangible. How practically can Christians fight for justice?

Many Christian organisations based in the UK work on behalf of the poor and oppressed in order to bring freedom, kindness and justice. Some might be supported by the church and if so, spend some time presenting the basic principles of the organisation or showing a short video or DVD about their work. For example: www.tearfund.org; www.stopthetraffik.com; www.christianaid.org.uk; www.barnabasfund.org.

Individuals can also 'shine' by being present in the lives of friends and family through kindness and generosity.

Lead into a time of quiet to reflect on the **Bible talk**.

Prayer time

With: items from the goody bags

This is a time for individuals to use items from their goody bag to help them pray for or actively put into action the challenge presented to be 'light in the world.' Each individual should work independently with children assisted by adults. Alternatively, a special table for children could be arranged for them to engage with the more child-friendly activities.

Activities could include:
- Eat the fair-trade chocolate and think about how you might look for fair-trade items in your weekly shopping or search the internet for fair-trade presents or clothes. Pray silently for those whose lives have been positively affected by fair-trade.
- Write a letter to someone not known well to you, inviting them to share a meal at your home, then pray for them.
- On the outline of the person, write the name of someone to whom friendship or forgiveness might be extended (the children can do this one easily) and pray for them.
- Sign the campaign postcard and pray for God's will to be done in that situation.
- Place some money in the charity envelope and pray for the work done in God's name to bring peace and justice in the world.

Ending the service

Before singing a final song or hymn, invite everyone to read out loud together or to listen to the words from the prayer of St. Francis of Assisi, making this a personal commitment to live out the message of the service in the coming week.

Lord, make me an instrument of your peace.
Where there is hate, let me sow love.
Where there is injury, Lord let me sow,
A pardon as deep as the flowing sea.

Where there is doubt, let me sow faith.
Where there is despair, let me sow hope.
Where there is darkness, let me sow light.

Where there is pain, let me sow joy.

O loving Lord, may I not seek
To be understood, but to understand,
To be consoled, but to console,
Or to be loved, but to love man.

For it's in giving that we receive,
It's in forgiving that we're forgiven
And it's in dying that we are born
To eternal life.

Helpful extras

Music and song ideas
'Light of the world' (here I am to worship);
'I the Lord of sea and sky' (Here I am Lord);
'May the fragrance of Jesus fill this place';
'I will offer up my life'; 'Make me a channel
of your peace'; 'Shine, Jesus, shine'; 'So cool'
(Reach up CD (SU); 'Whoopah Wahey'
(Whoopah Wahey CD Doug Horley)

Game
'Beans beans beans' is based on an idea on
the theme of fairness taken from Jaffa 3
(SU). Each person present should have five
jelly beans in their 'goody bag.' Participants
get up from their seats and walk around the
worship space as music is played. When the
music stops, (or when a whistle or hooter
is sounded), they team up with a partner
and compare the colours of jelly beans. The
leader shouts a colour from the front. This
is the colour to be 'traded.' So, for example,
whoever has red beans must give all their
red beans to their partner. Repeat and play
the game five or six times. At the end, invite
players to share how many beans they have.
Some will have a few, some will have none
and some will have lots more than they
started with.

(This game indicates that although all players
began with the same number of beans, the
final outcome was different. Parallels can
be drawn with the worldwide economic
situation where enough resources are
available for everyone, but the uneven
distribution of wealth means that there are
gaps between those that have and those that
don't.)

Notes and comments
To provide the contents of the goody bag
might prove expensive especially to a large
church, so some items might be omitted. If
the idea of a bag is not taken up, the items
needed for the prayer time might be placed
on tables around the worship area.

If using candles, ensure that each candle is
mounted on a circle of cardboard to catch
drips. Advise safety before lighting.

For deeper exploration of these topics, look
at Eyes wide open, (SU and Tear fund). Also
Rich Christians in an age of hunger (Hodders)
by Ron Sider, The Politics of Jesus (Eerdmans)
by John Howard Yoder and Multi-sensory world
(SU) by Craig Borlase provide an interesting
and relevant read.

In a service of Holy Communion, draw
attention to Jesus' act of justice in dying for
the sins of the whole world.

Alternative online options
Visit www.lightlive.org for additional
activities for children, young people and
adults.

FOURTH SUNDAY BEFORE LENT (also known as PROPER 2)

READINGS: **Deuteronomy 30:15–20; 1 Corinthians 3:1–9**
Psalm 119:1–8; Matthew 5:21–37

Bible foundations

Aim: to confront the choice that God gives us to recognise and obey him

When God rescued the people of Israel from Egypt, he made a special promise to them. This was a 'covenant' which is a serious agreement between two groups or individuals. In biblical times a covenant involved a list of promises – with the threat of what would happen if one party failed to keep it. As the Israelites prepared to enter the Promised Land, Moses reminded them that they were in a covenant with God and he would hold them to it (Deuteronomy 30:15–20). They had a simple choice. They could choose life, obey God's commands and receive his blessings, or they could choose death, follow other gods and find themselves living under a curse. This may seem to be a very clear and simple choice but, over and over again, the nations of Israel and Judah went on to choose curses rather than blessings.

Jesus offered a new covenant which he sealed with his own blood. In this new covenant God's people are offered a new choice: repent and believe. The new covenant requires us to make a decision to turn in his direction, to follow him and discover life. Our relationship with God could be described as a series of choices. Following Jesus is a daily process of choosing life over death – with the promise that he will work to heal our bad decisions so that new life is always open to us.

In his first letter to the Corinthians however, Paul tells the believers off for making unnecessary choices with unfortunate consequences (3:3–9). They were choosing between Paul and Apollos - the one who planted the seed of faith and the one who nurtured it. Paul reminds them that those who serve Christ have different gifts and different callings. The Church needs people to take on different tasks so it is foolish and immature, to choose between them. We are all fellow-workers in God's field.

Beginning the service

With: a series of appropriate props or words or images to represent pairs of objects, people or roles, such as salt and/or vinegar, chocolate and/or crisps, ice-cream and/or ketchup, a bicycle and/or car, male and/or female – both of which things we may choose/like/be or else things that we may only choose one of

Introduce the range of paired items. Explore whether these are 'I choose/like/am both in the pair' or 'I only choose/like/am one in the pair. It may not be obvious. For instance, some people may like sausages with marmalade while others may prefer mustard; or people will only be male or female but you might choose to entertain both or both would be welcome in church. Choose pairs that encourage lively discussion.

Explain that the theme of this service is about choices. Sometimes we are free to choose between different options. For example, we could choose to drink orange or apple juice. In fact we could mix them together and drink both. On other occasions we make serious decisions and we need to make a choice that matters: What job will we do? Where will we live? Will we steal what we want or save up for it? Will we eat all the ice-cream in the fridge, even if it might make us ill, or will we be more restrained?

God asks us to make choices and the biggest choice of all is about Jesus. Will we ask for his help to live his way and follow him – or will we choose our own way?

Bible reading

Many people are unfamiliar with Old Testament stories so will not know the context of the reading from Deuteronomy. Explain that Deuteronomy 30:15–20 is part of one of Moses' speeches that he gave after God had rescued the people from slavery in Egypt, but before they had entered the land where he had promised to bless them. Read this as a speech, preferably by someone with dramatic skills, dressed as Moses.

To emphasise the idea of choices, divide the congregation in two. One half cheers if they hear the words 'life', 'live', 'bless' or 'blessing', while the other half boos if they hear the words 'death', 'destruction', 'destroyed' or 'curses'. This concept of blessings or curses, life or death, is an important element of the covenant.

To emphasise the options that the Corinthians had created, 1 Corinthians 3:1–9 could be read as follows:

Narrator:	Brothers and sisters, I could not address you as spiritual but as worldly— mere infants in Christ. I gave you milk, not solid food, for you were not yet ready for it. Indeed, you are still not ready. You are still worldly. For since there is jealousy and quarrelling among you, are you not worldly? Are you not acting like mere human beings?
Voice 1:	For when one says, "I follow Paul,"
Voice 2:	and another, "I follow Apollos."
Narrator:	Are you not mere human beings?
Voice 2:	What, after all, is Apollos?

Voice 1:	And what is Paul?
Narrator:	Only servants, through whom you came to believe—as the Lord has assigned to each his task.
Voice 1:	I planted the seed
Voice 2:	Apollos watered it
Narrator:	but God has been making it grow.
Voice 1:	So neither the one who plants,
Voice 2:	nor the one who waters...
Narrator:	is anything, but only God, who makes things grow.
Voice 1:	The one who plants...
Voice 2:	and the one who waters...
Narrator:	have one purpose, and they will each be rewarded according to their own labour. For we are God's co-workers; you are God's field, God's building.
	1 Corinthians 3:1–9 (TNIV)

Bible retelling

One way to explore 1 Corinthians 3:1–9 would be to stage a talent competition, interview or debate which contrasts Paul and Apollos. What did they do? How did they contribute? Which one was best? Home groups or young people could work on this.

Bible talk

With: a pair of scissors; around 10 pairs of cards indicating choices/events (A) and their consequences (B) such as 'Drop a pot'(A) and 'Pot breaks'(B), linked as pairs by long pieces of string – (suggestions (YearA.4Sunb4Lent_1) are available from www.scriptureunion.org.uk/lightdownloads)

Choices and consequences

Distribute the cards around volunteers with the long pieces of string stretched across several people. This will create a complicated web of choices/events and consequences. Ask people to read out their A cards and invite others to think which B card this would be linked to. Untangle the web to discover which choice/event is linked to which consequence. For example, (A) 'Go to bed late' is linked to (B) 'Tired in the morning'.

As the pairs emerge from the web discuss how actions always have consequences and explore what other choices could have been made. (Those holding the cards should line up with each A card-holder facing their B card-holder. Ask them to stay still while you explain about 'God or idols?')

God or idols?

Remind everyone about the reading from Deuteronomy 30. Moses was explaining to the people of Israel that their future decisions would have consequences. God had rescued them from slavery and had given them freedom but they would now have to choose to *stay* free. They could worship God and live the way that he wanted them to, or they could turn to idols made of stone or wood.

They had a choice between life and death, blessings and curses. It sounds simple but the people were often tempted by the idols of their time and prayed to gods who were not really gods - simply because everyone else was doing it. Together think of things that we might choose rather than God: money, success, popularity or possessions? Why are these things tempting? What do we think they will gain for us? Why are they false gods?

Life presents a series of choices. It's easy to make the wrong choice and get lost in a knotted mess of decisions and consequences. For the people of Israel, their decision to follow false gods meant that they had been rescued from slavery in Egypt only to become slaves again to the false gods!

Choose life

Remind everyone that Jesus asks us to make a decision too. He offers us so much – forgiveness, a new beginning, new life. We have to trust him and ask for his help. If appropriate, refer to the reading from Matthew 5:21–37.

Cut the string or ribbon that links the A and B cards, representing choices and consequences. Gather up the B pieces of string and lead their card-holders (the consequences) to the cross. Explain that Jesus died for us and took on himself the consequences of our bad decisions. This means that we are free to begin again and start living.

It doesn't mean that the mess has gone and the consequences may still be there to deal with, but we do have someone who will help us find our way to freedom, healing and peace. (Ask all card-holders to return to their seats.)

Living as servants of God

Paul told the Corinthians to grow up. They were getting tied up again with controversies and arguments, even choosing between Apollos and Paul and fighting over who was best! Paul reminded them that he and

Apollos were both merely servants of God. The Corinthians shouldn't fight over who was best but seek to be servants of God themselves.

The challenge of decision-making is always with us. We are called to act in a mature way, respecting difference and diversity, attempting to see things from God's perspective.

Choices always have consequences. Jesus faces them with us and will be there even if we get it wrong. We need to ask for his guidance and listen to other people. We need to keep choosing the life and love that comes from God.

Prayer activity

With: one stone for each person; quiet music

Give out the stones and invite people to hold one and imagine that it represents a decision - an important decision, or an everyday one about something to do this week, or even the decision to follow Christ. Ask people to consider the consequences of their decision. What will happen if they don't make a decision?

Play quiet music and invite people to talk with God. They then add their stone to a pile in an appropriate place in the building if they feel able to make a decision, or if they want to offer their decision to God in prayer, or ask for wisdom if they have not yet made it. They may wish to take the stone away as a sign that they need to live with their choices and continue to pray about them.

Thank God for the gift of choice and for the

promise of wisdom. Ask him to help us make good decisions.

Prayer of confession

With: the words of the prayer (YearA.4Sunb4Lent_2), are available from www.scriptureunion.org.uk/lightdownloads, printed or displayed

The congregation responds with the emboldened words.

Prayers of intercession

Ask people to think about those in the news, or people they know, who have difficult decisions to make. This could be done as one big group, as small groups or as individuals. Then ask people to think of those affected by these decisions, who are part of the 'consequences'. If appropriate encourage feedback.

Ask two people to pray for those who are decision-makers and then for those affected by the decisions.

Ending the service

Finish with this declaration and prayer:

Wherever you lead us Lord: **We will go!**
Wherever you send us Lord: **We will go!**
Wherever you call us Lord: **We will go!**
Be with us Lord, in the decisions we make and in the choices that face us.
Be with us Lord, in the people we meet and in the places where we go.
Be with us Lord, when we are alone and when we are together
and give us all that we need to be your people.
Amen.

Helpful extras

Music and song ideas
Songs on the theme of choices and decisions include: 'All my hope on God is founded'; 'At the name of Jesus'; 'Be still and know'; 'Change my heart, O God'; 'Father, hear the prayer we offer'; 'Father we place into your hands'; 'Here I am'; 'Follow me' *Bitesize Bible Songs* CD (SU).

Notes and comments

At this time of year in the UK, children moving to secondary school will be hearing which school they have been allocated to. This can be a very challenging time for parents and children. How much choice did they have? Did they make the right choice? Continue to pray for those caught up in this.

In Holy Communion, emphasise that no-one has to participate, but that we choose to, at Christ's invitation.

Alternative online options
Visit www.lightlive.org for additional activities for children, young people and adults.

THIRD SUNDAY BEFORE LENT (also known as PROPER 3)

READINGS: **Matthew 5:38–48; I Corinthians 3:10,11,16–23**
Leviticus 19:1,2,9–18; Psalm 119:33–40

Bible foundations

Aim: to learn the values of the kingdom as we build our lives on the wisdom of God

Christians are intended to be different. Being God's temple (see I Corinthians 3:16), the place where God's presence was manifested among his people, demands it. Note that it is 'temple', singular and 'you', plural. We are not a collection of individual temples; we are together one temple (Paul uses the image differently in I Corinthians 6:19). As such we have a different wisdom, a new way of looking at the world. Wisdom is not a matter of acquiring information; it is about a practical response, a way of thinking that shapes our daily lives and conversation. So, in the face of global warming, terrorist threats, or personal pain we have a different set of attitudes and responses that can challenge and inform those around us.

Wisdom leads us to live by a different set of values. As Jesus makes clear throughout the Sermon on the Mount and as exemplified in today's verses, it is people and relationships that take priority. This is a hard call. Vindictiveness and the desire for revenge (often dressed up as justice) come more easily to us than loving and forgiving those who have wronged us. 'Going the extra mile' has passed into popular usage as an expression of going beyond what might be expected, sometimes grudgingly. But Jesus was asking for real, hard, sacrificial action that went against the grain – action that demonstrated a different way. It was also politically subversive, a demonstration that the kingdom of God, and not that of Caesar, had ultimate authority. We, who live with different challenges, will have to work out what it means, in practice, to live out the conviction that Jesus is Lord of all life and that in his kingdom, people matter supremely. If living differently, and being perfect as God is perfect, seems impossible – and it does – then we have the assurance that this temple is built on the sure foundation of what Jesus has done, rather than on the shaky foundation of what we are able to do.

Beginning the service

With: details of houses for sale – one set for each small group of people (Details of houses for sale can be obtained from estate agents or from local newspapers. Make sure there is a bit more detail than just the price.)

Welcome everyone, saying there is a special greeting for anyone who has recently moved house. You hope they will be very happy in their new home. Say that for anyone who is looking to move, that is great as you have some possible homes for them and many experts on hand (indicate around the congregation) to help them decide on a really good house.

Put people into groups and give out the house details, asking each group to study them - they will be quizzed on the houses in a couple of minutes. Think up four or five questions according to the information the groups have. For instance, newspaper advertisements may not say how many bedrooms are in the house, but you could ask for the colour of the door, how many windows are on the front of the house or whether there is a chimney. Other questions might include: 'How many reception rooms does it have?' or 'Is there space for a washing machine?' Tell the congregation that they may not guess, but can only answer according to the information they have. Congratulate them on their knowledge of 'their' house. As your last question, ask about the foundations, such as 'How deep are the foundations?' or 'What are they made of?'

Be 'surprised' that they don't know the answer to this very important question.

Without foundations the house could fall down! Comment that the foundations of our lives are important too, and we will be thinking about them – and about how and what we build on them – in our service today. Collect up the house papers during the next hymn.

Bible reading

Matthew 5:38–48 could be read aloud with two voices to give it greater impact. Sometimes the voices could read alternate sentences, but occasionally sentences could be broken into two parts as in: 'When someone slaps your right cheek...' / '... turn and let that person slap your other cheek.'

As 1 Corinthians 3:10 and 16–23 is read, someone could slowly write out, in attractive writing, verses 10b and 11: We must each be careful how we build, because Christ is the only foundation (CEV). Everyone joins together in reading this at the end, after verse 23.

Bible talk

With: a flip chart and pen; a display board (or use the flip chart), Blu-tack; four equal-sized squares of card with the following words: 'Don't try to get even', 'Be generous', 'Be willing to put yourself out' and 'Be loving and friendly to everyone'; a strip of card the length of two of the squares with 'Jesus Christ' written on it; a card triangle (roof shaped) the width of two squares with 'the Holy Spirit' written on it

Ask someone (adult or child) to come forward to draw a picture of a house on the sheet of paper. It doesn't need to be elaborate – a simple one will do. Ask the congregation to watch carefully. Congratulate the artist on their work of art and then ask where the picture was started. Make your following comments according to what the artist did. Very few people will draw a line (the foundation) first and then draw the house above it. Most will start at the top of one of the walls or possibly draw the roof first. Point out that, as in **Beginning the service**, we usually ignore the foundations and yet they are really important. Read 1 Corinthians 3:10 and 11 and fix the strip of card firmly along the bottom of the display board, showing the words 'Jesus Christ'. Talk about having Jesus as the foundation of our lives. If we don't have him, our lives will collapse.

Explain that you are going to make a picture of a house and that it does look odd starting a picture at the bottom. But that is one of the things about building our lives on Jesus: things often appear to be upside down or the wrong way round, but God knows what he is doing and it is best to learn from him.

One by one, build the four squares into a larger square above the foundations, talking about each phrase and saying how this way of life is different from the world's way. Read out the relevant verses from Matthew 5 and use illustrations from Jesus' own life:

- 'Don't try to get even' (Matthew 5:38,39). Jesus allowed himself to be abused and beaten, and didn't answer back.
- 'Be generous' (verses 42). Jesus shared whatever he had with others, particularly his time.

- 'Be willing to put yourself out' (verse 40,41). Jesus still ministered to others even when he was tired (for example, to the woman at the well) and he acted as a servant at the Last Supper.
- 'Be loving and friendly to everyone' (verses 43–48). Jesus made friends with all sorts of people, many of whom were shunned by society.

As you display each square, point out that this is how we should live our lives too, if Jesus is our foundation. Add the triangle as the roof, making sure that the words are hidden for the time being. Admire the house and say what a wonderful society ours would be if everyone built their lives in this way. Read out 1 Corinthians 3:18 and 19a to remind everyone of God's 'upside-down wisdom'.

Ask everyone to think for a few moments about living that way of life: not trying to get even, always being generous with our possessions, putting ourselves out and being friendly with everyone – yes, everyone! It seems impossible, even with Jesus as the foundation. Remind everyone that Jesus promised never to leave us. Someone is in the house with us. Turn the roof around to reveal the words 'the Holy Spirit' on the other side and read out 1 Corinthians 3:16,17a. Finish by saying that if the foundations of our lives are truly founded on Jesus, the Holy Spirit will help us to live God's wise way.

Prayer activity

With: a house brick (or toy wooden blocks) for each small group of people; felt-tip pens;

sticky notes (optional); 'Jesus' written on a piece of card and attached to the edge of a table

If you are not able to obtain house bricks, use toy wooden blocks, such as Lego or Duplo. As they are smaller, you may need to give these to individuals or pairs, rather than a group. You could use a cross to represent Jesus. In this case, make sure there is a suitable table or step, placed above it, to build on.

Point to the card saying 'Jesus' and remind the congregation that he should be the foundation for our lives. Talk briefly about the values of God's kingdom, which seem to be so different from the way we would normally want to follow. Say that we need God's help to build our lives on him. Ask everyone to think about the things we own. Is there something we have that we could share or give to someone in need? Ask them to think about our time. Could we spare some extra time to help others? Ask them to think about someone they don't like much or would avoid if they could. Could we ask God to help us love that person?

Give time for the groups to write prayers around these thoughts on the bricks, or on sticky notes to fix on to the bricks. The prayers need not be in words. Pictures and symbols could also be used, as some may be personal. After a few minutes one person from each group should carry their brick to the front. As each brick is laid above the foundation, everybody says, 'Lord Jesus, help us to build on you.'

Prayer of confession

Ask everyone to join in the emboldened response of this prayer of confession (YearA.3Sunb4Lent_1) that is available as a PowerPoint from www.scriptureunion.org.uk/lightdownloads.

Ending the service

With: a small card for each person (the cards could be shaped like bookmarks or credit cards, or they could be folded like a small greetings card that will stand up); felt-tip pens; Bibles

As we need God's wisdom to build our lives day by day, it is good to keep his wise words nearby. Many people have favourite Bible verses that they recite regularly or find helpful when problems arise. Ask if anyone has a favourite piece of God's wisdom that they would like to share. It could be 1 Corinthians 3:10b and 11 from today's **Bible reading**. Allow a few people to recite a favourite verse. Suggest that the congregation get into pairs or threes to tell each other one helpful Bible verse. Encourage them to look them up in their Bibles. Give out the cards so that each person can write down one of the verses.

Ask everyone to hold their card. Give them a moment to think where they will keep it. It could be in a book, in their wallet or on view, but it should be somewhere where they will notice it. Finish with the following prayer:

Thank you, God, for your wisdom. Help us to remember the values of your kingdom as we build our lives on you.

Encourage everyone to reflect on their own personal Bible reading habits as they prepare for Lent. You could have a range of

Bible reading guides available. For details of Scripture Union's provision, see page 293 or www.scriptureunion.org.uk, or www. wordlive.org. Do encourage parents to think about how they provide their children with the tools to read the Bible for themselves.

Helpful extras

Music and song ideas

Relevant songs include: 'A new commandment'; 'Christ is made the sure foundation'; 'Don't build your house on the sandy land'; 'For I'm building a people of power'; 'God of grace and God of glory'; 'Jesus put this song into our hearts'; 'Make me a channel of your peace'; 'Meekness and majesty'.

Statement of faith

This statement of faith (YearA.3Sunb4Lent_ 2) is available as a PowerPoint presentation from www.scriptureunion.org.uk/ lightdownloads. The words in bold should be spoken by the congregation. Practise, saying it with the emphasis put on 'his'. Use two voices to read the lines in between, to emphasise the paradoxical statements.

We believe in God's wisdom and the values of his kingdom.
We believe that Jesus, the Word of God, made heaven and earth.
We believe that this same Jesus left his home in glory and came to earth to be born as a man.
We believe in God's wisdom and the values of his kingdom.
We believe that Jesus has the power to work miracles, even to bring people from death to life.
We believe that this same Jesus himself died on a cross.
We believe in God's wisdom and the

values of his kingdom.
We believe that all people have sinned and are not worthy to live with God forever.
We believe that God accepts us because Jesus took our sins away on the cross.
We believe in God's wisdom and the values of his kingdom.

We believe that Jesus was raised from the dead and ascended to God in heaven.
We believe he lives in us now on earth through his Holy Spirit.
We believe in God's wisdom and the values of his kingdom.

Notes and comments

Leviticus 19:1, 2 and 9–18 show that God's 'upside-down values' did not start with Jesus' earthly ministry. Older children, teens and adults could discover other ways in which God's values are different from those of the world.

Instead of a quiz at **Beginning the service**, the congregation could study the details from the estate agents and decide which pieces of information are most important. Before you mention the foundations, you could ask if any important information has been left out.

In the **Bible talk**, instead of asking someone to come forward to draw a house, ask everyone to draw a house in the air. They can then think about where they started their 'picture'.

Alternative online options

Visit www.lightlive.org for additional activities for children, young people and adults.

SECOND SUNDAY BEFORE LENT

[handwritten: Prayer = V ?]

READINGS: **Genesis 1:1 – 2:3; Psalm 136:1–9,23–26**
Romans 8:18–25; Matthew 6:25–34

Bible foundations

**Aim: to marvel at God's creation, which is being restored from the
results of the fall**

God did indeed make a wonderful world. With the fragility of creation very much
in evidence through what we hear and see in the media and experience in daily life,
we can forget that in the beginning God's world was perfect. So he rested (Genesis
2:3), not because he was tired out but because his creative work was complete. His
rest was one of utter satisfaction and, one has to presume, joy! He was as pleased
as anyone could ever have been: in fact, a trillion times more! What is more, we do
not know how he made the world, and discussions about this can also sometimes
distract us from marvelling at the awesomeness of his creation.

This rather unusual service outline aims to lead a congregation in wonder, without
analysing the how, what or why of God's creative actions. Ultimately, it is a mystery.
Psalm 136:1–9 and 23–26 form a congregational song of praise, which God's people
sang long before the time of Christ - God's love never fails; his mercy endures
forever. Jesus reminded his listeners in Matthew 6:25–34 that God not only gives
beauty to be enjoyed but he cares for his created world in all its minute detail.

The Epistle reading, however, in Romans 8:18–25 reminds us of the fallen nature
of this world, as we long to be set free from decay (verse 21). The image of a
mother groaning in childbirth (verse 22) is so powerful, for there has to be the pain
in order that a new life (with all its hope and potential) might be set free to live
independently of her. We long for ourselves and our world to be transformed, but
we know that it is only God who can do that (although we play our part) and that
this will happen in God's time.

This Sunday, may you all enjoy your worship of our creator God.

Beginning the service

With: either: squares of tissue paper in various colours; a straw; parcel tape; two-sided tape; or: paint; paper; coloured pens; hand-washing facilities

Begin with a creative activity, being as messy as is possible! Ask everyone to choose their favourite colour of tissue paper and create a flower, using this and brown parcel tape wrapped around a straw.

Alternatively, invite everyone to create an insect (real or imaginary) by using a thumb dipped in paint to make prints for the body and head, with legs, arms and feelers added by pen.

Introduce the theme of the service by saying that the reason why we have just done something creative is because we are going to explore the wonderful world that God created.

Bible reading

As Genesis 1:1–2:3 is being explored in the **Bible talk** and Psalm 136 is part of the **Prayer activity**, read Matthew 6:25–34. One reader could read the questions in verses 25, 26, 27, 28, 30 and 31, while another person reads the rest. Both of the readers, or everyone, could join in verse 34 together.

Romans 8:18–25 would remind people of the present state of God's creation and his people.

Bible retelling

The *Wastewatchers* DVD, from the Scripture Union holiday club programme, has an imaginative retelling of the story of the creation in Episode One. For details, visit the Scripture Union website. The script itself (YearA.2Sunb4Lent_1) is available from www.scriptureunion.org.uk/lightdownloads.

Bible talk

With: props (suggestions are given in the text below) to explore the story of creation; a team of helpers to create the effects; a copy of the customised text (YearA.2Sunb4Lent_2) available as a word document from www.scriptureunion.org.uk/lightdownloads

This account could be done in a number of ways, depending on your facilities, imagination and helpers. This is a multi-sensory experience for everyone. You could lead from the front with everyone together, having set up sound effects and visual images on the screen or on display. You could invite people to find their own space and only come together when God has created human beings. Or, you could create small groups and give each group a container with various props that can be passed around the group, such as shining star shapes, soil, plants, fur, water, etc. Make the room as dark as possible without alarming anyone, and raise the lighting slightly throughout the story-telling until God has finished his creation. Slowly read the following statements, which are customised for everyone altogether.

Close your eyes to imagine you are surrounded by nothing; no one is anywhere near you. You are all alone. And it is gloomy and dark. (*Play gloomy music.*)

But in the middle of all this is God. He just is! And as God moved around, he began to create. Out of nothing, he began to separate things out. (*Create swishing sounds.*) He made day different from night.

He made the sky different from the earth. (*Shine a moving spotlight in flashes over the ceiling.*)
And God looked at what he had made and he was very pleased with everything. 'This is very good,' he said.

God made the dry land different from the sea. Just listen to this. (*Play some sea music.*) Mighty waves crashed over rocks, seas swooshed up the coast, little waves gently lapped on the beach, and rivers flowed out into the deep seas. And the dry land was like the soil in this bucket. (*Tip the soil onto the ground where all can see it.*)
And God looked at what he had made and he was very pleased with everything. 'This is very good,' he said.

God created plants and flowers and trees to grow; they were all different. He created red, yellow, pink, blue, and orange flowers with star-patterned petals, round floppy petals and sweet-perfumed petals; some had long stems, some had thorny stems and some had short stubby stems; he created tall trees and short ones, with rough, brown trunks, or with smooth, silvery trunks, some producing nuts, some producing soft fruit, some with five-fingered leaves and some with waxy copper-red leaves (*play wind in the trees sounds*); he created bushes and grasses and reeds; he created vegetables that grew under the ground and vegetables that grew above the ground; he created wheat and maize and

barley corn. (*If you are distributing some plant life, ask the following rhetorical question.*) Just look at the plants and grass; feel them and smell them: what do you notice?
And God looked at what he had made and he was very pleased with everything. 'This is very good,' he said.

God made the sun and the moon and the stars. High above, the sun was bright and glowing with blurred edges, and it slowly shifted across the sky. The moon was pale and silvery and it changed its shape as night followed night. It shone in the darkness. The stars were far away and mysterious, like tiny silver dots on a huge screen. (*Play a xylophone. Shine the spotlight on a sun and moon shape hanging from the ceiling, or show images of planets and stars, etc.*)
And God looked at what he had made and he was very pleased with everything. 'This is very good,' he said.

God created birds and fish and animals: all sorts, all different, some big, some small, some fast, some slow, some furry, some slimy, some bright-coloured, some dull-coloured, some fierce, some friendly. (*Play animal sounds. Show the pictures or models of the animals.*)
And God looked at what he had made and he was very pleased with everything. 'This is very good,' he said.

Finally, God created human beings. They were different from the animals because, unlike them, they were able to be friends with God. They could do all sorts of things with their bodies. (*Encourage everyone to come together to stand up, stretch, bend down, jump, blink, somersault - whatever body movements you can think of. You could run a short set of fitness*

exercises with suitably energetic music.) God gave these human beings a special job to do. He asked them to give names to all the animals. He also told them that they had to look after everything in the world - to make sure that fruit and vegetables grew healthily, that trees grew strong, that the animals, birds and fish were well cared for. This was a big job but God knew that human beings could do this properly.
And God looked at what he had made and he was very pleased with everything. 'This is very good,' he said.

And after this, God rested. It was not that he was tired out. It was just that he had created everything that was in his grand design. He was satisfied that it was complete. It was very good!

Prayer activity

With: squares of black card (8 cm x 8 cm) with one hole punched in a corner; small sticky stars; crayons or chalk or glitter pens that will write on the card; silver thread at least 50 cm long

Give everyone a card, a pen, and a star or stars. It might be easier if they come to tables around the church to create these. A star is placed in one corner of the card, which represents the night sky. The silver thread is pushed through the hole and tied in a knot. 'God's love never fails, Psalm 136' is written on the card, or people can add their own phrase of praise to God for his creation.

When everyone has completed their card, invite everyone to stand in groups. As the leader reads Psalm 136:1–9 and 23–26,

everyone joins in the refrain: **God's love never fails** (CEV) or **His love endures forever** (TNIV). The square can be hung above a window at home as a reminder of God's vast world that we are part of.

Alternatively, use this rhyme for young children.

I can hear and I can see;
Thank you, God, for making me.
(Cup your ears and point to your eyes.)
I am strong and I am free.
(Flex your muscles and fling your arms wide.)
You have made the earth and sea.
Thank you, God, for making me.
(Draw a circle in the air and then make some waves.)
Thank you, God, for making me.
(Finally, stretch up tall.)

Prayer of confession

Romans 8:18–22 remind us that right now the world is suffering. This is partly because this is how it has always been since the fall, but, also, we are aware that we ourselves have not been good stewards of God's world. Show some images of the results of our damaged climate and environment.

Ask two or three people to lead in prayer asking for forgiveness for our failure to be good stewards. They might also pray for those engaged at international level in responding to the challenges of climate change.

Ending the service

As it is springtime in the Northern hemisphere, you could plant some bulbs at the end of the service and comment that you are going to watch how they grow over the next few weeks. Invite people to notice signs of growth, new life and hope in the natural world as they go home.

For refreshments, you could encourage people to bring home-made (created) biscuits, cakes and fruit juices; also encourage them to bring anything else that they have made or created (which could be artwork, patchwork, photographical collages), so that others can enjoy them.

Conclude with a song of joy and praise and this prayer:

Go out into God's world, to love and to serve,
To enjoy all he has made,
To notice signs of new life and hope,
To rejoice in our creator God! Amen!

Helpful extras

Music and song ideas
Relevant songs include: 'All creatures of our God and King'; 'All things bright and beautiful'; 'Praise him, you heavens'; 'Let everything that has breath'; 'Who put the colours in the rainbow'; 'Now thank we all our God'; 'If I were a butterfly'. Saint Saens' *Carnival of the animals*, which is full of interest and variety, would be suitable to play before or after the service or during the **Prayer activity**. 'From heaven You came' includes

the phrase 'hands that flung stars into space', which combines the idea of the great creator God stepping into this small world.

Percussion instruments are also many and varied and, if used, would reinforce the variety of sounds in the world. A variety of instruments that are played to lead worship will have the same effect.

Notes and comments

A service that focuses upon the creation and new life is one that is immediately accessible to smaller children. So aim to make this service full of fun and wonder for all ages but especially for younger people present. *The Big Bible Storybook* (SU) contains some wonderful images of God's world, which are very accessible to children.

A Rocha is a Christian charity committed to environmental issues. To find out more, visit www.arocha.org.

Some of the material in this outline was originally published in *Wastewatchers* and *All-Age Service Annual Volume 3*, both by SU.

Alternative online options
Visit www.lightlive.org for additional activities for children, young people and adults. There are an amazing number of resources that you could use in this service.

SUNDAY BEFORE LENT

READINGS: **Matthew 17:1–9; 2 Peter 1:16–21**
Exodus 24:12–18; Psalm 99:1–9

Bible foundations

Aim: to have confidence in the truth about who Jesus is

The media will often try to pit science against religion or faith. Science uses reason to deduce theories that then form a paradigm or world view. Reason looks at facts and figures for its results. However, faith, they say, is based on esoteric thinking. Peter, though, is clear in pointing out that as far as he is concerned his faith is rooted in fact. The phrase 'cleverly devised stories' in the TNIV relates to one of the theological systems of Gnostic speculation – the real esoteric religion.

Peter states that he was an eyewitness to the events recorded in Matthew 17:1–9. The belief that Peter wrote the second letter that bears his name has long been contested because the language used is linguistically different from that of 1 Peter. But this internal evidence is used in favour of Petrine authorship.

The transfiguration in Matthew takes place 'after six days', which could be a possible allusion to Exodus 24:16. The mountain is most likely to have been Mount Meron; it is not too high, but it is remote enough for the event. Jesus is transfigured and this literally means transformed, metamorphosed. The appearance of Moses and Elijah again forms a strong link to the Law and the Prophets. They were also part of Old Testament times when miracles were prevalent, and were both Messianic forerunners.

The cloud that descends harks back to the cloud that visited Moses on Mount Sinai and that led the Israelites. The words that the voice says would remind the listeners of Deuteronomy 18:15. They are also the same words used at Jesus' baptism. God is endorsing the next step of Jesus' ministry, the journey to the cross. This is the last time that Jesus tells his followers not to tell anyone; however, this time there is a time limit. Hard times lie ahead, but here is a little taster of the glory that awaits.

Beginning the service

Explain the call to worship below before you begin. Practise the response so that everyone will be able to participate with enthusiasm!

You could use two readers for each section, but one will do. The call to worship, adapted from Psalm 99 (CEV) and using 2 Peter 1:16b as a response (YearA.Sunb4Lent_2), is also downloadable from www.scriptureunion.org.uk/lightdownloads.

> Reader 1: Our Lord, you are King! You rule from your throne above the winged creatures, as people tremble and the earth shakes.
> Readers 1 and 2: With our own eyes we saw his true greatness.
> **All: Holy is the Lord!**
>
> Reader 2: You are our mighty King, a lover of fairness, who sees that justice is done.
> Readers 1 and 2: With our own eyes we saw his true greatness.
> **All: Holy is the Lord!**
>
> Reader 1: The prophets of old prayed in your name, and you, our Lord, answered their prayers.
> Readers 1 and 2: With our own eyes we saw his true greatness.
> **All: Holy is the Lord!**
>
> Reader 2: Our Lord and our God, you answered their prayers and forgave their sins, but when they did wrong, you punished them. We praise you, Lord God. Only you are God!
> Readers 1 and 2: With our own eyes we saw his true greatness.
> **All: Holy is the Lord!**
>   based on Psalm 99 (CEV)
>   and 2 Peter 1:16b

Bible reading

Introduce 2 Peter 1:16–21 by saying that Peter, in this letter, is referring to the transfiguration of Jesus, which he witnessed. Ask why he was telling this story as he wrote his letter. To aid understanding, the epistle should follow the Gospel reading.

Matthew 17:1–9 could be read with a narrator, Peter, the voice of God and Jesus. Alternatively, use the **Bible retelling** script.

Bible retelling

With: the script (YearA.Sunb4Lent_1) available from www.scriptureunion.org.uk/lightdownloads; three actors (who should rehearse in advance)

Two people play the parts of Peter and the Questioner (who raises questions throughout). A third person takes the part of Narrator, to put the passage in context. The characters perform as if they are having a debate.

Bible talk

With: a line of laundry secured with clothes pegs, including: a pair of pyjamas; a pair of gloves; everyday clothes; favourite clothes; a suit or dress that would be worn on special occasions

If you have not introduced these items already in the **Game**, reveal them in a fun way, leaving the pyjamas until last. Each item of clothing relates to different Bible verses (scriptures) that we would find useful in our lives.

Everyday clothes: These represent scriptures that are useful for everyday living – for example, the Ten Commandments, proverbs or advice from Paul's letters.

Special clothes: These refer to scriptures that we recall on special occasions – such as the story of the birth of Jesus from the Gospels, or John 1, at Christmas, or the passage about love in 1 Corinthians 13 at a wedding.

Favourite clothes: These are like scriptures that encourage us and build us up. If you did the suggested **Ending the service** in the previous outline, refer to the verses you used then.

Gloves: Gloves represent scriptures of comfort or protection, such as verses about the peace and security that come from God.

Pyjamas: These are a reminder of Bible passages that are more private and personal to you. You probably wouldn't want to share them publicly because of what they mean to you, but they are very important.

All these clothes are no good hanging on the line or at the back of a wardrobe – they have no life in them unless they are worn and enjoyed. If we are to engage with the Bible, we need to 'wear' it – just as we wear our clothes – using and applying it within the context of our day-to-day experiences. Our clothes do not 'come alive' until we put them on and use them with confidence – so it is with the Word of God.

For Peter, this happened when his experience of seeing Jesus transfigured on the mountain (see 2 Peter 1:16–18) proved to him that the prophecies of Jesus were true (verse 19);

and the prophecies, in turn, proved that his experience was real, and not imagined. If you have not performed the drama from **Bible retelling**, then you may like to explain what happened to Peter on the mountain (see Matthew 17:1–9).

As individuals, because our personal experiences are limited (verse 20), we can only understand a small part of the whole truth. We need the Holy Spirit to help us to understand the Bible, alongside the testimony and experiences of both ourselves and others. In this way we can hear and apply God's Word and encourage one another (verse 21). When we put personal and shared experience together with a clear understanding of Scripture, we will have confidence in the truth of who Jesus is.

Prayer activity

With: large sheets of paper suitable for collage; smaller (A4) sheets of paper; glue or sticky tape; scissors; pens (for an alternative, see **Notes and comments**.)

Each person draws around one of their hands on an A4 sheet of paper and cuts it out. On it, they write, 'I trust Jesus when…' and add their own comment. This may be something day-to-day, a particular experience they have had, or something that has happened recently.

Stick all the hands onto the larger sheets and display them. (Some people may have written something deeply personal, so mention that it is fine to opt out.) Encourage the congregation to talk together about what they are writing on their 'hands' and to describe the ways in which they feel Jesus helped them.

Everyone can thank Jesus silently for the confidence they can have in him, whatever happens.

Ending the service

This would be a good opportunity to add a short testimony to show how personal experience is key to understanding the Bible and how we can be confident that it is the truth about Jesus. It is best to plan a testimony carefully to make sure that the person speaking is to the point and doesn't use the opportunity to deliver another sermon.

An alternative would be to use prepared questions and answers, which the leader and person giving the testimony could agree on and go through in advance. No more than three to five minutes is recommended. Make any appropriate links between the **Bible talk** and the testimony.

Alternatively, this is an appropriate time to encourage people to read the Bible throughout the week. Provide information on suitable Bible reading guides, for all ages. This is particularly relevant as Lent approaches and many people set time aside to reflect on their relationship with God. For more details visit www.scriptureunion.org.uk

Helpful extras

Music and song ideas
Relevant songs include: 'These are the days of Elijah'; 'Open our eyes, Lord (We want to see Jesus)' – this song could be sung without accompaniment if there are strong singers to lead; 'Lord Jesus Christ (You have come to us)'; 'How sweet the name of Jesus sounds'; 'O Jesus, I have promised'; 'I cannot tell how he whom angels worshipped'; 'At your feet we fall (Mighty risen Lord)'; 'Our confidence is in the Lord'; 'My Jesus, my Saviour'; 'Crown him with many crowns'.

Game
With: clothes including those to be used in the **Bible talk** (a pair of pyjamas; a pair of gloves; everyday clothes; favourite clothes; a suit or dress that would be worn on special occasions) scattered around the room, or hidden under chairs; clothes pegs; a washing line strung out across the front of the worship space (be aware of safety issues)

The leader should have a list of the clothing available. Two or more people (who have been warned in advance) stand in front of the congregation as 'shop dummies'. Each 'dummy' has a 'runner' to gather clothes from the congregation. As each item is called out in turn from the list, everyone looks for it. The 'runners' compete to retrieve each item as it is found. The 'runner' who gets the clothing, puts it on their 'dummy'. (It doesn't matter if it fits or not.) Once the game is finished, the items are taken off the 'dummies' and points are scored for each item. (Make up your own scoring system.) These items should then be hung out on the washing line ready for the **Bible talk**.

Statement of faith
With: paper and pens

Since this service has focused upon what we believe about Jesus, it would be appropriate to include a statement of faith. As an alternative to your usual creedal statement, invite everyone to get into small groups and make a list of all the things that you can say about who Jesus is. For example: he is the Son of God, he is the Lord, he is the creator, he is love, he is loved by God, he is chosen by God.

Everyone chooses two of these and then standing in the group, each person in turn declares what truth they want to say about who Jesus is.

Conclude by declaring 2 Peter 1:17.

If this service includes a baptism, you could comment on the fact that Christian baptism is in the name of the Father, and of the Son, and of the Holy Spirit. Draw attention to the reading in 2 Peter where Peter speaks about God the Father expressing his pleasure in his Son, Jesus, and where he says that it is the Holy Spirit who helps and guides those who want to understand the Scriptures. Believing in the Trinity is one of the central truths that mark Christians out from those of other faiths.

Notes and comments

A simplified **Prayer activity** could include drawing around a number of hands on one large sheet of paper (and not cutting them out).

Alternative online options

Visit www.lightlive.org for additional activities for children, young people and adults.

Top Tips on Explaining the Cross
(1 978 84427 330 0)

This book is full of ideas to use with people of all ages, including children, to help them understand what the Bible says about Jesus' death on the cross and what it means for us.

For more details, visit www.scriptureunion.org.uk

FIRST SUNDAY OF LENT

READINGS: **Romans 5:12–19; Matthew 4:1–11**
Genesis 2:15–17; 3:1–7; Psalm 32

Bible foundations

Aim: to rejoice because Jesus has defeated all our enemies – sin, death and the devil

All of us experience what it is to be tempted to do things we know are wrong. Often we fail. It is therefore very encouraging for us to know that Jesus was tempted just as we are (see Hebrews 4:15) but that unlike us he won the victory over the devil and succeeded in not compromising in any way or giving in to pressure. His victory was due to his complete dedication to God and his determination as a human being to obey God, at any price. He recognised the source and the folly of the devil's challenge, which could hardly be described as subtle. The devil even quoted scripture, to support his case, but Jesus recognised the strategy. It is not enough to know the words of scripture. It is their power and the God who 'spoke' them that make it possible to withstand temptation.

Of course, Jesus' greatest and final victory over Satan was on the cross. In Romans 5, the apostle Paul teaches that where Adam failed, Jesus succeeded. With a succession of contrasts focusing on the respective results of Adam's transgression of God's command, and Christ's act of obedience, Paul brings home the significance of their acts. Whereas through Adam's sin, death reigned (verse 17), through Christ's obedience, believers in him may 'reign in life' (verse 17). This is because they have been justified (verse 16) – made right with God through the death of his Son on their behalf. Having received 'God's abundant provision of grace' and 'the gift of righteousness' they do not fear Satan's accusations and have power to resist his temptations. Already they are experiencing eternal life (verse 21), which is the ultimate fruit of Christ's obedience. Verse 17 is a good verse to memorise to remind ourselves of these wonderful truths!

Beginning the service

Ask if anyone can name any superheroes. You could download images to show those who may say they do not know any. Then ask if anyone knows a man called 'Christus Victor'. Some people may get this straight away, but if not, you can string the question out with clues, such as, he's not a Russian secret agent or a famous Greek author!

Explain that 'Christus Victor' is actually another name for Jesus. Not a name that you hear very often these days, but when Jesus had just risen from the dead and people were beginning to follow him, the early Christians gave Jesus this name because it has a special meaning – ask if anyone knows what it means (Christ the conqueror).

'Christus Victor' describes Jesus' victory over our enemies. You will need to explain that when the Bible talks about 'our enemies', it does not mean the people we don't get on with at school or countries that we have been at war with! Rather it is referring to three things:

- Sin – human selfishness, which ignores God and wants what I want.
- The devil – God's enemy, the source of all that is wrong in the world.
- Death – being separated from God forever, the result of human selfishness and sin, decay and destruction.

If relevant you could refer to *The Lion, the witch and the wardrobe*, which illustrates this well. There is a battle going on between good and evil. That is the focus of this service.

See **Game** for an alternative **Beginning the service.**

Bible reading

Romans 5:12–19 should be read by two people, making the contrast between Adam and Jesus. Reader 1 reads about Adam's sin and its effects in verses 12–14, 16a, 17a, 18a, 19a while Reader 2 reads about Christ in verses 15, 16b, 17b, 18b, 19b, as below (CEV). Ask everyone to listen out for the contrast between Adam and Christ.

> Reader 1: Adam sinned, and that sin brought death into the world. Now everyone has sinned, and so everyone must die. Sin was in the world before the Law came. But no record of sin was kept, because there was no Law. Yet death still had power over all who lived from the time of Adam to the time of Moses. This happened, though not everyone disobeyed a direct command from God, as Adam did.
>
> Reader 2: In some ways Adam is like Christ who came later. But the gift that God was kind enough to give was very different from Adam's sin. That one sin brought death to many others. Yet in an even greater way, Jesus Christ alone brought God's gift of kindness to many people.
>
> Reader 1: There is a lot of difference between Adam's sin and God's gift. That one sin led to punishment.
>
> Reader 2: But God's gift made it possible for us to be acceptable to him, even though we have sinned many times.

> Reader 1: Death ruled like a king because Adam had sinned.
> Reader 2: But that cannot compare with what Jesus Christ has done. God has been so kind to us, and he has accepted us because of Jesus. And so we will live and rule like kings.
> Reader 1: Everyone was going to be punished because Adam sinned.
> Reader 2: But because of the good thing that Christ has done, God accepts us and gives us the gift of life.
> Reader 1: Adam disobeyed God and caused many others to be sinners.
> Reader 2: But Jesus obeyed him and will make many people acceptable to God.
> Romans 5:12–19 (CEV)

In reading Matthew 4:1–11, ask people to listen out for who quotes scripture.

Bible talk

With: Bibles or copies of Matthew 4:1–11, on screen or on paper; children dressed up in superhero outfits or with appropriate accessories, such as Spiderman, Robin Hood, Thunderbirds, Superman, Luke Skywalker (You will need to have arranged this the previous week.)

Heroes
Invite your 'heroes' to the front. Ask the children in the congregation to identify who the dressed-up children represent. Then ask everyone to shout out the arch-enemies of these characters. For example, the Sheriff of Nottingham was Robin Hood's arch-enemy.

Ask what makes someone a hero? How much did Jesus behave like a hero?

Fighting the enemy
Explain that all heroes have their enemies – people, creatures, or forces of evil who want to sabotage or disrupt the hero's good intentions. The enemies often try to tempt the heroes away from accomplishing their mission by suggesting an alliance. In Matthew 4:1–11 Jesus, who had a clear mission – to save the universe from death – was tested by his arch-enemy, the devil. He attempted to sabotage Jesus' mission by trying to undermine his confidence in God. Ask people to look at Matthew 4:1–11 and read out what the devil said to try to undermine Jesus' trust in God.

When these things didn't work, the devil tried another tack – the offer of power if Jesus would form an alliance with him. Ask people to read out what the devil said about power. Jesus fought his enemy not with his fists, nor with a sword, but with the truth about God.

Living and dying like a hero
Romans 5:12–19 tells us that Jesus did more than live like a hero (even though most of his actions did not seem very heroic – refer back to the earlier conversation at the start of the **Bible talk**); he died like a hero too. He was put to death as a criminal. He could have called down the angels to rescue him but he chose not to. That was God's plan.

He really and truly died but he came back to life in a new way. He was the victor. Satan could not put a stop to him! So being on his side means that ultimately we are on the winning side. (For children especially this is a very clear way to understand the cross, so take time to explore what it means for Jesus to stand up for us when we are bullied or feel weak and defeated.)

Show one of the shields that will be used next, in the **Prayer activity**. It is as though we are in an army, protected by what Jesus has done on the cross, as we race into battle.

Prayer activity

With: coloured pens and crayons; A6-sized shields with a cross outline at the centre – one for each person present – a cross template (YearA.1LentSun_1) is available from www.scriptureunion.org.uk/downloads.

Give everyone a shield and in small groups ask each person to colour or decorate their shield as brightly as possible and, as they do so, talk about the battles against evil that they face, either with personal temptation or in standing up for what is right in the wider world. Everyone then gathers at the front of church, or remains in their group; keep everyone bunched together in a crowd, as an army ready to charge. Each person holds their shield in front of them as you pray as follows, with everyone joining in with the words in bold:

Powerful Jesus, we are with you in a battle for what is right and good and true.
We are on your side.
Make us strong when we are tempted to do wrong.
(*Pause for individual silent conversation with God.*)

Courageous Jesus, we see many wrong things in this world.
We are on your side.
Make us strong to stand up for what is pure and just and fair.
(*Pause for individual silent conversation with God.*)

Mighty Jesus, we are ready for battle.
We are on your side.

(Close with a roaring 'Amen', which you should practise beforehand – begin quietly with the 'A' and as the 'Arrrrrrrrr…' gets louder and louder, it ends with an explosive 'men'!)

Ending the service

We are still waiting for the time when the devil will finally be totally defeated. But we know that he will be, one day. He is on the losing side! The Lord's Prayer sums it up so well. It would therefore be appropriate to close the service by saying that together. You could insert the following concluding lines to the prayer:

Yours is the kingdom, the power and the glory,
For you are the king, the ultimate victor and our hero,
For ever and ever.
Amen.

(If the roaring 'Amen' went well in the **Prayer activity**, repeat it here.)

Helpful extras

Music and song ideas
Songs on the theme of rejoicing and praise include: 'Thine be the glory'; 'And can it be

that I should gain?'; 'Oh happy day'; 'Fight the good fight'; 'We are marching in the light of God'; 'I am with you' *Bitesize Bible Songs* CD (SU), which is a Learn and remember song based on Joshua 1:9b.

You could use the following recording: 'For The Cross' by Matt Redman, for congregational singing.

Game

Play a game/drama where the rules are debated. For example, a game of noughts and crosses is known to most people. The person who gets three noughts or crosses in a line objects strongly when the other person (who has failed to get the three in a row) is declared the winner. The 'loser' then seeks to change the rules as declared by the 'referee'.

Then explain that in the account of Jesus' temptation, the devil tried to make up the rules, to his advantage. He wanted Jesus to bow down to him, and he even quoted the Bible to prove his point. You could include this in **Ending the service**, to reinforce the theme of the service, or as an alternative introduction in **Beginning the service**.

Notes and comments

The Bible explains death as far more than the end of bodily life. Rather, it is a state of decay and destruction where there is no evidence of God or of his goodness. Jesus ultimately has conquered the power of death that brings havoc to this world but we wait for his final victory. People still die, and decay is still all around us. Be aware that the word 'death' may be painful for people who are suffering bereavement.

Similarly, 'the devil' may conjure up images of horns and forked tails. We don't know what Satan looks like, but we do know he is the source of all evil. Be careful with the language you use, so as not to frighten younger children.

If this is a service of Holy Communion, include thanks that in Christ's death, evil has been defeated. The promises made in baptism acknowledge the battle that we are engaged in.

Alternative online options

Visit www.lightlive.org for additional activities for children, young people and adults.

SECOND SUNDAY OF LENT

READINGS: **Romans 4:1–5,13–17; John 3:1–17**
Genesis 12:1–4a; Psalm 121

Bible foundations

Aim: to put our faith in Jesus who has come to save the world and lead the way to eternal life

In Romans 4 Paul is concerned to defend his statement in 3:28 that people are 'justified by faith apart from observing the law'. Does the story of Abraham back this up or not? Paul goes back to the time when God established his covenant with Abraham, and points out that Abraham was exercising faith in God's promise before he was given any covenant requirements to obey. He was justified, put 'in the right' with God, on the basis of faith, not on the basis of any good deeds. God promised that he would be 'heir of the world' (verse 13) – that all nations would be blessed through his offspring (see Genesis 12:3; 22:17). Paul argues that all who share Abraham's faith, whether or not they are Jews, also share with him in the promise of acceptance by God (verse 16).

How can we hope to understand these things? Nicodemus found it all very difficult, despite his knowledge of the Hebrew Scriptures. Jesus tells him plainly that actually no one can understand spiritual things unless they are 'born again' (John 3:3). When Jesus says that everyone needs to be 'born of water and the Spirit' (verse 5), he is probably referring back to Ezekiel 36:25–27: 'I will sprinkle clean water on you, and you will be clean; I will cleanse you from all your impurities and from all your idols. I will give you a new heart and put a new spirit in you; I will remove from you your heart of stone and give you a heart of flesh. And I will put my Spirit in you...'

On what basis can all this happen? Just as all who looked at the bronze snake lifted up by Moses in the desert were healed (Numbers 21:9), so all who 'look' in faith to Jesus, God's Son, lifted up on the cross to bring us salvation, will receive the gift of eternal life (John 3:14,15).

Beginning the service

Much of the service will focus on what God has done for us in Jesus, so help everyone to focus on who God is. Playing a song for people to listen to would be a good way of encouraging that focus; a song such as Steve Curtis Chapman's 'Be still and know that he is God' would be ideal, or 'Our God is an awesome God' or 'Indescribable' (From the highest of heights).

Afterwards, invite members of the congregation to call out the great things we know about who God is, such as 'merciful', 'provider', 'strong tower', 'loving', 'faithful', and so on. Continue with a time of praise.

Bible reading

John 3:1–17 could be read as a conversation between Jesus and Nicodemus. It is suggested that John 3:16 is learnt as a Learn and remember verse to conclude the **Bible talk** (see **Music and song ideas**).

Romans 4 builds on the story of when Abraham was first called by God to set out on his journey of faith, as developed in the **Bible retelling**. It would help to set this in context by reading Genesis 12:1–4a. Explain that Abraham was living in the country around where present day Iraq is. His father, Terah, moved his family in the direction of the land that was eventually to become Israel. He got as far as a city called Haran and then settled there. He died and it would appear at this point that God appeared to Abraham with a stunning challenge. Draw attention to the fact that Abraham was already an old man, and it was known that his wife, Sarah, could not have any children. Then read Genesis 12:1–4a.

Bible retelling

This paraphrase of Romans 4:1–5 and 13–17 can be read as though someone is sitting in an armchair, explaining something important to those listening. The Bible quotations are from the CEV.

So, what can we say about old Abraham, the man God first called to take a journey of faith? Did he actually do anything to make God want to be his friend? If he did, he'd have been able to be pretty proud of such an achievement! But no, the Bible simply says, 'God accepted Abraham because Abraham had faith in him'.

It's a bit like this – you work hard all the hours you are employed to do and you get paid. It is only right that your employer pays you. But God doesn't accept us because of what we have done. The Bible simply says, 'God accepts sinners only because they have faith in him': in other words, they trust him.

Then the Bible says, 'God promised Abraham and his descendants that he would give them the world'. Again, Abraham didn't deserve this; he just trusted God. It was a promise from God with no conditions attached.

And this promise of being accepted by God, simply because of trusting him, wasn't just for Abraham. It was for you and me too! That's right – for you and me too!

Bible talk

With: a globe or world map; a cross made

of wood or cardboard; sticky notes; pens

Ask everyone to imagine that they are living at the time of Jesus and that it's night time. Imagine they are hurrying through the back streets of Jerusalem to find Jesus. They want to ask him some important questions, but would prefer to do it secretly. What questions would anyone want to ask Jesus? What questions might you want to ask Jesus at night? (Encourage the children especially to use their imagination and natural curiosity, with 'how' and 'why' sort of questions. It does not matter if there is no simple answer!)

A religious leader, called Nicodemus, did just this. Maybe he was a busy man and this was the only time available. Maybe he was afraid that people would think he was a follower of Jesus or wanted to become one, but he was not yet ready for that. He certainly had lots of questions. He believed in Jesus' miracles. And that was evidence that God was with Jesus.

Jesus spoke in a riddle to Nicodemus. He said that in order to be a part of God's kingdom, a grown-up man must be born again. Now that's impossible! Ask the children to imagine climbing back inside their mum! Ask their mums what that would be like! (This is a visually memorable image that Jesus is painting!)

Jesus was explaining that to become a child of God and belong to his family you have to start again. God would give people a fresh start to begin a new life, just like a newborn baby. Jesus went on to tell Nicodemus how anyone who has faith in Jesus would have life for ever. (If you talked about 'death' in

the previous outline, you can refer back to that.) This is the best promise that Jesus could give to anyone – and it's available to all.

Refer to God's promise to Abraham that was introduced in the **Bible retelling** from Romans 4. We don't know what Nicodemus made of all this but we do know that he believed enough in Jesus to help bury his body, identifying himself as some sort of follower. This was a brave thing to do. The promise of life with God, now and for ever, is still true for us if we believe.

John 3:16 is a key verse for everyone to know by heart. You could learn it by using the Learn and remember verse song 'So much' (see **Music and song ideas**) or by splitting the verse into phrases to print on separate cards, saying them altogether, and then gradually removing the cards one at a time until everyone can say the verse without any visual prompt.

Prayers of intercession

Ask three people to lead prayers for those who are exploring or are already putting into practice what it means to have faith in Jesus. This might include praying for:

- those coming to an Alpha-type course
- children who have been part of a holiday club or outreach event that introduced them to the good news of Jesus
- families who are growing together in their faith.

Prayer of confession

In this prayer of confession, the congregation responds with the line in bold:

Lord, forgive us when our focus and trust is not on you;
Bring us back to you.
Lord, forgive us when we lack the faith to trust in you;
Bring us back to you.
Lord, forgive us when we are proud of all that we can do and become boastful;
Bring us back to you.
Lord, forgive us when we think we are good enough for heaven;
Bring us back to you.
Lord, thank you for saving us and giving us new life by your Holy Spirit;
Amen.

Ending the service

Eternal life with God for ever begins NOW. We don't have to wait until we die. For all those who have faith in God, their lives are transformed NOW. God makes a difference NOW. Ask people to stand up if any of the following statements are true of them. After each statement, say, 'This week, God's everlasting life is for everyone who has faith in him.' They then sit down and you declare the next statement.

The statements could be: Everyone who is going to a school this week; going to work this week; visiting a friend this week; finishing off a project this week; coming to church this week.

Finish by using the doxology from Jude, verses 24 and 25 (either TNIV or CEV version).

Helpful extras

Music and song ideas
Songs and hymns about Jesus' offer of eternal life could include: 'Over the mountains and the sea'; 'The message of the cross'; 'Thank you for saving me'; 'We really want to thank you Lord'; 'Worthy, O worthy are you Lord'; 'And can it be'; 'When I survey the wondrous cross'; 'Love divine, all loves excelling'; 'So much' *Bitesize Bible Songs 2* CD (SU) – John 3:16 as a Learn and remember verse; Steve Curtis Chapman's 'Be still and know that he is God'; 'Our God is an awesome God'; 'Indescribable' (From the highest of heights).

Notes and comments

Consider interviewing a member of your congregation about how they became a Christian, but make sure they use the concept of faith as referred to in the **Bible talk** and use language that is accessible to all ages.

If this service includes Holy Communion, acknowledge that we eat bread and drink wine together because we have faith that God in Christ has accepted and forgiven us.

Alternative online options
Visit www.lightlive.org for additional activities for children, young people and adults.

THIRD SUNDAY OF LENT

27/3/11

READINGS: **Romans 5:1–11; John 4:5–42**
Exodus 17:1–7; Psalm 95

Bible foundations

Aim: to share how Jesus came to bring fresh new life

In the story of Jesus' conversation with the loose-living Samaritan woman, we see him disregarding normal conventions and breaking down barriers that divide people from one another. He begins by asking for a drink (John 4:7). This amazes the woman, who engages him in conversation. Jesus quickly turns the conversation on to the eternal life he can offer (verse 10), challenges her about her lifestyle (verses 15–18), and speaks of the worshippers that the Father is seeking (verses 23,24). The woman perceives that Jesus is both a prophet (verse 19) and, indeed, as he claims, the promised Messiah (verses 25,26). (The Samaritans were looking for a similar 'prophet like Moses' figure, called the Taheb, see Deuteronomy 18:15,18.) So she is willing to own up to her sinful past, and witness to Jesus (verse 39).

The Samaritans were the Jews' enemies, yet Jesus reached out to them in love. The apostle Paul shows how, in fact, by his death on the cross Jesus has died for all of us, for we are all God's enemies (Romans 5:10). We may not think of ourselves like that, but the truth of the matter is that because we are all 'ungodly' (verse 6), failing to please God by our lives, we all need to be 'reconciled to him through the death of his Son' (verse 10). The heart of the good news that the Bible teaches is that 'while we were still sinners, Christ died for us' (verse 8).

There is nothing we can do to recommend ourselves to God. All we are called to do is to respond to this good news as the Samaritan woman did, by confessing our sins and recognising that Jesus is Lord and Christ. Having done that, we will be able to rejoice (or, more literally, 'boast') in three things: in our hope of sharing the glory of God (verse 2b); in our sufferings, because in them we learn steadfastness and experience God's love poured into our hearts; and in God himself, 'through whom we have now received the reconciliation' (verse 11).

Beginning the service

With: jugs of water; drinking glasses or plastic cups

As people arrive, provide them with a drink of water. (They may need to use their cups/glasses again in the **Prayer activity**.) Have some contemplative music playing in the background and display some or all of the following verses: Psalm 42:1, 2; Psalm 107:9; Isaiah 55:1; John 7:37, 38; Revelation 21:6.

Explain that in the service you will be hearing how Jesus asked a woman for a drink of water. We don't know if she gave it to him or if he drank it but we do know that they ended up talking about some very significant things. It was a bit like Nicodemus, in last week's service, who talked with Jesus about something really important in the middle of the night. But this conversation took place in the middle of the day!

Bible reading

The focus is on the first part of the story in John 4, so the Bible reading should be verses 5–14 only. Read it with a narrator, Jesus and the woman. It could also be acted, with 'Jesus' seated beside something to represent a well, such as a small round table. The woman, who should have a bucket, could join him and sit next to him for the dialogue.

Romans 5:1–11 is full of amazing statements about God. Read it slowly, asking people to follow the reading in their own Bibles or Bibles in the pews.

Bible talk

With: a plastic bucket containing the following numbered signs printed onto individual cards: Water that is living; Never be thirsty again; Eternal life

Encourage everyone to have a Bible open at John 4:5–14, or have copies of these verses on show. Talk about how Jesus arrived at the well in the middle of the day when it was really hot. Most people would have gone home for a rest from the hot sun. Here he met a woman from Samaria. No one liked her, which was probably why she came to fetch her own water in the middle of the day so she would not have to meet anyone. Explain that Jesus was tired and thirsty. He had sent his disciples into the town to get some food.

Water that is living

Ask what Jesus first asked the woman to do (see verse 7). Explain that it was quite out of the ordinary for a Jew to speak to a Samaritan (whom Jews despised), let alone for a man to speak to a woman whom he didn't know. As usual, Jesus didn't do what people expected him to do.

Then ask what Jesus said that he could give the woman, in verses 10 and 11. Pull out the label from the bucket – 'Water that is living'. (Either display this in some way, or ask a child to hold it up.) The woman imagined that this water had special powers. She could not grasp what Jesus meant. He was of course speaking in picture language.

Never be thirsty again

Ask what Jesus told the woman she would

never be if she drank his water (see verse 14) and pull out the label from the bucket – 'Never be thirsty again'. Now the woman really thought that Jesus had an extraordinary power. She was intrigued.

Eternal life

Finally, ask what this living water would give people (verse 14) and pull out the final label – 'Eternal life'. The woman could not really understand but she did see that Jesus was offering her hope and new life, both for now and eternity.

Later on in the story it becomes obvious that, as Jesus chatted with the woman at the well, he knew all about her and the wrong things she had done, but he still offered her life-giving water. She went and told everyone around just what it was that Jesus had offered her.

God loves us while we are still sinners. He sent Jesus to die for us so that, if we want to, we can be forgiven and have new life as his friends, for ever. Read Romans 5:8–10 again to finish.

Prayer activity

With: one bucket/jugs filled with drinking water; an empty bucket; plastic cups (possibly the ones used in **Beginning the service**)

Jesus promised to give the woman living water, a life that was of a quality that it would never end. But she had to believe that he would keep his promise. She had to have faith in him.

Ask everyone to think what it means for them to receive the new life that Jesus offers, made possible because of his death on the cross. Then ask people in small groups to come to the front to thank Jesus for this new life. (This can be done as a small group activity or as an individual one.) Each person pours or scoops a little of the fresh water into their cup and then they stand as individuals facing the cross or they stand in a circle and thank Jesus for this new life. They can then either drink the water or pour it into the empty bucket.

Prayer of confession

Water also washes and cleanses and therefore in a time of confession it would be appropriate to use the imagery to enable people to ask for forgiveness and reassure them that God will wash clean those who repent.

Conclude by reading verses such as Psalm 51:7 and 10. After this, you could sing one of the songs in **Music and song ideas**.

Prayers of intercession

Jesus knew the needs of this woman. He knew all about her. Explain about her husbands for those who do not know the story (John 4:16–20,28,29). We cannot hide anything from Jesus either.

Ask everyone to get into small groups and identify one need each, and then pray for each other. (These could be the same groups as for the **Prayer activity**.) Draw this to a close by thanking God that he does meet all our needs. Pray too for those who are longing to know God for themselves, but who may be deliberately hiding from him. May they discover that they need never thirst any more!

Ending the service

Invite everyone to find Romans 16:25–27. Say that it is at the end of the letter Paul wrote to the Christians in Rome, part of which has been the focus for today's Bible teaching.

The person who preached should read verses 25 and 26. Encourage everyone to respond by reading verse 27 together as enthusiastically and joyfully as possible.

Helpful extras

Music and song ideas
'Great is the Lord and most worthy of praise'; 'Jesus Christ is risen today'; 'Jesus is Lord! Creation's voice proclaims it'; 'Lord, I come to you'; 'Purify my heart'; 'I hunger and I thirst'; 'I've come to wash my soul'; 'O breath of life'.

To conclude the **Prayer of confession**, appropriate songs include: 'You rescued me'; 'God forgave my sin in Jesus' name'; 'Only by grace'; 'My Lord, what love is this'. .

Notes and comments

Focusing upon the new life that Jesus offers with the challenge to take the living water should have an impact on all those present. If people respond to this, make sure that there are pastorally sensitive people available for them to pray and chat with afterwards.

In Holy Communion, where we are invited to drink Jesus' blood, there is an obvious development of the invitation to drink. In a service of baptism, the connections with water and cleansing are also very clear.

The significance of Jesus' meeting with a Samaritan woman of dubious reputation could be dealt with in more detail, if appropriate. The centuries-old feud between the Jews and Samaritans is highlighted in John 4:19–24. The issue that Jesus raises with his disciples in verse 34 emphasises the need to receive spiritual nourishment from doing God's will. We may be attending church, studying the Bible and praying faithfully, but we are nourished by what we give out in obedient service to God, as well as by what we receive. In John 17:4, as he anticipates his forthcoming death, Jesus refers to completing God's work on earth – his mission was accomplished.

Since water has played a central part in this service, it would be appropriate to pray for those in the world living in areas of drought or inadequate water supply and the initiatives there have been to make a difference. For relevant information, you can visit www.wateraid.org, www.waterforlife.net, www.tearfund.org or www.christianaid.org.uk. You could set up a fundraising venture, which would be appropriate in the season of Lent when Jesus fasted for 40 days.

Alternative online options
Visit www.lightlive.org for additional activities for children, young people and adults.

FOURTH SUNDAY OF LENT

READINGS: **Ephesians 5:8–14; John 9:1–41**
1 Samuel 16:1–13; Psalm 23

Bible foundations

Aim: to ask God for help and wisdom as we act rightly as followers of Jesus

John Newton's hymn 'Amazing grace' includes the lines: 'I once was lost but now am found, was blind but now I see.' In John's Gospel, the image of light is especially common, right from the start of the Gospel: 'The light shines in the darkness, but the darkness has not understood it' (1:5) or 'Jesus comes as light for the world' (8:12).

The story in chapter 9 has symbolic significance beyond the obvious storyline. In the blind man's experience, we see a growing understanding of who Jesus is. At first he describes his healer as 'the man they call Jesus' (verse 11). After being questioned he comes to the conclusion that Jesus cannot be a sinner (verse 16), and indeed must be a prophet (verse 17). He is a 'godly man' who must have been sent 'from God' (verses 31,33). Finally, when he encounters Jesus, he acknowledges him as the Son of Man to whom all lordship has been given (see Daniel 7:13,14) and worships him (verses 35,38). By so doing he shows that spiritually he has far more insight than the blind Pharisees.

In Ephesians 5, the apostle Paul also uses the imagery of light. As 'children of light' (verse 8), God's people are to 'have nothing to do with the fruitless works of darkness, but rather expose them' (verse 11). We are to refuse the seductions of the world, the flesh and the devil, choosing day by day to follow the values, attitudes, goals and priorities of the kingdom of God instead. We are to unmask the devil by revealing his lie that the way to live is, 'If it feels right, do it.' Our main concern should be to please the Lord, and to do always what is good, right and true (verses 9,10). In doing this we will truly be Jesus' followers, 'a city on a hill' (Matthew 5:14) giving light to all around.

Beginning the service

With: a mirror; some torches

Show the mirror to the congregation and point out that it has no light of its own. Give the torches to various people sitting near the front, asking them to direct the light onto the mirror. Angle the mirror to reflect the light back onto the congregation. Explain that in today's service we are going to reflect on the fact that when Christ shines his light on us we become lights.

Divide the congregation into two parts. The first half reads from Ephesians 5:14 (CEV): 'Wake up from your sleep and rise from death'. The second half repeats it back to the first, but louder. Continue for three or four repeats; then both groups shout triumphantly together, 'Then Christ will shine on you'. The obvious follow-on is the song 'Shine, Jesus, shine'. (See **Music and song ideas**.)

Bible reading

There is a drama script (YearA.4SunLent_1) that is available from www.scriptureunion.org.uk/lightdownloads. This passage lends itself to a dramatised reading for everyone. You will need five readers at the front for the narrator, disciples, Jesus, blind man and parents. Divide the remaining congregation into two to read the parts of the neighbours and the Pharisees.

By contrast, Ephesians 5:8–14 is best read by one confident reader. The CEV gives a clear, readable translation that younger listeners will appreciate.

Bible talk

With: a blindfold; a needle with a fine hole; some thread; three strips of card that could be used as blindfolds – on one is written 'What other people think', on another 'What I am missing' and on the third 'What I know best!'; a torch from **Beginning the service**

The challenge of a blindfold

Invite a volunteer to come forward. Explain that you are going to ask them to perform some tasks blindfolded. Blindfold them and then place two or three chairs to make an obstacle course. Ask them to find their way to the other side. When they've successfully accomplished this, and with the blindfold still on, give them a needle in one hand and a piece of thread in the other. Ask them to thread the needle. After a few tries explain that there are some things we can do without being able to see, but other things that are impossible.

Explain that when it comes to spiritual things, knowing God and his plans for our lives, we are like the man born blind. There are still lots of things we can do – eat, drink, sleep, work, play – but compared with living for God we are living in the darkness.

Take the blindfold off the volunteer and ask them to thread the needle. They may still find this difficult. Explain that when we meet with Jesus and our lives are changed by him, we don't suddenly become able to see and do all that God wants. We start a journey, a process. Every day, our job is to 'find out what pleases the Lord' (Ephesians 5:10).

Invite suggestions from the congregation as to

what those things might be, or, alternatively, ask them to get into small groups and to try and answer the question: 'What things could I do in this next week that would please Jesus?' As you receive answers, make the point that it's not about looking for special good deeds, but about pleasing Jesus in the ordinary and everyday things (Ephesians 5:9).

The impact of spiritual blindfolds

The Jewish religious leaders (Pharisees) knew a huge amount about God. They had tried to serve him all their lives. But when Jesus came they deliberately blindfolded themselves because they did not want to believe (John 9:40,41). Even a miracle of a kind that had never been seen before (John 9:32) couldn't convince them.

What other people think

Because we live in a world of spiritual darkness, we can be tempted to go back to our old ways, even after we have met with Jesus. Show the blindfold 'What other people think' and hold it loosely to cover your eyes. Ask someone in advance to share how they have failed God because they were worried about what friends, neighbours or family might have thought or said.

What I am missing

Show the second blindfold. Sometimes things that are wrong look very attractive. It may seem that our friends are having a much better time than us. Sometimes we are just so full of our own ideas that we don't stop to listen to God. Again, take suggestions and stories from the congregation.

What I know best

Show the third blindfold and ask how we

can determine what is the best way to go: for example, making a point of seeking God's way, asking advice from God's people and taking time to hear from God. God will help us know what is best. We have to trust him and learn how to enjoy and appreciate the good things that come from following him.

There are times when we need specific wisdom from God, such as, 'What do I do now?' and 'What shall I do with my life when I leave school, when I change jobs, when I retire?' But mostly, walking in the light is like going on a night-time walk with a torch (show the torch). Through our prayers, our reading and learning from the Bible, and the help we receive from one another, God gives us enough light to see just as far ahead as we need to. (If your building permits, draw the curtains, turn out the lights and switch on the torch. Use it to find your way around.)

Prayer activity

With: a string of Christmas fairy lights

This activity follows on from the **Bible talk**.

Ask a few people to prepare prayers for those who are seeking God's wisdom and who need the light of God to make decisions, such as changing jobs, courses, schools, moving, new initiatives at church, commitment to Christ.

These people should stand in a line holding the fairy lights, ideally standing in the body of the church with people all around them. After the prayers, the following verse is read while you encourage everyone in the congregation to reach out towards the light:

'Now you are people of the light because you belong to the Lord. So act like people of the light and make your light shine' (Ephesians 5:8b,9a, CEV).

Prayer of confession

With: a collection of newspaper articles from the previous few weeks showing 'the fruitless deeds of darkness' (Ephesians 5:11, TNIV)

Show or summarise the stories that reflect the darkness of our society. (You could scan some of the stories and images to project them.) Be careful that no stories alarm younger children. Encourage the congregation to form small groups of mixed ages to pray together, confessing to God the mess that our world is in. Draw the prayers to a close with these words:

We were once darkness,
But now we are light.
Help us to live as children of the light.
Help us to shine our light into the darkness,
So that darkness may become light.

Ending the service

With: some relighting candles (sold for birthday cakes; after you blow them out they light themselves again); a cake (optional)

Put the candles on a cake (or if you don't want to use a cake, fix them into Plasticine or anything else that will make them stand up). Review all that has been shared in the service as you light them. Remind people that God calls us to be light in this dark world. Ask two children to blow out the candles. As they do so, warn everyone that there will be all sorts of things that will try to put out our light.

Pause as the candles relight themselves; then say that however many times our light is put out (repeat the blowing out and relighting), the light of Christ is never put out and we can constantly be re-lit.

Finish by using the response you started with, 'Wake up from your sleep and rise from death. Then Christ will shine on you.' If you have coffee after the service, share the cake.

Helpful extras

Music and song ideas

Songs that pick up the themes of light and darkness include: 'Lord, the light of your love (Shine, Jesus, shine)';, 'Great is the darkness' and 'Darkness like a shroud' take the themes out into the wider world. 'Light of the world, you stepped down into darkness' and 'Open our eyes, Lord, we want to see Jesus' are more personal. 'Be thou my vision' is a challenging song of commitment. 'We are marching in the light of God' is a joyful celebration and could include percussion instruments with everyone marching around the building as they sing.

Garth Hewitt's song 'Mud on my eyes' is a simple song telling the story of the blind man in John 9 and could easily be taught to a congregation; alternatively, 'God is an awesome God' or 'Who was the man', both on *Light for everyone* CD (SU), could be used.

Statement of faith

Explain that this statement of faith is based on the increasing realisation of the blind man as to who Jesus is. This Statement (YearA.4SunLent_2) is also available from www.scriptureunion.org.uk/lightdownloads.

Jesus is a teacher
Jesus is a healer
Jesus is a miracle worker
Jesus comes from God
Jesus is the sinless one
Jesus is a prophet
Jesus is the Messiah – God's chosen one
Jesus is the judge of all the earth
Jesus is the Son of Man
Jesus is light for the world
Jesus is the Son of God
Jesus is the one I put my faith in
Jesus is the one who opens my eyes
Jesus is the light and his light shines in me

Notes and comments

If praying in small groups is not your usual practice, then for the **Prayer of confession** explain that there is no need to pray long, complicated prayers. Encourage as many people as possible to pray short, simple prayers. Give people permission to remain silent in the groups, if they wish to.

Mothering Sunday occurs on the Fourth Sunday of Lent so you may wish to use the following outline instead.

Alternative online options

Visit www.lightlive.org for additional activities for children, young people and adults.

MOTHERING SUNDAY

READINGS: **Jeremiah 29:1–14; Luke 2:41–52**
Psalm 127:1–5; Colossians 3:12–17

Bible foundations

Aim: to see how God has made us all unique with a purpose for life

God's people had been in Babylon, far from their homeland in Jerusalem. They must have wondered how much longer it would be before they could return home, if ever! But through the prophet Jeremiah they were to be reassured that God had a future for them (29:10–14). Some of them would not return but the time would come when God's plans for his people would move into a new phase.

Jesus' mother, Mary, and Joseph must have wondered how the strange events that surrounded Jesus' birth would turn out. How could they understand the meaning of the angels' words or the dagger that would pierce their hearts (Luke 2:35)? The visit to Jerusalem when Jesus was twelve years old was to clarify some things for them. It was obviously customary for Joseph's family to travel to Jerusalem from Nazareth, around 100km, and they would have walked in a larger group. It was like a village holiday. The age of 12 was when Jewish boys were accepted as full-grown adults, so this particular occasion may have been especially significant for Jesus, his first as a grown man. Children in the congregation will be familiar from their RE lessons, or from the experience of Jewish friends, with the custom of Bar Mitzvah.

It was easy for Jesus to become detached from his family or village group but it was no accident. Through this incident in Luke 2:41–52 he was to discover more of the calling that God had upon his life, more of his destiny. His parents were to discover more of this too. Psalm 127 reflects the sense that God is intimately engaged in the lives of his people, a care that was extended towards the twelve-year-old Jesus.

Beginning the service

Welcome everyone; then ask what twelve-year-olds want to be in the future and what plans they have for their lives. If it is possible to ask them before the service, ask some 12-year-olds in the church what they think they will be in their late teens. A teacher or youth worker could supply useful quotes. Write down comments to display on a screen or to read out. Alternatively, comments from some 12-year-olds in Coventry (YearA.Mother_1) are available from www.scriptureunion.org.uk/lightdownloads.

Alternatively, ask adults/parents if they can remember what they thought their future would be when they were moving on to secondary school.

Without specific reference to Jesus as a boy, ask what sort of ambitions a twelve-year-old carpenter's son, living 2,000 years ago, might have had for his life – (a job, wife, sons, avoid getting into trouble with the landlord or being forced to join the 'army'). Explain that in this service we shall be exploring what we all expect in life.

Bible reading

Invite everyone to listen to one example of God's plans for his people, as Jeremiah 29:5–12 is read. Explain that 2,500 years ago God's people had been dragged away from Jerusalem to Babylon as prisoners and had little idea how long they would stay there. Listen out for what God, through the words of Jeremiah, said they should do in the future, and what he would do. Answers include: settle down, build houses, plant gardens (verse 5); marry, increase in numbers as a people (verse 6); pray for peace for Babylon (verse 7); you will return (verse 10); you will have a future filled with hope (verse 11); I will answer your prayer (verse 12).

God's plans for his people at that time were to get on with life but not to lose sight of the long-term future. Life was just going to be very ordinary if not ideal.

Luke 2:41–52 could be read with a narrator, Jesus and Mary, pausing for the appropriate actions. Children and adults mime the parts of Mary, Joseph, Jesus, a crowd of three, and two senior teachers of the law (these could be older people).

- Mary, Joseph and Jesus dawdle up the aisle, with three of the crowd.
- All six stand with backs to audience and hands together in attitude of prayer.
- Mary and Joseph set off slowly down aisle while Jesus remains in the crowd.
- Jesus joins two senior teachers at the side but in such a way that the audience can see him.
- The 'crowd' blocks Mary's and Joseph's view of Jesus as they hurry down the aisle, looking anxious.
- Mary finally finds Jesus and wags her finger at him.
- Mary, Joseph and Jesus go down the aisle together, arms round each other.

Bible talk

With: six images of Jesus' life to illustrate (see below) the following verses (Luke 1:31; 2:16; 2:18; Matthew 1:21; Luke 2:35; 2:49), either as pictures or as a PowerPoint, (YearA.Mother_2), available from www.scriptureunion.org.uk/lightdownloads.

Ask what hopes parents have for their 12-year-old children. Remind them of the comments in **Beginning the service** and invite comments from all parents.

Mary's expectations

Ask what Mary's expectations might have been for her son, Jesus, such as, a safe job, a nice wife, lots of sons, someone to look after Mary in her old age, respectability. By the time he was twelve she did know some unusual things about him. Show the images from the PowerPoint or pictures you have found. Explain their significance as you go, remembering that some people present, both children and adults, will not know the full story.

- Mary knew her son was conceived in a miraculous way for she was not yet married to Joseph and Jesus was God's Son, not Joseph's.
- Mary knew that shepherds had been told about Jesus' birth by angels.
- Mary kept thinking about what the shepherds had said.
- Mary knew Jesus' name was to be 'Jesus' meaning 'he will save his people from their sins' because an angel had told Joseph this was how it was to be. What did that mean?
- Mary knew that being the mother of Jesus was going to bring her pain. Simeon had warned her and told her that her son would have enemies.
- Mary watched as Jesus grew up and saw him as an ordinary but wise boy and one whom God blessed (Luke 2:40).

What was she to make of this son of hers? Did she worry? Did she hope he would not be rejected and that she would not have to suffer, that Simeon's words would not be true?

The story in the reading from Luke is a key turning point in Jesus' life. Explain how Joseph's family went up to Jerusalem (see **Bible foundations**). Even though Jesus was a newly acknowledged grown-up, his mother's anxiety was great when she discovered that he was not with them. Maybe other people in their group, knowing Jesus was not with them, assumed he was old enough to look after himself. Maybe her reaction was over the top. They spent two days looking for him in the city. She must have been distraught. Her reaction when they discovered him is understandable.

Jesus' response

The young Jesus is calm and matter-of-fact, as though he was saying, 'Haven't you realized yet who I am and what God's plan is for my life?' And he might have added, 'I am not going to be the sort of son you would ideally like, not like your neighbour's boy or my cousins.'

Mary and Joseph did not understand but Mary did not stop thinking and trying to understand. It was another 18 years before her son's destiny became clear but from this point on, Jesus had established his independence from his parents. He was going to fulfil God's plan for his life, not the hopes and plans of his parents. Yet after this incident he returned home and God continued to be pleased with him. Refer back to the earlier discussion on the hopes of a carpenter's son 2,000 years ago.

Our expectations

For parents: Mary had to come to terms with the fact that God had a plan for her son's life, independent from her. No parent has ever had a son whose destiny was of such significance but every parent has hopes for their children, hopes that they may try their best to turn into reality. But these hopes may not be the best for their children, and, more important, they may not be God's plans. Parents should not live out their own ambitions and disappointments in the lives of their children. God has made each of us unique and his plans are formed by quite a different set of criteria.

For children: Jesus, for his part, knew what God had called him to be although he could not have known the full implications. God has a special purpose for the lives of each child present. He wants them to become the people he has intended. Children are special because he has made them unique and loves them.

For everyone: How far do people wish they were other than they are? Are they resentful of how life has turned out, or do they long to be or do something different? Learning to accept ourselves as God intended is an important way to grow spiritually.

For those on the fringe: The simple message of being loved and made by God for a purpose, which frees us from self-dislike or poor self-esteem, is very powerful. Encourage anyone for whom this is a fresh concept to think about it some more.

Prayer of confession

Invite everyone to reflect on the example of Mary and Jesus. Then ask two parents to read this prayer, based on Psalm 139, with everyone saying the emboldened response.

A: God our father, you know all about us. You watched us being formed inside our mothers.
B: Forgive us for the times when we have envied others and wanted to be different from how you have made us. Nothing is hidden from you.
Father God, forgive us.
A: God our father, you notice everything we do.
B: As parents we have sometimes tried to force our children to be what we want them to be, and not allowed them to develop in the unique way you have planned. Nothing is hidden from you.
Father God, forgive us.
A: God our father, we praise you for the wonderful way you created us.
B: Help us to celebrate the fact that you know and love each one of us, as we are. We know that nothing is hidden from you.
Father God, forgive us.

Prayer activity

With: pens or pencils; ribbons; copies of two different scrolls, one for children and one for adults (possibly one for under-fives too) – (YearA.Mother_3) available from www.scriptureunion.org.uk/lightdownloads

Give each child a scroll with the following words written on it:
Dear _____ Thank you for caring for me. Please help me become the person God wants me to be. Signed_____
(For under-fives simplify this with just the words: Thank you for caring for me. From _____)
Give everyone else a scroll with the following words written on it:
Dear God, Thank you for creating me as I am. Please help me accept this and allow me

to become the person you want me to be.
Signed _____

Give everyone a pencil or pen to sign their name and a ribbon to tie around the scroll. Children can give their scroll to their parents if they are present or take them home. If the church has a tradition of giving mothers some flowers, it would be appropriate to do so at this point in the service. Adults keep their scroll as a reminder of what they have said to God in this service.

Prayers of intercession

Pray for parents, asking God to give them wisdom in the demanding task of parenting.
Pray for those wanting a child but for whom it is proving not possible, for whatever reason.
Pray for children across the world without parents either because of HIV/Aids, war or social breakdown.
Pray for the hopes of everyone to be influenced by God's plans, which are always conceived in love.

Ending the service

Break into small groups, which may be family groups, to face each other. Repeat each phrase after the leader, as you request the following blessing from God for each other.

May the Lord be kind to you.
May the Lord bless you - with a future filled with hope.
May the Lord watch over you - as you grow up in him.
Amen.

based on Jeremiah 29:10,11

Helpful extras

Music and song ideas
'Now thank we all our God'; 'For the beauty of the earth'; 'Lord for the years'; 'God has a plan' *Bitesize Bible Songs* CD (SU); 'Be thou my vision'; 'I'm special because God has loved me'; 'Father let me dedicate' (Be glorified); 'Lord of the future, Lord of the past'.

Notes and comments

Mothers' Day or Mothering Sunday services can provoke strong negative reactions but the Mothers' Day event (an essentially secular festival) is an opportunity to build bridges into the community that surrounds the church. Try to identify what means of outreach you can use through this service.

'Mothering Sunday' itself is a term that probably finds its origins in people gathering in the Mother Church/Cathedral or in young women in service visiting their mothers with a simnel cake three weeks before Easter because they would be too busy to go home after that.

This outline has been adapted from *All-Age Service Annual Volume 1* (SU). *All-Age Service Annuals 2–4* include other services for Mothering Sunday.

A suggestion for giving out flowers to mothers/women present, if that is your custom, is included in the **Prayer activity**.

Alternative online options
Visit www.lightlive.org for additional activities for children, young people and adults.

FIFTH SUNDAY OF LENT

10/4/11

READINGS: **Romans 8:6–11; John 11:1–45**
Ezekiel 37:1–14; Psalm 130

Bible foundations

Aim: to explore the many kinds of 'life after death' that Jesus brings

Martha's faith in Jesus is very touching. As soon as she sees Jesus, she says to him, 'Lord, if you had been here my brother would not have died, but I know that even now God will give you whatever you ask.' In contrast to the story of the two sisters in Luke 10:38–42, in this passage Martha comes across even more positively than her sister Mary. In one of the most famous 'I AM' sayings in John, which link Jesus with the redeeming God revealed at the time of Moses (Exodus 3:13,14) and in the deliverance from exile in Babylon (Isaiah 43:10–12), Jesus declares himself to be 'the resurrection and the life' (John 11:25). Those who trust in him will live again even if they die, and that life will be eternal (verses 25,26). The calling of Lazarus back to life when he has already been dead for four days and the body has begun to decompose (verse 39) is a startling preview of what the Son of God will one day accomplish for all his true disciples.

The apostle Paul sees believers as united to Christ by faith. What is true of him is also true of them. Since, therefore, Jesus has overcome death and has risen in triumph, believers also (Romans 8:6–11) have died and risen with Christ. This implies that we are no longer slaves to sin, and death has no mastery over us (verses 6 and 9). Not only does our firm hope in a future resurrection deliver us from any fear of death, but we also have the power of the risen Christ in our hearts through the Holy Spirit to enable us to live the life of the risen Jesus in this world. Since we know (verse 6) that we are dead and risen with Christ we must count (or 'reckon' – Paul uses an accounting term here) that this is the case, for indeed it is!

123

Beginning the service

With: mobile phone with a flat battery; charger

Take out of your pocket a mobile phone that has no charge. Apologise and explain that you need to make a phone call. Be surprised and puzzled that you can't get the phone to work. Let one or two volunteers look at it to see what the problem is. Make the point that the phone is dead – it has no charge. Ask what you can do. Then plug in the phone in order to charge it and explain that you'll come back to look at it later in the service and see what has happened.

Introduce the theme of the service as 'Life – death – and life again' and sing the song 'We believe in God the Father' (see **Music and song** ideas).

Bible reading

With: a set of emoticons (simple pictures showing emotions, such as a smiley face, sad face, puzzled face and so on)

Comment that the Bible contains stories about real people, who experienced the same emotions that we do. Ask everyone to smile to show how we look when we're happy; then ask them to frown to show sadness. As the Bible is read, we are going to try to enter into the emotions of what was happening.

An expressive reader can read John 11:1–45 from the CEV, or the TNIV, if you don't want to lose the phrase 'I am the resurrection and the life' (verse 25). As the passage is read, display the emoticons and ask the congregation to show the appropriate emotions. Leave a short space for quiet reflection at the end of the reading.

Verses 1–3 (worried); 4–10 (puzzled); 11,12 (pleased); 13–16 (puzzled); 17–21 (upset); 22–31 (hopeful); 32–38 (upset); 39–42 (scared); 43–45 (excited).

Romans 8:6–11 is a difficult passage for an all-age service and will be served best by being read slowly and thoughtfully, with brief pauses after each verse to allow the meaning to sink in.

Bible talk

With: a mobile phone; charger; flip chart (if required)

This talk relies mainly on questions and answers with the congregation rather than props and visual aids. PowerPoint images would illustrate the opening part, if you wish.

Being dead

Ask the congregation what it means when someone says the following phrases:

they are dead tired; their hopes are dead; an idea is dead in the water; the sea is dead calm; this is a dead time of year; the phone is dead.

Imagine a football team (your local team, if they are doing badly!). It's the end of a disastrous season. They've lost pretty well every match. Their hopes of ever winning are dead. When they start the next season, do things have to be the same? How could things change (new players, new manager, new spirit, a takeover by a

Russian millionaire!)? All through life we find situations that seem to be dead but in fact can be brought back to life again. For example, what could we do if our phone is dead? Remind them of the phone you put on charge at the start of the service (see **Beginning the service**).

Prime a volunteer in advance to ring your mobile at this point. You pick your phone up as it rings. Hold the phone to the microphone to pick up the message, which should be along the lines of 'Your phone has come back to life. Remember to keep it charged in future!'

Ask what it means to be dead in our sins. (Our sins make us spiritually dead. We cannot relate to God. Our spiritual battery is flat.) How can we be raised to life if we are dead because of the wrongs in our lives? After the raising of Lazarus, the religious leaders began to plot to put Jesus to death (John 11:46–53). Talk briefly about Jesus' death on the cross for our sins, so that we can have new life.

Being alive

You could at this point ask someone to share their own experience of coming to Christ and receiving new life. Ask them what things have changed in their life. Alternatively, ask for suggestions of ways our lives change when we become Christians. You could brainstorm 'before' and 'after', and record the suggestions on a flip chart.

Make a link with Romans 8:6–11. What Paul is saying is that God's Holy Spirit gives us new life here and now, if we allow him to live and work in us.

Read Romans 8:10 and 11. We change from being dead, like the phone, and are given new life here and now, but eventually our bodies will all die. Jesus raised Lazarus after he had been dead for four days. Explain that Jesus only raised three people from the dead in the Gospels: Jairus' daughter, the widow's son and Lazarus. This was done to help people understand what would happen to Jesus after he died. For Christians, death is very sad, but it is not the end. Read John 11:25. Jesus is promising that those who believe and trust in him will have life after death – life for ever.

You could remind people of recent all-age services that have focused on new life in Christ.

Prayer activity

With: paper; pencils; felt-tip pens or crayons; two boards on which to pin or stick pictures

Hand out sheets of paper and ask people to fold their paper in half and then open it again. Encourage them to think of a situation that needs new life, such as someone who is ill, a part of the local community struggling with a problem, or a local church that is struggling. It could be something further afield, such as a mission situation, a developing world situation from the recent news, a tragedy or a disaster. On the left-hand side everyone draws something to represent the situation as it is now – for example, people fighting, or a church with only one or two people. Everyone then thinks about what God could do in that situation.

Draw on the right-hand side some things that show the new life that God can bring – for example, the fighting people shaking hands or hugging, or the church filled with people. When the pictures are complete, people tear their papers in half ('before' and 'after') to bring them to the front. Pin or Blu-tack the 'before' picture to the left-hand side of a board saying, 'Lord, bring comfort to those in need', and pin the 'after' picture to the right-hand side of the board saying, 'and give them new life'.

Prayer of confession

This is based on Romans 8:6–11.

Lord, so often we do the things we want to do
Instead of the things you want us to do.
So often we fight against you, God,
And won't obey your laws.
Then there is no real life in us.
Lord, we are sorry.
Help us to allow our lives to be ruled by your Spirit;
Help us to allow our minds to be ruled by your Spirit;
Help us to allow our desires to be ruled by your Spirit.
Let us live to please you,
Let the Spirit of Christ live in us,
Rule in us,
And give us life.
Amen.

Ending the service

Explain the idea behind the language in the hymn 'Come ye that love the Lord' (see **Music and song ideas**). If we love and trust Jesus, every day of our lives is a journey towards heaven, which is our true

home. Give out percussion instruments and march around the room, singing the hymn. At the end, shout triumphantly, 'Jesus is the resurrection and the life. Anyone who believes in him will live, even though they die.'

Helpful extras

Music and song ideas
Graham Kendrick's creed song, 'We believe in God the Father', is a good way of introducing the themes of the service, with Christ's death and resurrection in the first verse and the coming of the Holy Spirit (and new life) in the second.

Isaac Watts' hymn 'Come ye that love the Lord' is a celebration of our journey to heaven. The language is old fashioned but it can be explained. Set to the tune 'Marching to Zion', with a rousing chorus, it can provide a triumphant end to the service. This hymn can be found in Sankey's hymnbook or can be downloaded from www.hymnsite.com/pdf/733piano.pdf.

Other songs include: 'Thine be the glory'; 'Lord, I was blind, I could not see'; 'O for a thousand tongues to sing'; 'There's a place where the streets shine'; 'Beauty for brokenness'; 'Living one' *Bitesize Bible Songs* CD (SU), a Learn and remember verse based on Revelation 1:18.

Notes and comments

Death is inevitably a sensitive subject. Children may get the wrong message, such as 'If I pray hard enough, my hamster/dog/granny will come back to life.' Because the **Bible talk** is in the form of a dialogue with the congregation, you have an opportunity to pick up some of these things from the answers you get. However, don't allow yourself to be totally sidetracked. This kind of talk works best if you stand as close to where people are sitting as possible and don't use a lectern.

One of the very best explanations for all ages of what happens when we die is found in Patricia St John's book *The Tanglewoods' Secret* (published by Scripture Union). The part you need is Chapter 19, 'Mr Tandy explains'. Briefly outline the story so far. (Two children are staying with an aunt in the country; they make friends with a local boy who falls out of a tree and subsequently – despite their prayers – dies.) This extract comes just after the funeral when Ruth, one of the two children, is very upset and confused. You could use this at the appropriate point in the Bible talk or as a separate item in the service. Alternatively, play this clip from the DVD of *The Tanglewoods' Secret*. It's powerful and moving and well worth the effort of

obtaining the book or DVD. (The book is available from Scripture Union Mail Order.)

If you would like to include some practical activity in the service, plant bulbs or seeds such as mustard and cress on cotton wool, hyacinths in a glass container filled with water, or even carrot tops in a saucer of water. These could be taken home (one per family) as a reminder of new life. Alternatively, they could be kept in the church and observed each Sunday, watching the evidence of new life.

If a service of Holy Communion is included, emphasise that the only reason why we can celebrate the Last Supper, is because Jesus was resurrected.

Alternative online options

Visit www.lightlive.org for additional activities for children, young people and adults.

PALM SUNDAY

READINGS: **Psalm 118:1,2,19–29; Matthew 21:1–11**

Bible foundations

Aim: to worship Jesus as servant King and conquering King

Psalm 118 was probably sung by Jesus and his disciples at the end of the Last Supper (Matthew 26:30), as the conclusion to 'the Egyptian Hallel' (Psalms 113–118), which was sung at the great religious festivals. In the light of its New Testament fulfilment we can see various elements of the psalm as significant. The king who enters the inner court is righteous and has experienced God's salvation (Psalm 118:21). The people exult because the one once rejected is now enthroned (verse 22; see also Acts 4:11,12; 1 Peter 2:7). The 'day the Lord has made' (verse 24) is the day of rejoicing at God's victory through his anointed king. The crowd process to God's house with the king, thanking, exalting and rejoicing (verses 26–29).

All of this, of course, could be seen on Palm Sunday as Jesus entered Jerusalem to the sound of praise from 'a very large crowd' (Matthew 21:8). Their acclamation of Jesus as the 'Son of David' (verse 9) indicates clearly that they are viewing him as none other than the Davidic Messiah, the coming king who would deliver God's people from their enemies. The word 'Hosanna' literally means 'Save us, Lord!' There is joy and celebration, seen in their royal homage to Jesus as they strew his way with cloaks and branches (see 2 Kings 9:13), but also a sense of expectation. The crowds recognise that he is not merely 'the prophet from Nazareth in Galilee', a despised area of the country (see John 1:46; 7:41), but in him is one who comes with God's authority (verse 9), bringing salvation.

Jesus is still despised and rejected by most people. But because by faith we recognise that he is God's chosen Saviour, we can celebrate him with all we've got. The Lord may wish to use us in whatever humble way he chooses, just as he used the owner's donkey on the first Palm Sunday (verses 2,3).

Beginning the service

With: palm crosses or card crosses, enough for everyone; a copy of the prayer (YearA/PalmSun_1) for display or printed from www.scriptureunion.org.uk/lightdownloads

Depending on your custom, hand out palm crosses or cut-out card crosses as people arrive, or give them out as described below. People will need to have one to be able to participate in the **Prayers of intercession**.

You could invite people to come forward during the opening hymn or song to collect a cross from a basket. A few people could stand near the basket, waving large palm branches to add to a sense of celebration. Ensure that all people can easily access the basket, or that there is an alternative way for people to receive a cross if they do not come to the front.

After everyone has received their cross, invite them to join in the following words, pointing out the ways in which the phrases are divided up between different parts of the congregation:

Leader: Let us worship Jesus.
Men and boys: Hosanna to the king!
Women and girls: Who comes to reign.
All: We welcome him here!
Women and girls: Hosanna to the king!
Men and boys: Who comes to serve.
All: We welcome him here!

Bible reading

The words of the crowd could be displayed, so that when Matthew 21:1–11 is read, everyone can join in saying verses 9b and 11.

Bible talk

With: images of several football managers on the touchline, available through an Internet search; 2 images of a war horse and a donkey (YearA.PalmSun_2), available from www.scriptureunion.org.uk/light/downloads

Things are not always as we expect
Show the photos of various football managers and discuss how many of them are dressed as you might expect. Ask for the reason behind each answer.

Then show the pictures of a donkey and a huge war horse. Ask which animal you would expect a king to come on and ask for the reason behind each answer. People will probably suggest the horse, but you can tell them that at the time of Jesus a horse or a donkey could be ridden by a king. The difference was that the king who rode a donkey came in peace, whereas arriving on a huge battle horse gave a very different message. So the fact that Jesus needed a donkey to ride meant that he was coming as a king – but one who came in peace.

A conquering king
Explain that many in the crowd who welcomed Jesus into Jerusalem would have been expecting or hoping for a conquering king, someone who would free them from Roman occupation, and establish himself as their real leader. The word 'Hosanna' means 'Save us, Lord'. Many people were looking for someone who would simply make their lives better, and give them independence, saving them materially and physically. But Jesus had not come as a military, conquering king.

A servant king

Jesus came as a king of a different kind. He came as a servant king. He did not come to overthrow the Roman occupying force, but to demonstrate the reign and love of God. He would do this by dying on the cross – within days of this triumphal entry. Read Matthew 20:28, as a way of demonstrating that Jesus knew what he was coming to Jerusalem for, and that he was willing to do this.

Point out that although Jesus took the role of a servant, he was actually also a conquering king. Through his death and resurrection, he conquered sin once and for all, and set us free to enter his gates with thankful hearts. Refer to the themes of the recent lectionary services. Use the words of Psalm 118:19 to sum up how we can respond to him: 'Open for me the gates of righteousness; I will enter and give thanks to the Lord.'

To conclude, ask everyone to imagine themselves at the roadside on that day. Help them to picture what it would have been like to welcome Jesus into the city. They would have been filled with excitement, with hopes of freedom, drawn along by the exuberant atmosphere and shouting of loud 'Hosannas'. Then suggest that they imagine themselves in a different crowd just a few days later, shouting, 'Crucify!' Ask them to think of ways of answering the question, 'Who is this?' (a servant king). How far do they see Jesus as both a conquering king and a servant king?

Prayers of intercession

If you normally give out palm crosses, you will need to have done so by this point in the service. If you do not normally give out palm crosses, consider buying some for this activity (although crosses made of card would do).

Ask the congregation to stand, if they are able to and, holding their palm crosses high, turn towards the direction you point them to, beginning with the north. (You may need to ascertain where north is, using a compass and a couple of children to help.) Teach everyone the emboldened response before you start.

We hold our crosses to the north, from whence cold winds come, and we pray for all who experience life as a bitter wind: those suffering because of broken relationships, painful memories, low self-esteem... (*Add as you feel appropriate.*)
Come, Servant King, come and reign.

We hold our crosses to the east, from whence the sun rises, and we pray for all who wait for a new day: those seeking new employment or vision, those struggling for peace or justice, those accepting a new challenge... (*Add as you feel appropriate.*)
Come, Servant King, come and reign.

We hold our crosses to the south, from whence stories of poverty often come, and we pray for all who struggle to make ends meet: those whose land produces no harvest, or whose labour produces no reward... (*Add as you feel appropriate.*)
Come, Servant King, come and reign.

We hold our crosses to the west, where the sun sets, and we pray for all who are facing darkness: those who are ill in body, mind or

spirit, or whose lives in this world are ending, those who... (*Add as you feel appropriate.*)
Come, Servant King, come and reign.

Prayer of confession

Explain that everyone needs to repeat the response that both leaders say together.

Leader 1: Lord Jesus, when you came into Jerusalem, people gathered to welcome you. They shouted 'Hosanna' and hope filled their hearts.
Leader 2: A few days later, the same people called for your death. They shouted, 'Crucify!' and hate filled their hearts.
Leaders 1 and 2: Forgive us, Lord, for the times when we change our hearts towards you.
All: Forgive us, Lord, for the times when we change our hearts towards you.

Leader 1: When you came into Jerusalem, people treated you as a king. They waved branches in celebration and asked you to save them.
Leader 2: When you hung on the cross, people treated you as a criminal. They waved their fists and asked you to save yourself.
Leaders 1 and 2: Forgive us, Lord, for the times when our praise of you becomes a protest.
All: Forgive us, Lord, for the times when our praise of you becomes a protest.

Leader 1: When you came into Jerusalem, people stood as one, shoulder to shoulder in their hopes and dreams.
Leader 2: When you were taken down from

the cross, people scattered, divided by their fears and failures.
Leaders 1 and 2: Forgive us, Lord, for the times when our belief in you turns to betrayal.
All: Forgive us, Lord, for the times when our belief in you turns to betrayal.

Leader 1: This week, Lord, and every week, let us know your compassion, your understanding and your forgiveness.
Leader 2: Let us be made new: sure in hope, certain in faith, and strong in love.
Leaders 1 and 2: Hosanna, Lord! Hosanna! Save your people. Amen.
All: Hosanna, Lord! Hosanna! Save your people. Amen.

Ending the service

As people look at their palm cross, ask them to tell their neighbour where they will display it during the week, encouraging them to find a place where others will see it and be drawn to think of the reason it is there. It could stimulate a conversation about Christ this week, and possibly an invitation to come to a special Easter service or event.

Use the following words to sum up your worship and prepare to go into the world:

Lord Jesus, Servant King, you came into Jerusalem.
May you go with us as we seek to serve others.
Lord Jesus, Conquering King, you came into Jerusalem.
May you go with us as we seek to live for you.
Hosanna to you, Lord! Hosanna!
Amen.

Helpful extras

Music and song ideas

Encourage the music group to use the talents of young and old together, which will reflect the celebratory occasion when everyone shared fully in making Jesus welcome as he rode into Jerusalem.

Classic Palm Sunday hymns include: 'My song is love unknown'; 'Ride on, ride on in majesty'; 'All glory, laud and honour'. But as well as these, there are many relatively contemporary songs, such as: 'Make way, make way for Christ the king'; 'Hosanna, Hosanna, Hosanna in the highest'; 'King forever, Lord Messiah'; 'Prepare the way of the Lord, make his paths straight'; 'You are the King of glory'; 'Praise is rising (Hosanna)'; 'Hear the call of the kingdom (King of heaven)'.

Game

There is a 'Guess the word' game (YearA. PalmSun_2), based on the Gospel story, available from www.scriptureunion.org. uk/light/downloads. Instructions for how the PowerPoint works are on the first screen, which you don't need to show to everyone!

Notes and comments

Palm crosses provide an opportunity to share the meaning of the cross with those who don't know Christ. Why not order twice the amount you normally do, and invite people to take two, so they can give one to a non-Christian as a gift? If done sensitively, this could be given to people of other faiths without being offensive.

For details of how to explain the meaning of the cross, read *Top Tips on Explaining the cross* (SU). For more details see page 99.

Alternative online options

Visit www.lightlive.org for additional activities for children, young people and adults.

GOOD FRIDAY

READINGS: **Isaiah 52:13 – 53:12; John 18:1 – 19:42**
Hebrews 10:16–25; Psalm 22

Bible foundations

Aim: to use our imaginations to enter into the events surrounding the death of Jesus

As we consider the events culminating in the death of Jesus, it is helpful to ask how these events show us Jesus' character, identity and purpose. As God's Son, Jesus resists all attempts to stop him doing what the Father wills (John 18:11). Before Annas, Jesus maintains his poise. He responds to his questioning by saying he has nothing to hide. Before Pilate he is happy to talk in private, and to state clearly that he poses no threat to him since his 'kingdom is not of this world' (verse 36). Again he takes the initiative in the conversation (verses 36,37).

Pilate wishes to release Jesus, but, since the crowd do not want Jesus, he has him flogged, hoping this will satisfy them (18:38 – 19:5). But the crowd bay for his blood, and eventually Pilate gives in to their political blackmail (19:12) and agrees for Jesus to be crucified. Did anyone at the time think that Isaiah's words, written centuries before, were finding their fulfilment: 'He was oppressed and afflicted, yet he did not open his mouth … By oppression and judgement he was taken away…' (Isaiah 53:7,8)?

Pilate does at least ensure that Jesus is recognised on his cross as 'the King of the Jews' (John 19:19–22). As the soldiers unwittingly fulfil prophecies concerning him (verses 23,24), Jesus still has time to think of his mother's needs (verses 25–27). Under the most severe stress, his loving unselfishness is apparent. Having drunk wine vinegar, he proclaims, 'It is finished!' These words are to be understood as meaning 'paid in full'! Throughout John's Gospel there has been reference to the 'time' for the completion of the 'work' the Father has given him (2:4; 17:4). This is now done. Theologians speak of 'the finished work of Christ', by which they mean his once-for-all sacrifice that has accomplished eternal atonement for our sins (Hebrews 9:26).

Beginning the service

With: an image of the cross; scenes set up as below; cut-out card crosses for everyone

Before the service, set the scene in your worship area, also to be used in the **Bible talk,** with either an image of the cross projected at the front, or a physical representation (such as a wooden cross, painting or fine art image). This should be large enough to act as an immediate and unmistakeable focus for the service. Around your meeting area (or different parts of your church building) display large signs and simple props indicating different scenes from the Easter story, as follows: the olive grove, the high priest's courtyard, outside the palace, Golgotha, the garden tomb.

Arrange to have 'actors' in the following roles: Jesus, Judas, religious leaders, one or two soldiers, Simon Peter, other disciples, a maid, the high priest, one or two other religious leaders, Pilate, Barabbas, Joseph of Arimathea and Nicodemus. They should wear simple costumes to suggest their roles and should mix with the congregation until it is their turn to participate.

As everyone arrives, give each person a cross-shaped card. Introduce the theme of the service, explaining that you are going to 'travel' with Jesus from the garden where he was arrested to the garden where he was buried. Ask everyone to imagine themselves as the crowd who followed the events in Jerusalem that first Easter. Indicate the different points around your meeting area. As you begin your journey, ask everyone to look out for this question: 'Who is he?'

Explain that you'll meet many different characters involved along the way. Introduce some of these characters. Ask adults and children to guess which character they think the actor is representing and which scene they have a part in, giving clues and help as needed. A volunteer then leads each character to the scene where they first appear.

Bible reading

This service focuses on excerpts from John 18 and 19. Each of the following verses should be read by narrators during the appropriate 'scenes' as indicated in the **Bible retelling** drama script (see below).

The olive grove: John 18:1–3, 12–14
The high priest's courtyard: John 18:15, 16, 27
Outside the palace: John 19:1–6
Golgotha: John 19:17,18, 31–37,38–40
The garden tomb: John 19:41, 42

Isaiah 53:1–12 could be used to follow the **Bible talk**.

Bible retelling

With: the drama script (YearA.GoodFri_1) available from www.scriptureunion.org. uk/lightdownloads; volunteers to read, act as producer and play the characters; props as indicated

The drama, including the Bible readings, should be well rehearsed before the service. If possible, encourage the congregation ('the crowd') to walk from scene to scene as though physically participating in this journey. Start by directing attention to Scene 1: 'The olive grove'. Continue as indicated in the drama script.

As the drama ends, play some of the music suggested to encourage quiet reflection.

Bible talk

With: 8–10 large, cut-out 'speech bubbles' on which are written the questions: 'Who is he?' or 'Who are you?'

Explain that in each of the scenes acted out there was a question being asked – either spoken, or underlying the action. The question is: 'Who is he?' or 'Who are you?' As we think about Jesus dying on the cross, it's an important question for us to ask ourselves. Our answer will affect what we believe about why Jesus died, our relationship with God, and the way we live our lives. Imagine yourselves in each of the scenes. Who is he? How would you respond?

Give out the speech bubbles for children and young people to hold. Encourage interaction with all age groups as you comment and raise questions.

Scene 1: The olive grove

Ask all the characters in Scene 1 to take up their positions, as if for a tableau. Which characters in the scene were asking the question 'Who is he?' or 'Who are you?' about Jesus. Ask for a speech bubble to be taken to those characters (a soldier and religious officials) to hold so it is visible to everyone.

Talk about the characters. The soldiers and religious officials were probably just doing their job, wanting to get the right man. But also present was the person who had led the soldiers to Jesus. Ask who that was

(Judas). Point out that Judas had spent years with Jesus and had heard his teaching. He had been learning who Jesus was, along with Peter and the other disciples. What do his actions in betraying Jesus tell us about his answer?

Scene 2: The high priest's courtyard

Do the same as for Scene 1. Give a 'Who is he?' and a 'Who are you?' speech bubble to the high priest and religious officials. Give a 'Who are you?' speech bubble to Peter.

Other Gospel accounts (such as Mark 14:55–64) make it clear that the religious officials wanted to trick Jesus into saying he was the Messiah (God's special servant, the one whom the Jews had been waiting for) or God's Son (making himself equal with God). The Jewish law said that anyone who did that should be killed. Like others in Jerusalem, they had already heard Jesus' teaching and seen the miracles, which made it clear who he was, but Jesus was a threat and an embarrassment. The Romans might take action against the Jews if they thought that here was a rebel leader. Also, Jesus had criticised the hypocrisy of the Jewish leaders. What answer to the question 'Who are you?' did they want?

Point out that Peter was also asked a 'Who are you?' question. He did believe Jesus was the Messiah and the Son of God (Luke 9:18–21), and he had sworn he would always stay true to him (John 13:37), so why does he deny knowing him here?

Scene 3: Outside the palace

Do the same as before. Give 'Who are you?' and 'Who is he? speech bubbles to Pilate.

What did Pilate think of Jesus? Talk about why Pilate agreed to crucify Jesus.

Scene 4: Golgotha
Do the same as before. Remind everyone that Pilate wanted to call Jesus 'the King of the Jews'. Others watching the crucifixion had different answers. Ask: 'What's our answer?'

As Christians, we believe Jesus is God's Son, given by God to take the punishment for our sins. If we truly believe this, then we'll want to show that it's true as we live for him with thankfulness. Like some of those we've read about, that response isn't always easy to demonstrate.

Scene 5: The garden tomb
Finally, focus on the garden tomb, with Joseph of Arimathea and Nicodemus standing at the tomb. Ask if anyone can remember another occasion when Nicodemus had been wanting to find out who Jesus was (John 3:1,2). Both Joseph and Nicodemus had been watching Jesus carefully, wanting to discover the answer. Give speech bubbles to them. It was costly for them to risk their reputations and possibly their positions by caring for Jesus as they gave him a dignified burial. What answer do you think they had decided on?

If appropriate, follow this activity by reading Isaiah 53:1–12.

Prayer activity
With: cut-out cross-shaped cards, given out to everyone as they enter the service

Read slowly the words from Isaiah 53:4 and

5. Ask everyone to hold their cross and, in a time of quiet, think about what it meant for Jesus to die on the cross. Invite everyone to think of their own 'infirmities, sorrows and iniquities' (explain these terms as appropriate) and those of others. They might think of personal things, troubles in the family, or suffering in the world. Remind everyone that Jesus died to lift these things from us, so that our sins and failings could be forgiven. Invite everyone to talk with God about their sorrows. It might be something they want to pray for or they might want to ask for God's forgiveness.

Read Isaiah 53:5 again. Conclude by thanking God for his love and forgiveness.

Encourage everyone to take their cross home to put it where they'll often see it over this Easter weekend as a reminder of what Jesus has done for them on the cross.

Ending the service
Remind everyone that the people involved in these events, unlike us, didn't know what would happen next. They had seen Jesus die a terrible death, and didn't know what would happen on the Sunday. How do you think they were feeling on Friday evening and during Holy Saturday (the Sabbath)? What did they think would happen next? Say that you're going to ask some of the people who were there.

Briefly interview some of the characters you've already introduced. You could include: a soldier, a religious official, the high priest, Judas, a disciple, Pilate and Peter. Answers could be improvised (for example, 'Just another execution'; 'Glad to have got rid of him'; 'Sad and puzzled'; 'But he said he'd come back to life on the third day'). Or, you could ask each character to prepare their responses in advance of the service. There are some ideas (YearA.GoodFri_2) available from www.scriptureunion.org.uk/lightdownloads. End with the response from Peter, referring to the fact that Jesus had said he would rise again (Mark 8:31; 10:32–34).

Conclude by inviting people to return on Easter Day to celebrate the good news that Jesus didn't stay dead but rose again – and lives for ever.

Helpful extras

Music and song ideas
'From heaven you came' ('The Servant King'); 'There is a green hill far away'; 'On the cross'; 'Led like a lamb'; 'When I think about the cross'; 'When I survey the wondrous cross'; 'Oh, to see the dawn'; 'Thank you, Jesus'; music associated with the Passion (such as Stainer's *The Crucifixion*, Fauré's *Requiem*, Bach's *St Matthew Passion*).

Notes and comments

The tone of this service is reflective and solemn. Even so, there's plenty of opportunity for everyone (including children) to get involved as they enter into the events surrounding Jesus' death.

You will need to set up the five different scenes described in the outline. This could be done simply or more elaborately, depending on available resources. It would be most effective if the congregation as 'the crowd' moved from scene to scene. If your building, seating, size of congregation or mobility issues make this difficult, focus the attention on each appropriate scene in other ways (for example, by asking them to look in the direction of each scene as it is played out). If it is dark, use lighting to direct attention.

Characters for the drama should wear costumes to suggest their role. The number of characters is flexible. Some characters could take on different roles in different scenes, suggested by a different prop, or item of clothing.

The question 'Who is he?' about Jesus is a theme throughout John's Gospel. In chapters 18 and 19 it is present in each of the scenes you will consider. Encourage personal thoughtfulness about this and prompt reflection about the implications of our response. You could include music for quiet reflection at various points in the service (for example, following the crucifixion scene, when the drama finishes).

Alternative online options
Visit www.lightlive.org for additional activities for children, young people and adults.

EASTER DAY

READINGS: **Colossians 3:1–4; Matthew 28:1–10; John 20:1–18**
Jeremiah 31:1–6; Psalm 118:1,2,14–24

Bible foundations

Aim: to experience the suddenness, wonder and mystery of Jesus' rising again

Before the latest film or TV series is released, you'll probably be able to find out exactly what happens in it by previews in various forms. The Easter story is a little similar for us. We have read it, we have watched it and listened to it and we know exactly how it is going to end up and exactly what will happen.

Baptism is alluded to in Colossians 3:1. Previously in Colossians 2:20 the believer is linked to Christ's death. Now in verse 1 the believer is linked with the resurrection; there are always two sides to the Easter story - death and resurrection. Our futures will parallel Christ's, but our lives should also parallel this truth in the here and now, in the way we live: hence Paul's words. We should 'seek' things above. The future glory awaits us. For us, this side of death's mystery, it can be difficult. However, we have glimpsed, through Christ, what lies beyond.

Our aim is to experience this resurrection event. To experience something we need to commit ourselves to engage with what happened, and how, as well as appreciate the emotions surrounding it. The Easter event, although known to us, is a unique event in history. It is witnessed by the two women in Matthew's account: in itself proof of the authenticity of the resurrection for no one at that time who wished to convince someone of an event would use female witnesses.

The Greek verb used is passive and should be translated 'he was raised'. Jesus never raised himself; God was the author of this event. The followers and disciples are called brothers by Jesus; they are now co-workers in the ministry to spread the news. It is time for us to take a fresh look at the resurrection, to let it shock us again.

Beginning the service

With: two sealed envelopes for each group or row of people

Prepare envelopes labelled '1' and '2' and 'Do not open until told'. Envelope 1 contains party poppers; envelope 2 should contain brightly coloured paper-chain strips (seven strips approximately 3 cm x 21 cm made from an A4 sheet), plus pens, and staplers or glue sticks

Wish everyone a very happy Easter and say you are going to begin with a surprise. Invite each group to open the envelope marked '1' and share out the party poppers. Remind them to point them into the air, then join together in an impressive countdown, and pull the strings! When the excitement has subsided, point out that what happened on the first Easter day was even more noisy and impressive, and even more exciting. We can still feel the effects today.

Remind the congregation not to open the other envelopes until they are told to. There are even more surprises to come!

Bible reading

As Matthew 28:1–10 is read, ask the listeners (or followers in their Bibles) to look out for any words or phrases that suggest surprise or suddenness. Invite them to call these out at the end of the reading. Give hints about which verses (verses 2,3,4,7,8,9) to look at, if necessary.

Matthew 28:1–10 is available as a PowerPoint presentation (Year A. Easter_1) from www.scriptureunion.org.uk/lightdownloads. This highlights the 'surprise' or 'sudden' words and phrases.

Bible talk

With: a 'mystery', decoratively wrapped package consisting of three parcels each inside a larger one and all inside a fourth (as in Russian dolls); the first parcel contains the second parcel and a message saying 'Freedom from fear'; the second contains the third parcel and a message saying 'Peace'; the third contains the fourth parcel and a message saying 'A message to tell'; the fourth contains a message saying 'You have been raised to life with Christ … your life is now hidden with Christ in God'. Remember to pack them in reverse order, with parcel 4 first.

Commiserate with the congregation that although we celebrate at Easter we don't get presents. Talk briefly about birthdays and Christmas when we might get very special gifts. Say that even an elaborate Easter egg can't compare. At this point your assistant should rush forward with the package. Create a feeling of excitement and anticipation that Easter does bring gifts after all. Try to maintain the excitement and anticipation throughout the talk.

Invite someone to open the outer package. Take out, read and display the message: 'Freedom from fear'. Refer to Matthew 28, where both the angel and Jesus himself tell the women they need not be afraid. Think about things people might be afraid of and remind them that because Jesus rose to life, they have no need to be afraid again.

'Discover' parcel 2 inside the first parcel and

invite someone to open it. Take out, read and display the message: 'Peace'. Remind everyone of all the turbulent events that occurred that first Easter morning – an earthquake, stones rolling, soldiers shaking with fear and falling down, an angel appearing, people running around – and yet Jesus said, 'Peace be with you'. Maybe turbulent or upsetting things have happened to people present. Here is another great Easter gift: peace in our hearts, whatever happens around us.

'Discover' parcel 3 inside the second parcel and invite someone to open it. Take out, read and display: 'A message to tell'. Talk about this gift being one to be shared. The women in the Bible story were not to keep the news to themselves. The angel was anxious that the disciples were told quickly. The women hurried off although they hadn't seen Jesus for themselves. Their message was so important. When Jesus appeared to them, he reiterated the angel's instructions. Challenge everyone to think about how important this message is to them. Would they rush to tell anyone? Who might that be? What would make them want to do that?

'Discover' parcel 4 and invite someone to open it. Take out, read and display the message: '…you have been raised to life with Christ … your life is now hidden with Christ in God.' Although this was in the smallest box, it tells us about a truly amazing gift. It wasn't just Jesus who was given new life on that great day. Use the verses from Colossians 3:1–4 to explain the tremendous news that we share in Jesus' resurrection and will go to live with him one day.

Finish by looking again at the wonderful

Easter gifts that God has given us, gifts that will last for eternity!

Prayer activity

With: sealed envelopes marked '2' (see **Beginning the service**); a standing cross

Point out that the cross is empty, indicating that Jesus is no longer dead, but has risen to life. Ask the congregation to open the envelopes marked '2' and share out the paper strips. Then ask people to draw or write on these their praises and thoughts about Jesus being alive for evermore. Invite them to join their prayers together by making paper chains with the strips. If possible, end up with one long chain. As everybody holds these up, use words from Matthew 28:6 to praise God that Jesus rose from death. Then remind everybody that Paul says in Colossians 3:1 that we share in Jesus' resurrection.

Helpful extras

Music and song ideas
Suitable songs and hymns include: 'All heaven declares'; 'I believe in Jesus'; 'Jesus, we celebrate your victory'; 'Sing a song' (Celebrate); 'Lord, I lift your name on high'; 'Thank you, Jesus, for loving me'; 'Jesus Christ is risen today'; 'Jesus lives!'; 'Christ the Lord is risen today'; 'Christ triumphant, ever reigning'; 'In the tomb so cold they laid him'; 'Low in the grave he lay'; 'Led like a lamb to the slaughter'; 'Thine be the glory'; 'He has risen'.

Suitable extracts from Handel's *Messiah* or Haydn's *Surprise Symphony* (no. 94) could be used as introductory music or as the service finishes.

Game

With: a stopwatch (optional)

Remind everybody of how the women were told to pass on the message that Jesus had risen from the dead. In the story everything happened very quickly, and you are going to see if you can pass the message on very quickly too. Choose two people to be 'starters' in different parts of the room. Set the stopwatch, if you have one, and at the word 'go' (or 'earthquake!') the 'starters' must each grab the hand of somebody close by and say, 'Jesus is alive'. This person should hold on to someone else and give the same message. Continue until there are no people left not holding hands. Decide which group has told the most people. If you wish, have a replay with different people being the starters to see if you can be even quicker.

Statement of faith

The following statement of faith (Year A. Easter_2), also available from www. scriptureunion.org.uk/lightdownloads, uses material contained in Matthew 28 and Colossians 3. Divide the congregation into two groups, if possible facing each other. One group should read the lines of the statement, with the other group responding each time in agreement. Encourage young children to listen carefully to each statement and nod in agreement. If you have time, repeat it, exchanging each group's statement.

Group 1: We believe that Jesus died on a cross.
Group 2: Yes, we believe that too.
Group 1: We believe that God raised Jesus from the dead.
Group 2: Yes, we believe that too.

Group 1: We believe that after his resurrection, Jesus' friends saw and touched him.
Group 2: Yes, we believe that too.
Group 2: We believe that Jesus' death sets us free from our sins.
Group 1: Yes, we believe that too.
Group 2: We believe that we have new life in Jesus.
Group 1: Yes, we believe that too.
Group 2: We believe that one day we will live with Jesus in glory.
Group 1: Yes, we believe that too.
Together: Alleluia!

Ending the service

Often services on Easter Day begin with the Easter acclamation: Christ has died! Christ is risen! Christ will come again! Alleluia!

For a change, conclude the service by splitting the congregation into three parts. Group A makes the first statement, Group B says the second and Group C, the third, while everyone then joins in with 'Alleluia!' Group B then begins with the first statement, Group C says the second and Group A says the third. Finally, Group C begins with the first statement and so on. Repeat this, at least twice, with a rising crescendo of joy!

Notes and comments

Often visitors come to church on Easter Day who may be unused to all-age worship. So include at least one well-known traditional hymn amongst your selection.

Some churches also make Easter a special time for baptisms. If this is so in your church, make greater use of the passage from Colossians (see **Bible foundations**). Do ensure that the celebration of the Eucharist is truly joyful.

The Dramatised Bible could be used for the **Bible reading** from Matthew 28. Alternatively, the actions of the women, angels and guards could be mimed as the story is read directly. Consider using music from Handel's *Messiah* to enhance the drama.

A short clip from *The Miracle Maker* or another film about the life of Christ could be shown in addition to the **Bible reading**. Choose a section that shows the drama, surprise and joy of those who witnessed the resurrection.

If the parcels in the **Bible talk** are going to be opened by children, they could also each contain a small Easter gift, such as a chocolate egg, sticker or bookmark.

If your congregation consists mainly of adults and young people, use short times of discussion during the **Bible talk** to think of occasions when we are fearful or lacking peace in our lives, and to whom we might pass on the message of the resurrection.

Party poppers in **Beginning the service** should be treated with respect, handled at arms' length and held away from people's faces. They can also create a considerable amount of mess, so provide rubbish bags and volunteers to clear up at the end of the service.

Alternative online options
Visit www.lightlive.org for additional activities for children, young people and adults.

SECOND SUNDAY OF EASTER

READINGS: **1 Peter 1:3–9; John 20:19–31**
Exodus 14:10–31; 15:20,21; Psalm 16

Bible foundations

Aim: to praise Father, Son and Holy Spirit for the reality of life after death

Financial worlds can be rocked by crises. Life is uncertain. How different is the transitory nature of wealth (with all its potential for corruption as well as possibilities for good), compared to the inheritance we are promised as Christians (1 Peter 1:4). What God has stored up for us in heaven will never decay or be ruined or disappear. Salvation offers us life after death. It is a future inheritance that we have already gained. As Peter describes this, he pours out praise. There will be trials and struggles. Faith will be tested. But the promise of protection (verse 5), salvation (verses 5,9), and Christ's return (verse 7) enable the followers of Jesus to persevere. Such promises impact present reality, clothing us in joy with an even greater future realisation.

Thomas could hardly be described as a super-disciple type. Most people can relate to his questioning and uncertainty. He wanted proof. How trustworthy were the reports of his fellow disciples? We can look towards Thomas and his example and find some relief that one of Jesus' disciples doubted that he had been raised from the dead. (This thought process can be dangerous, though, especially as we think further and realise that one of Jesus' disciples also betrayed him, and we wouldn't like to feel an affinity to Judas.) There is no denying that Thomas did question what was said about Jesus. However, when he realised that Christ had been raised and was alive he launched into a spontaneous outburst of worship.

Jesus commends Thomas for his personal confession of faith, as the reality of life after death sinks in: a reality that is still very much ours. Let this lead us, too, into praise.

Beginning the service

With: scissors; sticky tape; a thick felt-tip pen; five sheets of A4 card fixed together to form a cross, which can be folded into an open box to represent the empty tomb

Hold up the cross for everyone to see. While everyone is watching, write on the front: 'Christians believe that...'

Invite the congregation to complete the sentence. (Answers could include: 'God made the world'; 'God sent Jesus to earth'; 'Jesus died on a cross' and so on.)

Explain how, at Easter time, we remember that Jesus was raised to life by God, and he is alive today. Turn the cross over and write, 'Jesus is alive!' down the middle of the cross.

Fold the cross to form an empty box and secure the sides with sticky tape. Place it on its side so that the opening is visible to the congregation.

Ask the children to tell you what they think it represents (the empty tomb). Talk about how some of the disciples had seen Jesus die on the cross and seen the empty tomb, but it took them a while to realise what had happened. Encourage everyone to shout, 'Jesus is alive!' as loudly as possible.

Bible reading

The reading from John 20:19–31 is an example of the faith that Jesus' disciples needed after the Resurrection. As it is read, a group of people could mime Jesus' initial encounter with his disciples, followed by a 'Thomas' excluded and on the edge. From verse 26 he moves into the centre of the action.

1 Peter 1:3–9 expresses something of what Thomas experienced. Verse 8 resonates with John 20:29. Make that connection for people.

Bible retelling

With: the script below, spoken by one of Jesus' disciples

Ask someone to practise this in advance. They do not need to dress up. The more natural it appears - the better. He can rephrase things to match his normal speech, if necessary.

We were meeting in secret. OK, I admit it – I was scared. We were all scared. After all – once they've murdered the top guy, what's to stop them hunting down the rest? Of course we were scared.

We'd had such hopes too. How strange to go from jubilation to depression in less than a week. We had to meet up, just to keep going. Any one of us alone would have slunk off home, like a dog with his tail between his legs.

We just sat around with some of us eating, although I didn't have much appetite. And fish – of all things, why cook something that told everyone in the street where we were? We might as well have hung out a flag! But mainly we were chatting. Sitting around in quiet groups. And sighing. I remember there was a lot of sighing.

But suddenly the atmosphere changed. It wasn't possible, but Jesus was there! Through a locked door. No fuss, no announcement, he was just – there. He said, 'Peace be with you'… and it was, of course. He was there! He ate some fish. And he showed his hands. And it really was him!

We were so happy! He told us he was giving us his Holy Spirit! He's alive! And what he said would happen, did happen! The Father did raise him! Death is not the end! And I've never heard such good news before – have you?

Bible talk

With: several items that have a function, such as a torch or calculator

This talk works best if it follows the **Bible reading** or the **Bible retelling**.

Display the items and ask the congregation to tell you how we know they are really there:

- We can see them: invite some children to come to the front, point to an item, and then describe it.
- We can touch them: choose other children to come and hold the items and say how they feel.
- We can watch them doing something: ask people to come and demonstrate each item's function.

Explain that it was a bit like this when Jesus appeared to his disciples. Display the Bible verses, or ask everyone to find John 20:19–31 in their Bible. Read verse 19 to illustrate that the disciples saw Jesus. Suddenly he was there, standing among them. They heard his voice as well, because he spoke to them. Ask

someone from the congregation to tell you the first thing Jesus said.

Later, Thomas touched Jesus and, as a result, he believed that Jesus was alive. Take some time to explore how Thomas must have felt over the days after Jesus died. If people mimed the actions of Jesus' disciples in the reading from John 20, ask what people noticed about where Thomas stood and how he was drawn into the crowd, from the outside. (**Notes and comments** give some suggestions about this.) The disciples knew they weren't imagining it and, as we are told by Luke in his account of what happened (Luke 24:41–43), they watched him eat fish. He really had been raised to life after dying on the cross!

Finish by reading Revelation 1:18 together, preceding it with the words, 'Jesus says…'

Prayer activity

With: Sticky notes; pens or felt-tip pens; a shallow basket; quiet background music

This activity relates to the emotions felt by the disciples when they realised that Jesus was not dead, but alive. Explain that after overcoming their amazement at seeing the risen Christ, the disciples were overjoyed.

Play the music and ask the congregation to write or draw things on the sticky notes that make them glad at Easter time.

Encourage people to bring their notes and place them in the basket at the front, as a symbol of all that they want to thank God for. Finish with the following prayer:

Father God, we thank you for always giving us good gifts.
Please accept our praise and thanks for these things that gladden us.
Help us to keep you first in our hearts and to be joyful because Jesus is alive. Amen.

Prayer of confession

Explain that each section of the following prayer comes in two parts: the first part, A, where we sit with palms downwards on our laps, symbolises putting things down and 'letting go' of them; the second part, B, with palms facing up, symbolises receiving from God. In each section, the leader will use general words and then leave a short silence for each person to tell God silently what they hope to 'put down', or 'receive'.

A: Father, we know that fear and other emotions get in the way of our friendship with you. We want to let go of all the things that get in the way. (*Silence*)
B: Father, we thank you that your love casts out fear. We want to receive your love. (*Silence*)
A: Jesus, we know you are holy and the things we do wrong spoil our friendship with you. We want to put down our bad habits and the things we do that get in the way. (*Silence*)
B: Jesus, we thank you that you have paid the price for all the things we do wrong. We want to receive your forgiveness. (*Silence*)
A: Holy Spirit, we want to put down and let go of all our wrong attitudes and thinking. (*Silence*)
B: Holy Spirit, we thank you that you comfort and guide us into all truth. We want

to receive your wisdom. (*Silence*)
Amen.

Ending the service

Conclude by saying that the resurrection showed how God has conquered death, once and for all. Death is not the end for Christian believers – it is the beginning of a new life with God, for ever!

Finish with this prayer:

Father, Son and Spirit, thank you for creating a beautiful world.
Father, thank you for sending Jesus.
Jesus, thank you for choosing to die to save us.
Spirit, thank you for coming to guide us into the truth.
Father, thank you for raising Jesus to show us the reality of life after death.
Jesus, thank you that you are praying for us in heaven.
Spirit, thank you for coming to live in us as our comforter and helper.
Amen.

Helpful extras

Music and song ideas
Songs that fit the theme include: 'Thank you, Jesus'; 'Led like a lamb (You're alive)'; 'Praise God from whom all blessings flow'; 'Now thank we all our God'; 'Let all the world, in every corner sing'; 'The price is paid'.

Music in the **Prayer activity** should be quiet and unobtrusive. Musicians could play songs such as 'I will enter his gates' or 'Come bless the Lord'. You could use CDs of classical pieces such as Bach's *'Jesu, joy of man's desiring'*, the adagio from Marcello's *Oboe Concerto*, or 'Nimrod' from Elgar's *Enigma Variations*.

Statement of faith

Since this service has focused on what we believe, it would be appropriate to make a statement together of what you believe about Jesus. Use your usual creed or the one given for Easter Day (YearA.Easter_2) that is available from www.scriptureunion.org.uk/lightdownloads.

Notes and comments

Ask the congregation how they would have felt in Thomas' position when it appeared that all his friends seemed to have gone mad! Why did Thomas doubt the people he had spent three years with? Was it because he thought they were hysterical? Or did he think that their hopes had somehow deluded them?

Is there a problem with scepticism? (How far was Thomas sceptical or doubting? It could be argued that it is wrong to label him 'Doubting Thomas!') Or is it sensible to want evidence? When he saw, Thomas came out with the deepest response – he grasped that Jesus was God, and worshipped him. Jesus accepted the worship but he gently chided Thomas for needing the evidence rather than accepting the word of his friends. Peter picks up on what Jesus said in John 20 in his own letter. In 1 Peter 1:8 and 9 he commends his readers for believing without seeing and implies that their faith will carry them through great trials (verses 6,7).

Remind everyone that they are in a similar position to those who received Peter's letter – they believe without seeing and God commends them. His promises of salvation, relationship with him and of eternity will be fulfilled in us.

Alternative online options

Visit www.lightlive.org for additional activities for children, young people and adults.

THIRD SUNDAY OF EASTER

READINGS: **Acts 2:14a,36–41; Luke 24:13–35**
Psalm 116:1–4,12–19; 1 Peter 1:17–23

Bible foundations

Aim: to discover how the risen Jesus brings life and hope

This is one of the great stories of the New Testament. The transformation that
occurred in the disciples' journey on the road is staggering (Luke 24:13–35). At the
start these two people are weary, disappointed and puzzled, with all their hopes for
the future dashed. By the end they are invigorated with strength and renewed hope
to take the seven-mile journey back to Jerusalem. What has made the difference?
The realisation that Jesus, whom they had given up for dead, is alive and among
them!

They should have been prepared, but, as with all the disciples, this truth dawned
slowly; they failed to read the signs or hear the words. Now this new reality comes
to them in three ways, which still have the same transforming power. It is found
in the company of Jesus; as we spend time with him we gain a fresh perspective. It
develops through the exploration of the Scriptures; as we read them we discover
that they bear testimony to Jesus. It is experienced in the breaking of bread; as we
remember the crucified one, so we celebrate the risen one who is with us – and
this is Peter's point at Pentecost (Acts 2) – by the Spirit. In him all our hopes and
longings are met.

For us, too, there is the assurance that Jesus is all he claimed to be and that he
can bring transformation to our lives. This means that whatever our age, or our
life situations, we can have hope. We cannot simply see Jesus as the soother of
individual pain (although he may well do that); he is not a commodity whom we can
use at will. But, in him, the new future has arrived and we can look forward with
hope to something better and can live each day now in the light of that anticipated
future. When the pressures of life wear us down, as they did the disciples on the
road to Emmaus, we can discover the life-changing presence of Jesus in the Bible, on
the road with us, and in the broken bread.

Beginning the service

The psalm set for today's lectionary readings is Psalm 116; the words of the call to worship are taken from it. The natural rhythm of the psalmist's words has been retained in the bidding and responses, so, if possible, emphasise this, perhaps using percussion, although this is not vital.

It's you, Lord:
You've kept my soul from dying.
It's you, Lord:
You've saved my eyes from crying.
It's you, Lord:
You've held my feet from stumbling.
It's you, Lord; it's you, Lord;
It's you.

Bible reading

Luke 24:13–35 lends itself to be read by a narrator, Jesus and two disciples. If possible, display a copy of Caravaggio's painting, *Supper at Emmaus*, which is in the National Gallery in London. After the reading, talk about how far the painting reflects the story. At exactly what point in the story has the artist set his painting?

Set the reading of Acts 2:14a, and 36–41 in its post-Pentecost context.

Bible talk

With: a pair of walking boots; a large question mark on a piece of card; a loaf of unsliced bread

Using the boots, question mark and bread as visual aids, ask the congregation to decide which, out of the following three, they prefer:

- Going for a walk
- Having a good discussion about something interesting
- Enjoying a meal with friends

Ask people why they have made the choice they have. Through their answers, draw out the fact that although there may be different reasons for choosing one over another, each of these activities are sometimes really good ways of finding out things. When we go for a walk we find out about where we are going, or, often, about the people we are walking with, or meet along the way. When we have a really good discussion about something, we learn what other people think, and also reflect on our own opinions. When we share a meal with friends we find out about what's new or significant in their lives.

Talk about the journey to Emmaus that the disciples were taking. Explain that although Jesus had died, they had heard that he had risen again – but they seemed unsure about this. Ask what emotions they may have been feeling as they walked along together. Then begin to talk about the point where the stranger joined them and talked with them. Make sure people realise that the two friends, at that time, did not know that the stranger was Jesus.

Recap the story, including the following points:
- The stranger walked alongside them (Luke 24:15). (*Show the boots.*)
- The stranger listened to them and answered their questions (verses 17,27). (*Show the question mark.*)
- The stranger accepted their invitation to stay for a meal (verse 29). (*Show the bread.*)

Then make the point that when the stranger broke the bread (*break the bread at this point*), the two friends recognised that it was Jesus who had been walking with them. Ask again what their emotions would have been at this point, and remind people of what the disciples said (verse 32): 'Were not our hearts burning within us…?'

Suggest that the story helps us to understand certain things about how Jesus wants us to think about him now. We should know that:

He walks at our speed (*show the boots*). Jesus does not race ahead expecting us to be clever, or to understand, or to know all the answers. He walks by our side.

He answers our questions (*show the question mark*).
He wants us to think about the things that puzzle us, and talk to each other about them. Sometimes, when we do that, it will be just as if he is speaking to us.

He accepts our hospitality (*show the bread*).
He wants us to know that he loves to be invited in – to our lives, our journeys, our hopes and fears. He does not force his way in, but waits to be invited. Suggest that people take a moment to think how they would choose to finish this sentence: 'I would like Jesus to walk with me when…' Then ask them to complete another sentence: 'If I could, I would ask Jesus about…' Finally, do the same with: 'I'd like to invite Jesus to…'

Whether or not we realise it, Jesus walks with us on our journeys through life. He knows what we are thinking about. He waits for us to open the door of our lives to him. Are there times when we do not recognise him? At these times we need to remember to keep looking, asking and seeking – and our eyes will be opened!

To conclude, either focus on our response to Jesus, who walks with us, or suggest that we might be able to represent Jesus to others as we walk alongside them – listening, sharing and helping them to see the life and hope that can be found in knowing the risen Christ. The **Game** could follow on from here.

Prayer activity

With: pens or pencils; pictures on cards of boots, a question mark and a loaf of bread (YearA.Easter3_1) available from www. scriptureunion.org.uk/lightdownloads (Print enough for a set for each person.)

This **Prayer activity** is based on the points made in **Bible talk**, using the same visual aids – the boots, the question mark and the bread. Explain what each picture might suggest about the ways in which we can pray (see below), and invite people to take one or more cards and write or draw something they are praying for on the reverse. As the cards are completed, people can place them around the three items used in the **Bible talk**, perhaps on three separate tables.

The three items can help us to pray in the following ways:
Boots: Pray for people who are on a journey of some sort. Maybe they are travelling to a new home, or country. Maybe they are on an emotional journey such as grief, illness, or

excitement at the arrival of a child.

Question mark: Pray for people who are facing difficult questions in their lives about family life, work, or their faith. Perhaps you can pray for people in the international community who deal with difficult questions about war and poverty.

Bread: Pray for people who have a gift or ministry of making people welcome – communities, counsellors, welcomers at church. What about those who work with refugees, or with the immigrant communities – how do they need our prayers?

Sum up the prayers by using the following words, displayed on PowerPoint or OHP. The response (YearA.Easter3_2) is available from www.scriptureunion.org.uk/lightdownloads. Everyone says the emboldened words.

As Jesus walked by the side of the two friends in their sadness and confusion,
So may we learn to walk with others when they need us most.
As Jesus listened to the questions of those struggling to understand and believe,
So may we learn to listen to people as they ask questions about their faith in you.
As Jesus was willing to spend time with the two friends over a meal,
So may we learn to offer hospitality and welcome to everyone we meet.
In our journeying,
Lead us.
In our listening,
Teach us.
In our welcoming,
Meet us.
Amen.

Prayer of confession

Very often, a prayer of confession focuses on the wrong things we have done. This prayer focuses on the difficulties we sometimes have in believing, just as the disciples on the Emmaus Road found it difficult to understand and believe that Jesus had been raised from the dead. (Refer back to Thomas in the previous service outline.)

The structure of the prayer is based around six excerpts from Luke 24. This needs to be explained before the prayer begins. Everyone should be encouraged to join in with the response after Voice 2 – **Forgive us, Lord, and heal us**.

Voice 1: 'We had hoped that he was the one…'
Voice 2: Sometimes we begin to lose hope in God…
All: Forgive us, Lord, and heal us.
Voice 1: 'It is the third day since all this took place…'
Voice 2: Sometimes we feel that God goes too slowly for us…
All: Forgive us, Lord, and heal us.
Voice 1: 'But him they did not see…'
Voice 2: Sometimes we expect evidence that God is still there…
All: Forgive us, Lord, and heal us.
Voice 1: 'How foolish you are, and how slow of heart to believe…'
Voice 2: Sometimes we act foolishly and cannot see when God is moving…
All: Forgive us, Lord, and heal us.
Voice 1: 'Were not our hearts burning within us…?'
Voice 2: Sometimes we ignore the Spirit at work within us…
All: Forgive us, Lord, and heal us.

Voice 1: 'The two told what had happened on the way…'
Voice 2: Sometimes we keep quiet for too long…
All: Forgive us, Lord, and heal us.
Voice 1: Lord Jesus, you walk with us, listen to us and come into our lives when we welcome you;
Voice 2: Thank you for your love, your grace and your forgiveness.
All: We receive your mercy with burning hearts. Amen.

Ending the service

Use the footprints that were laid down on the floor earlier for the **Game** and give one to everyone in church. Encourage people to take their footprint home to use as a bookmark, to remind them that Christ is walking with them.

Helpful extras

Music and song ideas
Sing hymns and songs that promote the resurrection theme. For example: 'Alleluia, alleluia, give thanks to the risen Lord'; 'Lord, I lift your name on high'; 'I know he rescued my soul (My Redeemer lives)'; 'In Christ alone'; 'Celebrate Jesus'.

Game
Prepare plenty of cut-out footprints from card or paper in three different colours.

Stick them on the walls, hide them under seats, or put them in strange places! At the appropriate point in the service invite the children to move around the building, finding as many footprints as they can, as quickly as possible. Then invite them to bring these to the front and together lay them down on the floor to make three 'journeys' in footprints, representing the two disciples and Jesus walking together. As this takes place, talk with the children about the journey that Jesus made with his disciples along the road to Emmaus.

Notes and comments

You may need to explain to the children that although the disciples did take a literal journey with Jesus, you are using the word 'journey' in a non-literal way.

Children may be returning to school after the Easter holidays, so remember to pray for them and for their teachers and all staff in schools.

If the service includes Holy Communion, make a link with the bread that Jesus broke in Emmaus.

Alternative online options
Visit www.lightlive.org for additional activities for children, young people and adults.

FOURTH SUNDAY OF EASTER

READINGS: Acts 2:42–47; John 10:1–10
Psalm 23; 1 Peter 2:19–25

Bible foundations

Aim: to explore what it means to be part of the Church

Jesus' illustration of the shepherd, the gate and the sheep (John 10:1–16) would have been immediately familiar to his listeners. Every day the shepherd would lead the sheep to the best pasture and every evening bring them back to a place of safety. In the course of the day they would meet other flocks, but would stay with the shepherd they knew. This is a picture of belonging and identity. To be with Jesus is to know where we fit in the order of things, to be valued, and to be safe. These verses come as good news in a world in which people long to know who they are, where they belong and where they have value. The world values us on the basis of what we do – wearing the right brands, going to the right clubs, listening to the right music. But for Jesus none of this matters. It is when we follow him that we find security, worth and acceptance.

The picture of the early Church in Acts 2:42–47 is of a group who felt that they belonged together and who found deep satisfaction in meeting. They seem to meet informally. They are in houses; they eat, drink, talk, remember Jesus and tell stories; they pray, share bread and wine. Probably all ages are present. They are not measured by what they own, but by what they share with one another. They are held in high regard by others; they show the love of Jesus in practical ways and in the power of the Spirit.

The Church is where people of all ages feel safe, enjoy one another's friendship, experience the presence of the risen Jesus, learn about him and live for him. This picture may well challenge current practice, but it is worth facing up to and asking where we need to change.

Beginning the service

The theme of today's service is what it means to be God's people, so it would be appropriate to use Psalm 100, which has been arranged below for congregational use. Before you start, point out the various ways in which it is divided up, so people can join in fully. The words of this psalm (YearA.Easter4_ 1) are available from www.scriptureunion. org.uk/lightdownloads.

People on the right: Shout for joy to the Lord, all the earth.
People on the left: Worship the Lord with gladness.
All: Come before him with joyful songs.
Men: Know that the Lord is God.
Children: It is he who made us, and we are his.
Women: We are his people, the sheep of his pasture.
People on the right: Enter his gates with thanksgiving.
People on the left: Enter his courts with praise.
All: Give thanks to him and praise his name.
People on the right: For the Lord is good.
People on the left: And his love endures for ever.
All: His faithfulness continues through all generations.
Psalm 100 (TNIV)

Bible reading

Before reading Acts 2:42–47, ask the children to devise signs of actions for the following: people learning together, eating together, praying and praising God together, sharing with each other. These will also be used in the **Bible talk**. When these phrases occur during the reading, pause for the children to enact the signs. They should reinforce the community element of the life of the early Church.

Ask people to listen to the reading from John 10:1–10 with their eyes closed, imagining a shepherd with his sheep.

Bible talk

With: pictures (YearA.Easter4–2) available from www.scriptureunion.org. uk/lightdownloads or your own pictures of: a church building, notice board or notice sheet with the times of the services, a lot of people, a shepherd's crook

This talk aims to remind us of how the early Church was about people and values, rather than buildings and services. Don't fall into the trap of knocking the Church of today, but encourage those present to have positive expectations of being part of a church community.

Display the pictures of your church building, your notice board, and a lot of people. Ask the congregation which of these pictures best represents the word 'church'. The congregation will probably say the people (they know the 'right' answer by now!). Then ask whether people in the community around you would have given the same answer. They would probably say the building or the services. They may not understand that the people are the Church.

You have another image for the Church.

Show the picture of the shepherd's crook. Remind people of the reading from John 10. Explain how a shepherd looked after the sheep day and night. He would lead them from the front, not herding them from behind. Ask for any experiences or observations from people of herds/droves of sheep and sheep dog trials.

The Church belongs to the Good Shepherd (John 10:1–5)

Jesus described himself as the Good Shepherd and all those who belonged to him would know his name and would trust him. That's one way to describe the Church – the people who belong to the Good Shepherd. That's why the Church praises God together, to remind one another of who we are and to whom we belong. Sing a song(s) of praise at this point, preferably one based on Psalm 23, today's psalm.

The Church is kept safe by the Gate (John 10:7–9)

Jesus went on to describe himself as a gate. This kept the sheep safe in the fold, safe from wandering away or being harmed. Jesus wants to keep the Church safe from roaming away from him and from one another and safe from those who would seek to harm them or cause them to turn away from him. That's why it is always important to read the Bible when a local church meets together, to remind one another of what it is that we believe, the truth of God, and how he wants us to live. Pause to read a few verses from the Bible, such as part of Psalm 23.

The Church is given life by the Life-giver (John 10:10)

Jesus wanted to give life, full life, to those who belonged to him. This was what the early Church experienced, as we read from Acts 2. Use the signs from the **Bible reading** to explain this – they learnt together whom they belonged to, they ate together (which included celebration of the Last Supper), they praised and prayed together and they shared with each other.

This is a very different picture of the Church from a building or a series of services or a notice board. This is a group of people, full of life, being part of each other's lives. As a result, many more people joined them.

Prayer activity

With: shepherd's crooks in card (enough for each person); pens and pencils

As a response to the **Bible talk,** give each person a shepherd's crook and a pen. Ask them to write or draw on it the one thing they would like to see more of in the church community. It could be more friendship, honesty, laughter, creativity, sharing or worship. Encourage everyone to talk with God about this.

Finish by praying that God will bless the growth of the Church as you become more and more of a community of God's people.

Prayer of confession

The following prayer is more of a poem and will require some practice by a good reader, to be effective.

Lord, how come you love your Church as you do?
How come you are still the Good Shepherd?

Here we are – a bunch of people who get it wrong more often than we get it right.
Pilgrims who, though safe in the fold, will still want to wander.
Saints who, though made clean, still sin.
Yet love us you do – and will, eternally.
Lord, was there not supposed to be a Plan B?
Surely you never thought that entrusting the good news to your Church was such a great idea?
Or, in fact, would it not have been better if we had been Plan B?
For so often Lord, we misrepresent you, compromise you, limit you, deny you, hide you,
And you still go on loving us – and will, eternally.
Lord, how come, that even with the fire of God, we burn so dimly?
That even with the wind of God, we remain unmoved?
That even with streams of living water, we remain dry and dusty?
Lord, we long for you.
We long to serve you, to bless you, to please you, to make you known.
Forgive the emptiness of our words,
The powerlessness of our resolve,
The lifelessness of our church.
Forgive and renew, Lord.
Forgive and bless;
Forgive and ignite.
Amen.

Prayers of intercession

Since the outcome of the early Church's life together was that many others joined them as believers, it is important that you pray for those known to you who do not know Jesus

as their Good Shepherd or Gate or Life-giver. Pray for any outreach events, ongoing and planned for the future. For details of Scripture Union's outreach to children and young people visit www.scriptureunion.org.uk.

Ending the service

Some people will not realise that the words of 'The grace' are taken from Paul's second letter to Corinth (2 Corinthians 13:14), where he blesses the church with the words of this great Trinitarian prayer. Explain that our prayer for each other when we use these words goes back two millennia to join with Paul's prayer. With this is mind, invite the congregation to join with you in the words of 'The grace'.

Helpful extras

Music and song ideas
Ideas for songs include: 'Thy hand, O God, has guided'; 'Who is this?'; 'I will build my church'; 'For I'm building a people of power'; 'Teach me to dance'; 'The Lord's my shepherd' or other songs based on Psalm 23.

As the reading from Acts mentions the breaking of bread, it might also be appropriate to use songs on that theme, especially if you are sharing in Holy Communion together. For example: 'Jesus Christ, I think upon your sacrifice'; 'Let us break bread together'; 'Broken for me'.

Notes and comments

This is a post-Easter and pre-Pentecost service, coming four weeks before we celebrate Pentecost, yet the role of the Holy Spirit is key to understanding what it meant to be part of the early Church. This service could be the beginning of a series where the person and work of the Holy Spirit are explored, leading up to the Church's celebration of his coming at Pentecost.

To break bread in a service of Holy Communion would tie in very naturally with the theme of this outline.

Alternative online options

Visit www.lightlive.org for additional activities for children, young people and adults.

The ten Bible stories in the *Must Know series*, have been voted the ten stories that must be passed on to the next generation. In three different formats they are suitable to be read in all-age services or read at home by children, parents and adults.

The 10 Must Know Stories (978 1 84427 326 3)
For junior-aged children and ideal for school assemblies.

The Green Book of Must Know Stories (978 1 84427 324 7)
The Red Book of Must Know Stories (978 1 84427 325 6)
For infant-aged children – five stories per book.

Must Know Stories (978 1 84427 320 1)
Dramatically told stories for adults, to read and to hear.

For more details, vivit www.scriptureunion.org.uk

FIFTH SUNDAY OF EASTER

READINGS: **Acts 7:55–60; John 14:1–14**
Psalm 31:1–5,15,16; 1 Peter 2:2–10

Bible foundations

Aim: to think about the challenges and blessings that come to followers of Jesus

It was not long before Jesus' followers found themselves in trouble and for Stephen, he paid the ultimate price (Acts 7:55-60). That is hardly surprising, for Jesus, himself, had faced opposition and had told them that they could expect it too. Opposition takes many forms. There are still Christians who face imprisonment and death for their faith. For most of us, however, it is more subtle. Being a Christian is not cool and may bring ridicule, disbelief, and sometimes isolation. The last few years have seen increasingly militant attacks by atheists like Richard Dawkins and Christopher Hitchens. Something of this for children and young people can be seen in the writing of Philip Pullman. None of us is immune from the personal attacks, the pressures to conform, or the intellectual assaults.

It is against that background that Jesus gives his words of reassurance. In the terms of this world and its values, Christians are often seen as a minority, but are in fact the people who have been shown the way to God. We have a secure destiny and can live through pressures because we take a long view. We know that in the age to come we will be with God. This hope sustained Stephen and has provided hope and encouragement to God's people down through the ages.

The only way to God, and therefore to this hope, is through Jesus. This presents difficulties in a multi-faith world where we do not want to give offence to others. We accept the teaching of Jesus, yet we must treat people of other faiths with respect and dignity, even as we disagree. We will do all we can to share our faith with others with both urgency and sensitivity.

Beginning the service

With: enough 'Cadbury's Heroes' chocolates, one for each person

Give every member of the congregation a 'Cadbury's Heroes' chocolate to eat. As they are chewing, ask them to think who are their heroes and heroines, people in dangerous jobs or who have done something bold and risky. This could be an opportunity to greet one another and talk about our heroes. Then sing (once mouths are empty!): 'The world is looking for a hero.'

Bible reading

In reading Acts 7:55–60, contrast the fury of the Sanhedrin with the calmness of Stephen, with a simple dramatisation. Using the TNIV or GNB ask a single, good reader (perhaps a child or a woman) to read Acts 7:55, 59 and 60, and the congregation to read verses 57 and 58 together. Encourage the congregation to be loud and angry. If you wish, include verse 54, to be read by the congregation.

John 14:1–14 should be read thoughtfully by someone who has had a chance to prepare it beforehand.

Bible talk

With: pictures of heroes/people who are admired or are in dangerous jobs; a flip chart; a pen for making a list

Heroes

Begin by referring to the brave heroes who were talked about in **Beginning the service**. Accept suggestions without comment. Pose the question: 'What would make someone in real life, a superhero?' After a short discussion, point out that, in real life, it's not about having invincible powers that you can use, but being willing to give everything you have (however great or weak), even to the extent of giving your own life. You may wish to include a story at this point – either a local example or one from *Jesus Freaks* (see **Notes and comments**). Explain that today we'll be looking at a superhero of the New Testament.

A superhero for God

Give out the following references: Acts 6:3, 5, 8, 10 and 15 (project them, if you use a projector); encourage members of the congregation to use their Bibles to find out what kind of person Stephen was. Ask adults to work with younger children so they can be fully involved. Make a list of his 'super powers', which could include 'full of the Holy Spirit', 'wise', 'full of faith', 'full of God's grace and power', 'able to work miracles' and 'a convincing speaker'.

Show the images of people in dangerous jobs, such as fire-fighters, police, or members of the armed forces. If you are able, show a short recruiting advert from the TV. Ask why people sign up to do these jobs when they know they might be injured, or killed. In small groups where they are sitting and in two or three minutes ask people to think of as many reasons as they can why people choose to 'sign up' to follow Jesus. What are the benefits and blessings? The reading from John 14:1–14 is a good starting place.

Make a list of responses on the flip chart. Jesus promised to prepare a place in heaven for his disciples and Stephen was to discover this was so true. He actually saw Jesus (Acts 7:56) standing to receive him. (Point out that this is unusual since most references to the ascended Jesus are of him sitting.)

We are all superheroes!
Summarise as follows: signing up to follow Jesus does bring blessings and benefits, but it also brings many challenges – in some cases life-threatening ones. Show the images of superheroes again. But if we trust in God, he has plans to use us in very special ways. He gives us the power and strength we need to achieve his purposes. It may be tough. It may hurt. For some it may lead even to death. But that's how to be a real superhero – to be a follower of Jesus.

Prayer activity

With: information about situations where Christians are being persecuted for their faith, one situation per sheet of paper – see **Notes and comments** for source suggestions

Divide the congregation into groups and give each group one situation for prayer. Ask each group to pray for their situation.

Prayer of confession

Give an opportunity for people to think in silence about situations in which they feel they have let God down by not speaking or acting for him when they could have done so. Some examples may be necessary, especially to make this concrete for children. Then use this prayer, encouraging everyone to join in with the response: **Lord, we are sorry.**

Where we could have spoken for you and

failed to do so…
Lord, we are sorry.
Where we could have been an example for you and failed to do so…
Lord, we are sorry.
Where we could have invited someone to church and failed to do so…
Lord, we are sorry.
Where we could have intervened in a difficult situation and failed to do so…
Lord, we are sorry.
Where we could have shown love and practical concern and failed to do so…
Lord, we are sorry.
As we face a new week, Lord give us grace and give us strength to stand for you, to speak for you, and to live for you…
Lord, let us live for you,
Amen.

Ending the service

Use the second version of the **Statement of faith** to send people out into the world, boldly committed to face the challenges of the week, with God.

Helpful extras

Music and song ideas
Suitable songs could include: 'The world is looking for a hero'; 'Jesus is greater than the greatest hero'; 'Fight the good fight'; 'I sing a song of the saints of old' (old-fashioned, but picks up the idea of our personal involvement in following Jesus); 'Who would true valour see?' (which could be sung immediately after the **Bible talk**).

Other songs can include: 'For all the saints who from their labours rest'; 'God in my living' (by Tim Hughes – would be a helpful response to follow the **Prayer of confession**); 'God of justice' (by Tim Hughes – offers a challenging act of commitment for the end of the service); 'Be bold, be strong'; 'I am the way, the truth and the life'; 'Take my life and let it be'; 'I will offer up my life'.

Statement of faith

Use either version of this statement of faith, both of which are based on Psalm 31, (Year A. Easter5_1) that are available from www.scriptureunion.org.uk/lightdownloads. The first version should be read by everyone together. The second version, which is very much simpler, should be read by a leader with the congregation responding with the emboldened words.

In you, O Lord, I have taken refuge;
You do not let me be put to shame;
You come quickly to rescue me.
You, Lord, are my rock, my refuge, my strong fortress;
You protect me,
You guide me and lead me,
You help me to steer clear of traps and dangers.
I trust in you, Lord.
My times are in your hands.
You deliver me from my enemies.
Your love for me is never ending;
How great is your goodness, O Lord.
It is stored up for those who fear you;
You give it to all who trust in you.
Praise be to the Lord!
Love the Lord, all his people!
Be strong and take heart all you who hope in the Lord!

from Psalm 31

Whom do we trust?
Jesus!
Why do we trust him?
He's strong. He loves us!
How will he help us?
He'll keep us safe from trouble.
He'll help us when other people are out to get us!
Will he do it?
Yes, he will!
What shall we do?
We'll praise him. We'll love him.
We'll live for him!

based on Psalm 31

Notes and comments

If you search for 'superheroes' on Google Images (on the Internet), there are many useful montages that could be printed off or projected. Right-click with your mouse to save the image. Then either print it, turn it into an acetate, or use it in a PowerPoint presentation.

The books *Jesus Freaks* and *Jesus Freaks II* by DC Talk (Eagle Publishing) have a very useful compilation of short stories about people from all generations and countries who have suffered or died for their Christian faith. Examples could be read or retold as part of the service.

The **Prayer activity** requires material relating to Christians suffering persecution. The mission societies you regularly support may be able to provide this. Other sites that may be helpful include: www.opendoorsuk.org; www.persecution.org; www.persecution.com; www.csw.org.uk.

It may be that you have in your congregation

(or know from another congregation) an asylum seeker who has fled persecution or will face it on return. A short, personal interview could be very powerful (taking care that questions and answers are on a level all ages can understand).

You may wish to follow up the **Prayer activity** by brainstorming practical ways in which the church could support persecuted Christians. These could be considered by your leadership team with a view to one or more of them being put into action.

Alternative online options

Visit www.lightlive.org for additional activities for children, young people and adults.

The summer of opportunities

Summer is coming, with all its attendant opportunities for outreach events to children, young people and families – holiday clubs, beach missions and residential holidays! For Scripture Union this is an important time for ministry as volunteers give of their time (and often money) to be involved in such events. To find out more of the story, visit www.scriptureunion.org.uk/holidays. Make sure that in your services you regularly pray for any outreach events that affect the church.

Remember too those who face new beginnings in the autumn, whether starting school for the first time, moving to secondary school or going to university. It is not too late to get hold of *Get ready go* (for those starting school), *It's your move* (for those moving on to secondary school) and *Life actually* (for those in Year 11, making significant life choices). These are all gift books that support people at times of transition. For more details, visit www.scriptureunion.org.uk/itsyourmove.

SIXTH SUNDAY OF EASTER

READINGS: **Acts 17:22–31; John 14:15–21**
Psalm 66:8–20; 1 Peter 3:13–22

Bible foundations

Aim: to celebrate the way the Holy Spirit makes Jesus known to us

In a world of many faiths, it can be difficult to say that Jesus is the only way to God. Paul lived and worked in just such a world (see Acts 17:22,23). Having spent some time in Athens observing the city, catching something of the local flavour and seeing the many gods on offer, Paul goes to the Areopagus. This was where new ideas were discussed and assessed. It is always important to understand how others think and to look for bridges. Paul sees that God is already at work in Athens and finds a point of contact in the sense of wonder at something beyond our world that all people experience. Even ardent atheists have such a sense of wonder – perhaps directed towards the natural world. It comes naturally to children, but can often diminish with age. Perhaps this is one of the ways in which we can make Jesus known in our world. Paul teaches us to be looking for points of contact and never to underestimate what God has already done in preparing people.

Often we do not speak out because we are afraid that we don't have all the answers. Paul probably didn't think that he had all the answers when he started out. It is not always easy to make sense of the world, especially when confronted by conflicting claims to the truth. We need help. Jesus has promised that the Spirit will help us (John 14:15–21). He is the Spirit of truth who helps us to know more about God and his plans. He helps us to see and know God. And he will help others to see the truth, too. So when we step out like Paul and begin to tell others about Jesus, we need not worry that everything depends on us. We can be confident of the help of the Spirit, who lives in us and constantly reminds us that God is with us.

Beginning the service

Start the service by asking people to think of one thing this week that has made them thankful to God. Invite a few responses and then sing a thankful hymn or song.

Bible reading

Paul's speech in Athens in Acts 17:22–31 should be read in a declaratory way, using a modern version such as The Message or NLT.

As John 14:15–21 is read, divide people into two halves and ask one half to listen out for what Jesus says about the Spirit and the other half for what he says about himself. It might help to project the verses onto a screen. A copy of this passage (YearA.Easter6_1) is available from www.scriptureunion.org.uk/lightdownloads.

Bible talk

With: four flip charts; pens

Evidence for Australia

You will need someone to work with you at the start, having rehearsed in advance. If you have projection facilities, display an image of Australia (or another country, as appropriate) and adapt the following dialogue with your helper. It's probably best if you (the main speaker) are Person 2 and your helper is Person 1, as this makes a smoother link into the rest of the talk.

Person 1: I don't believe in Australia.
Person 2: What do you mean you don't believe in Australia?
Person 1: Well, people say it exists, but I've never seen it.

Person 2: But you've seen photos and TV pictures.
Person 1: Yes, but you can fake things like that.
Person 2: But what about people who've been out there on holiday?
Person 1: They might have been conned. After all, you sit in a tin box for 24 hours. You could be flying round in circles for all you know. When you land, it could be anywhere.
Person 2: You mean it could really be (insert name of local town)?
Person 1: Yes!
Person 2: What about the kangaroos?
Person 1: Brought in from the zoo to fool you.
Person 2: What about the hot weather? What about the different scenery, and food and people and….
Person 1: It's no use. I don't believe in Australia and I'm never going to believe, whatever you say.

Continue by asking, 'Is anyone convinced? Does anyone think that Australia doesn't really exist?' If we changed 'Australia' to 'God', there are lots of people who will argue in the same way. 'I've never seen God', 'I've never heard God', and so on. Today we are going to think about how we know that God is real and how we know what he is like.

Evidence for God

Set up the flip charts at the front and have some pens available. Label one sheet of paper, 'Evidence we can see'; another, 'Evidence we can hear'; another, 'Evidence we can understand'; and the fourth sheet, 'Anything else'. Ask people to talk to one another about what evidence they can think of that shows that God exists and what he is like. Encourage as many people as possible to briefly write their evidence on the sheets of paper. For example, 'Nature helps us see God', 'We hear about God in church', 'The Bible tells us about God', and so on.

When everyone has written what they want to, look at the sheets and read out the answers and comment on them. Be positive; but at the end ask, 'Does this prove God exists?'

Acting on the evidence

Invite someone (whom you've warned beforehand) to come to the front dressed in a football strip holding a football. Allow them to 'show off' with the ball, in any way that isn't going to cause major damage. Then ask if people think they could learn to play football by reading a book about it, by listening to stories about it or by watching other people. Not many people will rate these methods, so ask what is needed and draw out the answer that we actually have to play.

But what do we need once we start playing? We need a coach: someone to come alongside us, show us new ways to play, teach us new skills and bring out the best in us.

Take a straw poll. How many people play football? How many people go to football matches? How many watch football on TV? How many are not interested at all?

Point out that the same pattern is true as far as believing in God is concerned: some people aren't interested at all; some people keep their distance - they come to church at Christmas and Easter or they watch 'Songs of Praise'; some people come along to church but haven't really signed up for the team – haven't accepted Jesus as their team captain – and aren't living for him; some people are actively involved in living (playing) for God.

Ask: where are you? For those who have joined the team and are following their captain, Jesus, there is a bonus: we have the best coach in the world, the Holy Spirit. Ask someone to read John 14:15–17 from the Good News Bible, which describes the Holy Spirit as 'another Helper'. (It is more difficult to make the link with 'coaching' from the words 'advocate' or 'counsellor' found in other versions.)

Finish by challenging those who are not already Christians to 'sign up' and those who have 'signed up' to allow the Holy Spirit to guide them and lead them in all they do.

Prayer activity

With: 4 large labels: 'Making a decision', 'Feeling weak or afraid', 'A bad relationship', 'Other'; 4 candles

Place the four labels in different parts of the building with a lighted candle. Remind people that Jesus promised that the Holy Spirit would come to us as a helper. Ask people to identify one area in which they need the help of the Holy Spirit. Once they have done this, invite them to go to one of the labels, as a sign that they want him to help them.

Conclude by reading John 14:16 and 17 again.

Prayer of confession

Use the following simple responsive prayer (Year A.Easter6_2), which is also available from www.scriptureunion.org.uk/lightdownloads. Everyone joins in the emboldened lines.

When we've looked at the world around us and not seen you, Lord…
We are sorry for our blindness.
When we meet with people who love you and we don't see you living in them…
We are sorry for our blindness.
When we read the Bible and hear its message preached but we don't draw closer to you…
We are sorry for our foolish disobedience.
When we listen to all the other voices around us but we don't listen to your voice…
We are truly sorry. Help us to see. Help us to listen. Help us to meet with you through your Holy Spirit every day.

Helpful extras

Music and song ideas
Songs and hymns about the Holy Spirit include: 'Breathe on me, breath of God'; 'O breath of life come sweeping through us'; 'Spirit of the living God, fall afresh on me' (either version); 'Give me oil in my lamp'.

Songs and hymns about seeing God in creation and elsewhere include: 'Who put the colours in the rainbow?'; 'All things bright and beautiful'; 'How great thou art'; 'Loved with everlasting love'; 'Tell me the story of Jesus'.

Other appropriate songs and hymns include: 'I believe in God, the Father'; 'There is a Redeemer'; 'Higher higher'; 'I know not why God's wondrous love'; 'In Christ alone'.

Game
Project various images that portray the Holy Spirit. Sitting in small groups, encourage the congregation to decide what each image tells them about what the Holy Spirit is like, and what he does. When you've been through all the images, take answers from the groups. Images might include: the wind, fire, a helper, a dove, oil, water, light. If you do not have facilities for projection, give each group a printed sheet with the images on or collect objects to show from the front.

Ending the service

Ask people to think about ways in which God has been at work recently in their lives. People may be more used to identifying things to be thankful for (see **Beginning the service**) than looking for where God has been active in life, but do persist. In advance you could ask two people, including a young person, to briefly share their experience.

Encourage people to be thankful to God, looking for him to be active in their lives in the coming week.

Notes and comments

You can expand the Australian section at the beginning of the talk by showing Australian fruit, a bottle of wine, and so on. If someone in the congregation has been to Australia, they could 'give evidence'.

The **Bible talk** follows Paul's method in Athens without specifically referring to it. You may wish to make a more explicit link to the reading from Acts; when the flip chart evidence section is being explained, mention that Paul in Athens used evidence that people would be familiar with in order to convince them about Jesus.

If you are searching for images of the Holy Spirit on Google Images, 'olive oil' produces better results than 'oil'. The other words all produce a good selection of images. It is also worth entering 'Holy Spirit' and looking through the results.

You could incorporate this old prayer (which can be said or sung) into the service:

Day by day, dear Lord,
Of thee, three things I pray:
To see thee more clearly,
Love thee more dearly,
Follow thee more nearly,
Day by day.
(Richard of Chichester, 1197–1253)

Make more of the celebratory element at the end of the service by having a party, or lunch, or another special event to celebrate God's goodness in sending his Holy Spirit.

Alternative online options

Visit www.lightlive.org for additional activities for children, young people and adults.

ASCENSION DAY

READINGS: **Acts 1:1–11; Luke 24:44–53**
Psalm 47 or 93; Daniel 7:9–14

Bible foundations

Aim: to experience the wonder and mystery of the ascension

The account of the ascension forms a bridge between Luke's two books – a brief account at the end of Luke and a fuller account at the start of Acts. For Luke, this is a crucial point in God's activity in the world. Jesus has come, has taught, healed, loved and died. Now his work is completed. Jesus' cry from the cross was, 'It is finished.' The resurrection confirms it, and the ascension seals it. Victorious, Jesus now returns to the Father and will continue his reign from the Father's side - until his return when every knee will bow and every tongue confess Jesus is Lord.

Our first response will be to follow the disciples in their worship of the risen, victorious King Jesus. We can feel weak and fallible – we are – but we are also children of the King. We need to capture a sense of victory and of Jesus' glory. We are not following failure. But we are not only called to worship; we are called to witness and so we will want to hear again the challenge to tell others what Jesus has done for us.

The work of mission, God's mission, now passes to the disciples. A ripple effect is set in place whereby the gospel is preached in ever-increasing circles. They are to be witnesses, empowered by the Spirit, and we are their natural successors with the same call – a calling for the Church as a whole, and for each individual. We witness to what God has done in Christ (Luke 24:44–48; Acts 1:8). We proclaim that, in Christ, God has established his reign in the world (Acts 1:3). We announce forgiveness and call people to repentance (Luke 24:47), all in the light of the fact that one day the King will return (Acts 1:11). Our authority is the word of the risen Christ and the testimony of the Scriptures (Luke 24:44). Our power is the life of the Spirit (Luke 24:49; Acts 1:8). But it is still a tough business and we need to support and encourage one another.

Beginning the service

Start by saying that the theme is based upon one of the most important events in the Bible. However, do not say what the theme is – namely, the ascension. After speaking for some time about how important the topic is, say 'Sorry, I've got to go – but I'll be back!', and ask a member of the congregation to take over from you. Then walk out of the nearest door. (Make sure that you tell your replacement beforehand what you plan to do, so they are prepared.)

The congregation should be bemused as your replacement continues to speak from your notes and introduces the theme of the ascension. Come back into the room after about a minute, thank them, and ask them to sit down.

Explain that the ascension of Jesus into heaven showed that he had conquered death for us and gone back to heaven, but that he had only started the job of telling people about this new life that is at their disposal. He has left it for his disciples (us) to continue his work. (This was the reason for your earlier departure.)

The ascension also points to the future – a time when Jesus will come back as King to complete his mission and take us home with him. We can therefore trust God not only to finish what he started, but to be with us while we wait upon him.

Bible reading

The ascension narrative describes a visually astounding and dramatic event. If you are not using the drama from **Bible retelling**

(or even if you are), it would be good to choose a reader or readers who can read Luke 24:44–53 and Acts 1:1–11 dramatically. Try involving two or three older children or young people who are confident readers – but make sure they are well prepared.

Bible retelling

With: the script (YearA.Ascension_1) available from www.scriptureunion.org.uk/lightdownloads; about seven actors for Luke, Jesus, apostles (at least three), two angels; props (a scroll, a quill pen, a large blue or white sheet and two volunteers to hold it, white clothes for angels, appropriate clothing for other characters)

To start with, the characters are frozen in tableau: Luke is sitting at a table, writing on a scroll; the apostles are sitting with Jesus, listening to him teaching them. Luke picks up his scroll and reads from it. The other characters 'come to life' when it is their turn to speak.

Bible talk

With: five sheets of card (about A3 size), each with one of the following phrases and an optional illustration (suggested in brackets):
- 'Jesus came' (*a drawing of a manger*)
- 'Jesus went' (*an empty cross*)
- 'Jesus came back' (*an empty tomb*)
- 'Jesus went again' (*a cloud over the top of a mountain*)
- 'Jesus will come back again' (*an outline of a crown*)

This talk is to be positive and hopeful. The

ascension points Christians to the fact that Jesus has conquered death, and has gone to be with God in heaven. He has sent the Holy Spirit to be our Helper instead. One day he will come back and take his followers to be with him for ever.

Begin with a 'True or false' quiz (see **Game**). State that a lot of people believe the story of Jesus' ascension into heaven to be like a fairytale that can't possibly be true. We can gain comfort that it is true. This should make a difference to every one of us.

Display the cards in the wrong order and invite people to arrange them into the correct order (as shown above).

The reliability of the Bible means that those who know God can trust in him and the ascension of Jesus. Acts 1:1–11 tells us that Jesus was taken up to heaven (indicate the card 'Jesus went again'), and will come back again one day (indicate the card 'Jesus will come back again'). Share with the congregation that the ascension is evidence once and for all that Jesus is the Son of God. He is now in heaven looking after us and interceding for us.

However, Jesus has left us with the task of finishing off the work that he started and has sent the Holy Spirit to help us. This might sound daunting, but we know that God will be with us to share his perfect will for us and to help us achieve life in all of its fullness. Refer to the service outline for the Sixth Sunday of Easter based on John 14:15–21.

Finish by sharing a testimony with the congregation. It might be something from your own life, or you could choose a church member to share a time when they have had to trust in God, and he proved trustworthy. The power of a personal encounter with God should reinforce the fact that God can be trusted in all situations, and that he looks after all of his children.

Prayers of intercession

With: the words of the prayer (Year A. Ascension_2) printed or displayed - they are also available from www.scriptureunion.org.uk/lightdownloads.

Invite the congregation to respond with the words in bold.

Lord, as your disciples waited to receive the Holy Spirit,
We wait for you to fill us again.
As expectant parents wait for their child to be born,
We wait for you to give us new life.
As those suffering drought wait for the rain,
We wait for you to refresh us.
As the unemployed wait for a job offer,
We wait for you to reveal your will for us.
As the sick wait for healing,
We wait for you to heal our nation.
As the bankrupt wait for restoration,
We wait for you to forgive our debts.
As the homeless wait for a place to belong,
We wait for you to take us home.
As we wait…
Lord, in your mercy, hear our prayers.
As we wait for you…
Lord, in your mercy, hear our prayers.
As we wait for you to come…
Lord, in your mercy, hear our prayers.

As we wait for you to come again…
**Lord, in your mercy, hear our prayers.
Amen.**

Ending the service

Think about the impact of the ascension on your own lives. What difference does it make that Jesus is alive in heaven and has promised to return? Allow for a time of silent reflection, or invite people to pray together in pairs.

Bring the service to a close with the following prayer, introducing the response in bold.

Lord, you made the heavens and the earth…
Thank you, Lord, for loving us.
You were rejected by Adam and Eve, but you did not reject mankind…
Thank you, Lord, for loving us.
You came down to earth as a baby to save us…
Thank you, Lord, for loving us.
You were crucified without ever having done wrong…
Thank you, Lord, for loving us.
You rose again, and now you are watching over your children…
Thank you, Lord, for loving us.
Thank you, that we have hope in you…
**Thank you, Lord, for loving us.
Amen.**

Helpful extras

Music and song ideas
Choose songs that point to the fact that Jesus is alive, looking after his people and coming back one day. These could include:

'When we walk with the Lord (Trust and obey)'; 'There is a redeemer'; 'There's a place where the streets shine'; 'In Christ alone'; 'These are the days of Elijah'; 'The Lion of Judah' or 'O Lord, my God (How great thou art)'.

You could also play the song 'What a friend I've found' by Delirious? It points to how Jesus is our friend for all time. This perfectly accompanies the story of the ascension.

Game
Read out the statements shown below and ask people to say whether they believe them to be true or false.

* Elephants are the only mammals to have four knees – TRUE
* One in ten babies is born before breakfast – FALSE (It's six out of ten!)
* Birmingham has more miles of canal than Venice – TRUE
* Bingo is the most popular pastime in Britain – FALSE (It's fishing!)
* A hailstone once fell in Italy that contained a fish – FALSE (It fell in Germany!)
* Prince Charles and Prince William never travel on the same plane in case it crashes – TRUE
* The can opener was invented 15 years after the can was introduced – FALSE (It was 48 years afterwards!)
* A lightning bolt is five times hotter than temperatures found at the sun's surface – TRUE
* Most lipstick contains fish scales – TRUE
* Crocodiles can whistle – FALSE

Explain that all of these statements seem like make-believe, but some are in fact true.

Notes and comments

The **Bible retelling** script uses text from the CEV of the Bible and can be performed as simply or elaborately as you like. Costumes and props are not essential but may help people to visualise the events more effectively. The actual moment of ascension is difficult to convey well, but try to avoid it looking like a comical disappearing act! Consider carefully the best way to achieve this.

If you have a large number of children and young people present, make the **Game** more active. Do this by asking people to stand up if they think the answer is true, and remain seated if they think it is false. Alternatively, if there is room to move around in your church building, designate one side of the room as true, and another as false, and encourage people to choose for each statement the 'true' or 'false' side to run (or walk) to.

Although it is possible to explain some aspects of the ascension, many of the 'How?' and 'Why?' questions remain a mystery. We may never know all the answers. However, people may have questions or comments they would like to discuss. If there is time, break into small groups to allow time for such discussion around the issues raised.

It is also possible that the themes of the service may prompt people to ask for prayer, perhaps feeling that their faith and hope in Jesus are weak. If you have a prayer ministry team, allow time at the end of the service for them to pray with people, or ensure that you or other leaders are available.

Alternative online options

Visit www.lightlive.org for additional activities for children, young people and adults.

SEVENTH SUNDAY OF EASTER

READINGS: **Acts 1:6–14; John 17:1–11**
Psalm 68:1–10,32–35; 1 Peter 4:12–14; 5:6–11

Bible foundations

Aim: to pray for all followers of Jesus, as Jesus prayed for us

Prayer was clearly important for Jesus. John 17 is the longest recorded prayer we have and reveals profound truths. As Jesus approaches death his followers are on his mind; he demonstrates the depth of his love for them. He knows that after he has gone they will face difficulty and opposition. The new life that he has given them (verse 2) will not guarantee them immunity. They will find themselves in a spiritual battle, and he prays for their protection. They will face division and he prays for their unity. Later in the prayer, it becomes clear that this is a prayer that is not just for the first disciples but for others who will believe through them (John 17:20). We face similar problems today – young and old in different ways. We can take this as an ongoing prayer for ourselves, remembering that the risen and ascended Jesus continues to pray for his followers (Romans 8:34; Hebrews 7:25) and does so from a position of understanding (Hebrews 4:15).

The account of the ascension in Acts 1 presents a Jesus who has completed all that he came to do and is now returning to a position of power and glory. Glory, as the prayer of John 17 makes clear, is intimately connected with the work of the cross. Jesus has died, has risen, and has returned victorious to the Father. He has accomplished our salvation and reigns – but still has our interests at heart. It seems highly likely that the prayer of John 17 indicates what Jesus prays for us now.

This should be a source of strength and encouragement, especially when we find the going tough. If Jesus cares this much about our unity, we should reflect that in the way we live and pray. Like it or not, we are in this together and that involves supporting and praying for one another. While much of Jesus' prayer must remain unique to him, other aspects can become a model for our own praying; as Jesus prayed for his followers so we pray for our fellow Christians.

Beginning the service

Pretend to make a call on your mobile (to your mother, although she should not be identified by name during the 'call' as you will be asking everyone to guess to whom you were talking), with an ad-lib script along the following lines:

Hi, it's me. (*Pause*) Yes, I'm fine. (*Pause*) Don't worry! I know you can't help worrying, but I am fine, honestly. (*Pause*) Yes, you did tell me about Aunt Margaret. (*Pause*) Yes, I am eating properly. (*Pause*) Well… it's not too untidy – I did make my bed this morning, you'll be pleased to hear! (*Pause*) Yes, I love you too. I'll phone you again later. (*Pause*) I promise! Bye.

Challenge the congregation to identify whom you were calling. Ask if they know that Jesus talked to his Father. But he didn't talk much about himself. He talked mostly to God about his followers – and that includes us!

Bible reading

If you did not use the script on Acts 1:1–11 (YearA.Ascension_1) available from www.scriptureunion.org.uk/lightdownloads, on Ascension Day, you could use it here.

As John 17:1–11 is being read out loud, ask people to listen out for what Jesus says about his followers. It might help to have the passage (YearA.Easter7_1) on the screen; it is available from www.scriptureunion.org.uk/lightdownloads. Gather up the observations once the verses have been read.

Bible talk

With: the following letters printed on 14 individual sheets of paper: A, C, E, F, I, N, O, P, R, S, T, T, U, Y; a board and pins or a 'washing line' with pegs to display them; scissors; a string of paper figures folded in a zigzag fashion and ready to cut out

Remind everyone of the discussion about the importance of prayer at **Beginning the service**. How often do we remember that Jesus prayed? Although he was already so close to his Father, he made sure that he spent time in prayer. We are going to discover what Jesus prayed for us, how to respond to his prayer, and how to pray for each other in the same way.

In John 17:1–11, Jesus prayed for his followers. Encourage everyone to find the passage in the Bible and keep it open in front of them. Display the 14 letters. Jesus asked his Father to do three things for his followers; these are hidden in the letters on display. (This only works with the TNIV and any other Bible versions that include the word 'sanctify' in verse 17.)

Explain that you will give a clue for each one.

Clue 1: The first word is something that a sports team should do if they are to play well. It's referred to in verse 11 as 'being one', and it begins with 'U'!
Answer: Jesus asked God to unite his followers so that they would be as one, and strong as a result. (*Make the word 'unite' from the letters by inviting volunteers to sort out the letters and then hold the relevant sheets of paper for everyone to read.*)

Clue 2: In verses 11 and 15 Jesus asked God to do for his followers the same thing that he did for Daniel when he was in the lions' den. **Answer:** Jesus asked God to protect them – spiritually, as well as physically. (*Make the word 'protect', using 'T' and 'E' from 'unite' and the rest from other letters on display.*)

Clue 3: This word is in verse 17 and it means 'to be set apart for God, and made holy'.
Answer: Jesus asked God to sanctify them, which means to help them be more and more like Jesus. (*Make the word 'sanctify' from the remaining letters, using 'N' and 'I' from 'unite', and 'C' and 'T' from 'protect'.*)

Ask everyone to tell you what the three things are that Jesus asked God to do for his followers – unite, protect and sanctify them. Jesus prayed for his disciples, but he also prayed for people who would become his followers in the future; so Jesus prayed this prayer for us too (John 17:20)!

(*Take the string of paper figures and hold it up folded, so that the outline figure of a single person can be seen.*) Ask a child how many people they can see on the paper. Then cut out the figures (or ask a volunteer to do this for you), being careful not to snip the folds where they will hold together! Hold the figures up again, still folded up, and ask again how many can be seen. Explain that although we feel like just one person, we are united with every other Christian in the world as a part of Christ's body. (*Ask a volunteer to take one end of the chain and open it out, showing all the figures.*)

Talk about how there are many figures, but still one sheet of paper – they are all joined. Ask a child to rip one of the figures, and show how easy it is to damage them when they are alone. Fold the figures up again and ask the child to try again. It is very difficult to damage the figures folded together. If we pray for each other the way that Jesus prayed for us, asking God to unite us, protect us and sanctify us, we will be like the figures – strong together (with God helping us as well!).

Challenge everyone to answer the following questions in their minds:
• How can we become united as a church family? Are there differences we need to pray about and sort out with each other?
• How can we make sure we are protected by God? Do we read his Word and pray regularly, as well as meet together as the body of Christ?
• How can we encourage each other to become more like Jesus? Do the house groups encourage and motivate members to live God's way and pray for each other?

Finish by reading the first part of Acts 1:14, explaining that this refers to the disciples when they met together after Jesus had gone back to heaven. It should be true of us, too.

Prayer activity

With: a large world map; information sheets about Christians in different continents; tea lights; alternatively a large map of the parish or local area with information and photographs about local churches

Set aside different areas of the church building to represent different continents, including your own. In each area, place information such as photographs, news, prayer requests and letters from missionaries or brochures from Christian organisations that work there. (Ask members of the congregation to contribute to an area if they have family or friends living abroad, or if they sponsor a child.)

Ask people to travel around the areas, individually or in small groups, and pray at each station. Alternatively, suggest that individuals move to the area for which they feel the most concern and remain there for the time given. Play some quiet music. Leave tea lights in each area as people pray silently, or voice their prayers aloud.

To close, ask the congregation to bring the tea lights back to a central area and to place them on the large map in the continent for which they have prayed. Explain that this is a visual representation of all our prayers coming together to enable God's light to shine through Christians all over the world. Tim Hughes' song 'Whole world in his hands' would be a good one to sing or play as this happens (see **Music and song ideas**).

If you would prefer to focus on Christians in the local area, set up a similar arrangement by displaying photographs and information about the churches closest to you, their leaders and their work. Ask them for particular prayer requests to be made known to your congregation.

If you expect a lot of children to be present and would prefer not to use candles, return to the image of the paper figures, giving a string of figures to each child and asking them to visit the different areas of the church building and write or draw on each figure a prayer concern from one of the areas. Ask them to save one figure and decorate it as themselves, representing their part in the family of God when they pray for each other. Let the children bring the figures back to the central area and encourage them to read or say aloud what they have prayed for.

Ending the service

Remind the congregation that, in praying for each other and remembering that we are members of Christ's body, we are responding to Jesus' prayer for us. Encourage them to continue in their prayers for each other as followers of Jesus. If your church has house groups, the information from the **Prayer activity** could be divided among them as a way of ensuring that every area continues to be prayed for.

End the service with Jesus' parting words to his disciples from Acts 1:8: 'You will receive power when the Holy Spirit comes on you; and you will be my witnesses … to the ends of the earth.'

Helpful extras

Music and song ideas

Songs that reflect themes of unity and the Church around the world include: 'Brother, sister, let me serve you'; 'O let the Son of God enfold you'; 'For I'm building a people of power'; 'Bind us together'; 'A new commandment'; 'When all around is fading' ('Whole world in his hands' - Tim Hughes); 'Thy hand, O God, has guided'; 'Onward, Christian Soldiers'; 'Father, hear the prayer we offer' and for an evening service, 'The day thou gavest'.

For churches that use music from Iona, the song 'A touching place' would fit the theme well. One of the two Taizé settings of 'Ubi Caritas' would be appropriate for contemplation, or as a refrain for prayers. If the congregation is unfamiliar with Taizé worship, link a few words of introduction to the theme by explaining that the words are in Latin because it is seen as a universal language of prayer in a community that welcomes young people from all over the globe. More information can be found on the website: www.taize.fr.

Alternatively, background music from churches in other parts of the world could be played during the **Prayer activity**.

Statement of faith
If you used the paper figures in the **Prayer activity**, recall the image here and ask people to join hands as they state their faith, reminding them that this is the common belief that unites all Christians and makes us one.

Use the liturgy or creed that you would usually employ. You could introduce it with Jesus' words from John 17:2 and 3. Alternatively, a statement of faith that is based on the readings for the day (YearA.Easter7_2) is available from www.scriptureunion.org.uk/lightdownloads. The congregation joins in the emboldened response.

Notes and comments

The theme provides a good opportunity to talk about any mission partners that the

church has, any links with other churches or church plants, or work that members of the congregation do in the local area. Draw attention to these with video links, photographs, interviews or testimonies and pray for those specific people and groups.

If the service includes Holy Communion, emphasis could be placed on the response 'We are one body, because we all share in one bread' and the communicants could be asked to imagine other churches all over the world in which people are sharing in the same bread, and to pray for them.

If your church has a prayer ministry team, this service should provide plenty of opportunities to encourage people to ask for prayer as well as to pray for each other.

The paper figure activity suggested in **Bible talk** and **Prayer activity** could be expanded further and made into a focal image for a baptismal service: the candidates for baptism are entering the family of God. In particular, attention could be drawn to the part of some baptism services in which the congregation is asked to continue supporting the candidates in prayer. If you decide to do this, you could also change the **Prayer activity** to one in which the congregation prays for all those who have been baptised in the church within the last year.

Alternative online options
Visit www.lightlive.org for additional activities for children, young people and adults.

PENTECOST

READINGS: John 20:19–23; Acts 2:1–21
Numbers 11:24–30; Psalm 104:24–34,35b; 1 Corinthians
12:3b–13

Bible foundations

Aim: to explore the role of the Holy Spirit in forgiveness, peace and the sharing of the good news about Jesus

The Old Testament promises that the arrival of the kingdom would be accompanied by a fresh outpouring of the Spirit (see Ezekiel 36:26,27). With the fulfilment of these promises at Pentecost, we have further confirmation of the presence of the kingdom. With the coming of the Spirit, people are empowered in new ways. A group of disciples, who only a few weeks ago had been hiding away in fear, are now out on the streets, telling of the wonders of God's salvation. Peter, who a few weeks earlier had denied knowing Jesus, is now standing in front of a large crowd explaining who he was and what God was doing through him. The change is remarkable! They see things in new ways and they are enabled to speak out with new courage and authority.

Jesus sent his followers out with the authority to forgive sins and in the power of the Spirit. But before we assume that all will therefore be easy, we need to see that Jesus is the model for the way we go into the world: with power (yes!), with authority (certainly) – but also in weakness and humility, to live lives of service and to identify with others in their pain, loneliness, suffering and need. Into such situations we bring peace – and the thought reflects more of the Hebrew shalom. This is not merely the absence of conflict, but the presence of a positive sense of well-being. To those separated from God we announce the forgiveness of sins. We embody the good news of Jesus to those for whom there is little good news. And we do it because we are agents of the kingdom of God, marked by the outpouring of the Spirit.

Beginning the service

At the beginning of the service, ask people to answer the question 'Who is the Holy Spirit?', and note down the responses. Use some of the responses to illustrate the range of thoughts and ideas given. Make sure that the children and young people's answers are represented.

Bible reading

Acts 2:1–13 is a very familiar and dramatic passage. There are a number of ways in which you could bring it alive to the congregation:

- Use at least two voices for the reading, with one telling the narrative and the other saying the verses and phrases that were spoken (for example, verse 7 onwards).
- Arrange for a small group to do various sound effects, such as a gentle breeze, chattering, excitement and laughter, as appropriate. Use large candles to demonstrate the tongues of flame.

Bible talk

With: a letter 'P', as large as possible, made out of card

Ask for two volunteers to carry the 'P' across the front the first time you mention one of the key 'P' words – or this could be done every time a 'P' word is mentioned but that might get tedious! Begin by asking anyone to suggest any words that begin with the letter 'P'. Be open to fun suggestions, and thank everyone for their contributions.

Explain that today we are thinking about a special occasion called '**P**entecost', which was an annual Jewish festival to celebrate harvest. But the most well known Pentecost happened after Jesus had returned to heaven.

Peace

The Bible is full of promises, and we know that God keeps his promises! Jesus promised that he would beat death and after he died on the cross he came alive again. He wanted the world to have peace. Some of his followers understood, but others were confused and didn't quite believe it all.

The disciples were all together in a locked room for fear of being arrested, and they didn't really feel the peace of God at all! Then suddenly Jesus was with them! He appeared in the room and spoke to his followers. Jesus said, '**P**eace be with you', and greeted them all. Then he went on to offer them peace again, before breathing on them and encouraging them to receive the Holy Spirit.

Jesus came to the world to bring peace, and that's not just about an end to big wars! We can all do our part to live peacefully with others, to think of others rather than ourselves, and to bring peace into friendships and relationships. At school we can help people who are arguing or fighting; in our families we should bring peace; and at work we can offer the peace that Jesus gives us.

Power

It was a few weeks later, and the disciples had continued to worship and pray together, trying to hold on to Jesus' promise of peace. They chose leaders, and gathered often to worship and talk about how to bring God's peace to the world. What they needed was some power… and that's what they got!

As they prayed they heard the sound of a wind blowing through the room, and then they saw what looked like flames landing on their heads. They were confused and possibly even a little afraid, but they soon discovered that they had a new **P**ower through the Holy Spirit. This power meant that they were able to talk in the many languages of the crowds that filled the city of Jerusalem for the Pentecost celebration. They also had the power to speak up about the peace of Jesus in a way they hadn't before.

The power that the followers of Jesus received from the Holy Spirit changed their lives. The Holy Spirit can give us power too. He can give us the strength to speak out and share what we believe with our friends and others who don't know Jesus as we do. His power can help us pray for other people. That power is given by God, and is part of God's purpose.

Purpose

When Jesus came to his disciples and offered them peace, he explained a little about the purpose of the Holy Spirit. He wanted the disciples to bring peace to the world, and peace to all situations.

Jesus also said that the **P**urpose of the Holy Spirit was to help the disciples forgive others. He gave them power to forgive, and to bring forgiveness to the lives of others.

The Holy Spirit's purpose, after the Pentecost celebration, was to help those who believed in Jesus to share their faith with others. The disciples suddenly found they had the power and the confidence to do that with the crowd.

The Holy Spirit had a number of different purposes then, and he still has the same purposes now. As followers of Jesus, we can see what the Holy Spirit does, and allow God to help us through the Holy Spirit. We can have the peace, and the power, to share our faith – today and in the coming week!

Prayer activity

With: two large sheets of paper (on the walls or floor) labelled 'Peace' and 'Power'; marker pens; quiet music on CD or played by musicians

Peace

Ask everyone to stand in one large circle or turn to others in smaller circles, and invite them to stand silently and peacefully for one minute asking God to be with them. Explain that as we are peaceful we can receive the peace that Jesus offers. Then ask each person to turn to the next and say, 'The peace of the Lord be with you', and the other to offer the response, 'And also with you'. You may want to demonstrate this and practise it, particularly for children and young people present, if it is not your usual practice to share the peace with one another.

Then play some quiet music while you invite people to talk briefly in small groups about places in the area, country and world that need more peace. Then one person from each group can go and write what they have identified on the 'Peace' sheet.

Power

Invite everyone to picture in their minds all the people they think may not know much about Jesus and so may not love him. Help children by reminding them of their friends at school, staff, and others with whom they have contact. In addition, they could think of situations where God's power is needed.

Invite them to join in with the response:
Give us the power to share our love for you.

Thank you, God, that you sent your Holy Spirit to the followers of Jesus.
Give us the power to share our love for you.
Thank you, God, that you send your Holy Spirit to us.
Give us the power to share our love for you.
Help us, God, to invite the Holy Spirit to help us.
Give us the power to share our love for you.
Help us, God, to tell others of your greatness.
Give us the power to share our love for you.
May we see your power changing apparently hopeless situations.
Amen.

Play quiet music as volunteers write on the 'Power' sheet the name of a friend, colleague or family member, with whom they would like to share their faith.

Ending the service

The Holy Spirit came for all people, and his peace and power are available to us now so that we can fulfil his purposes. A great way to draw the service to a close is to invite the children and young people to stand and pray for the Holy Spirit to help the adults.

If appropriate, and in line with your church tradition, they could gently lay their hands on the adults around them. They could pray silently, using their own words, or simply pray as follows:

'Holy Spirit, we ask you to help all of us to bring peace, to have power, and to fulfil your purposes.'

This action can be reversed, with the adults praying that the Holy Spirit will help all the children and young people in a similar way.

Finish with the following prayer, based on the speech that Peter gave to the crowd in Acts 2:14–21 when he quoted Joel 2.

The Holy Spirit gave the followers new power, and helped them speak of their faith:
We give thanks for the Holy Spirit.
The Holy Spirit will come to all people, and be poured out on everyone:
We give thanks for the Holy Spirit.
The Holy Spirit will help everyone – the old, the young, the women, and the men:
We give thanks for the Holy Spirit.
The Holy Spirit will show amazing things, and perform wonders of earth and heaven:
We give thanks for the Holy Spirit.
The Holy Spirit will prepare the world for the return of Jesus:
We give thanks for the Holy Spirit.
The Holy Spirit will help everyone, all those who call on the name of Jesus:
We give thanks for the Holy Spirit.
based on Acts 2: 14–21

Helpful extras

Music and song ideas

Songs that focus on the Holy Spirit, include: 'Holy Spirit, we welcome you'; 'There is a Redeemer'; 'Breathe on me, Breath of God'; 'Spirit of the living God'; 'Spirit of God, unseen as the wind'; 'We are marching'; 'God's Spirit' *Bitesize Bible Songs 2* CD (SU), a Learn and remember verse song for 2 Timothy 1:7.

Game

With: scissors; orange, red and yellow paper; pens; staplers; the flame template (YearA. Pentecost_1) from www.scriptureunion.org. uk/lightdownloads.

Ask everyone to get into groups of mixed ages, preferably where they are sitting, and ensure that there are adults to supervise the children when using scissors and staplers. Explain that the followers of Jesus saw what looked like flames above their heads when the Holy Spirit came. Then remind everyone of the three points of the talk – the 'Peace', 'Power' and 'Purposes' of the Holy Spirit.

Ask everyone to cut out three flame shapes, one of each colour. These could be prepared in advance. When everyone has cut out their flame shapes, invite them to write one of the three 'P' words on each flame. Staple the three flame shapes together at the base.

Once everyone has made their 'flames', they should all be held high and waved, as the phrase 'We welcome the Holy Spirit' is repeated. This could be done as a 'Mexican wave' across the church. Divide the church into five sections (for example, from left to right). The first section starts by shouting the word 'We' and raising their flames. In turn, each section shouts the next word until the final word ('Spirit') is shouted by the group at the other side of the church. You might need to practise this, a couple of times, before you do it for real.

Notes and comments

The Old Testament reading from Numbers 11:24–30 gives a foretaste of what the Spirit does. The Spirit fell on Moses and his elders, and they prophesied and testified to the power of God. This passage could be read and briefly explained early on in the service, and the parallel between this and Pentecost referred to in the main Bible talk.

Acts 2:1–21 mentions many languages and nations. An additional activity could be to see how many different languages can be spoken by people in the congregation, and how many different nations or birth nations are represented.

If the service includes Holy Communion, make appropriate links as you share the peace.

Alternative online options

Visit www.lightlive.org for additional activities for children, young people and adults.

TRINITY SUNDAY

READINGS: **2 Corinthians 13:11–13; Matthew 28:16–20**
Isaiah 40:12–17,27–31; Psalm 8:1–9

Bible foundations

Aim: to explore the way followers of Jesus are called to make disciples

The idea of a God who is 'Three', but also 'One', is a mystery. Few of the analogies really help our understanding and it is better to live with the truth and the mystery. Christian witness and fellowship are bound up with the worship of the one God in three persons. When others come to faith, they are brought into union with a God who encounters them as the loving Father, as the redeeming Son and as the energising Spirit – not three gods, but one God, present to us in three persons. Baptism into the threefold name (singular) meant that, early in their Christian life, new converts were introduced to the understanding of God that distinguishes Christianity from the other monotheistic faiths.

Discipleship continues as it starts, in the service of Father, Son and Spirit. Disciples in the first century spent time with their rabbi or teacher, travelling, sitting, talking, observing, questioning, and aiming to become like the rabbi. This is how Jesus has been working with the twelve and he now sends out the eleven as rabbis who will, in turn, call a group of disciples to themselves to teach them by word and example (Matthew 28:16–20). Christian faith is characterised by trust in God; it is demonstrated by baptism, and with a new lifestyle of obedience to the pattern of life laid down by Jesus and lived in the power of the Spirit. That is what we are about when we make disciples.

Disciples cannot exist in isolation – they are always part of a group. So it is with those whom we disciple; they join a church in which they are united with one another because they are united with the Father, Son and Spirit. The words of the grace (2 Corinthians 13:13) are a constant reminder that we live together because of the grace of the Son, the love of the Father and the shared life we have in the Spirit.

Beginning the service

Welcome everyone by addressing them as 'disciples'. Display the word 'disciple' on a PowerPoint or on a board at the front. Alternatively, jumble up the letters of 'disciple' and invite people to guess the word. Then ask for a definition of what a disciple is. Explain that a disciple is a learner, a follower, a student. If we follow Jesus and listen to him, we are all his disciples. Today's service explores what it means to be a disciple of Jesus, and how we, as disciples, are called to make others disciples.

Bible reading

The reading of Matthew 28:16–20 includes the instructions Jesus gave to his disciples after the resurrection. The commands in verses 19 and 20a could be printed out on separate strips of paper, labelled: A – Go to the people of all nations and make them my disciples; B – Baptise them in the name of the Father, the Son, and the Holy Spirit; C – Teach them to do everything I have told you. Distribute these around the congregation. In order, the three commands can be read as addressed to one another. Everyone should then be urged to listen carefully to Jesus' final promise in verse 20b.

Ensure that the prayer known as 'the Grace' (2 Corinthians 13:13) is said at least once in the course of the service. Verses 11 and 12 put it in its context, the ending of Paul's second letter to the church in Corinth.

Isaiah 40:12–17, and 27–31 include some awesome statements about the character and activity of God.

Bible retelling

With: a copy of the script below – an account by one of the disciples of what happened as the disciples waited for Jesus on the mountain

Explain that this service focuses upon Matthew's account of the story.

So there we were, the eleven of us, sitting on the side of a mountain. We were there because Jesus had told us to be there. And what better reason is there to be anywhere? But this time wasn't like the other times – when we used to sit there waiting for him to appear with his stories, his miraculous powers and his wonderful ways of caring for people and seeing exactly what they needed. In those times there used to be excited crowds pressing on us, buzzing with anticipation. Then he would arrive, and there would be an expectant calm. Everyone sat waiting, listening.

This time, though, it was just us – just the eleven of us, sitting on the side of a mountain. There were still some of us, you see, who were not sure what was going on. We all knew that he'd been arrested after the Passover supper. Most of us had made ourselves scarce at that point, but everyone heard about what happened next. How he died. And our whole world fell apart.

The story became stranger after that. Some of the women claimed to have seen him – alive and well. They said the grave was empty. They said things about earthquakes, and light, and stones rolling away and shining people and other things none of us understood, but

you follow…?'; 'I, the Lord of sea and sky'; 'We have a gospel to proclaim'; 'Great is the darkness'; 'Days of Elijah'; 'Holy, holy, holy'.

Ending the service

Include Jesus' words from Matthew 28:19 and 20 in the dismissal: 'Go and make disciples of all nations … and surely, I am with you always, to the very end of the age.' Conclude by saying 'The Grace' (2 Corinthians 13:13) together, reminding everyone that it is Trinity Sunday.

Notes and comments

Fitting all the resurrection appearances from the four gospels together is a challenge, so there may appear to be some gaps in this outline. The gospel writers included different details in their own account. Bear that in mind as you prepare for this service which is based around Matthew's account. There is remarkable similarity between the four writers, but the fact that they are not identical is evidence that this was not a story concocted by the early Church. If it had been, the stories would have been almost identical!

If your service includes a baptism, make more of Matthew 28:19 and the reference to the Trinity. The account of Jesus' own baptism is the only scene in the Bible that includes all three persons of the Trinity. At the end of his ministry, Jesus is recalling the beginning of it and showing how his work continues through his disciples. 'Making disciples' is the work of the Trinity – the Father sends his Son, the Son dies and rises to call people to himself, and the Holy Spirit inspires us.

At the end of the **Bible talk** you could make

a comparison to Facebook, where, in order to 'make a friend', you first have to send an invitation to the person with whom you wish to be friends. But you are not linked up until that person responds and clicks 'add friend'. In the same way, Jesus' invitation to discipleship requires a response from us. Our job, as disciples, is to invite others to discipleship, but it is only through God's Holy Spirit that they will respond. The task of 'making disciples' is one that we will always share with Jesus.

The **Bible retelling** is written as a 'witness account' from an unnamed disciple, evoking the atmosphere of the moment, including some background to the story and placing the events in the context of the crucifixion and resurrection of Jesus. It could just be read, but it would be more effective if learnt by heart. It could easily be turned into an interview by breaking it up into phrases and paragraphs, with people of mixed ages reading introductory questions (in the style of a journalist or newsreader).

Today is a good opportunity to pray for mission partners or discipleship courses running in the church or locality. Also recognise the value of home groups, cell groups and small prayer groups where people mature in their discipleship of Christ.

For a clear guide to explaining the Trinity read *Top Tips on Explaining the Trinity to young people* (SU) see the Scripture Union website.

Alternative online options
Visit www.lightlive.org for additional activities for children, young people and adults.

PROPER 7

READINGS: Romans 6:1b–11; Matthew 10:24–39
Jeremiah 20:7–13; Psalm 69:7–10,16–18

Bible foundations

Aim: to consider the decisions that we need to make about Jesus

In previous services we have seen that following Jesus is a rewarding but costly business. To follow Jesus is to take up the cross. To first-century listeners in a rebellious outpost of the Roman Empire, this could have meant only one thing – death. Crosses were not fashion items, or church furniture, but instruments of protracted, painful death. Few of us will face a call to such sacrifice, but publicly acknowledging and following Jesus may involve facing opposition even from those closest to us. It will, at the very least, mean that we adopt a totally new way of living, giving up the ambitions, dreams and goals that we cherish.

Paul takes us behind the scenes for a deeper understanding. Jesus died as our substitute and our representative. His death was in some way ours, and when we follow him we are accepting that he not only died for us, but we identify with that death and make it our own (Romans 6:3,4). This means that his life is also ours (verses 5,8).

Our baptism (whatever our practice and underlying theology) represents our death to an old way of living and our entry into a new life, lived in obedience to, and for the glory of, God. This cautions us against too easy a view of our baptismal promises, whether undertaken on our own behalf or on the behalf of others. Baptism marks a profound change, and our baptismal vows need constant reaffirmation. Every day we determine to live in the light of those vows. This means that the motivation for our behaviour, the driving force of our decisions and the determining factor in our relationships, is the desire to live for God. The practical outworking of this will be different at different stages in our lives, and particularly challenges us at points of transition or in the light of new circumstances. But the underlying principle is the same for all of us whatever our age or life experience.

Beginning the service

In small groups, encourage people to share a recent important decision that they have made. Perhaps it is a life-changing decision. It may have been a decision that was made in the last week or some time ago. If appropriate, use a 'roving' microphone and ask if people would be willing to say publicly what they have done. Alternatively, interview someone who has prepared a comment on their decision.

Introduce the aim of the service: to consider the important and sometimes hard decisions that we make when we follow Jesus.

Bible reading

It would help people to understand if they follow the reading from Romans 6:1b–11 in their own Bibles or on a screen or notice sheet because it is one of Paul's tightly argued parts of his letter to the Christians in Rome. A copy of this (YearA.Proper7_2) is available from www.scriptureunion.org. uk/lightdownloads.

Matthew 10:24–39 is a difficult passage. A copy of these verses with three cartoon illustrations (YearA.Proper7_2) is available (see above); alternatively, as it is read, use three mimed actions to illustrate the visual images in verses 27, 29 and 30 – someone standing on a rooftop, two sparrows held up by a large hand, someone counting the hairs on their head. Introduce the verses by explaining that Jesus is saying that things may get very tough for his followers, but we have God on our side!

Bible retelling

In addition to the **Bible reading** and **Bible talk**, you could read or perform a modern-day story that explains the meaning of the Bible passages (YearA.Proper7_1), available from www.scriptureunion.org. uk/lightdownloads. The story can be read, or retold; if you choose to perform it, you can do so with only a little rehearsal and a minimum number of props.

You don't have to keep the suggested names. If people in the congregation support different teams use these team names instead. If the story is going to be acted out, you need someone to be 'Dave' (in a football strip, with a hat and scarf), 'Sid' (preferably in the same football strip) and some really big people to be the supporters of the opposing team.

Bible talk

With: items that are used or worn by a football fan; the words 'Stand up', 'Shout out' and 'Follow' on three separate cards, or displayed on a screen or flip chart

We all have to make decisions and some are easier than others. Ask for and give some personal suggestions. Hard decisions may make us feel unhappy even though they are the right ones to have made. If you haven't performed the **Bible retelling**, invite a volunteer to come out dressed as a football fan, but don't tell the congregation just yet what they are. Ask, perhaps with humour, what they think the volunteer is dressed as. Alternatively, ask the 'Dave' character from **Bible retelling** to stand at the front.

Ask how you all know that the person is dressed as a football fan. It should be fairly obvious that they are wearing all the right gear so that they can be identified with their team. Ask what football fans do when their team scores a goal. A really enthusiastic fan will clap, make lots of noise, and jump up and down. Check what else happens at a football match – you are looking for the answer of singing songs or shouting. Your football fan could sing a 'clean' football chant loudly. (*Ask if fans ever sing quietly.*)

Then ask how a really keen fan follows their team, such as buying the new strip, sticker albums, magazines, collecting the match day programmes, buying a season ticket or going to away matches. When they play football (if they are more than a couch supporter!), they might pretend to be one of their football heroes, perhaps doing a well-known celebratory action after they have scored a goal.

If you have told the story of the football fan in the **Bible retelling**, relate the next section to that story. Otherwise follow the suggestions below.

Stand up

Ask how the football fan would behave when they are in the crowd and discover that they are surrounded by supporters of the other team. How will it make them feel? Should they stay quiet and not admit which team they support? This might be a bit difficult if they are wearing their team's football colours.

As Christians who are living for the Lord, Jesus tells us we shouldn't be afraid to stand up for him (Matthew 10:26). You might decide to be quiet in a football crowd because you don't feel safe, but living for Jesus is much more serious (verse 28). We can be brave because God loves us so much that he even knows the individual hairs on our head (verse 30) – who else, but God, would know the answer to that one? The phrase 'stand up and be counted' means to let people know your views, even though they might not be popular. In football, by the colours you wear, you stand up and are counted as a fan. In the same way Christians should also stand up and be counted for Jesus. This means being open about their faith and sharing Jesus with others.

Shout out

Point out that football fans know the songs and chants and sing and shout them loudly, declaring publicly which team they belong to and support. Jesus says that we need to shout out, declare or proclaim for him. If we do so, then he will shout out for us before his Father in heaven. He also warns us that if we stay quiet then he will reject us before God (Matthew 10:32,33). Point out, however, that the person who is a follower of a football team, no matter what, will always shout out for his team because he loves them so much and is so committed to them. Are we able to respond to Jesus in the same way?

Follow

Remind everyone how they spotted the football fan and what they said a fan would do to follow their team with real commitment. When Jesus speaks about following in his steps (Matthew 10:38), he means that we should imitate him and choose his way over all others (verse 39).

Each time we encounter a situation that challenges our Christian faith, we have a decision to make. Will we stand up, or choose not to make a fuss? Will we shout out when we need to speak up for Jesus, or be silent? Will we follow by imitating Jesus' way, or will we choose what we think is acceptable? We can have confidence that God cares for us (verse 31); that Jesus will speak up for us when we speak up for him (verse 32); and that when we follow Jesus, we will win the prize of eternal life (verse 39). Another way of thinking about it would be this: would we think a football fan was really the fan they said they were if they didn't stand up for their team, didn't know the songs, didn't speak up for their team, and didn't have the strip?

Prayer activity

Use some of the following ideas to pray for your mission partners and their activities in making disciples and also for those who have had to make difficult decisions as a result of their faith in Jesus.

The following are prayer suggestions relating to 'Stand up', 'Shout out' and 'Follow'. Break into small groups to address each of the suggestions. Alternatively, they could all be led from the front, with activity as appropriate.

Stand up

Print out visual information to help the congregation to pray for people for whom it is a challenge to stand up for their faith, both internationally and at home. Don't forget to create some information that younger children can relate to. Prayers could be written onto foot-shaped Post-it notes or hand-cut pieces of paper and stuck onto a board. You could also have a pile of dominoes that children could attempt to stand up on one end when they have said their prayer.

Shout out

Interview your missionary – get the most recent prayer letter or email. Use a telephone, or even webcam link-up. What is the country like where they are? What problems do they face? Are they allowed by law to speak openly about their faith or do they have to be careful? Use the Internet for research into the temperature, government, and what pastimes there are. Have pictures available. Encourage the person linked to the mission partners to lead these prayers.

Follow

Take a very long rope and stretch it out as long as possible, paying particular regard to safety. (You could simply lie it along the floor. The rope can run down a central aisle or run across the front or back of the church.) Along the rope, attach some simple pieces of information and/or relevant pictures on strips of card and string. Describe clearly what it is like to follow Jesus in the countries where your missionaries are and pray for the people whom they are discipling. This could include praying for children in schools, patients in hospital, and all normal aspects of living. People reach out to touch and read the piece of card that is closest to them as they pray.

Helpful extras

Music and song ideas
Appropriate songs include: 'Stand up! Stand up for Jesus'; 'Guide me, O thou great

Jehovah'; 'O Sacred King'; 'Oh Jesus, I have promised (to serve you to the end)'; 'We shall stand (with our feet on the rock)'; 'May the words of my mouth (and the thoughts of my heart)'; 'Show me the way of the cross'; 'He who would valiant be'; 'Be bold, be strong'.

Ending the service

Commission the congregation to grow in their faith and go forward in faith.

May we stand up for you, Lord Jesus!
May we shout out your good news, Lord Jesus!
May we follow you as closely as we can this week, Lord Jesus!
Amen.

You could use the enthusiastic 'Amen' explained on page 103.

Notes and comments

You could link the Old Testament reading from Jeremiah with the **Bible talk**. Point out that Jeremiah felt afraid, but was brave (Jeremiah 20:7,8). He couldn't keep quiet about it (verse 9) and he stood for God knowing that in the end God would win through (verses 11 and 13).

Holy Communion is a constant reminder of Jesus' death and resurrection. We celebrate his death until he comes again. It is evidence of our discipleship.

Alternative online options

Visit www.lightlive.org for additional activities for children, young people and adults.

PROPER 8

READINGS: **Romans 6:12–23; Matthew 10:40–42**
Jeremiah 28:5–9; Psalm 89:1–4,15–18

Bible foundations

Aim: to explore what it means to live for God

The nature of the change that comes about in our lives when we trust in Christ becomes clearer as Paul continues his complex argument. Outside of Christ, we find ourselves controlled by desires that we do not always like. When we come to Christ, we change our allegiance. We are no longer involuntary slaves but willing servants, motivated by our desire to serve the God who has saved us in and through Christ (Romans 6:13). We no longer live to serve ourselves – we live to serve Christ. This develops the idea of taking up our cross. It means that in the small decisions of each day, many of which may seem to have no massive moral implications, we are always asking ourselves if we are serving our own purposes or those of Christ, who calls us into his righteousness. Righteousness is a state in which we exist before God; we are put right with him through Christ. But it is also the nature of the life we live. To be right with God means having the desire to live in ways that please him (verse 18).

The followers of Christ are so closely identified with Christ that those who receive and welcome them are receiving and welcoming Christ (Matthew 10:40). There is a reward for servants and there is a reward for those who receive them. But if we are this closely identified with Christ, it means that this must be evident. We are to live out the life of the risen Christ so that others may see it and receive their reward, just as we receive ours. Our lives should be such that people want to welcome us. It is sad that Christians so often live in ways that encourage unnecessary hostility rather than welcome, by condemning in others the things that we condone ourselves. Our aim should be to live in ways that reflect our allegiance to Christ and genuinely attract others.

Beginning the service

With: two different flags – one to represent God, and the other, sin

Explain that you will be looking at the choices we have to make between God, and sin. It can sometimes feel as if we have to decide between two worlds or two kingdoms.

Introduce the two flags. One represents life under God (this could be golden); the other represents life under sin (this could be grey or dirty). Invite two volunteers to come forward and wave the flags. As you do so, invite people to comment on what life might be like in the two kingdoms. Put the flags in a place where they can be seen.

Bible reading

Matthew 10:40–42 could be read by five people who are connected together by holding hands or a rope. Each states one phrase or sentence that begins with 'anyone' or 'whoever', depending on the Bible version. One statement follows on from another.

As in the previous outline, it would help people to understand if they follow the reading from Romans 6:12–23 in their own Bibles or on a screen or notice sheet because it is one of Paul's tightly argued parts of his letter to the Christians in Rome. Alternatively, use the suggestion in **Bible retelling**.

Bible retelling

With: two notice boards to represent life under sin and life under God; cards with

key words from the **Bible reading**: sin, evil, desire, wickedness, life, death (and so on…)

Turn the reading of Romans 6:12–23 into an activity. Remind people of the idea that there are two kingdoms: of God and of sin (see **Beginning the service**). Give out the cards with the key words on them that are associated with either life under God, or life under sin. As the reading is read (*slowly*), they should jump up if they hear their word and put it on one of the notice boards, representing the kingdom of God or of sin. At the end of the reading, comment on the lists that have emerged.

Bible talk

With: a cut-out figure on a board, or a large rag doll, which can be pulled apart and put together again (You need to be able to remove the legs, hands, eyes and mouth. The figure doesn't have to be overly accurate, and could be constructed from bits of old clothes, stuffed and stuck together with Velcro, depending on how creative you want to be.)

Introduce your figure, which represents an average human being. It has various parts that enable it to do different things. Human beings are amazing creations and we can do many different things. But nothing we do is entirely neutral. We make all sorts of decisions and these decisions have consequences. Give some real-life examples.

Eyes enable us to see
Being able to see is so important. We make decisions about what we look at and what we look for. If we choose to focus on things

that we want, even to the point of being obsessed, we can fail to look at anything else. You could say that we become slaves to the things we long for. Point out some examples, such as concern for good looks and fashion, obsessive fascination with a type of car or a particular colour. It's as if we no longer own our eyes. At this point remove the eyes from the figure and put them somewhere safe.

Hands enable us to do and make things
Do we use our abilities to help other people, or do we concentrate on our own good? Are we self-centred in our activities? We can train our hands to serve others, or to be creative, such as playing a musical instrument. We can train them to do good, or to serve our own interests. Our hands can become tools of selfishness – then they no longer belong to us, but to sin. Take the hands from the figure and put them somewhere safe.

Work your way around the body, removing various bits: the mouth, which can be used to bless or hurt other people (refer to James 3:1–10); the legs, which we can use to run purposefully can also take us to places we should not go, and so on… Soon there will be very little left. The figure no longer owns its own parts. They belong to sin. Explain that we are just the same and can easily allow ourselves to become slaves to sin – as Paul says in the reading from Romans – but the good news is that Jesus can rescue us from this slavery and give us our lives back. We can be forgiven for our selfishness and given a new start. Stick all the bits back on the figure.

But there is still a temptation to slide back into selfishness. Paul says that we can choose to be slaves of sin, or we can choose to be slaves of God. If we choose to offer ourselves to our own self-interest, we end up losing ourselves; but if we offer ourselves to God, we discover that he brings wholeness and life. Point out that the figure is now in one piece and make sure it has a smile on its face.

A series of choices
We have to choose between our own way, and God's way. The consequences of our decisions can be really significant, but being a follower of Jesus is not just about avoiding bad decisions. We are also called to take positive action. In Matthew's Gospel, Jesus says that the disciples represent him in the world and that those who welcome followers of Jesus are really welcoming him. Living for God brings freedom, wholeness and life; it also brings purpose and responsibility.

Finish by asking God to help us in our decisions.

Prayer activity
With: glasses or cups of water – one for each person

Give each person a cup of water. (Be careful of spillages.) As you do so, remind people of the reading from Matthew's Gospel. Explain that we are going to give our cup to someone else in the congregation, just as the reading suggests.

First, think about the needs that disciples have. Invite people to think about their friends and neighbours, fellow church members, mission partners, and so on. What needs do these people have? Ask them to give their cup to another person in the church. As they do so, they should think of

God blessing that person and all the other people they have thought about.

Everyone should now have a cup that someone else has given to them. Invite them to think about their own needs. How might God bless them? Ask them to drink the water as a way of showing that they are open to receiving God's blessings.

Prayer of confession

During the following prayer, the congregation is invited to point first to themselves, then down to the floor, then at other people, and, finally, up towards the sky. This pattern is repeated twice and then reversed. Explain this carefully. It may help to say the prayer twice, so that people can make it their own.

When we are selfish (*point to ourselves*)
we fall into sin (*point down*);
we forget others (*point to others*)
and we forget God (*point up*).
We hurt ourselves (*point to ourselves*)
and fall down deeper (*point down*);
we hurt others (*point to others*)
and we hurt God (*point up*).
But God will forgive us (*point up*)
and draw us together (*point to others*).
He'll rescue us from sin (*point down*)
and give us peace (*point to ourselves*).
Amen.

Here is an alternative responsive prayer.

Lord, forgive us when we put our own needs first.
Jesus, lead us into life.
Lord, forgive us when we choose to do wrong.

Jesus, lead us into life.
Lord, forgive us when we treat others badly.
Jesus, lead us into life.
Lord, forgive us when we forget those in need.
Jesus, lead us into life.
Lord, set us free from sin, and teach us to serve you.
Jesus, lead us into life. Amen.

Reassure people that God has heard their prayer and has taken away their sin.

Helpful extras

Music and song ideas

Songs might include: 'I am a new creation'; 'Amazing grace'; 'Shout for joy and sing'; 'God forgave my sin'; 'Just as I am, without one plea'; 'Only by grace can we enter'; 'You laid aside your majesty'.

Statement of faith

The following statement of faith is based on Romans 6 (YearA.Proper8_1) and is available from www.scriptureunion.org.uk/lightdownloads. Encourage the congregation to read it through carefully before saying it.

> We will not let sin reign in our bodies
> so that we obey its desires.
> We will not offer any part of ourselves to sin
> so that we become instruments of wickedness.
> We will offer ourselves to God,
> for we have been brought from death to life.
> We will offer every part of ourselves to him
> as an instrument of righteousness.

For sin shall no longer be our master,
because we are not under the law, but
under grace.
We used to be slaves to sin,
but we will obey, from our hearts,
the pattern of teaching that has now
claimed our allegiance.
We have been set free from sin
and have become slaves to righteousness.
We have been set free from sin
and have become slaves of God.
The benefit we reap leads to holiness,
and the result is eternal life.
For the wages of sin is death,
but the gift of God is eternal life in Christ
Jesus, our Lord.

based on Romans 6 (TNIV)

Ending the service

With: the two flags used in **Beginning the
service** and small flags or streamers for each
person (similar to the flag that represents
God)

Remind people of the flags used at
Beginning the service. Ask two volunteers
to wave them. During the service we have
thought about life under God and life under
sin, and how we might pass from one ruler to
the other. We are now preparing to go back
out into the world – will we be slaves to sin,
or servants of God?

Give out the small flags and invite people to
wave them when they say their response in
the following prayer:

Lord, you came to rescue us
from the mess we made for ourselves.
We are God's people. Alleluia! (*Wave flags.*)

Lord, you want to lead us
from death to life, from despair to hope.
We are God's people. Alleluia! (*Wave flags.*)
Lord, you call us to serve you
and to be witnesses for you in the world.
We are God's people. Alleluia! (*Wave flags.*)
Lord, you promise to be with us
and to remain with us always.
We are God's people. Alleluia! (*Wave flags.*)
Lord, we now go out from this place,
but we shall remain yours.
We are God's people. Alleluia! (*Wave flags.*)

Invite people to take their flag home with
them as a reminder that they are called to
live for God.

Notes and comments

Some congregations may be sensitive to the use
of flags, seeing them as a symbol of nationalism
or exclusivity. Consider using alternative
symbols for the rule of sin or of God, such as
crosses, candles, badges or stickers.

The **Statement of faith** could be used
to help people internalise the message of
the reading from Romans 6. This would be
less helpful for a congregation with a high
number of younger children because of the
complexity of the language and concepts.

In a service of Holy Communion emphasise
that God has set us free from our sin
because of Jesus' death on the cross.

Alternative online options

Visit www.lightlive.org for additional
activities for children, young people and
adults.

PROPER 9

READINGS: Romans 7:15–25a; Matthew 11:16–19,25–30
Zechariah 9:9–12; Psalm 145:8–14

Bible foundations

Aim: to explore the difference between being a slave to sin and new life in Jesus

Romans 7:7–25 is one of the most controversial chapters in the New Testament. For many people, both ordinary Christians as well as top class scholars, it appears to be describing the common experience of believers. For them, it describes the despair that many of us seem to feel about our inability to triumph over sin. But is this the best reading? Paul has actually already told the Roman Christians that they need no longer be enslaved to sin (Romans 6:6–10). As Christians they share in Christ's death and are effectively dead to sin. Of course they must work hard to ensure that this remains a reality for them and not slip back into the old patterns of enslavement. As is sometimes said, 'You can take the prisoner out of prison; it is harder to take the prison out of the prisoner.'

This struggle between the flesh and the Spirit is dealt with in Romans 8. In Romans 7:7–25 Paul seems to be describing how he struggled with sin before he became a Christian. It is all about how, though he loved God's Law, it merely served to condemn him and drive him to despair. He is not describing his experience as a Christian at all. Indeed, unlike chapter 8, Romans 7 has no mention of the Spirit, but plenty about the Law!

In Matthew 11 Jesus criticises the Jewish people of his own day. They have criticised both John the Baptist and Jesus for their different approaches to holiness. John was thought to be too ascetic and severe; Jesus was thought to be too liberal. In Matthew 11:25–30 Jesus points to a new way. This new way is revealed through him and involves becoming his close follower. In one sense it is not complicated or difficult, as the scribes and Pharisees made it. You could say that their minds resemble that of Romans 7. But for the Christian it is all about relationship to Jesus and taking on his way of life. Romans chapter 8 also says plenty about that – see next Sunday!

Beginning the service

Introduce the theme by showing a neutral picture of an animal wearing a yoke. Ask the congregation whether they think the animal is happy or sad, comfortable or uncomfortable. Does it like its master? Is it well rested and well fed? Is it possible to tell just by looking at the picture?

Explain that today we are exploring the difference between being a slave to sin and a servant of Christ, and discovering the way that obedience can mean two very different things depending on who the master is.

Bible reading

Romans 7:15–24 is a catalogue of woe and frustration that climaxes with verse 25a. This final verse could be shouted out by several readers or even introduced by a loud gong or concluded with a round of applause! You may wish to suggest that Paul may either have been talking about what life was like before he came to follow Christ or may be talking about the struggle all followers of Christ still face – see **Bible foundations**.

Introduce Matthew 11:16–19, 25–30 by explaining that Jesus was under constant criticism. Here is how he once responded.

Bible talk

With: images of yokes on oxen either from the Internet or images (Year A. Proper9_1) available from www.scriptureunion.org.uk/lightdownloads

Ask what it might mean to be a slave. You may wish to explore or answer this by reading a story (see **Notes and comments**), listening to a song (see **Music and song ideas**) or by asking people to share their thoughts out loud. Alternatively, go straight on to the following activity.

Two masters

Ask a child or teenager to stand at the front between two people who will have been forewarned! Tell the child that one of the people is their 'master' and they must do whatever the 'master' says, whatever anyone else might try to tell them. The 'master' gives some physical instructions, such as 'Touch your head!', 'Sit down!' or 'Do a star jump!' Next, the child must continue to follow instructions from the 'master', but now the other person gives alternative instructions, which are more appealing, such as 'Eat this chocolate!', 'Sit down!' or 'Have a rest!' But the child must only follow the instructions of the 'master'.

Afterwards, ask the child how easy or difficult it was to keep following the 'master'. Did they wish they could follow some of the instructions from the other person? Explain that in the passage from Romans, Paul describes himself as a 'slave to sin' and complains that 'what I want to do I do not do, but what I hate, I do' (verse 15). In verses 21–23, he says that he feels as if his body is at war with his mind – just as the child longed to follow the alternative instructions. Paul was caught between two conflicting 'masters': he wanted to follow God, but in his body and his sinful human nature he was stuck as a prisoner of the law of sin. With reference to **Bible foundations**, you may wish to apply this either to how we were before we came to Christ or as part of the struggle we experience now. What is important is that we live as people who know we are joyfully saved by Christ.

Wearing a yoke

The reading from Romans finished with Paul thanking God through Jesus Christ. Remind people of this, if you followed the dramatic suggestion above. But what was there to thank God for? Compare Romans 7:15–25a with Matthew 11:30 where Jesus says, 'My yoke is easy and my burden is light.' Show some pictures of yokes and explain what they are and how they work. A good yoke is made to fit the measurements of the animals that use it, to help them pull the load evenly and with maximum power. It is not meant to be a burden.

To illustrate this, ask some mixed-age members of the congregation to have a go at lifting heavy (not too heavy!) buckets with different handles – a rope one, a metal one and a padded one. (The weight is much easier and more pleasant to lift with the padding to spread the load, even if all the buckets weigh the same.) Jesus' yoke is easy because his commandments are made lovingly and fittingly, with our best interests at heart. Jews at the time thought of the Old Testament law as a yoke. But the yoke of Jesus was not heavy and demanding – quite the opposite!

Jesus' yoke is liberating

You could finish here, or go on to point out that the image of the easy yoke does not always mean that life following Jesus will be easy, or that we will want to do everything he asks us to do. (You could refer back to what has been observed in previous weeks.)

Give the example of a child following the rules at school. Ask for suggestions. It's not always easy, and it certainly isn't always what you want to do! But making the right choices is also about recognising who is in charge and deciding whether we trust them to make the right decisions for us. If we do, then we should follow them even when it gets tough. If possible, invite someone to share how the yoke of Jesus, far from being burdensome, has been liberating. You will need to ensure that their language is jargon-free, using tangible examples that connect with children and young people.

Prayers of intercession

Use the following response after each bidding: **Thanks be to God – through Jesus Christ our Lord!**

Father, we pray for your world, and today we pray for those who can't choose how to live their lives because of slavery, poverty, war or oppression. We thank you for the people who are working to free them, especially... (*Response*)

Father, we pray for our community. We thank you that we are free to choose to follow you. We thank you for people who look after us in our schools and at church, especially... (*Response*)

Father, we pray for people who are slaves to sin because they have not yet heard about the new life that you offer. (*Ask the congregation to name people silently.*) Help us to tell them about your light and easy yoke. We thank you for rescuing us from our slavery and giving us the freedom of serving you. (*Response*)

Father, we pray for the sick, the weary and for those who are sad, especially... Help us to share their burdens in the way that you do. Thank you for your promise of rest for the weary and heavy burdened. (*Response*)

Use the spaces prayerfully to name people or groups of people belonging to the community, events taking place in the news or places and people close to the hearts of your church. You could prepare lists of appropriate topics to give to those reading the intercessions; or invite the congregation either to call out names or name people silently, before beginning each response.

Prayer of confession

Use the following response:
Jesus, break these chains holding me. In serving you I will be free.

A leader (or several people of mixed ages scattered around the church building) say the first line, followed by the response. The response could be accompanied by an action that symbolises freedom, such as joined wrists being forcefully separated. The final reading of Matthew 11:28 and 29 could be used as an absolution or, together with an absolution from the liturgy, would be most appropriately spoken by the service leader. (The first part of the response is reminiscent of a line from the song 'I wish I knew how', recommended in the **Music and song ideas**. You could listen to it reflectively before or after these prayers.)

Father, we confess that we are slaves to our own hopes and wishes. We follow the things that we want, and ignore your plan for us.

(*Response*)
Father, we confess that we are slaves to our pride. We deny you and follow others when it makes us look better. (*Response*)
Father, we confess that we are slaves to our bodies. We listen to our own appetites and weaknesses more than we listen to your Word. (*Response*)
Father, we confess that we are slaves to this world. We care more about our possessions and our lifestyles than we do about following you. (*Response*)
Jesus said, 'Come to me, all you who are weary and burdened, and I will give you rest. Take my yoke upon you and learn from me, for I am gentle and humble in heart, and you will find rest for your souls.' (*Response*)

Leave silence for the congregation to consider Jesus' invitation in the light of their confession.

Ending the service

Make some simple 'yokes' out of paper – a picture printed on a square of paper would do, or a cut-out shape. On the shape print Matthew 11:29a or verse 30.

Place the 'yokes' by the door and invite people to pick one up on their way out as a symbol of their choice to pick up Jesus' yoke over the following week. Encourage them to put it where they will often see it and read the verse this week as a reminder – on the fridge, or the bed, or use it as a bookmark.

Helpful extras

Music and song ideas
Appropriate songs include: 'Teach me, my

God and King'; 'And can it be'; 'I heard the voice of Jesus say'; 'I am a new creation'; 'Amazing Grace'; 'O let the Son of God enfold you'.

If you have used Psalm 145, set for today, or wish to replace it with a song, try 'The Lord is gracious and compassionate' (from Psalm 145:8) by Graham Ord.

Nina Simone's song 'I wish I knew how it would feel to be free' is a powerful song about slavery and longing for physical and spiritual freedom. It could be listened to reflectively, for example at the beginning of the **Bible talk**, before or as part of the **Prayer of confession**, or as a voluntary at **Beginning** or **Ending the service**. Ask people to listen to the words as the singer imagines freedom. As Christians, do we know how it feels to be free? What could we say about it to others?

Notes and comments

The topic for this session is ideal for an exploration of the theme of slavery and what we can do to help stop the slavery that continues today. You may need to explain the concept of slavery at the beginning of the **Bible talk**. The website www.stopthetraffik. org has some excellent resources including facts and figures, videos and media and suggested projects. Bob Hartman's story 'Chaga and the Chocolate Factory' can be downloaded from www.stopthetraffik.org and may help to explain in child-friendly terms something about what slavery is like.

In the **Prayers of intercession**, include prayers for charities such as Amnesty International. You could take up a special collection for an appropriate charity.

An invitation to Holy Communion could be linked to the Gospel reading, in particular verses 28–30.

For a baptism, specific mention could be made in the **Bible talk** of an adult candidate's movement from being a slave to sin, to becoming a servant of Christ. At an infant baptism, you could explain that although the child is too young to make this choice for themselves, parents are making it on the child's behalf, in the child's best interests. But we pray that one day the child will make the choice for themselves, because Jesus' yoke is one to be chosen and taken on every day.

Alternative online options

Visit www.lightlive.org for additional activities for children, young people and adults.

PROPER 10

READINGS: Romans 8:1–11; Matthew 13:1–9,18–23
Isaiah 55:10–13; Psalm 65:1–13

Bible foundations

Aim: to explore the relationship between hearing, growing and living in Christ

Jesus burst onto the scene in such a way as to cause an immense amount of questioning and speculation. There were exorcisms (see Matthew 8:28 – 9:1), healings (Matthew 9:2–8), other miracles (Matthew 8:23–27), crowds of onlookers, close followers and opponents. He taught his disciples to replicate his ministry in the villages (Matthew 10:1–42). Not everyone became a disciple and not everyone approved of his actions or his teaching (Matthew 9:34). Some even sought to kill him. Eventually even his closest followers were asking, 'Who is this man?' (Matthew 8:27).

There was a variety of responses to him and Jesus clearly wanted to explain to his followers how it was that people could react to him and the arrival of the kingdom of God in such unpredictable ways. That's why he told them the so-called Parable of the Sower. In fact, although the sower is important to the story, we could also call it the Parable of the Seed as it demonstrates how God's words and actions are received in the world. Best of all it could be called the Parable of the Soils because the real focus is on how the path, the rocks and the soil are either unable or able to receive the good seed. This was true of Jesus' ministry; it is also true for the Church across the ages. Some hear, grow and live. Others, for various reasons, do not.

In Romans 7 Paul has demonstrated how the Law could never deliver the righteous life that it laid before people. In fact it ended up condemning people. But Christians are not condemned and a righteous life is possible because God has sent his Son (Romans 8:3), setting them free from slavery to sin and death and fulfilling all that the Law intended for God's people (Romans 8:4). However there is still a battle on. Human beings, even Christians, are still troubled by sinful thoughts and desires and the Spirit is in conflict with this state of affairs. But Christians are on the winning side! The Spirit gives power to live that life (Romans 8:9). Indeed he is the same Spirit who raised Jesus from the dead (Romans 8:11). That's real power!

Beginning the service

If you have enough space, ask everyone to arrange themselves in order of age, in a line looping round the church. Or have a group of 10–12 (chosen beforehand) at the front arranged in order of age. Ask them to put up their hands if they can do the following and add other abilities, as appropriate:

- Tie their own shoelaces
- Read
- Ride a bike
- Drive a car

Point out that as we grow we are able to do more things. Ask some of the younger ones what they most want to do when they grow up. Ask some of the older ones what are the benefits and the problems of growing up.

Sing 'Praise my soul the King of Heaven', pointing out the imagery of verse 4: like flowers we grow, we flourish, we die, but God never changes.

Bible reading

The first part of the reading from Matthew 13:1–9 lends itself readily to a series of mimes by the whole congregation – see below. Someone at the front will need to demonstrate the mime. Alternatively, a few people could practise the mime for everyone's benefit. This version is taken from the CEV. The congregation is seated at the start.

> That same day Jesus left the house and went out beside Lake Galilee, where he sat down to teach.
> Such large crowds gathered around him that he had to sit in a boat, while the people stood on the shore.
> Then he taught them many things by using stories. He said:
> A farmer went out to scatter seed in a field. *(Stand. Mime scattering seed.)*
> While the farmer was scattering the seed, some of it fell along the road and was eaten by birds. *(Mime birds swooping.)*
> Other seeds fell on thin, rocky ground and... *(Crouch down.)*
> ... quickly started growing because the soil wasn't very deep. *(Leap up quickly.)*
> But when the sun came up, the plants were scorched and dried up, because they did not have enough roots. *(Shrivel up.)*
> Some other seeds fell where thorn bushes grew up and choked the plants. *(Half congregation (seeds) grow slowly. Half (weeds) grow quickly and choke seeds who die.)*
> But a few seeds did fall on good ground ... *(Everyone grows as tall as they can.)* ... where the plants produced a hundred or sixty or thirty times as much as was scattered. *(Wave arms to show fruit.)*
> And Jesus concluded, "Listen, then, if you have ears, pay attention! *(Congregation sit for the remainder of reading.)*
> Matthew 13:1–9 (CEV)

Then read Matthew 13:18–23.

Introduce the reading of Romans 8:1–11 by explaining that Paul was describing what it means to live by the Spirit, bearing fruit.

Bible talk

With: some actors with relevant props; an envelope; a symbolic post box; a flip chart and pens; some chairs for an obstacle course; a blindfold; a large pile of empty boxes

Begin with an improvised drama. The leader stands at the front holding an envelope. One or two people pass by with an iPod and earphones in their ears or playing with a mobile phone. The leader asks, 'Could you take this letter to the post box for me?' They pass without hearing. Another person passes and is asked the same question. They agree but before taking it someone shouts, 'Ere, I want a word with you,' and the person runs off. The next person passes and agrees to take the letter but wanders off, getting distracted by talking to someone else (this could be someone in the front row of the congregation). They put the letter down and go off having forgotten it. The leader sighs and picks up the letter. The final person is asked to take the letter and posts it.

On a flip chart write down the answers from the following brief brainstorm:

- What things stop us from **hearing** what God is telling us?
- What things stop us from **doing** what God is telling us?

Draw parallels with the reading from Matthew 13, the different way in which the seeds are received that leads on to the different ways that people hear and respond to God's message.

Invite someone to the front who has recently learnt to do something like tying shoelaces, riding a bike or mastering a computer programme. Ask how they finally managed to succeed. Draw out the idea that to succeed we need to:

- Be clear what we are trying to do.
- Keep on until we succeed.
- Know that God will help us.

Apply this by explaining that if we are to follow Jesus Christ, as Paul said, we need to:

- Know what God wants us to do. (Expand on this to include belonging to a church community and reading the Bible.)
- Keep on trying even when we fail. This is the way we go on learning and grow to bear fruit.
- Rely on God's Spirit to help us – which Paul explained in the reading from Romans 8.

Illustrate this final point by asking someone to move a large pile of boxes from the back of the church to the front. They need to do this in two journeys. Give them directions that take them all round the building carrying just a few of the boxes. After this first journey to the front, ask if they would like some help. With several helpers, and maybe even using a wheelbarrow, give similar instructions that need to be listened to as they go round the building, but the task should be completed with one more journey. Explain that although we struggle to do things on our own, if we listen to what needs to be done and accept an offer of help, a task becomes much easier. God gives us clear instructions about how he wants us to live and we need to obey them. But we also have the Holy Spirit within us to help us listen and obey, however tough life may seem. Encourage everyone to read aloud together Romans 8:9–11.

Prayer activity

With: sunflower or pumpkin seeds; a tub of soil

Give everyone a sunflower or pumpkin seed.

Explain that each seed stands for someone who has heard the message of Jesus but has not yet responded. Ask everyone to think of someone like this, which could include friends at school, neighbours, work colleagues, or a group of people whom the church community has a particular concern for (such as those in a parents and toddlers' group or a lunchtime school club). Lead in a prayer asking God to help them respond to him.

Invite everyone to bring their seed to the front to plant in a tub of soil. As they do this, each person could say, 'Help me to help them respond to you, Lord God.'

Prayer of confession

Use this responsive prayer (YearA.Proper10_1), which is also available from www.scriptureunion.org.uk/lightdownloads.

Dear Lord
We are sorry for when we have opportunities to learn and don't pay attention.
Lord, help us to listen, help us to grow, help us to live for you.
We are sorry that when we know what we should do, we are afraid of what our friends might say and don't do it.
Lord, help us to listen, help us to grow, help us to live for you.
We are sorry when we think that living for you is too difficult and don't do what we know we should.
Lord, help us to listen, help us to grow, help us to live for you.
We are sorry that so often we just allow ourselves to get distracted by all the good

things we have – computer games, iPods, friends and family, work, having fun – and forget about living for you.
Lord, help us to listen, help us to grow, help us to live for you.
We thank you that you go on loving us despite our faults. We ask you to forgive us and give us a fresh start today.
Lord, help us to listen, help us to grow, help us to live for you.

Ending the service

Use a hymn or song of commitment like 'Be the God of all my Sundays' or 'O Jesus, I have promised'. As it is being sung, encourage people to come and collect a seed (see **Prayer activity**) from the front and take it away with a promise to pray during the week for the person they thought of.

Helpful extras

Music and song ideas
'Lord for the years' picks up the theme of God's Word (verse 2) and the distractions that cause us to ignore it – 'Spirits oppressed by pleasure, wealth and care' (verse 3). Although it's not harvest, the hymn 'Fair waved the golden corn' is a prayer for growth in our lives. 'Be the God of all my Sundays' picks up the idea of taking what we gain on Sunday out into the world every day. The tune is the familiar Ode to Joy. Other songs could include: 'Lord of all hopefulness'; 'O Jesus, I have promised'; 'I'm special because God has loved me'; 'God in my living'.

Play the song or show a clip of 'The Ugly Duckling' from the film *Hans Christian*

Andersen with Danny Kaye. Explain that he became what he was always intended to be. That's what God wants for us. But sin prevents this, so it's only in Jesus that we can become what we are meant to be. Even when we become a Christian we are not the finished article. Like the Ugly Duckling, we still have a lot of growing to do.

Game

Compile a series of images of young and adult animals and birds, which can be run in a fast-moving sequence, for example lamb/sheep, tadpole/frog, caterpillar/butterfly, seed/flower, etc. Have the images in random order with adult images separated from juvenile ones. Once the sequence has been shown ask the congregation to form groups and list as many of the young and old pairs that they can recall seeing. This explores the idea of growing and changing.

Notes and comments

Explain the mime before the start of the **Bible reading**. You may wish to practise quickly the various elements. You will need to divide the congregation into two (roughly equal) parts to be weeds and seeds. This could be male and female. Or quickly number people off, weed, seed, weed, seed, etc. Don't use left and right hand side because the weeds and seeds should be mixed up together.

Images of adults and juveniles for the **Game** can be found on Google Images. Type in caterpillar, or butterfly, etc. (Don't search on the word 'adult' unless you have a very good filter!)

The improvised drama that starts the **Bible talk** could be done with different people for each character or by a leader and two actors who play all the other parts. Make up your own dialogue to suit those taking part. Use any particular fears or distractions that may be relevant to your congregation.

'The Ugly Duckling' clip is available on YouTube (search for Ugly Duckling Danny Kaye) for those tech-savvy enough to use it.

Alternative online options

Visit www.lightlive.org for additional activities for children, young people and adults.

PROPER 11

READINGS: Isaiah 44:6–8; Matthew 13:24–30,36–43
Psalm 86:11–17; Romans 8:12–15

Bible foundations

**Aim: to explore what it means to be different, as children of God, in a
world that does not acknowledge Christ**

To be a member of God's people means you are different. This has never changed.
When Isaiah prophesied to Israel, he emphasised how God is completely unique.
Nothing can stand alongside him (Isaiah 44:6–8). No wonder he makes it clear that
his people should be no less unique. Their experiences and behaviour are simply
not like that of other people. Paul understood that completely. In fact, he says
that Christians are obliged to be different and live according to the promptings
of God's Spirit (Romans 8:12–14). That, indeed, is how they will know that they
belong to God and have the dignity of becoming his children and heirs of all that
is to come (Romans 8:15–17). This may well entail suffering. Isaiah was addressing
the experience of Israel as they went into exile and suffered the effective loss
of everything and all security. For Paul, suffering was a hallmark of Jesus, and his
followers could expect no less. If the Master was misunderstood, opposed, rejected,
deserted, betrayed and finally done to death, can his followers expect anything
much less? In fact, Christians live lives that are part of the general sufferings of this
age. They will be recognised for who they truly are at the start of the new creation
when God makes all things new.

According to Jesus in the Parable of the Weeds (Matthew 13:24–30,36–43), it is
impossible to separate out the good from the bad before this final harvest. This
parable clearly expands upon the Parable of the Sower (Matthew 13:1–23) – see
last Sunday. In God's field both good seed and bad is sown. It may not be obvious
which is which, nor possible to separate good from bad, until it is harvest time. As
in Romans 8:12–15, God's people live in the midst of suffering and overwhelming
opposition. But in the final analysis they will triumph. They will suffer and be
unrecognised, but God sees, preserves and faithfully brings them to share in his
glory.

Beginning the service

With: pieces of single-colour card (two colours only); safety pins (optional); photos of people of different nationalities who all share the same skin colour – a PowerPoint (YearA.Proper11_2) is available from www. scriptureunion.org.uk/lightdownloads

As people come into the service give out small pieces of card in two colours only. People are to hide these in their pockets or you could even give them a safety pin so that they can pin the piece of card to the inside of their coat, trousers, inside pocket. They are not to tell anyone what colour they have. If you use hymn books or song books you could hide one piece of card in each book before it is given out. The object of this is to be able to separate the congregation into two parts in a way that is not too obvious. This will be used in the **Bible talk**.

Begin by showing the photos or PowerPoint of people from different nationalities but with the same skin colour. Discuss how you can tell (or cannot tell) which nationalities they hold. Often it is difficult to tell what people are like inside. When we first meet a group of people everyone may initially look very similar. You might be able to tell who is rich or poor, who is healthy or not healthy, but you cannot tell who is musical or artistic or… invite a mixture of musicians and non-musicians to the front to demonstrate this point. You have to allow time to get to know people to know what they are like inside. Talk about how, just by looking, you cannot easily tell what people are like or what is their identity.

Bible reading

The reading from Isaiah 44:6–8 contains many strong statements about God's timeless and awesome power in the face of Israel's disaster. It lends itself to a choral reading as follows (using the CEV). This reading (YearA.Proper11_1) is available from www. scriptureunion.org.uk/lightdownloads.

Voice 1:	I am the LORD All-Powerful,
Voice 2:	the first and the last,
Voice 3:	the one and only God.
Voices 1,2:	Israel, I have rescued you! I am your King.
Voice 3:	Can anyone compare with me? If so, let them speak up and tell me now.
Voice 1:	Let them say what has happened since I made my nation long ago,
Voice 2:	and let them tell what is going to happen.
Voice 3:	Don't tremble with fear!
Voices 1,3:	Didn't I tell you long ago?
Voices 1,2,3:	Didn't you hear me?
(*Pause*)	
Voice 1:	I… (*with Voice* 2) alone (*three voices*) am God – no one else is a mighty rock.
	Isaiah 44:6–8 (CEV)

The reading from Matthew 13 could be read as a dramatic reading. If you are going to tell the story in the **Bible talk**, read Psalm 86:11–17 instead, as another statement of God's protection from the enemy.

Bible talk

With: small pieces of single-colour card (two colours only); safety pins; a collection of wild plants (a mixture of what we would call non-weeds and weeds); a really large badge made with one of the colours of the cards above (given out earlier) with 'WELCOME' written across the middle as well as a bit of scribble on the badge that will need to be covered up by card of the same colour being stuck onto it; glue; rubbish bin; photos of people of different nationalities who all share the same skin colour – a PowerPoint (YearA.Proper11_2) is available from www. scriptureunion.org.uk/lightdownloads

If you have not already used the PowerPoint and other ideas in **Beginning the service**, establishing the hidden differences of people, do so now. You will already have handed out the different pieces of card.

Show the plants and ask how you can tell which of these are good, fruit-bearing plants and which are weeds. One dictionary definition of a weed is, 'A wild (not deliberately cultivated) plant growing where it is not wanted'. People may choose to disagree, but establish the point that for a farmer there are some things that grow in their fields that they do not want. It is not always obvious and these unwanted plants may be hard to get rid of.

If you have not already done so, tell the story of the weeds among the wheat. Initially it may have been hard to tell which was which but over time they all grew together and it was difficult to separate them. But the fruitful plants were different from the weeds. It was only when the time came to harvest the whole field that the separation between the weeds and the wheat could happen. The weeds were destroyed.

Jesus told this story to demonstrate that there are those living in the world who belong to him and those who don't. Everyone rubs along together and you cannot always tell who is who. But God knows, and at the end of time there will be a division between those who belong to him and those who don't. At this point, bring out the giant badge. Ask everyone what colour it is and then invite everyone to look inside their pockets, trousers, or jackets to see if they have a colour that matches. If they do, invite them to stick their piece of card onto the large badge to cover up the scribbling, but not the word 'WELCOME'. Everyone with the other colour of card cannot help and the best thing they can do is throw their piece of card away – it is useless! They could come to the front to put their wrong colour in a rubbish bin.

Explain that no one knew which colour card was the colour that was of any use when they came into church. But the leader knew although they did not know who had got which colour! The farmer knew which plants were weeds and which were not, although probably not when they first started growing. We do not always know who are the people who belong to Jesus and who are not, but we do know whether or not we ourselves love Jesus. If appropriate, explain what it means to belong to Jesus and invite people to talk with a church or children's and youth leader and/or offer a booklet for any who would like to know more. Scripture Union produces Me+Jesus, one of a series of booklets for children and young people. For more details visit the Scripture Union website.

Prayers of intercession

Many people find it a challenge to work, study, or live among those who scorn the Christian faith. It would be good to use this time to ask God to help people in situations like this, making the words of Isaiah 44 real for them. We live in a world of other faiths and also a very secular world. You could invite someone to share their situation and ask for specific needs for prayer.

Helpful extras

Music and song ideas

Relevant songs include: 'Our God is an awesome God, he reigns from heaven above'; 'Our God is an awesome God and he's full of amazing wonderful love'; 'From the highest of heights'; 'Be bold, be strong'; 'Fight the good fight'; 'He who would valiant be'. Singing a song which is a round or is easily sung in two parts would reinforce the theme of the service, for example 'The Lord's my shepherd' (Stuart Townend).

Game

Devise a game in which people are sorted into two groups, and only two – to relate to weeds and fruitful plants. This could include: those who were born in your town and those who have moved in; those who go to school (including staff in a school) and those who don't; those who had breakfast and those who didn't; those who came to church last week and those who didn't. Explain that we cannot always tell who has said, or done, what, just by looking at them. We need to allow time to pass and also get to know them. The leader can talk about knowing who has had breakfast in their home because they know the people who live there; they may know who was in church last week, or they may have a guess at who does or does not go to school, but they may not know who has lived in the town all their lives. People can be asked to stand up with the first option of a suggested group. Alternatively, a large group of people could come to the front and walk either to the left or the right depending on which option applies to them.

Ending the service

Since this has been a service of sorting people into two groups, it would be fitting to divide people once more so that they can ask God to bless the other half that they do not belong to. The split could be in terms of age, gender, people who live in one part of the town, even people who are wearing blue and black (and the rest).

All together say: **Thank you, Lord, that you are All-powerful**.
One group says: May the All-powerful God be with you, the (women and girls/people wearing black/left-handed people, etc.) this week.
The other group says the same, filling in the gap with the description of the alternate group.
All together: (*loudly*) Amen!

Notes and comments

Jesus' words of a fiery furnace and gnashing of teeth are very graphic as a means of describing just how awful it is going to be for those who do not know Christ at the end of time. However literally you may take this to be, it emphasises the importance of the message that Jesus was teaching.

However, this is not an opportunity to sort out who does or does not belong to Christ, because that is not always obvious (and it's not our job, but God's)! But it is a challenge to everyone to consider where they stand with God. Paul's words in Romans 8:12–15 speak of the role of the Holy Spirit assuring us that we are God's children. You may wish to expand on this.

If you are using this outline as part of a baptism service, invite adult candidates to talk about how they have chosen to belong to Christ's kingdom, separating themselves from identifying with the evil one. Parents and godparents or sponsors of younger children could also share their own experience of being separated from those who do not belong to Christ. Link this

into the actual words that are said in the baptismal part of the service.

It is interesting to ask people when they first became aware that they knew God. Was it when they were under 10, 11–14, 15–25 or older? Often when this is suggested, it is amazing how many people in church were aware of their relationship with Jesus before they reached the age of 14. This is a challenge about the importance of youth and children's work. If you do ask about this, pray for your children and young people and those who work with them.

Alternative online options

Visit www.lightlive.org for additional activities for children, young people and adults.

PROPER 12

READINGS: **Psalm 119:129–136; Romans 8:26–39**
1 Kings 3:5–12; Matthew 13:31–33,44–52

Bible foundations

Aim: to celebrate the hope that God has promised us in Christ

Hope is in short supply in the twenty-first century. Positive thinking and developing
a strong self-image masquerade for substantial hope. Lasting hope can only be found
in the God who is alpha and omega, who knows the beginning from the end and
who can be known and related to. That is why the writer of Psalm 119 didn't stint
upon expressing his joy at God's word. These are the oracles of God, the Almighty's
very words, which reveal him and teach his followers how to live to please him.
There is hope because the psalmist puts his trust in a trustworthy God. No wonder
he is glad! Jesus picks up that sense of hope and anticipation in the parables of
the treasure and the pearl merchant (Matthew 13:44–46). Once the man and the
merchant discovered what they had hoped for, they sacrificed everything to acquire
it.

As Paul reaches one of the climaxes of his letter to the Romans, his confidence is
not in himself. Nor is he full of wishful thinking. His trust and his hope are in God.
God's Spirit supports believers in their deepest difficulties, including those moments
when even prayer itself seems impossible (Romans 8:26–27). It is the Spirit who
works together with the believer for their good. He works along with believers to
bring about the very best they could possibly hope for. Nothing in all of creation
can separate believers from their God (Romans 8:29–31). The proof of God's
trustworthiness is that he has not even stopped short of giving up his own Son.
No wonder Paul is triumphant in his assertion that the hope of Christians is totally
secure (Romans 8:33–39).

Beginning the service

Psalm 119:129–136 is the set psalm for today. Use the following verses as a call to worship, with everyone joining in with the emboldened words. These verses (YearA. Proper12_1) are also available from www.scriptureunion.org.uk/lightdownloads.

> Your teachings are wonderful,
> **and I respect them all.**
> Understanding your word brings light to the minds of ordinary people.
> **I honestly want to know everything you teach.**
> Think about me and be kind,
> **just as you are to everyone who loves your name.**
> Smile on me, your servant,
> **and teach me your laws.**
> Psalm 119:129–132,135 (CEV)

Bible reading

Romans 8:28 from the TNIV is available as a PowerPoint (YearA.Proper12_2) from www. scriptureunion.org.uk/lightdownloads, which could be shown during the reading. This is used in the **Bible talk** and comes in several versions: i) the whole verse, ii) with words going missing (as it is memorised), and iii) a version where just the word 'love' is missing (YearA.Proper12_4). The wording of Romans 8:28 on the PowerPoint is: We know that in all things God works for those who love him, who have been called according to his purpose.

Use part of the reading from Psalm 119 in **Beginning the service** as a call to worship, see above.

Bible talk

With: Romans 8:28 written out on a large sheet of paper or use the downloadable version (YearA.Proper12_2), see above; the words 'Promise', 'Love' and 'Purpose' written out on three cards that are rainbow, heart and arrow shaped respectively (also to use in the **Prayer activity**), or use the shape outlines (YearA.Proper12_3) available from www.scriptureunion.org.uk/lightdownloads; Romans 8:28 written in sets of words on card cut out for groups to rearrange in the correct order – note the missing word 'love' in the download (YearA.Proper12_4)

The focus of today's talk is around learning and knowing the words of Romans 8:28. There are various parts to the talk, which could either be used together, or are more likely to be interspersed with songs or other items. They should be used in the order suggested here.

- Learn and remember PowerPoint
- Talk 1 – Promise
- Activity – Organise word cards into order (omitting the word 'love')
- Talk 2 – Love
- Talk 3 – Purpose
- Prayer response – rainbow, heart and arrow cards

Learn and remember Romans 8:28, from Paul's letter to the Romans. If possible, use the Learn and remember verse PowerPoint. This shows the whole verse and then a series where blank spaces appear, as different words are missed off. Can people remember the missing words? Alternatively, if you are not using PowerPoint, arrange the same sort of thing with a whiteboard, or in other ways, for example putting the words of the verse onto individual cards, hanging them on a washing line and then removing them one at a time.

Talk 1 – Promise

The first talk should only last a couple of minutes. Show the word 'Promise' either by PowerPoint or on a rainbow-shaped card. Explain that the verse you have learnt is a promise from God. (You could explain the significance of a rainbow as a sign of God's promise to Noah.) Through Paul, God was speaking his word to his original readers and also to us today. So it is God who tells us that 'in all things everything works together for the good'.

Ask everyone to think how it feels to make a promise – serious, special, etc. Ask how it feels to have a promise made to you – precious, personal, etc. Use either of these suggestions, or the suggestions that come from the congregation, to describe how God's promises are similar in the way they are made to us. God is serious, and his promises are special. They are precious and personal too. Encourage each person to think about the words of Romans 8:28 and to imagine Paul standing in front of them, telling them this promise of God, as if just for them.

Activity

Distribute the words of Romans 8:28 (omit the word 'love' on card 8 if you are using 12 cards, see below, TNIV). You will either need to print the words from the PDF or make your own sets – enough sets for one between six people. If you make your own, it is better not to put all 24 words on individual cards (there will be too many to arrange) but break the verse down as below:

Romans 8:28 / We know / that in / all things / God works / for the good / of those who _____ / him, / who have / been called / according to / his purpose

Mix up the cards before asking the groups to work together to rearrange them on the floor or on a pew. They should notice that the word 'love' has been missed out. Don't tell anyone this before asking them to complete the task, but let them point it out to you when they have completed it. If no one notices, say this yourself. Use this as a link into Talk 2, but thank everyone for managing to complete the task, despite the difficulty.

Talk 2 – Love

At the start of the second talk explain that when love is missing, the promise is incomplete. Show the word either by PowerPoint or on the heart-shaped card. Read the promise once again (Romans 8:28) and notice together that 'all things work together for the good of those who love him'. Say how important loving God is. It is not enough just to know we are loved by him – he wants us to love him in return. If there has been a wedding recently in your church family, use this to illustrate the relationship that promises and love have to one another. When we love someone we make them promises. God is like that too – his promise is based on his love for us, but it is also reliant on us loving him. If you have used Psalm 119, read verse 132, which says 'Think about me and be kind, just as you are to everyone who loves your name', as a way of strengthening the point.

215

Talk 3 – Purpose

God's promise to each of us is made because he loves us, but it is important for us to love him too. This is not because he would not want the best for us, but because when we love him, we are better able to understand what his purpose for us is. Show the word either on PowerPoint or on the arrow-shaped card. Point out that when people love one another they tend to know what the other person would choose. If you have not done so already, you could play the Mr and Mrs **Game**.

Conclude by making the point that if we love God we are better able to understand his purpose and direction for our lives. Knowing what God wants us to do is vitally important – he has a purpose for our lives and loves it when we find that out and get stuck in! Summarise the three talks, using the words 'Promise', 'Love' and 'Purpose'.

Prayer activity

With: prepared rainbow, heart and arrow-shaped cards (YearA.Proper12_3) available from www.scriptureunion.org.uk/lightdownloads

Ask a group of people to prepare prayers that are symbolised by each of the shaped cards.

Rainbow: Thank God for his promises and his trustworthiness, especially…
Heart: Thank God for his love for us and how he helps us love him and others, especially praying for those who need to know God's love, including…
Arrow: Thank God that he has a purpose

for our lives and guides us, especially those who are facing decisions at the moment including…

Prayer of confession

Invite people to join in the following emboldened words. Use as many other voices as appropriate.

Leader: Lord, you have promised to forgive us when we come to you and say that we are sorry for the wrong we do. We come now, knowing that we need to be forgiven, and are ready to say we are sorry.
Voice 1: We are sorry for the times when we forget that you know us and care for us.
All: Forgive us, Lord.
Voice 2: We are sorry for the times when we forget to trust your promises.
All: Forgive us, Lord.
Voice 3: We are sorry for the times when we forget that you are working in all the things that happen in our lives.
All: Forgive us, Lord.
Voice 4: We are sorry for the times when we forget to love you.
All: Forgive us, Lord.
Voice 5: We are sorry for the times when we forget to follow you.
All: Forgive us, Lord.
Voice 6: We are sorry for the times when we don't recognise that you have a purpose for our lives.
All: Forgive us, Lord.
Leader: Loving God, help us to remember that in all things you work for our good as we love you, and as we follow your purposes for each of us. Let us remember that God hears us, sees our hearts, and grants us forgiveness.

All: Amen.

Ending the service

Encourage people to read the words of
Romans 8:28 together, one more time.
Then encourage them to try really hard to
remember it this week, looking for ways that
God's promise is fulfilled. Remember to ask
them next week how they got on!

Helpful extras

Music and song ideas

Songs on this theme include: 'In every
day that dawns (I'm grateful)'; 'There is a
Redeemer'; 'I want to serve the purpose of
God'; 'I'm gonna worship my God (He's so
cool)' from *Reach Up!* CD (SU); 'All I once
held dear' fits well after the Talk 2 about love,
as a lead into Talk 3 about purpose; 'Jesus, be
the centre' fits well into Talk 3.

Game

A short game of Mr and Mrs should illustrate
the point in **Bible Talk** 3 that when you
know someone well you probably know what
they like or dislike! Invite a couple out to the
front, and ask one of them to leave the room.
Ask the remaining person questions like:

- When out for a two-course meal in a
  restaurant, would your partner prefer a
  starter or a dessert?
- Which does your partner do first in the

morning – brush their teeth or brush
their hair?
- If your partner had tickets for a show
  in London would they choose *The
  Sound of Music* or *Billy Elliot*? (change as
  appropriate)

Invite the other person back into the room
and ask them how they would answer the
three (or more) questions. This should
illustrate the point!

Notes and comments

The **Bible reading** from Romans 8 is quite
hard for an all-age worship service. Whoever
reads it will need to practise it beforehand.
Once it has been read, you may feel it is
appropriate to explain briefly some of the
harder concepts, but bring people's minds
clearly to the verse that today's teaching is
focused around, verse 28.

For the Mr and Mrs **Game** during the **Bible
talk**, make sure you have asked a couple in
advance whether they would be happy to
take part.

Alternative online options

Visit www.lightlive.org for additional
activities for children, young people and
adults.

PROPER 13

READINGS: **Romans 9:1–5; Matthew 14:13–21**
Isaiah 55:1–5; Psalm 145:8,9,14–21

17/8/14

Bible foundations

Aim: to celebrate the way God generously provides for us

One of the greatest themes of Scripture is God's special choice (election) of a
people to be his own, to worship and obey him and to receive his blessing, provision
and protection for ever. He chose the people of Israel not because they were the
biggest and best but simply because that was his sovereign decision; he had made a
promise to their ancestors and he loved them (Deuteronomy 7:7–11). Fundamental
to this theme is that he is an unfailingly generous and loving God (Deuteronomy
8:1–20). The people of Israel were encouraged by God to expect that, if they kept
his commandments, they would be blessed, both spiritually and materially, way
beyond what they could have hoped for.

At the time of Jesus it was expected that when the Messiah came he would
inaugurate a time of incredible blessing on all levels. Each of the four Gospels
records the incident we refer to as the feeding of the 5,000 (Matthew 14:13–21).
It is a fantastic miracle and clearly made a great impact on Jesus' followers simply
at the level of miraculously providing food. However, there is more to it than
that. Most Jews knew their ancestral history very well and would have detected
the resonances with how God had miraculously fed them in the wilderness
(Deuteronomy 8:3,16). John 6 brings out this deeper meaning very well as the
author describes how Jesus moved on to talk about himself as the Bread of Life.
The twelve baskets left over recall in a strange way the twelve tribes of Israel who
constituted the people of God.

When Paul comes to write Romans, one of his main aims is to explain how God,
while not rejecting his people Israel, has made it possible for the Gentiles to
share in their blessing. At the beginning of Romans 9 Paul celebrates the fantastic
privileges accorded to Israel – adoption, divine glory, covenants, Law, temple,
promises and patriarchs. His deepest grief is that so few of them seemed prepared
to acknowledge the Messiah now that he had come.

Beginning the service

Start the service with the following sketch (YearA.Proper13_4) that is also available from www.scriptureunion.org.uk/lightdownloads.

Four men are sitting in the waiting room of a hospital. It is the maternity unit. They are all reading books that had been placed on the table. It is important that the congregation does not see the covers of the books.
Nurse: (*Offstage*) Mr Smith? (*Nurse enters the room.*) Ah, there you are. I've got some wonderful news for you. Your wife has given birth to a beautiful baby boy!
Mr Smith: Oh, fantastic. Can I go in and see her?
Nurse: Of course. Come and meet your new son. (*They both walk off stage.*)
Mr Jones: I'm so nervous. I couldn't stay in there. (*Looking towards the ward*) I would have been a right nuisance. (*The nurse walks in again.*)
Nurse: Mr Jones. Your wife has given birth to two lovely girls – twins! Come and see them! (*Mr Jones gives the other two remaining fathers a worried look and walks off with the nurse. After two seconds, she rushes back in and taps one of the remaining men on the shoulder.*)
Nurse: Triplets!
Mr Morris: Oh my word. (*He puts his head in his hands.*)
Nurse: Come along then!
(*They walk off stage, and the one remaining father carries on reading. The nurse walks back in and he gives her a worried look. However, she's just come in to tidy up the books.*)
Nurse: That's funny. Mr Smith was reading **One** *Flew Over The Cuckoo's Nest*, and his wife had **one** baby, and Mrs Jones had **two** babies while her husband was reading *A Tale Of* **Two** *Cities*. And Mr Morris was reading *The* **Three** *Musketeers*, and his wife had **three** babies. Erm, what are you reading?
(*The remaining father looks at the cover of his book and dramatically collapses to the floor gasping and holding his heart. (Remember to make this funny!) The nurse picks up the book.*)
Nurse: Oh no! (*She shows the audience the book*) Jesus feeds the **5,000**!

Explain that the light-hearted nature of this sketch is in keeping with the theme of the service, a celebration of all of God's generous provision for us and a thanksgiving for his blessings. The feeding of the 5,000 is evidence of God's attention to our individual needs.

Explain that God cares for his children just as a parent cares for a newborn baby (in fact, even more so). Ask parents to think about how they felt when they first held one of their children. They would have felt an overwhelming love and a desire to do anything for them – but they might have been scared stiff with the responsibility! God longs to bless his children, and does so in many different ways.

Bible reading

Matthew 14:13–21 is a very well-known story, so read it from a contemporary Bible translation such as *The Message* to enable people to hear it in a fresh way.

Invite people to follow Romans 9:1–5 in their own Bibles, or Bibles in the pews, if at all possible.

Bible retelling

As an alternative to reading Matthew 14:13–21 you could read a retold version of the story from one of the *Must Know Stories* books, see page 157. These are the ten Bible stories voted as the ones that must be passed on to the next generation. They are available for adults as *Must Know Stories*, for 8s and over as *The 10 Must Know Stories* and for 8s and under in *The Green Book of Must Know Stories* and *The Red Book of Must Know Stories*. For more details, visit www. scriptureunion.org.uk.

The version 'And the rest' (YearA.Proper13_ 1) from the over-8s book *The 10 Must Know Stories* is available from www.scriptureunion. org.uk/lightdownloads. It is important to emphasise that this is a fictional retelling of the event, and not an accurate detailed account. The story itself is true!

Bible talk

The story of when Jesus fed over 5,000 people is one of the most dramatic events in history. It is one of the greatest, and certainly one of the best-known miracles, performed by Jesus, the Son of God. It is no ordinary tale. Therefore, the tone of the talk needs to be of a celebratory nature, emphasising the wonder of God's care for his children.

Go through Matthew 14:13–21 and explain the events of the miracle in detail. It is easy for people to be blasé about such a familiar passage, so this approach should help to remind them of how amazing this event was.

Explain that Jesus initially went to a place to rest on his own (verse 13). He had heard about the beheading of John the Baptist and had gone to lie low for a while and probably to grieve. He was also no doubt glad of a rest, which was something he wouldn't have experienced too often with 12 disciples and crowds around him. However, when he saw that a crowd had followed him, he had compassion on them. This point must be emphasised. Most people in Jesus' position would have told them to leave him in peace – not Jesus. Even though he was putting himself at risk (given what had happened to John) he chose to help and heal, not because of any obligation. He simply wanted to.

Explain to the congregation that the feeding of over 5,000 people is so well-known that it is easy to forget the context of the events. Evening was approaching and the disciples advised Jesus to tell everyone to go home. After all, the crowd had come to him for healing, not for dinner! Point out that Jesus did not have to feed them. But again, he chose to do so.

This miracle also shows the power of Jesus. Jesus could have thought 'Oh I see. Let's forget the whole food thing', when he discovered that only five loaves and two fish were at his disposal. But he doesn't even flinch. He gets on with the job, and everyone in the crowd eats and eats until they are stuffed! Nothing is impossible for God. His will cannot be stifled by circumstance, and his will is to bless his children. This needs to be highlighted.

It might be useful to end by stating that this miracle was performed for Jews, but even this could not bring the people of Israel to reconciliation with God. Romans 9:1–5 tells of Paul's frustration with Israel's disobedience towards God. Jesus was a Jew and preached to Jews and engaged with the Jewish authorities. But they did not all respond positively to Jesus. It is easy, therefore, for believers, both Jews and non-Jews, to forget what God has done for them. It is important for us to focus continuously on God's blessings upon our lives.

Prayer activity

With: lots of paper cut into fish and bread shapes (templates (YearA.Proper13_2) available from www.scriptureunion.org.uk/lightdownloads); up to 12 baskets; pens

Before the service, prepare enough pieces of paper cut into fish and bread shapes so that each person can have at least one of each. Divide everyone into mixed-age groups, with about six to eight people in each group. Give each group a selection of fish and bread shapes and some pens.

Encourage people to think of some things that God has provided them with. On the bread shape they write or draw anything God provides that is essential for our needs, such as food and water. On the fish they write or draw the extra things that God generously gives us, such as family and friends. Invite people to share ideas within their group, and to say short prayers of thanks for all the things God provides for us.

Ask for 12 volunteers (or less if your church is small) to collect all the fish and bread in the baskets to bring to the front. Show how much 'food' has been collected, symbolic of how generous God is and how much we have to be thankful for.

See **Notes and comments** for a creative way to make use of the fish and bread after they have been collected.

Prayer of confession

This prayer (YearA.Proper13_3) using the words of Psalm 145 with a response after each section is available from www.scriptureunion.org.uk/lightdownloads.

> **All: Lord, we are sorry for the times when we have not recognised that you give us what we need and have taken your good gifts for granted.**
> Voice 1: The LORD is gracious and compassionate, slow to anger and rich in love.
> **All: Lord, we are sorry for the times when we have not looked after the gifts you have given us, using them thoughtlessly.**
> Voice 2: The LORD is good to all; he has compassion on all he has made.
> **All: Forgive us, Lord, for ignoring the needs of others, and for selfishly thinking only of what we want and need.**
> Voice 1: The LORD upholds all those who fall and lifts up all who are bowed down.
> **All: Forgive us, Lord, for our greed and wastefulness, when so many people in our world are starving.**
> Voice 2: The eyes of all look to you, and you give them their food at the proper time.
> **All: Help us, Lord, to be thankful for the good things you provide, and give us wisdom to use them well.**
> Voice 1: You open your hand and satisfy the desires of every living thing.
> **All: Help us, Lord, to be generous with our resources, remembering**

the needs of others and not just our own.

Voice 2: The LORD is righteous in all his ways and loving towards all he has made.

All: My mouth will speak in praise of the Lord. Let every creature praise his holy name for ever and ever. Amen.

based on Psalm 145

Ending the service

It is important to remember the blessings of God throughout the week and not just in church. Finish the service with a prayer such as this:

Lord Jesus, we thank you for all of your blessings in our lives.

You love to bless your children with good things, and today we have been reminded of all of your provision for us.

Lord, we truly thank you for this, and we are sorry for those times when we moan and forget about your blessings. You are a God who provides for us.

During this week, please enable us to think about your love for us. Help us to rest in that love and remember that we have so many more blessings to come, in this life and the next.

Amen.

Helpful extras

Music and song ideas

'5000+ hungry folk' by Ishmael is a good song for children on the theme of the feeding of the 5,000; another relevant song is 'Who took fish and bread?'; 'Praise God from whom all blessings flow'; 'He brought me to his banqueting table'; 'We really want to thank you, Lord'; 'Give thanks to the Lord, our God and King'; 'Come on and celebrate'.

'The Lord is gracious and compassionate' by Graham Ord is based on Psalm 145 and could be sung or played on CD after the **Prayer of confession.**

Notes and comments

Ask people to bring food to share with others. As it is summer in the northern hemisphere, you could hold a picnic in a suitable outdoor location. Alternatively, arrange a 'hunger lunch', where you serve a basic meal of soup and bread and ask people to give the money they would normally spend on their Sunday dinner to a charity.

After the fish and bread shapes from the **Prayer activity** have all been collected, they could be used to make a prayer collage to display in church as a reminder to be thankful for God's provision. If appropriate, children could begin making this during the **Bible talk** or worship time. If you are holding a lunch after the service, children could create the collage while food is being prepared or after eating it. Alternatively, this could be done during a children's midweek group and presented to the rest of the church on the following Sunday.

Alternative online options

Visit www.lightlive.org for additional activities for children, young people and adults.

PROPER 14

READINGS: I Kings 19:9–18; Matthew 14:22–33
Psalm 85:8–13; Romans 10:5–15

Bible foundations

Aim: to recognise the importance of trusting God, discovering just how trustworthy he is

'Trust' may seem a stronger word in English than 'faith', implying practical and applied action rather than simply what is assented to in the mind. Certainly Elijah trusted God when he encountered Ahab and then the prophets of Baal on Mount Carmel (I Kings 18). This tested his trust in God. But the threat from Ahab's wife, Jezebel, comes as the last straw to his strung out nervous system (I Kings 19). He flees, and runs into hiding. Like Job or Jeremiah, though things have got very bad and Elijah is at his wits' end, he has not lost his ability to believe and trust in God, however small the mustard seed of his faith (Matthew 17:20).

In fact, in what is often referred to as 'prevenient grace', God takes the initiative. That is always the case, and it is humanity's responsibility to respond to God's approach. Elijah turns to God if only to complain that things have turned out so badly. But that is enough, as it proves to be for Job, Jeremiah and many psalmists. It is the beginning of God's saving action. God reveals himself to Elijah and restores his vision and hope. God still has great things for Elijah to do (I Kings 19:15–18). Like all of us, he is saved for a purpose – to serve God, not to enjoy his own comfort or ease.

The experience of Peter and the other disciples in Matthew 14:22–33 is similarly terrifying to that of Elijah. Being God's servants is not for the faint-hearted (see Hebrews 12:28,29). To be out on the water at night was cause enough for basic courage but Jesus' appearance terrifies them (Matthew 14:26). Once again, however, an encounter with God leads not to destruction but to salvation and growth. Peter at least is wonderfully eager to throw himself into Jesus' care. His trust is amply rewarded as Jesus saves him from sinking. No one ever threw themselves into God's care to be lost.

223

Beginning the service

With: a rubber ring or a float to hold someone up in the water; flip chart; marker pen

Ask how many people in church can swim, even just a little?

Note the number down on the flip chart. Then ask the following questions and write the number of those who answer positively as a rough percentage of the number who can swim. (Ask a mathematician to help.)

- How many learnt to swim by being thrown in at the deep end?
- How many learnt to swim by someone standing with them in the pool?
- How many learnt to swim by someone instructing them from the side?
- How many learnt to swim by using a rubber ring or float?

Comment on the percentage of answers.

Learning to swim involves a lot of trust. Ask for suggestions as to the sort of trust involved (trusting a person, an instruction, a float or our own ability to float or make progress through the water). Explain that trust is the theme of this service.

Bible reading

Introduce the story in 1 Kings 19 by explaining that Elijah, the prophet, had been under extreme pressure as he stood up for God against the evil queen, Jezebel, and false prophets. Exhausted and scared he went away on his own and, 40 days later, God met him. Elijah had to trust that God knew best. As a confident reader reads the story,

another person could mime the different natural elements in verses 11–13.

Bible retelling

In addition to the **Bible reading** and **Bible talk**, you could use this interactive version of the story (YearA.Proper14_1) that is available from www.scriptureunion.org. uk/lightdownloads. This brings out the main features of Matthew 14:22–33 and engages the imaginations of younger members of the congregation.

Invite six volunteers to stand at the front to lead everyone else in actions and sounds as the story is read. Each time the word in bold is read, the volunteer to whom the action has been assigned leads everyone in the correct response. One action for each volunteer works well, so that people only have to listen out for one phrase. Explain that each volunteer responds to their phrase as soon as they hear it.

Volunteer 1: **calm** – say, 'Shhhhhh' to the person next to you, and put a finger to your lips.
Volunteer 2: **wind** – rub hands together and blow out air.
Volunteer 3: **waves** – say, 'Splish splash.'
Volunteer 4: **ghost** – make spooky 'whooooo' type noises.
Volunteer 5: **walking/walked** – give a short gasp and throw hands up in a gesture of surprise.
Volunteer 6: **Jesus** – shout, 'Hurrah!'

It was a lovely sunny evening at the end of an exciting day. All the people who had gone to listen to **Jesus** had seen an amazing miracle!

It had been a long day and everyone was hungry. So they were amazed when he had given them a picnic from just five small loaves and two fish. There were about 5,000 people, not including the women and children, so this was a lot of food for a lot of people! But now it was time for everybody to go home, and Jesus wanted to be alone to pray. He sent everyone off, including his friends, saying to them, 'Why don't you set sail across the lake, and I'll see you later.' That's what they did. Off they went across the calm Lake Galilee.

Jesus went up a hill to think and pray. He was up there a very long time.

But the disciples hadn't been long out from shore when Peter said, 'Feels like there's a wind starting to blow.' And sure enough there was. Soon they were rowing against a strong wind, blowing against them. They kept going, right through the night until about three o'clock in the morning. But the wind blew stronger and stronger; and the waves bounced the little boat up and down. The wind and waves got bigger and bigger, stronger and stronger, wetter and wetter. The disciples were very afraid, and utterly exhausted.

Peter screwed up his eyes and peered into the distance to see how far they were from land. Suddenly he spotted a sight that made his already exhausted legs turn to jelly. He had seen… a ghost! Now Jesus' disciples, including Peter, were fishermen, men of the open lake. Such men shared stories on long dark nights of people drowning at sea and stories about ghosts that came out in winds and storms. And right now Peter was seeing a ghost! It couldn't be anything else but a ghost walking across the waves. All

the disciples screamed, until a voice drifted across to them: 'Don't worry! It's just me! Don't be afraid!'

'What?' said Peter. He knew that voice. It sounded very much like Jesus. At that moment he forgot about the wind and waves. Frightened and excited he called out, 'If it is you, Lord, tell me to walk out on the water to you!' Peter knew that if it was a ghost, it wouldn't reply.

But there was an answer. 'Come on then!' Jesus called out. Peter, needing no more encouragement, jumped out of the boat as if he was jumping into a puddle, not into the waves on a deep lake with fish in it. If Jesus told him to do something, Peter trusted him. He found he was walking on water! It was crazy! With a big grin he walked boldly over to where Jesus was… but then he heard the strong wind, and saw the big waves, and he took his eyes off Jesus' face and he started to sink. 'How can I be walking on water?' he thought. 'Lord!' he cried out. 'Save me!'

Straight away Jesus reached out and grabbed Peter's hand before he sank. 'What little faith you have! Why did you doubt?' he said gently. Together, with Jesus holding on to Peter, they walked through the wind and waves to the boat.

As soon as they got into the boat, the sea calmed down. The disciples looked at Jesus amazed. And they worshipped him. 'Truly you are the Son of God!' they murmured.

Bible talk

The story of Jesus walking on the water is broken up into three parts – (1) up to the point where the 'ghost' is spotted, (2) Peter walking and sinking and (3) Jesus rescuing Peter. As you tell the three parts, invite people to suggest suitable hand movements to accompany the story. (You will probably need to ask one expressive person in advance to think of some hand movements.) Some examples might include: for the disciples in part 1 (trembling, hands over ears and screaming, peeping through their fingers); for Peter on the water in part 2 (tentative balancing, excited and then panicking); and for Jesus pulling him out of the water and accompanying him back to the boat in part 3 (stretched up arms, hugging with gratitude). All the time ask how the different characters in the story might have been feeling.

Explain that Jesus is God as a human being. Peter had been in the presence of God and had discovered that not only could he trust God but even when he did not trust God, God was still trustworthy and rescued him. Comment that Elijah had had a tough time but he discovered that he could trust God too. You could explore the Elijah story and ask for suggestions for hand movements or you could duplicate the ones used in the **Bible reading**.

Your expressive person shows the following hand movements as you explain:

* We may find it hard to trust God. (*Clench fists around the chin and look glum.*)
* We may not want to listen to what God is telling us to do. (*Put palms over ears.*)
* We may feel we are too weak to do what God says. (*Move hands feebly.*)
* We may be afraid and cannot believe that God really will protect us and rescue us. (*Shake hands in fear.*)

But it is only when we truly trust God (and that may be risky) that we discover how trustworthy God is. The leader takes the trembling hands of the expressive person firmly in their hands and shouts out, 'God can be trusted!'

Prayer activity

On PowerPoint slides, or with several acetates, show contemporary pictures of people or situations where there is a need to trust Jesus; either use specific or symbolic ones, such as sick people you know or in general; places of war; people facing challenges. Invite everyone to hold out their hands high above their heads as though they are about to sink into the sea, as Peter was.

Lord God, we pray for those in our community who are finding it hard to trust you. (*Mention names*) Help them to know you are trustworthy.
We pray for those in our world who may find it hard to trust you – those suffering for their faith, those who are victims of injustice. Help... (*Mention names*)
We pray for ourselves when we find it hard to trust. (*Allow a time of silence*) May we know that you are always there to rescue us. Amen.

Ending the service

Encourage everyone to hold onto each other, whether it is simply holding a hand or grabbing a piece of their clothing, reminding them of the part of the story where Jesus grabbed hold of Peter to stop him from sinking beneath the waves. Jesus holds tightly onto us and through that faith he saves us.

Use a suitable prayer from your own tradition that reflects a trust in Christ or use the following prayer of blessing, with everyone joining in the emboldened response.

When we struggle with the hard times and difficulties, we can put our trust in Jesus.
God will bless us.
When we cry out to Jesus we can be sure his strength is in us.
God will bless us.
All this week we can trust God in everything.
God will bless us.

Helpful extras

Music and song ideas
'Thank you, Jesus (For loving me)'; 'Can we walk upon the water? (If our eyes are fixed on you)'; 'Everybody has a wobble from time to time' (The wobble song); 'O soul, are you weary and troubled (Turn your eyes upon Jesus)'; 'I'm gonna walk by faith (Each step I take)'; 'I will offer up my life'; 'Thank you for saving me (What can I say?)'; 'O Jesus, I have promised'; 'When I'm sinking'.

Statement of faith
Romans 10:5–15 includes the creedal statement of 'Jesus is Lord' in verse 9. Read out this statement of faith (Year A.Proper 14_2), which is as an expression of your trust in God. It is available from www.scriptureunion.org.uk/lightdownloads.

You will be saved if you declare with your mouth, 'Jesus is Lord'.
Jesus is Lord.

You will be saved if you believe in your heart that God raised Jesus from the dead.
God raised Jesus from the dead.
You will be saved if you call on the name of the Lord.
We call on his name and believe that he will save us.
based on Romans 10:9 (TNIV)

Game
With: a blindfold; a volunteer; obstacles

Place various obstacles in the aisle or at the front. Blindfold a willing volunteer and say that you will guide them verbally through the course. After you have done that, ask them how much they needed to rely on you? Did they think you would let them down?

Then personally guide someone else who is blindfolded through the obstacle course. After this, ask them if they thought it would be better to be guided or instructed or did it not matter? Explain that in the story Jesus both instructed and personally guided Peter. Peter had every reason to trust him.

Notes and comments
The **Statement of faith** could be used as a final expression of trust in God, to conclude the service.

Alternative online options
Visit www.lightlive.org for additional activities for children, young people and adults.

PROPER 15

READINGS: **Romans 11:1,2a,29–32; Matthew 15:[10–20] 21–28**
Isaiah 56:1,6–8; Psalm 67:1–7

Bible foundations

Aim: to declare that God's love and salvation are available to everyone

Jesus' encounter with the Syro-Phoenician or Canaanite woman has a number of surprises and points that demand clarification. It is somewhat surprising to find Jesus leaving Israel at all. He didn't do this very often and on this occasion it seems simply a matter of withdrawal, perhaps to find space for himself and his followers. As he says later in the story, his mission was to Israel (Matthew 15:24). We are so accustomed to thinking of all nations being welcome before God that it is a surprise to find Jesus affirming this limitation to his audience. The disciples had little sympathy for the woman and wanted Jesus to dismiss her (Matthew 15:23). At this point they seem to lack missionary zeal. It is not really until the Council of Jerusalem in Acts 15 that the early Jewish Church embraced the idea of a mission to the Gentiles. There was nothing new in this. Read Jonah for a critique of this attitude.

What is more, Jesus' own words to her seem uncharacteristically harsh (Matthew 15:26); a dog was an unclean animal, not a household pet as we might think of it today. His words, however, bring out the best in the woman who is to be numbered among the many feisty women of the Bible. Her point that even dogs pick up scraps beneath the master's table conceals a profound understanding of God and an even deeper faith, as Jesus recognises. It had always been God's intention that Israel should be a witness to the nations and that they would be blessed through Israel's faithfulness to him (see Genesis 12:1–3).

Paul, the apostle to the Gentiles, understood this better than anyone. He points out in Romans 11 that God has not rejected Israel (though some of Israel may well have rejected him…) but has made it possible for people from all nations to receive the mercy that God wanted to extend to them.

Beginning the service

With: words of Psalm 67

Welcome everyone in the Lord's name. Ask them to greet each other too. When they have sat down, ask if they would be happy to greet every single person who might walk in. Mention some controversial people in the news or figures like school bullies. Explain that today we are celebrating the fact that God welcomes everyone – even us. Split the congregation into two groups and use the words of Psalm 67 antiphonally (in parts). The version from the CEV below (YearA. Proper15_1) is also available from www.scriptureunion.org.uk/lightdownloads.

Our God, be kind and bless us!
Be pleased and smile.
Then everyone on earth will learn to follow you,
and all nations will see your power to save us.
Make everyone praise you
and shout your praises.
Let the nations celebrate with joyful songs,
because you judge fairly and guide all nations.
Make everyone praise you
and shout your praises.
Our God has blessed the earth
with a wonderful harvest!
Pray for his blessings to continue
and for everyone on earth to worship our God.

Psalm 67:1–7 (CEV)

Bible reading

In reading Romans 11:1, 2a and 29–32 ask everyone to listen out for what God has done.

To emphasise this, verses 1a, 2a, 29 and 32b could be read by a different person (or by the whole congregation) from the person who reads the rest. This reading (YearA.Proper15_2) is also available from www.scriptureunion.org.uk/lightdownloads. The emboldened words focus on what God himself has done.

Am I saying that God has turned his back on his people? Certainly not!
I (Paul) am one of the people of Israel, and I myself am a descendant of Abraham from the tribe of Benjamin.
God did not turn his back on his chosen people.
God doesn't take back the gifts he has given or forget about the people he has chosen.
At one time you Gentiles rejected God. But now Israel has rejected God, and you have been shown mercy. And because of the mercy shown to you, they will also be shown mercy. All people have disobeyed God, and that's why he treats them as prisoners.
But (God) does this, so that he can have mercy on all of them.

Romans 11:1,2a,29–32 (CEV)

Bible retelling

With: actor, script (YearA.Proper15_3) available from www.scriptureunion.org.uk/lightdownloads

Ask a woman with some dramatic skills to prepare this. Explain the context of historical enmity between Jews and Canaanites and the downtrodden role of women in both cultures. The teller can use their own words to convey the woman's emotions and reactions, but cover the same material as the webpage script.

Bible talk

With: globe; a picture of a group turned away from someone in an act of rejection and another picture of this same group welcoming this person (YearA.Proper15_4) available from www.scriptureunion.org.uk/lightdownloads

God's concern for the 'in' crowd

Are you in the 'in crowd' or the 'out crowd'? In some places you may feel 'in' and in others you may feel 'out'. What about your friends or neighbours? Have you ever thought about whether they are 'in' or 'out'? Style magazines and TV programmes set the trends for what (and who) are 'in' and 'out'. (*Show the picture of the person being rejected.*) Ask for other suggestions, which might include football teams that may or may not be doing well.

Some countries are 'in' and others 'out'. (*Spin the globe.*) By accident of birth or great hard work, people living in the west are definitely 'in' in global terms, with adequate food, shelter, sanitation and health care. We are not often devastated by earthquakes, volcanoes, tsunamis or war on our doorstep, though some of our families are affected by these events in other places. Do these favourable circumstances mean that God loves us more than others, or that we are more holy? Of course not! God loves each person he has created along with every part of his amazing creation.

God's concern for the 'out' crowd

In earlier times, God chose one nation, Israel, to be his light and show his way to all nations (Isaiah 42:6). But even though his people were privileged, the invitation was always there for outsiders. For example, Ruth, who was King David's great grandma, came from

Moab and so she was a foreigner. (*Show the welcome picture.*) Sadly, Israel focused so much on being the 'in' crowd that they shut everyone else out. (*Show the rejected picture again.*) This was not what God had required! All through their history, God kept reminding the Israelites of their role, for example in Psalm 67; God also reminded them through the prophets, for example Isaiah 56:1 and 6–8. These alternate readings for today are full of references to 'the nations', with God's light and message being for other nations too. (*Show both pictures and keep them on display.*)

The Church does not always make everyone feel welcome. Think about who might have arrived this morning and felt rejected. You will need to do this sensitively. You might suggest noisy babies, people who smell, a blind person with their guide dog, someone who was drunk, or who talked loudly to themselves, the person from school who terrifies you, or who people laugh at. Would they feel rejected or welcomed?

A common phrase used today to act as shorthand in reminding us of how to act is the acronym WWJD or 'What Would Jesus Do'. In Matthew's account of the meeting with the Canaanite woman, Jesus shows us what to do – engage, accept and bless. Jesus' words might seem harsh to our ears, but the response of the woman shows us that she did not feel rejected, though she may have felt tested! So here's the challenge – when we meet those on the edge, the 'out' crowd, how are we going to let the light and love of God show in us so that those who think they are unwelcome sense their welcome, acceptance and blessing?

Prayer activity

With: film clip from *Bruce Almighty* (see **Notes and comments**); pencils; paper; the unwelcomed and welcomed pictures from the **Bible talk**; cross(es) or picture of a cross

Choose one of the following two activities.

* Show the welcomed and unwelcomed images from the **Bible talk**, asking people to think of those who are unwelcome. Then ask God to fill your hearts with compassion for them and help you to see them with God's eyes.
* Share out the paper and pencils and ask everyone to draw a person (it need not look accurate, as it is symbolic) who symbolises all those they exclude or ignore (like the Canaanites or women for first-century Jewish men). Each person should ask God to fill their heart with love for this person to see them as someone loved by God, as people whom Jesus came to save. Each person could bring their picture to a cross (or number of crosses depending on the size of your congregation) and, as they put the picture down, ask God to bless those people or groups richly with all the gifts he wants to pour upon them.

Ending the service

We know that God pours constant blessings on all people, but it is good to close the service with a blessing. Choose one from your church's published resources, or the blessing below.

Thank you, for you accept us, Lord.
Thank you, for you bless us, Lord.

Bless us with the ability to see others with your eyes.
Bless us with welcoming hearts to accept others.
May we never forget that you welcome all people.
Amen.

Helpful extras

Music and song ideas

Songs and hymns on this theme include: 'Let all the world in every corner sing'; 'Hills of the north rejoice'; 'Far round the world'; 'Love divine all loves excelling'; 'Blessing and honour (Ancient of Days)'; 'Jesus Christ is waiting'; 'All who are thirsty'; 'My Jesus, my Saviour'; Tim Hughes' 'He's got the whole world in his hands'; 'Salvation belongs to our God'.

If people from other nations, or who speak other languages, are present, ask them to lead a praise song in their own language. Words could be given correctly, but a phonetic version may help people to sing, and a translation will encourage everyone to recognise that God does not 'just speak English'. This could naturally lead into people sharing about their 'home church' and different ways of worshipping, sharing prayer requests, or encouraging a partnership with a church in another part of the world.

Suitable music for the **Prayer activity** might include the Adagio from Mahler's *Symphony Number 5*, an excerpt from *The Lark Ascending* by Vaughan Williams, or 'Oh the love of my Lord' by The Northumbria Community (on the *Waymarks* album), though this may be a little short (just over 2 minutes).

Game

With: information from *Operation World*; a world map; Post-it notes with names of countries

Using information from *Operation World* to give clues, identify countries where there are (or are not) churches. Make the clues interesting. Someone can then come to put the name of the country in the correct place on the map. Here is an example: this country used to be a colony of Denmark; it has full employment but is not Communist; its capital city has a statue donated by the US government; the nation is sometimes known as 'the land of fire and ice'. The country is Iceland, where there is an established Christian community. (This could be a team activity or something to do altogether.)

Once you have established that there are Christian communities all over the world, draw the conclusion that God does not favour white Europeans, and in fact most of the global Church is in the developing world! Focus, too, on the fact that he loves people in places where there is no established church and loves people who are not believers in places where there is a Christian community.

Statement of faith

A statement of faith (YearA.Proper15_5) is available from www.scriptureunion.org.uk/lightdownloads.

Notes and comments

Music for a more mature group might include

quiet meditation within the service using the song 'He was despised' from Handel's *Messiah* with appropriate PowerPoint imagery to help people connect with Jesus as a 'rejected' person. This can be very comforting for those who do feel despised or rejected by society, or the Church.

If there is to be a baptism, emphasise that God seeks to engage, accept and bless every person who comes to him. Promises made by, or on behalf of, the one being baptised focus on the developing of a relationship with the living God, which is a reciprocal thing. This should also help parents and godparents or sponsors to see the importance of their role in living 'as Christ' on behalf of the person being baptised.

To introduce the **Prayer activity**, play the clip near the end of *Bruce Almighty* where Bruce and God are talking about Bruce's girlfriend, Grace. Bruce prays that she will meet someone who 'always sees her as I do now – with your (God's) eyes'.

If this is a service of Holy Communion, people could bring their pictures or symbols, made during the **Prayer activity**, to the cross as they come forward to receive bread and wine.

Alternative online options
Visit www.lightlive.org for additional activities for children, young people and adults.

PROPER 16   _C. Phillippi_

READINGS: **Romans 12:1–8; Matthew 16:13–20**
Isaiah 51:1–6; Psalm 138:1–8

Bible foundations

Aim: to think about different gifts that we have all been given to help us serve God

Matthew's Gospel is divided into three sections. The second and final sections are introduced with the phrase 'From that time on Jesus began to...' (4:17; 16:21). Matthew 16:13−20 comes at the end of the second section and is a pivotal moment. Once Peter has acknowledged who Jesus is, Jesus immediately sets his face to go towards Jerusalem and the cross.

Peter is able to discern who Jesus is, and Jesus confirms that this is so. His understanding has come from God and immediately leads to Peter being given the task of serving God with his foundational rock-like role in the early Church – not that he would have understood it when Jesus first gave him his name change. Isaiah 51:1, from today's Old Testament reading, acknowledges the foundations upon which God's people had been built.

Paul has just spent the chapters leading up to Romans 12 explaining foundational doctrinal issues such as justification, sanctification and election. On the basis of that, he turns to some practical matters that he introduces with the word 'therefore' (12:1). This is what we are supposed to do and be. We are called to be transformed, offering ourselves to God and discerning what are our roles in the body, which is the Church. There are many roles that we could take on, but Paul makes it clear that it is the abilities God has given us that determine which tasks we take on. We are to seek God's will for our lives and ask for his strength and empowering to fulfil these roles. Key questions to ask in the context of an all-age service are: do we think these roles include all ages in the church or just adults? What do Paul's words here mean when applied to children, young people and families?

233

Beginning the service

With: a pebble for each person or one large stone

Ask everyone to study a pebble, feeling and looking at it. Or invite one or two people to study one large stone on everyone's behalf. Ask for words to describe the stone. Agree that it is hard, firm and strong. Remind everyone about Jesus' friend Peter. He would have been a strong fisherman physically, but when it came to behaviour, things were different. Ask for examples of Peter's actions, such as saying things without thinking first, putting his foot in it and denying Jesus in his hour of need. Even though Jesus knew all about Peter's weaknesses, he described him as a rock, a strong, firm stone. Read out Matthew 16:18. Peter, in spite of all his faults, was given the gift of being a strong leader of Jesus' followers. God has given us gifts too. Today we will be thinking about the gifts God has given us, some of which might be surprising.

Bible reading

With young children present, Romans 12:1–8 could be read aloud from the CEV. Use two or more voices. Voice 1 can read up to verse 4; verse 5 should be read by all the voices together; then alternate voices should read the sentences in verses 6–8.

Bible talk

With: a 'Pass the Parcel' with three wrappers (see below); music; a sketch pad or flip chart; a very large sheet of paper (for example, two 1.5 m lengths of lining paper

fixed together side by side); pens; scissors; sticky tape

Pass the parcel – discovering gifts
Prepare the parcel, wrapping it with three layers as follows: the 'prize' in the centre should be some felt-tipped pens or colouring pencils with a label attached (not very noticeable) saying, 'Draw a picture for everyone'. The wrapping around the prize should be blank. The next outer wrapping should have a smiley face drawn on the inside of the paper; and on the outer layer, some musical notes drawn on the inside of the paper. Again these should not be very noticeable. Choose children in advance making it clear which child will open which wrapper. One needs to be good at (have a gift in) welcoming others, one needs to be musical (have a gift) and the last one needs to be good at drawing or colouring (similarly gifted). You may need to agree a signal with your musician if you are using live music for passing the parcel.

Lay the large sheet of paper on the floor and ask for a child volunteer. Choose one wearing trousers to come and lie down on the paper. Ask an adult to draw round the child to make a simple person shape and cut it out carefully. The shape should have arms and legs that spread out slightly.

While this is being done explain that you are going to begin with a party game, Pass the Parcel, but only three children can play. Choose your three children to come to play the game. When the music stops for the first time with the child gifted at welcoming others, be very disappointed that there appears to be nothing and toss aside the wrapping paper in disgust. Do the same with the second wrapper. When the third wrapper is opened exclaim with delight for the child who has won the prize (the one gifted in drawing) and say that it is typical of how things sometimes seem to be. Some people appear to get nothing while others seem to have everything.

But then wonder if there is more to it than what seems to be the case at first. Ask to look carefully at the prize. 'Notice' the label that says 'Draw a picture for everyone' and then invite the child to draw something for everyone. Comment on their gift of drawing: something that God has made possible, something to share with everyone.

While the child is drawing on the flip chart or sketch pad, suggest that the other two children look again at the discarded wrapping paper. 'Discover' the smiley face and the musical notes. Talk appropriately to and about the two children, acknowledging their musical and welcoming gifts, gifts that God has given them for everyone's benefit. Remember to admire the drawing too. Point out that all the gifts were ones to share with others. Thank the children and ask them to sit down.

Each part of the body has special gifts
Look at the cut-out figure. Remind everyone of how the Bible reading from Romans says we should offer our bodies as a living sacrifice.
Whatever gifts we have, we should offer to God. Read Romans 12:4 again, asking people to listen out for what Paul says about the body. Comment on the fact that a body is made up of many parts. Take up the scissors and dramatically cut the figure into sections:

two arms, two legs, the head and the trunk.

Each part of our bodies has special gifts. Hands do things that feet can't. Heads can see, hear and speak. Sometimes we need our whole body. Distribute the parts around the congregation with remarks such as, 'Can I give you a hand?' or, 'Do you want to get a head?' Encourage everyone to think of as many things as possible that we can do for God and each other, using the part of the figure that is nearest to them (either do this all together, or do it in small groups). For instance, a hand might prompt ideas of writing, hugging and offering; a foot might suggest ideas of visiting or taking a dog for a walk. Think of special gifts that particular named people may have, such as music, cooking, preaching and so on. If people are in groups, each group could write or draw their ideas on 'their' one part of the body.

Collect up the parts of the figure and read out some of the ideas on each. Be amazed that God has given so many gifts to you all. Read out Romans 12:6–8 to illustrate your point. Then say that of course these are all parts of a body. Read out verse 5 and then fix the body back together with sticky tape. Write the name of your church across the back, adding 'Christ's body'. Say that each of us has at least one gift mentioned here, given to us by God and for us to use for him and for others.

Prayer activity

Ask everyone to join in the following response between each section (Year A. Proper 16_1) that is also available from www. scriptureunion.org.uk/lightdownloads.

**Thank you for your gifts this day,
Gifts to use and give away.
Take our hearts and lives we pray.**

Open your hands and look at them.
Father God, we thank you that our hands
are a gift from you. Thank you that we
can use them to clasp someone's hand in
friendship... that we can use our hands to
give and receive... that we can use our hands
in praise and worship...
Look down at your feet.
Father God, we thank you that our feet are
a gift from you. Thank you that we can use
them to come to church... that we can tap
our feet or dance to the rhythm of the songs
of worship... that we can use our feet to
visit others or run errands for them...
Feel your head with both hands.
Father God, we thank you that our heads
are a gift from you. Thank you that we have
brains to learn about you and know you...
that we can think of good ideas for serving
and inspiring others... that we have ears to
listen to other people and mouths to speak
about you and sing your praise...
Hug yourself.
Father God, we thank you that our bodies
are a gift from you. Thank you that we can
serve you with our whole body and love you
with our whole heart...

Ending the service

With: the pebble(s) from **Beginning the
service**; felt-tipped pens (optional)

Ask everyone to swap pebbles with someone
sitting near them. As they hold the pebble,
ask them to think about their neighbour and
the gifts they have; then write one of these

gifts on the pebble. Young children could
draw or make patterns instead. Ask the
congregation to give the pebbles back to the
original owners, telling them what they have
written and why they appreciate that gift so
much.

Or ask people to pair up with a neighbour to
think about this person's gifts before telling
them of one in particular that is appreciated.

Say the following prayer:

Lord, we thank you for each other and the
gifts we all have. Help us to use these gifts to
help each other know you better.

Helpful extras

Music and song ideas
Songs might include: 'Make me a channel of
your peace'; 'Brother, sister, let me serve you';
'Hands, hands, fingers, thumbs'; 'I will wave my
hands'; 'Will you come and follow me?'; 'Forth
in thy name, O Lord, I go'.

Game
With: a prize to share (optional); sets of
cards saying 'hand', 'hand', 'foot', 'foot', 'body',
'head'; there should be enough cards so
that everyone can have one, and a good
number of complete sets can be made
(Cards to print off (YearA.Proper16_2) are
available from www.scriptureunion.org.uk/
lightdownloads.)

Ask everyone to get into groups, ideally
each with six people. Hand out the cards
making sure that complete sets are not made
straight away. Each group will need six cards
regardless of how many people are in it. The
best way would be to give a whole group

cards with the same word.

Tell everyone that the idea is to collect a whole body: a head, a body, two hands and two feet. They should decide which cards they will keep and which they will need to replace. Members take a card that is not needed and swap it for one they do need from another group. They may only ask, 'Please may I swap a card?' They may not ask for something specific. If they swap it for one they need, they should take it back to their own group until the body is complete. If they are given a card they don't need, they should ask somewhere else. The first group to produce a whole body is the winner.

Link the game with the idea that a body needs to have every part to function properly. It would be no use being all hands or having three heads. Each person has a place and function in the body of Christ.

Statement of faith

This statement of faith (YearA.Proper16_3) is also available from www.scriptureunion.org.uk/lightdownloads. Divide into two groups. The leader says the lines in bold and the groups read the other alternate lines.

We believe in the gift of creation.
God created us and all this beautiful world.
He has given us the gift of being creative too.
We believe in the gift of love.
God loves us and gave his only Son for us.
He wants us to use the gift of love towards everyone we meet.
We believe in the gift of sharing.

Jesus came to earth and shared his life with others.
He has given us many things and wants us to share with others.
We believe in the gift of forgiveness.
Jesus died for us on the cross so that we can be forgiven.
He wants us to use the gift of forgiveness towards those who have wronged us.
We believe in the gift of prayer.
The Holy Spirit of God helps us to pray in Jesus' name.
He wants us to use the gift of prayer in worship and service to others.

Notes and comments

Ask two actors to mime the 'We believe …' statements in the **Statement of faith**.

Use the cards from the **Game** in other ways: with one card between two, take turns to say a gift someone may have that uses that part of the body. See how many ideas you have before one person cannot think of any more. Or with one card for each small group, pass the card around, each thanking God for a gift using that part of the body, such as 'Thank you, God, that I can think with my head', 'Thank you that I can sing with my head' or 'Thank you that I can listen with my head.'

Alternative online options

Visit www.lightlive.org for additional activities for children, young people and adults.

PROPER 17

READINGS: Romans 12:9–21; Matthew 16:21–28
Jeremiah 15:15–21; Psalm 26:1–8

Bible foundations

Aim: to be prepared for the fact that following Jesus is a challenge

In Matthew 16:16–19 Peter has had insights that could only have come from God. Jesus acknowledges this. But almost immediately Peter comes crashing back to earth. (A similar pattern is seen in the Transfiguration in chapter 17.) As was pointed out in the **Bible foundations** for Proper 16, Matthew 16:21–28 marks a new direction for Jesus' ministry: it is focused on Jerusalem and the cross. Peter acknowledges that Jesus is the Christ, but doesn't see the implications of what the Christ has to do. He has misinterpreted Jesus' mission and probably wants to share in the glory of the Messiah. Thus he is horrified to hear that it means humiliation and death! Peter, in challenging Jesus, is in fact being used as an instrument of the devil, attempting to thwart God's master plan. Jesus adjusts Peter's perspective.

In Jeremiah 15, the prophet, under severe stress, speaks to God in a similarly aggrieved tone, wanting to put things right. God wants to adjust his perspective too: 'If you turn back to me,' he says, 'I will make you strong.' Whenever our perspective wobbles, the answer is to turn back to God. God tells him to stop speaking like a fool.

In Romans 12, continuing his practical outworking of God's grace, Paul focuses on the quality of love that is required to live in a Christlike manner in a fallen world. He gives many instructions that undoubtedly challenge any follower's behaviour. Paul is also making it clear that there will be hard and difficult times. Following Jesus is not the ticket to an easy life. He includes specific examples of what Jesus told his disciples to expect (Matthew 16:24–28). In this service there is the opportunity to present the challenge of the cost of discipleship. Think carefully how you will present this, in a way that takes seriously the words of Jesus.

Beginning the service

With: three visual aids – in a red circle, like a road sign, write the word ME, crossed out; in a rectangular sign create an arrow pointing to the word 'Jesus'; a large cross made of firm card that will not bend when carried (This will be used in the **Bible talk** so it needs to be large enough to stick other words on.)

Ask if anyone can work out which Bible verse these signs are referring to. Then read out Matthew 16:24 to begin the service.

Bible reading

Matthew 16:21–28 and Romans 12:9–21 can be combined in a dramatic reading using a mixture of voices. Use up to nine different people. It would work effectively if they stood up to read where they are sitting, or at least if they were spread around the worship space. A CEV version of Romans 12:9–21 (YearA.Proper17_1) is available from www.scriptureunion.org.uk/lightdownloads.

Begin with Matthew 16:21–28, split between a narrator, Peter and Jesus. At the end of verse 28 the narrator (or Peter) says: 'So how do I deny myself, take up my cross and follow Jesus?' Up to six scattered voices read from Romans 12:9–21.

Bible talk

With: the large cardboard cross from **Beginning the service**, or make one big enough to have words stuck on to it and to look cumbersome when carried; the emboldened words on the next two CHECK pages on separate pieces of card to stick on the cross

The two Bible passages focus on the difference between thinking as the world thinks and the Christian's challenge to think as God thinks, and to behave differently.

Thinking God's way

Imagine telling one of your best friends that they are a stumbling block or obstacle! That's what Jesus said to Peter. Think of an example such as it is raining but your friend has deliberately hidden your coat, umbrella or boots. They are stopping you from doing what you want, or need, to do.

Jesus wasn't really being rude to Peter! Jesus knew that he must soon face his death on the cross, something that he was afraid of. It was no help to him when his friend told him it wouldn't happen. Peter talked just as a friend would: he was horrified that Jesus would think of being killed. What did he say? Remind everyone of Matthew 16:22.

But Jesus' death was exactly what God did want! God sees and does things completely differently from how we might think, see or do things. But then, God has the big picture – past, present and future. Jesus could see that Peter was a stumbling block or obstacle, thinking the way the world thinks and not the way God thinks. To follow Jesus means forgetting about ourselves and putting God first. Ask for suggestions as to what forgetting about ourselves really means.

Living God's way

Paul expands on this in Romans 12. Stick the emboldened words on the large cross as you go along:

First of all, forgetting ourselves and putting

God first, affects the way we behave towards other people. This is the real opposite of how the world works.

- We are to **love** each other: and not just our **friends** and people we like, but our enemies too. We are not just to treat our **enemies** well, but we are to pray for them and leave them in God's hands – we are not to think bad thoughts about them, and we are to have **no revenge**. This is often a real challenge!
- We are to **welcome strangers** into our group, and this doesn't just mean people we don't know who come on a Sunday, or new people at school but perhaps people whom others see as strange. Jesus loved the outcast and the people no one else did.
- We are to look at **how others are feeling** and not just how we are feeling: rejoicing with those who rejoice and being sad with those who are sad.
- We are to live **at peace** with everyone, and this doesn't just mean not starting wars; it means not answering back when we feel like it, or starting arguments, or being unkind and so making others unhappy.

Living like Jesus

Living God's way is a real challenge. As well as denying ourselves, Jesus said that to be his true followers we must take up a cross and follow him. This doesn't sound very comfortable, does it? Jesus never said that going his way would be easy. Behaving as God wants is really difficult because the world notices that we are different. (*Walk around with the cross over your shoulder.*) If I walked around like this, people would give me strange looks! But what if they can't see the actual cross, but we're still doing what's written on here? People may laugh at us, or talk about us behind our backs, or try to trick us into doing wrong things. We may not be able to be friends with someone because they would lead us away from God. Worse, we might get bullied because we're Christians, or even persecuted. It might be really tempting to put the cross down and go back the other way. (*Act this out if you wish.*)

The difficulty of putting God and others first, and the tough way people may treat us, may become a stumbling block or obstacle to stop us following Jesus. So how do we avoid the temptation to trip over the stumbling block and not go God's way? (*Stick the following emboldened words on the other side of your cross.*)

Here's Paul's advice.

- **Pray constantly** – not just every now and then. We should make it our aim to pray whenever we can, especially when life is hard. And if we are finding it hard to pray, then we can ask someone else to pray for us.
- **Be patient** – when things are going badly. It's hard to be in the middle of it but let God's hope give you perseverance.
- **Keep going** – keep holding on to that cross even when it hurts.

But why should we live this way? What makes us want to go Jesus' way? What will make us stay clinging on when it might be easier to let go? Ask for ideas – these could give a real encouragement. Then read out Matthew 16:27. A reward from Jesus means eternal life with him for ever. So is it worth it?

Prayers of intercession

Use the phrases in Romans 12:9–21 as a stimulus for either open prayer or asking for prayer topics and suggestions that can be led from the front.

For example:
Verse 13: Take care of God's needy people – who in our world, community or fellowship are in need of God's care today?
Verse 15: Rejoice with those who rejoice – is there anyone who is particularly happy? For example, there may be a new baby who has been born, or an engagement, in the church. Give thanks together.
Verse 15: When people are sad, be sad – pray for people you know who are suffering bereavement or other sadness.
Verse 12: Be patient in times of trouble – who in your community is ill or having trouble? Ask God to give them his patience and peace.

The other verses could stimulate further thoughts and topics. If someone is leading these prayers from the front, write down the topics people suggest. It's a good way to include those who feel uncomfortable in an 'open prayer' situation. The list could get very long if lots of people have ideas, but it's important to get a range of suggestions: young people can have very different but equally valid perspectives on who, or what, needs prayer!

Prayer of confession

This would work best if you can split into groups of about ten, each with a leader who has been briefed beforehand. (Or adapt it to individual use or ask a drama or dance group to 'perform' it at the front of the church.)

As an active confession, the movements need to be explained beforehand. A leader needs to read the words (which could be repeated by the group):

Stand in a circle, facing inwards.
Leader: Lord, we are sorry for times when we've loved evil and held tight to the bad.
Everyone should tense their muscles and then relax.
Everyone now holds hands.
Leader: Lord, we are sorry for times when we haven't loved each other as we should.
All loose hands suddenly.
Leader: Forgive us, Lord, for times when we haven't taken care of others or welcomed strangers.
All turn with backs to the circle.
Leader: Forgive us for when we have been proud, believing ourselves to be better than others.
Take a step away from the circle.
Leader: Lord, we are sorry for times when we have mistreated others and not honoured your name.
Everyone should cross their arms, with their fists clenched in front of their face.
Leader: Don't let evil defeat us, Lord, but help us defeat evil with good.
Put arms down and relax.
Leader: Fill us with your Spirit so that we may live at peace with each other.
Turn back into the circle and join hands again.
Leader: And help us to love others more than we love ourselves.

If appropriate, share the Peace at this point.

Helpful extras

Music and song ideas

Use songs and hymns that refer to following Jesus and/or serving others, such as: 'I, the Lord of sea and sky'; 'Take up thy cross the Saviour said'; 'In my life, Lord, be glorified' (make up your own appropriate verses to this); 'Jesus, take me as I am'; 'Take my life and let it be'; 'Make me a channel'.

Statement of faith

A statement of faith (YearA.Proper17_2) is available from www.scriptureunion.org.uk/lightdownloads.

Ending the service

If possible, give everyone a small paper or card cross during the service (or at the start). At the end of the service invite people to take their cross home, but, before they do so, ask them to write on one side some of the ways in which they might be able to 'forget themselves'. From Romans 12:9–21 they could choose a few words or one phrase from Paul and write it on the other side of their cross. These might be particular things they believe God is calling them to or situations they need help with. Alternatively, this could be done at home, but at the end of the service the leader shares what they would write on their cross.

Ask everyone to hold their cross as you say:

May our Lord Jesus Christ, who died on the cross for you, give you the courage to forget about yourself and the courage to take up your cross and follow after him.

Take the large cross (used in **Beginning the service** and the **Bible talk**) with you as you leave and invite the congregation to follow you, holding their crosses.

Notes and comments

If you have a cross that is prominent in the church building, think of ways you could incorporate that into the **Bible talk**.

In the UK, the academic year is about to begin; for some children, students, parents and staff who work in schools this can be a challenge to their faith. In **Prayers of intercession**, pray for any who are about to make a fresh start; pray that they will be willing to take up their cross to follow Jesus.

In **Beginning the service**, ask how many people are wearing a cross or have one in their possession (a bookmark, on a book cover or in a pocket or bag). Talk about the cross as a religious symbol.

Alternative online options

Visit www.lightlive.org for additional activities for children, young people and adults.

HARVEST

READINGS: **Psalm 65:1–13; 2 Corinthians 9:6–15**
Deuteronomy 8:7–18; Luke 12:16–30

Bible foundations

Aim: to recognise that God's generosity prompts us to praise him

When God's people were about to settle in the land God had promised them, God also promised to bless them. But that promise came along with a command not to forget the Lord, and to obey his teachings. God's blessing so often is accompanied by the need to remain faithful to God. It is all to do with our attitude. We cannot see God simply as a benevolent giver who goes on dipping into a sack of goodies! Failure to remain faithful would lead to punishment, as God's people were to discover.

Psalm 65, which is the focus of this service, uses powerful picture language to acknowledge God's generosity. The writer declares so many of God's characteristics that draw people to thanksgiving and praise. So it is not surprising that this psalm is often seen as a harvest song. It is worth noting that the people of Israel, in what was essentially an agrarian society, celebrated three harvests: Passover, the first barley or grain harvest (March–April), Pentecost, the wheat harvest (May–June), with the third harvest, the harvest of grapes, called Tabernacles (September–October). This offered plenty of scope each year for thanksgiving, which is lost in modern society where harvest is usually only associated with late summer, and in urban areas where there are not even those symbolic reminders.

Harvest is a time to respond to God's generosity and not just in praise and thanksgiving. Paul highlights this in the reading from the epistle: 2 Corinthians 9:6–15. This passage is part of a section that began at the beginning of chapter 8, concerning a gift to the church in Jerusalem. But verses 6–15 can be universally applied for any giving that the church, either corporately or individually, is involved in. We should give to those in need to the best of our ability and not begrudgingly. It is all to do with attitude!

Beginning the service

With: a CD of birdsongs or music with nature sounds such as folk music by Vaughan Williams including the *Overture to the Wasps* and *The Lark Ascending*; the French composer Messiaen's music, inspired by bird song; Beethoven's *Pastoral Symphony* or some of John Rutter's versions of hymns inspired by the creation, such as 'For the beauty of the earth'

Play this music in the last five minutes as people arrive. Stand at the front just listening to the sound as it gets louder and louder. As you begin, ask what pictures this music puts in people's minds. You could jot them down or just repeat the list a couple of times. Then read Psalm 24:1.

Bible reading

Psalm 65 will be read in the course of the **Bible talk** but you may like to hear it read as an introduction to the talk.

The epistle reading from 2 Corinthians 9:6–15 is part of Paul's letter to the Christians in Corinth, whom he loves and admires. He is urging them to be generous in their attitude. This reading would benefit from being read, in a modern version, in a dramatic way as though from a scroll. It was, after all, originally read out to a group of people meeting together to worship.

Bible talk

With: either a long strip of strong paper or an old sheet; a piece of card folded in half, one for each person; glue; pictures of mountains, waves, plants growing ready

to be harvested (which could be grain or grapes), livestock, food (the size of these will depend upon whether it is for the central image or individual ones); pieces of material; glitter pens; pens for writing the following words, 'God gives his gifts generously. We too need to be generous.' Some images (YearA.Harvest_1) are available from www.scriptureunion.org.uk/lightdownloads. Use coloured ones if at all possible.

This talk is very simple. You are going to create a collage banner to be displayed in the church and used to stimulate worship, and you are also going to create a card for everyone to give to someone else at the end of the service. (The people creating the big banner will not be able to do both!) The size of your congregation will affect whether you do this all together or break into smaller groups.

God's world is great
Explain that Jesus came to earth as God in human form. Because he was God, he was able to control the created world in a way that was to benefit those he was with. Briefly tell the story of Jesus calming the storm in Mark 4:35–41. The power of the waves and the fury of the storm scared Jesus' followers but he was not afraid and, having been woken up, he calmed the storm.

God's creation is great and vast. We can marvel at it but we can also be fearful. Thunder and lightning, waterfalls and storms, and mountains and sharp crags can make us afraid. But the God who made all of them is with us and is able to take away our fear.

Read Psalm 65:5–8 and then invite people to

stick pictures of powerful things in creation onto their personal cards or onto the large sheet or strip of paper. As they do that, encourage conversation about how God has helped us to be brave, but also enthuse about the beauty of God's world.

God's world is full of variety
Then tell the story in Mark 8:1–9 when Jesus fed over 4,000 people, who were hungry after a day listening to him. Jesus provided them with what they needed. Read Psalm 65:9–13 and talk about the richness of the harvest. You may wish to acknowledge that climate change is affecting how the seasons and harvests happen, much of which is the result of human negligence, not God's responsibility.

Ask people to stick pictures of growing things, livestock and food on the banner or on their personal card. As they do so, encourage conversation about what foods people like and dislike, trying to draw the conclusion that there is a rich variety of foods from creation that we can enjoy and benefit from.

God's world is to be shared with others
Finally, take your marker pen, for the large version, or show people a sample of the individual one and write on it: God gives his gifts generously. We too need to be generous. If your handwriting is not attractive, find someone else with a creative ability to write these words. It would be a shame to spoil everyone's handiwork! Draw attention to what Paul wrote to the Corinthians in 2 Corinthians 9:6–15. That group of Christians were very generous but Paul wanted them to have the right attitude: not to be mean or martyrs in their giving but to be sure that God would bless them in their generosity. That's how God wants his people to behave – generously.

Admire the finished pieces of artwork and then explain that at the end of the service everyone is invited to give their card to someone else to enjoy, as a symbolic recognition of wanting to be generous, as God is.

Prayer activity
Traditionally, people bring gifts of food to a harvest festival service. These are brought to the front, usually quite early in the service. The food is distributed to those in need in the community. Usually the focus is on the gift rather than the giver. This activity also places a focus on the giver.

Assuming this is your custom, invite people to bring their food gifts to the front but to do so in three groups – for example, from three different parts of the building, in three different age groups (5s and under, 5 to 11s, and the rest) or in groups of boys, girls and adults. Each group stands at the front holding their gift for the service leader to pray for them as givers. Only then will they place their gift on the appropriate table or box. The leader prays along these lines:

Father God, we thank you for all you have given us.
We thank you that we too can give to others. Bless all these boys/people from the back of church/toddlers as they give these gifts of food to others.

It would then be appropriate to pray for those who will be receiving the gifts of food in your community and any other projects that the church supports. Pray too that those who will be distributing the gifts will be blessed by God in their generosity, as they have given up their time and energy.

Prayer of confession

With: a large picture of something beautiful from the created world stuck to a flip chart; a paintbrush and paint that will stand out when painted on this image; floor covering

We are all aware of the delicate balance in the created world as issues of climate change and ecological imbalance are always in the media, so it is appropriate to examine our own attitudes to God's world and, where necessary, to ask God to forgive us. Ask people to pray with their eyes open.

Lord God, you have made a wonderful and beautiful world. (*Show the beautiful picture.*) We thank you that we can enjoy your world. But we know that sometimes we take your world for granted and sometimes we even do things that damage the environment: we throw away things that are good and that could be used again, or we cause damage in some other way. (*Take the paintbrush and dramatically splash paint over the image. For dramatic effect, a cymbal player could crash the cymbals.*)
Pause to think of ways in which each person has been guilty of spoiling God's world. Then continue:
Lord God, we are sorry when we have been like this and we ask for your forgiveness.
(*Leave the paint dripping from the picture.*)
Explain that we often cannot undo what we have

done but we can seek to do things differently from now on!
Lord God, help us to take care of your world from now on! Amen.

Ending the service

Invite people to give their card to someone in church, or they may wish to give the card to someone who is not in church. Younger children who are used to taking home a piece of craft may be reluctant to part with their card! They, however, may benefit from someone else's generosity!

Conclude by singing the chorus of 'We plough the fields and scatter'. If anyone knows sign language for this song, it is an effective way of reinforcing the theme of God's generosity.

If you are going to have refreshments or even a harvest supper, include thanks to God for the food and drink you are about to consume!

Helpful extras

Music and song ideas
Michael Saward's song 'The earth is yours, O God' is a modern version of Psalm 65. Include traditional hymns, such as 'All things bright and beautiful'; 'Now thank we all our God'; 'We plough the fields and scatter', especially the chorus.

There are many modern songs that celebrate God's creation, such as 'Praise him you heavens'; 'From the highest of heights to the depths of the sea'; 'Let everything that has breath' and any of the many new versions of Psalm 23.

Statement of faith

Use Psalm 24 as a statement of faith as follows. The statement based on the CEV (YearA.Harvest_2) is also available from www.scriptureunion.org.uk/lightdownloads.

We believe that:
- The earth and everything on it belong to the Lord.
- The world and its people belong to him.
- The Lord is a strong and mighty warrior.
- The Lord saves those who do right for the right reasons.
- The earth and everything on it belong to the Lord.

based on Psalm 24

Notes and comments

Creating a harvest service that is a bit different is always a challenge. The craft features of this outline may be more interactive than you have space or inclination for. As an alternative, in advance create a banner or PowerPoint presentation with images of the rugged parts of creation and the food-producing elements of creation. Members of the congregation could read out the two stories of Jesus from Luke's Gospel. You could prepare little cards for everyone in the church, which they could personalise and then give away at the end of the service as suggested in **Ending the service**. Of course, a monetary collection or offering is another example of generosity.

If this service includes Holy Communion with bread and wine brought to the front, comment on how this is brought as a gift. Draw attention to the generosity of Jesus, who ultimately gave his life for the whole world – the supreme example of God's generosity. If you want to make more Trinitarian connections, God the Father gave his one and only Son and has also given us the Holy Spirit to be with us for ever.

In the **Prayer activity**, as you pray for a charity or for those who will receive gifts, think about how you can do that in an informative way that is relevant to all ages. This might inspire prayer and commitment long after the harvest festival.

Several other harvest all-age service outlines are available in the *All-Age Service Annuals*, Volumes 1–4. For more details see page 320 or www.scriptureunion.org.uk.

Alternative online options

Visit www.lightlive.org for additional activities for children, young people and adults.

PROPER 18

READINGS: **Romans 13:8–14; Matthew 18:15–20**
Ezekiel 33:7–11; Psalm 119:33–40

Bible foundations

Aim: to explore the choices that there are in lovingly resolving disagreements

In *The Hitchhiker's Guide to the Galaxy*, Douglas Adams places his story 'nearly two thousand years after one man had been nailed to a tree for saying how great it would be to be nice to people for a change'. This is, of course, a gross understatement of Jesus' mission. However, how close is this to the practical focus of God's revelation? Of the many theological issues that we spend time discussing, the one thing that is constant in the gospel is God's love and what this means to people.

Paul makes it clear in Romans 13 that love is the most important practical application of the gospel. God has shown love to us and we should show love to one another and back toward God. Love quite literally makes the world go round. Love is at the heart of the Law (verse 10), at the heart of how God has always wanted his people to live. An attitude of love and service towards others undergirds all practical actions – and Paul gives some examples.

One example of what love means in practice is explained by Jesus in Matthew 18. The process and order of things is important when issues of judgement are involved. Two people who are in disagreement should try to sort things out on their own before letting anyone else know. Verse 19 should also be seen as part of this process. When the two meet initially, we should remember that God is there with them.

When God is brought into the centre of any dispute between Christians, there should only be one outcome. Love should be the overriding factor. We will get things wrong, we will sin, and we will sin against others, but the beauty of the gospel is that we can be forgiven and be enabled to offer forgiveness. Younger members of your church family need to learn this and see it in action. This will make your community of believers appealing to an outside world where anger over personal rights, legal disputes and demands for compensation are the norm.

Beginning the service

With: film clip

Play the opening scene from *Love Actually*, where all kinds of people greet each other at the airport, and all kinds of 'love' are demonstrated. Ask the congregation for ideas about what 'love' might mean and explore the fact that sometimes love is tough. It may even mean confronting someone who offends us.

As an alternative, read Psalm 119:33–40, introducing it by saying that rules and being told off are not always bad things. Ask for examples of occasions when being told off has resulted in something positive. God has given us rules and directs us in the way he wants us to live. It may be hard, but it leads to life, as verse 40 concludes. This could be read antiphonally or by two readers taking alternate verses. Love and getting along together can be tough!

Explain that in today's service we will explore what it might mean to love our neighbours, even those we disagree with.

Bible reading

The reading from Matthew 18:15–20 is written as several points in an argument. It would help to clarify this, if one person reads verses 15 and 18, another, verses 16 and 19 and a third, verses 17 and 20, although verse 20 could be read altogether as a summary. A similar approach could be taken with reading Romans 13:8–14.

Bible talk

With: six actors to mime to the following rough script

Introduce the two main characters, Misery and Mouldy. They can be dressed appropriately. They have lived next door to each other for years and have gone to the same church for years but… Mouldy decided he was going to open up a cheese factory in his garden shed. He employed three people who worked all through the night, with bright lights and loud noise to keep them awake. His business was a great success but Misery was not happy. He could not sleep at night and the smell of cheese that was going off got worse and worse. The lorries that came to deliver the goats' milk and collect the cheese blocked his driveway at the most inconvenient of times!

So what should Misery do? (*The two scowl at each other!*)

Here are the choices.
- Misery goes to see Mouldy and angrily asks him to close his cheese business immediately! (*Misery waves his fist in Mouldy's face.*) But Mouldy is not convinced and ignores Misery. (*Mouldy turns away.*)
- Misery goes to see Mouldy and tries to explain how he sees things and suggests that the business only operates for three nights a week or just in the daytime and that the lorries come at more convenient times. (*Misery enters into a conversation.*) But Mouldy ignores Misery.
- Misery goes to the town council and lodges a complaint. (*Misery goes in the*

opposite direction and talks with two officials with a clipboard.) The councillors say that they will see what they can do.

- Misery goes to the leaders of his local church and asks them to help him sort it out. (*Misery goes to the front of the church to meet with two church leaders – not necessarily actual church leaders. They hold a conversation.*) They call Mouldy over and begin a conversation. (*Misery listens quietly. Mouldy looks a bit sheepish. He offers Misery a lump of cheese and Misery is undecided whether or not to accept it. But the two go back to their original spots talking together.*)

There are four options and there is something to be said for all of them. Sorting out disputes is never easy and everyone has to be willing to see the other person's point of view. Mouldy could have refused to listen. Misery could have lost his temper. Ask for other possible endings.

Jesus made it clear how people who loved God should settle disagreements. Run through the three stages of settling a dispute from Matthew 18 – personal discussion, taking along someone else and then reporting it to the wider group of Jesus' believers. Jesus concluded by saying that God was right there in the middle of the discussion. This is love put into practice. Read Matthew 18:20 again.

Getting on with others is demanding, as we all know. Paul made that clear in the reading from Romans 13. Sometimes the other person does not want to accept any offer of making peace. You could talk about how others settle disputes, including what happens in the playground or in the classroom or in the office. How different is that from what Jesus says? Read Romans 13:14 to conclude.

Prayers of intercession

We live in a world where there are fierce and violent disputes and those seeking to make peace are often hindered at every point. Select a number of disputes in the news at the moment, especially any local ones or ones that younger people can identify with. It may even include bullying in a classroom. If you can supply visual images, put them on PowerPoint slides. After each topic or image pray the following:

O God, the source of all peace and wholeness, may your peace rule in our world.

You could conclude by reading the following prayer from the *The Book of Common Prayer*. You will need to explain that this is in old language but it is as true now as it was nearly 350 years ago. God is the author of peace and he does love peace and he can defend us.

O God, who art the author of peace and lover of concord, in knowledge of whom standeth our eternal life, whose service is perfect freedom; Defend us thy humble servants in all assaults of our enemies; that we, surely trusting in thy defence, may not fear the power of any adversaries, through the might of Jesus Christ our Lord. Amen.

Prayer of confession

With: some quiet music on a CD

An obvious response to the **Bible talk** is

to give people the opportunity to make peace with those with whom they have had a disagreement. But long-term disputes take more time to sort out than the time available in an all-age service. But this service might make a start.

Ask everyone to be quiet and listen to the music and think of someone in church whom they find a little difficult in some way. If there is no one, they can think of someone outside the Christian community. Children may find it easier to think of someone in school with whom they struggle.

Read the following four statements and allow a pause after each for personal conversation with God.
Lord God, if I am honest, I find _____
____really difficult because _____.
I know that there are times when I have not always done my best to get along with them and help them, like the time when _____
_____.
Please help me to do something about that because bad relationships between Christians, and between any people, affect everyone else, and after all, I know that I am not perfect. So, from today, to make things better, I am going to _____
_____.

May our church be a place of acceptance and love and full of peacemakers!
Amen.

You could provide paper and pens and encourage people to write a note to someone to acknowledge that they have resolved to begin the process of putting things right.

Ending the service

Remind everyone that love and judgement are not exclusive – God does both. However, he has commanded us to love others and not judge them. As we leave, can we think of people around us who could do with a little more love and a little less judgement? Are we able to intervene to offer that love? If not, can we at least pray for them on a regular basis?

We have a big challenge before us, and will need to go in the strength of God. Use an appropriate blessing from your published resources, or the following:

Oh, Lord of love,
Help us to follow your example and love our neighbours.
Help us to know your love for us and to love ourselves too.
Help us to grow in our love for you, for who you are as well as what you have done.
Bless us with clear minds to hear your Word.
Bless us with big hearts to love your world.
And bless us with clear consciences to live as you ask.
We ask this so that you may be seen in us as we go in your name.
Amen.

Helpful extras

Music and song ideas
Songs might include: 'Make me a channel of your peace'; 'More love, more power'; 'O Lord, your tenderness'; 'How deep the Father's love for us'; 'The steadfast love of the Lord never ceases'; 'There is none like you'; 'Wonderful, so wonderful'; 'Restore, O Lord'.

Hymn suggestions are: 'Here is love vast as the ocean'; 'Come down, O love divine'; 'Love divine, all loves excelling'; 'Brother, sister, let me serve you'; 'Forth in thy name, O Lord, I go'.

Game

With: cartoon images to match each 'crime'

It is easy to make snap judgements about how to deal with different people. (Don't spend ages analysing the following situations! It is just for fun – and to provoke thinking later on.) Explain that each person can be dealt with in three ways:
1. Telling the police
2. Warning the individual
3. Hugging them without saying anything

The congregation will vote each time by moving to different parts of the building (for example, left, centre, right), but individuals should mentally keep track of what they thought the best response would be in each case.
- A child who was caught stealing sweets
- An office worker who 'throws a sickie' several times a year
- A burglar who was caught in the act late at night
- Someone who has gossiped about you
- A teenager who broke a favourite vase
- A child who blackened someone's eye fighting in the school playground

Ask people whether they tended to judge harshly or softly. Remind them that God judges fairly, but he also wants people to choose the right way and, with it, life (Ezekiel 33:11).

Notes and comments

The **Bible talk** and **Prayer of confession** would be especially effective in a service of Holy Communion where the Peace is part of the service. Allow extra time for people to greet each other and begin any necessary process of reconciliation. If you have refreshments after the service, encourage people again to make peace with those they may need to. Draw attention to any help that church leaders can offer in mediation and alert the children's and youth workers to the possibility that their support in mediation may be called for, because settling disputes does not just apply to adults.

A suitable piece of music for either the **Prayer of confession** or a closing song of blessing is 'My prayer for you', by the Northumbria Community, on the CD *Songs of Blessing*. It runs to 3:32 minutes and may therefore be deemed too long for the final blessing in some congregations.

Alternative online options

Visit www.lightlive.org for additional activities for children, young people and adults.

PROPER 19

READINGS: **Romans 14:1–12; Matthew 18:21–35**
Genesis 50:15–21; Psalm 103:[1–7] 8–13

Bible foundations

Aim: to explore the fact that knowing that God has forgiven us motivates us to forgive others

In Romans 14, Paul is most probably addressing specific issues in the church in Rome. However, the principles found here can be applied to all Christian fellowships because the primary principle is love toward others. Two issues Paul addresses are the eating of particular food and the observance of holy days. Both issues were not fundamental for salvation, but had the potential to cause division within the church. Paul wanted to avoid that.

We are all very good at adding extra beliefs or practices to the gospel message, whether from personal preference, culture or tradition. We expect people of all ages in our churches to act in certain ways and do certain things. Very rarely are these 'extras' essential to salvation. Paul is adamant that divisive issues shouldn't harm anyone within the church. Ultimately it is God who determines right or wrong. As we find in the Matthew 18, judgement is God's domain.

Matthew introduces the idea of forgiveness with questions from Peter. Jesus, having effectively shown that forgiveness is limitless, continues with a parable. This parable is about treating and forgiving others as we have ourselves been treated and forgiven. It comes with a stern warning. If we don't forgive others, how can God forgive us? The question for us as individuals and as communities is: how forgiving are we? From a very young age we all have a sense of fairness. The parable from Matthew is an example of fairness in action. Everyone can identify with the injustice of what the 'unforgiving' servant did. This can help even the youngest person present to live in a way that not only pleases our Father in heaven but has an impact on the world, which does not live by God's standards.

Beginning the service

With: a collection of old shoes, or pictures of shoes – have a broad range of shoes that might have been used by all sorts of people

Introduce your collection of shoes. As you do so, invite people to think about the people who may have worn them. What can we tell about these people from their shoes? Were they tall or short? Were they builders or supermodels? You could make this into a bit of a game. You could invite different members of the congregation to lend you their shoes. Can people guess which shoes were given by particular people?

Remind the congregation of the famous saying that you shouldn't criticise someone until you have walked a mile in their shoes. Today we are going to remember that people think and behave in many different ways. We are called to treat each other with understanding, and forgive each other as God forgives us. Draw attention to the fact that Jesus said we were to forgive 'not just seven times but seventy-seven times'.

Bible reading

Matthew 18:21–35 lends itself to a dramatic presentation, so you may wish to use a dramatised version, or ask volunteers to mime as the story is told.

Bible talk

With: three volunteers; three large envelopes; six cards – on three cards write the words 'money', 'good looks' and 'success'; on the remaining three cards, write the phrase 'God forgives me' in full on each card

and then hide them inside the envelopes so that they can be switched during the talk

This talk is a version of the famous trick with cups and peas. You will need three 'volunteers', who should be well briefed beforehand.

Invite the three volunteers to stand at the front. Give each one an envelope. Explain that each person is going to be given a card to put in their envelope. This card will have a word on it that indicates an issue that can cause people difficulties in their relationship with others and God.

Money can cause difficulties in relationships
Start with the word 'money'. Give this card to the first volunteer. As you do so, make sure that the congregation can see that this volunteer has this particular card. Discuss the issue of money. How can money affect our relationships with other people and cause us to sin? We can share our money generously or spend our money selfishly. We can envy those who have more than we do or we can be glad for them. Invite comments and then ask this volunteer to slip the card into their envelope.

Good looks can cause difficulties in relationships
Take the card with the words 'good looks' on it. Give this to the second volunteer. Have a conversation about good looks. How can what we look like affect our relationships with others and cause us to sin? How envious are we of others? When we look in the mirror, do we dislike what we see, someone whom God has made? Are we

driven by the desire to look fashionable at any cost? Ask this volunteer to slip this card into their envelope.

Success can cause difficulties in relationships

Finally, take the card with the word 'success' on it. Give it to the third volunteer, once again making sure that everyone can see that they have that card. Talk about the issues people have with being successful that cause us to sin. Again, envy will emerge along with jealousy; other issues might include: disappointment that we may fail, unrealistic expectations of what we can achieve, being apologetic when we succeed as well as failing to be content. Ask this volunteer to slip this card into their envelope.

Each of the three volunteers should now be holding an envelope. If people have been following carefully, they should know which volunteer has which card. Ask them to point to each in turn, just to make sure. Ask which issue they think is the most problematic – this is a rhetorical question!

Explain that you're going to muddle things up. Ask the three volunteers to swap envelopes. They must do this slowly and visibly so that the congregation can follow what's happening and keep track of the cards. Allow the swapping to go on for long enough for there to be a small chance of confusion. Now ask the three volunteers to stand in front with their envelope in their hand.

God forgives me

Invite someone to point to the person they think has the card with the word 'money'. The volunteer should look inside their envelope. They shake their head to say 'no'. Ask someone else to have a try. This will produce the same response. By a process of elimination it should now be clear which of the three volunteers has the word 'money' in their envelope. Ask this volunteer to show people what they have. Instead of the card they were given, they reach into the envelope and pull out a card that says, 'God forgives me'. At this point ask the remaining volunteers to do the same.

It's a fairly obvious trick and most people will have guessed what you did. Explain that our attitudes to money, good looks and success can affect our relationships with others and cause us to sin. We may not know why people behave as they do and we may not know the full story of why we respond to them in the way that we do. But God is willing to forgive us. And if we know we have been forgiven and that God has also forgiven others, then we should be willing to ask God to help us forgive others too. We need to see people as God sees them and see ourselves as God sees us. The fact that God has forgiven us should motivate us to forgive others. It is so serious that God will judge us if we fail to do so (verse 35). And Jesus said we had to go on forgiving 77 times – in other words on and on and on and on!

Prayer activity

With: paper footprints, one for each person; pens, pencils or crayons

Remind people of the shoes that you had for **Beginning the service**. If you haven't used that image already, use it here. Shoes and footprints can be a symbol for the journey that we take through life.

Give everyone a paper footprint. Ask them to write or draw something on the footprint that represents a person or situation that they would like to pray for today. Explain that this might be seen by other people.

Collect the footprints and use them to mark out a path around your church or worship space. You have been thinking about some things that negatively affect relationships with others and how we need not only to know God's forgiveness for ourselves but also ask him to help us forgive others. Invite people to walk around the footpath as a way of praying for the people and situations, especially that, where necessary, there will be forgiveness. You could play appropriate music as you do this.

Prayer of confession

With: small pieces of paper with the letters IOU written on them; enough chocolate money for everyone to have a coin placed in a bowl at the foot of a cross

Give everyone a piece of paper. What do the letters IOU mean? (I Owe yoU!) If you give an IOU, it means that you are in debt to someone. The two servants in the story Jesus told were in debt, one (the official or unforgiving servant) to the king and the other to the unforgiving servant himself. In the Bible sin is often described as the debt we owe to God. Our selfishness and bad behaviour puts us in debt to God. Invite people to hold their IOUs and think about what they may have done wrong over the past week or more. Have they been unwilling

to forgive someone?

The good news is that Jesus has paid this debt for us by dying on the cross. If we accept his forgiveness, our debt is cancelled. More than that, God is overflowing with generosity. He gives us more back than we ever owed.

Invite people to put their IOU in the bowl as a sign of their willingness to be forgiven, and then to take out a chocolate coin as a sign that they want to receive God's blessing. You could then sing 'The price is paid'.

Ending the service

With: a sheet of paper with a mixture of small pictures of shoes and feet, roughly 5 cm in length, (Year A. Proper 19_1) available from www.scriptureunion.org.uk/lightdownloads, one for each person (Depending on how creative you want to be, use laminators, colouring pencils, bracelets, necklaces, etc.)

You have already used images of feet, footprints and shoes. The following creative exercise should help you think of other people and the unique challenges they face. This could also be used during the coffee time after the service.

Distribute the sheets of paper and invite everyone to decorate and personalise them so that they represent people whom they commit to pray for. You could laminate them or punch holes in them. They could be used to make bookmarks, necklaces, or bangles. Think about health and safety when it comes to materials and tools, especially if small children are present.

Helpful extras

Music and song ideas

Relevant songs include: 'Be still and know'; 'Great is thy faithfulness'; 'A new commandment'; 'Here in this place'; 'Longing for light (Christ be our light)'; 'Beauty for brokenness'; 'God forgave my sin'; 'When the music fades (The heart of worship)'; 'You laid aside your majesty'; 'How I love you'; 'The price is paid'.

Notes and comments

Many churches celebrate Holy Cross Day on 14 September. You could choose to use the collect and readings for this day as part of this service or in place of the normal lectionary readings.

Holy Cross Day is associated with Helena, the mother of Emperor Constantine, who is said to have unearthed a cross in Jerusalem. On the site of this discovery the church of the Holy Sepulchre was dedicated on 14 September 335. It is a good day to think of churches in the Holy Land, or to concentrate on the centrality of the cross in the story of Jesus. *All-Age Lectionary Services Year A* does not provide a session for Holy Cross Day, but you could create a display focused around a large cross. This could be used in the **Prayer of confession** especially with the reference to the debt being paid on the cross.

Top Tips on Explaining the Cross (see page 99), will help you give a fuller explanation of the forgiveness Christ's death made possible.

Alternative online options

Visit www.lightlive.org for additional activities for children, young people and adults.

PROPER 20

READINGS: **Philippians 1:21–30; Matthew 20:1–16**
Jonah 3:10 – 4:11; Psalm 145:1–8

Bible foundations

Aim: to rejoice in the joys and challenges of following Jesus

Paul is in prison in Rome writing to the Christians in Philippi. You will recall that he had faced challenges in Philippi, with imprisonment and an earthquake, but also he had developed some very warm relationships. He has a soft spot for this church, so he is very open about his own sufferings, hopes and fears.

He wrote to them in Greek and sometimes in translation graphic language can lose its sharpness. The **Bible talk** is based on the translation of the Greek word 'analuo' in Philippians 1:23, which means 'to pull up the anchor' or 'dismantle a campsite': in other words, to set off again on a journey. It is variously translated as 'die', 'depart' or 'leave'. Paul was using the word to refer to his death, his final departure, which he foresaw as imminent. But until his death, he was going to make the most of the life that God had given him, with its joys and challenges.

The parable Jesus told in Matthew 20:1–16 offers more insight into what life in the kingdom of God is like, where values are not as one might expect. Who would have thought that workers employed for only a small portion of the day would get the same payment as those who have been working all day? But that was the agreed rate of pay. It is not a case of the length of time of service, but the terms and conditions of employment. God may accept anyone into his kingdom, however old or young, or however close to death. The Old Testament reading from Jonah also demonstrates God's values that Jonah did not find acceptable.

How refreshing that Paul embraces all that God has for him, in life and death. May his example inspire you all in this service!

Beginning the service

Choose one of the following options. Begin with an air of mystery, wondering why the tent or boat has been left in a corner of the worship area; perhaps you could ask for suggestions.

Alternatively, begin by stating the theme.

In Ingham Church in Norfolk there is a stone effigy of a knight. Often such carved knights rest with their head and feet on carved, supposedly soft, cushions, but in this case the knight lies on a bed of cobblestones. It is something of a shock and surprise. This expresses the theme of our service. The Christian life is not just an easy walk; it will bring challenges. In both the joys and the challenges, however, we can rejoice that Almighty God is with us.

Bible reading

Philippians 1:21–30 can be read as a choral reading. A version using the CEV (Year A. Proper20_1) is available from www. scriptureunion.org.uk/lightdownloads. The following introduction would help understanding:

Paul writes to the Christians who lived in Philippi. He looks at the delights as well as the difficulties of the Christian life. He considers the joys as well as the challenges of facing death as a Christian. Paul finds the choice between going on with life and dying to be with Jesus a difficult one.

Bible talk

With: a small, self-supporting tent (like the ones that young children play with indoors) or a small boat; flip chart or OHP; four envelopes labelled 'Life joy', 'Life challenge', 'Death joy' and 'Death challenge', with the words from the different verses written on separate pieces of paper and inserted in the relevant envelope

The talk is based on the fact that in Philippians 1:23 the Greek word for 'leave' (GNB) 'depart' (RSV) 'die' (CEV – and the version on the web page has been amended to take this into consideration) is used to describe a ship weighing anchor or people striking camp. Explain this. It is probably easier to focus on just one of these images. Position either a tent or a boat in part of the worship space. The key Bible verses that follow can be numbered in envelopes for children to fetch from the boat or the tent as the talk develops.

Making reference to the tent or the boat, explain that holidays spent camping or sailing can bring joys and challenges. Invite comments and personal experiences on both the joys and challenges, writing down comments for all to see on a flip chart or acetate. It would help to know beforehand whether there are camping or sailing (barge/ river boat/cruising/ yachting) experiences within the congregation. Make use of recent experiences that people may have had, even showing photos on the screen.

The joys of a tent holiday might include freedom, the open air, togetherness and new scenery. The challenges might include wind, rain, a lack of comfort, cramped conditions, unexpected wildlife (insects) and the stability (or instability!) of the tent.

Moving on to what Paul wrote from prison in Rome to the Christians in Philippi, note that he highlights the joys and challenges of life and the joys and challenges of death. He loves these Christians and is very proud of them. He wants the very best for them. He also knows that he is nearing the end of his life.

The joys and challenges of life

Ask a child to pick out the phrases from the 'Life joy' envelope and explain the different advice that Paul says about the joy of living. Do the same with the 'Life challenge' envelope.

In life

Joy	Challenge
	verse 13 in prison
verse 22 fruitful	verse 22 labour
	verse 30 conflict and suffering
verse 26 meet with Christian friends	verse 27 live a life worthy of the gospel
	verse 27 stand firm
	verse 27 one mind/ unity
	verse 29 suffer for Christ's sake

The joys and challenges of death

There comes a time when we move camp for a final time and on this occasion move through and beyond death. Talk about pulling up the tent pegs at the end of a holiday or leaving the quayside for the final time (you might want to refer to Frodo leaving by boat towards the end of Volume 3 of *The Lord of the Rings*). Ask someone to pick out the phrases from the other two envelopes as you talk about Paul's perspective on the joys and challenges of dying.

The prospect of death

Joy	Challenge
verse 21 to die is gain	
verse 23 desire to depart to be with Christ, which is 'far better', shown by Jesus' resurrection and transformed body	verse 24 leave friends behind who might need your help and encouragement

Whether in life or in death, the emphasis is on joy in verse 25 and on glorying in Jesus in verse 26.

Paul is confident that whatever we do and wherever we are, God is with us, at all times and in all circumstances. Christians came to believe that Jesus was their anchor in good times as well as difficult ones. Reflect on what that means to you or for others in the congregation.

Prayer activity

With: a selection of pictures as follows – a crown, a calendar, stars or earth, a family, a landscape scene, lightning, a selection of foods, the cross. These images (YearA. Proper20_2) are available from www. scriptureunion.org.uk/lightdownloads.

These prayers are based on Psalm 145:1–8. The congregation join in the words in bold.

(A picture of a crown on the screen.)
God our Father, we praise you because you are our God, our King.
Rule in our lives we pray.
We praise and bless your name for ever.

(A picture of a calendar.)
God our Father, every day we bless you.
Guide and protect us day by day.
We praise and bless your name for ever.
(A picture of the stars or earth.)
God our Father, you are greatly to be praised.
Your wisdom is unsearchable.
Give us a spirit of joy and praise.
We praise and bless your name for ever.
(A picture of a family.)
God our Father, we thank you for our families:
grandparents, parents, brothers and sisters.
Help us to love and appreciate them.
We praise and bless your name for ever.
(A picture of a landscape scene.)
God our Father, we thank you for your
wonderful works.
Help us to appreciate them.
We praise and bless your name for ever.
(A picture of lightning.)
God our Father, we praise you for your
power and might.
Help us to honour and revere you.
We praise and bless your name for ever.
(A picture of foods.)
God our Father, we thank you for supplying
our needs.
Help us to share your good gifts to us.
We praise and bless your name for ever.
(A picture of the cross.)
God our Father, we thank you for sending
Jesus to show us the extent of your love.
Help us to love one another.
We praise and bless your name for ever.

Prayers of intercession

These prayers are based on tracking signs.
The signs are available from scouting
handbooks or search scout tracking signs

from www.scoutbase.org.uk/library/hqdocs/
facts/pdfs/fs170058.pdf. Note that the
tracking sign 'Gone home' is on the grave of
Lord Baden Powell at Wajee Nature Park,
Nyeri, Kenya.

Four significant signs are 'This way', 'This way
over obstacle', 'Water in this direction' and
'Gone home'. These signs pick up ideas from
the reading in Philippians, especially the final
one with the idea of going home to Jesus.
Set up four groups to suggest names and
situations for prayer.

Group 1: Think about how we know we are
in the right way. Who helps us to know? The
group leader collects names of people such
as teachers, parents and church leaders.
Group 2: Think about times when obstacles
seem to have held us back. They list those
who are ill or persecuted.
Group 3: Collect ideas of people who are
short of food and water. Newspapers or
news from Tearfund or Christian Aid can be
resources.
Group 4: Think of those who are old or
dying, and those who care for them.

When the tracking sign for 'This way' is
displayed the leader of Group 1 prays:
Lord, thank you that you have given us
instructions to guide us.
Thank you that you have given us teachers
to…
Thank you that you sent Jesus to show
us the right way to live. We particularly
remember…

When the sign for 'This way over obstacle' is
displayed the leader of Group 2 prays:
Lord, we remember that life does not run

smoothly. There are things that happen unexpectedly. There are events that we did not plan. We pray for those frustrated by illness, especially…
We pray for those who feel tied down by the many demands on their life, especially…
We pray for those who are persecuted for their faith, especially…

When the sign for 'Water in this direction' is shown the leader of Group 3 prays:
Lord, we remember those who are short of water, especially…
We pray for those who only have polluted water, especially…
We bring before you those who are short of food, especially…

When the sign for 'Gone home' is displayed the leader of Group 4 prays:
Lord, we thank you that you are the God of life, the God of resurrection. We thank you that we can never escape from your presence. We remember those who are dying and we pray for those who mourn. Especially we think of…
You are the God who never leaves us – never ever leaves us. Make your home with us we pray and help us to feel at home with you.

Ending the service

Look again at the boat or the tent:

God our Father, we thank you that you are with us wherever we pitch our tent (or moor our boat). We praise you that you are with us in life, life both before and after death. Strengthen us in the challenges we face day by day as we seek to honour you. We ask this in the name of Jesus. Amen.

Helpful extras

Music and song ideas
'Father, hear the prayer we offer' (this contrasts the joy of 'green pastures' with the challenge of the 'rugged pathway' and the 'still waters' with the 'rocks'. All should be done 'courageously'. The tune reflects the ups and downs of life); 'In heavenly love abiding' (similarly this refers to 'green pastures' but also 'dark clouds'. The continuing reassurance is that 'my Saviour ... will walk with me'); 'The Lord's my shepherd (or another version of Psalm 23); 'When the road is rough and steep'; 'Be my everything' (God in my living); 'Tender Saviour' by Nick and Anita Haigh on *Celtic Roots and Rhythms 2*.

Notes and comments

This service theme is especially relevant if there are those in church today who are recently bereaved or it is around the time of the anniversary of the death of someone whom they loved. Unlike many of their peers, children and young people who are part of a Christian community are more familiar with people dying simply because they are part of an all-age congregation. Be aware of this in the planning of the service.

If there is a baptism, then a picture of the baptised person and the baptised person's family could be included in the **Prayer activity** based on Psalm 145.

Alternative online options
Visit www.lightlive.org for additional activities for children, young people and adults.

PROPER 21

READINGS: **Philippians 2:1–13; Matthew 21:23–32**
Ezekiel 18:1–4,25–32; Psalm 25:1–9

Bible foundations

**Aim: to celebrate the way Jesus came down to our level so that he can
lift us up**

Paul is tackling an issue of division within the Christian community in Philippi.
Humbly serving one another is the way to bring about unity, putting other people's
interests before your own. So he offers the example of Christ for them to follow.
Thus he makes it clear that seeking unity in an attitude of humility is extremely
costly. Paul takes an early Christian hymn and includes it in his letter. The structure
of the hymn is no more complicated than the most basic of Christian choruses and
yet it contains a profound summary of who Jesus is and what he achieved on the
cross.

In Matthew 21:23–32, Jesus is questioned about his authority by the chief priests
and Jewish leaders. They did not think he had been given authority from God (as
John the Baptist would claim) let alone that he was God himself. Jesus refuses to
answer them directly. They have no desire to put their faith in him, only to trip him
up. In the Old Testament reading, Ezekiel declares that the Lord God is not to be
doubted or questioned. Judgement will come on those who do evil but those who
seek to do good will be saved.

So Jesus comes back to the story of two sons, neither of whom do what they say
they will. It is what you do, rather than what you say, that matters in God's eyes.
Jesus was utterly consistent in what he said and what he did. He was both God and
human and he came to identify with the human condition. Ultimately this led to his
death, resurrection and glorification. There is plenty for people to engage with in
this service, recognising and celebrating Jesus as well as examining what it means to
serve others.

Beginning the service

Leave part of the worship space deliberately untidy or messy. Just as the service starts, a volunteer is asked to tidy things up. The service leader can then refer to this as an example of 'serving' others. The idea of being willing to serve can be introduced.

Bible reading

The reading of the passage from Philippians could be accompanied by a simple but expressive mime.

Verse 6	*an actor removes a crown from their head*
Verse 7	*…takes off a cloak*
Verse 8	*…kneels down to represent humility*
Verse 9	*the same actor stands to suggest exaltation*
Verse 10	*…puts on the cloak*
During verse 11	*…retakes the crown*

These six actions represent the key elements of the Christ Hymn, a balance of three stages down and then three up. With each verse the reader would need to wait for the relevant mime to be completed. The slower the presentation the more dignified it will be. A practice should ensure coordination between the reader and the one or two people involved in the mime.

There are two refinements:

• It would be appropriate for the actor to perform the actions themselves in verses 6, 7 and 8 because it emphasises voluntary submission. It is more appropriate theologically if in verses 9, 10 and 11 someone (representing God the Father)

raises the person, returns the cloak (putting it on them) and, finally, hands them the crown and places it on their head.

• If it is possible, the main actor could start in the pulpit or raised area in verse 6 and then descend to take off the cloak. In verse 11 the person could ascend into the pulpit. This physically highlights the 'coming down and lifted up' theme.

Bible talk

With: a flip chart and marker pen to highlight the key ideas from the TV programme *The Secret Millionaire*.

As the talk develops, one column on the flip-chart highlights ideas from the programme and the other column highlights how far they are paralleled in Philippians.

Secret millionaire

Remind the congregation that from time to time millionaires have lived unannounced and unrecognised among ordinary people. They have often assumed some kind of disguise and they have tried to understand the difficulties involved in leading a normal life. Sometimes they have given away money to help the people they have met.

The congregation may recall the Channel 4 programme *The Secret Millionaire*. (Check up on the latest details on the website and related Blogs.) Depending on the recentness of the last series, there would be a need for more or less background. If appropriate and technical facilities are available, play a clip from a recent programme. (Note that the programme only provides an illustration. The aim is to highlight Jesus, not to draw attention to the programme for its own sake.)

Ask for some phrases that might describe the series. Key ideas from the programme might be:
- a person of great wealth and power
- taking on a humble role, often a servant lifestyle, for example working in a care home
- understanding the difficulties and frustrations of everyday life receiving insults or ridicule when their advice is rejected
- showering a chosen few with wealth beyond their imagination or expectation
- bewilderment and astonishment and wonder from those who benefit

In the series, someone stepped down from their luxury lifestyle, and lived outside their comfort zone for a couple of weeks, to lift a few people up from a deprived, poor, lonely existence to a more dignified one. This is the point – coming down to lift others up.

Jesus – the secret millionaire?
This parallels the theme of the service. The similarities and differences can then be discussed and highlighted by recording them in two columns on the flip chart. Remind people about the reading from Paul's letter to the Philippians. What did Paul say to them about who Jesus is and what he did? What parallels can people see with the secret millionaires? Comments might include: Jesus has the Father's wealth (rather than being self-made); he took on a humble lifestyle (for about 33 years not just a week); he understood the difficulties of everyday life (with no camera crew following); he is ready to shower on us the good things that come from a love relationship with him (not money

– but gifts that matter and that cannot be bought); he is not restricted to favouring a few, nor is he limited by space. Jesus experienced terrible ridicule, humiliation and torture (not just verbal mockery).

An alternative, or additional, way into the theme (especially if you do not want to use *The Secret Millionaire*) is to ask the congregation what messy jobs they have had to do for other people – sweeping up, cleaning up after a party (some have cleaned up vomit after student parties – but use discretion), clearing drains and cleaning toilets, tidying someone else's bedroom, washing someone else's clothes, carrying someone's shopping. (A list of these could be compiled on the flip chart and used later in the **Prayer activity**.) And what does it feel like? To do these we have to surrender our comfort and we have to recognise the needs and identify with the person in order to help them.

This might be the time for a testimony or interview where a member of the congregation describes the way they care for others when the work is unpleasant. (See **Helpful extras**.) On a big scale, Jesus did this for us. He stepped down from heaven and identified with human beings in order to help us and to sort and solve our problems. This should inspire us to grateful worship and inspire us to follow Jesus' example (which is the reason why Paul included this hymn in verses 6–11: some of the Philippian Christians were not getting on with each other).

Prayer activity
Either the congregation are invited to suggest people who fill the following categories and

the answers are recorded from the front, or groups with a balance of ages (young and old) are invited to think around one task. You could use the list made during the **Bible talk**. A group leader makes a list of:

- Those who serve us with meals and food
- Those who serve us with time and conversation
- Those who serve our health needs
- Those who help us grow spiritually

The lists can be collected and then offered in prayer either by one voice or a voice from each group.

Prayers of intercession

Use the following four prayers to lead the congregation in intercession:

Father, we thank you for the example of Jesus.
He served his disciples with a meal of fish and bread.
We remember those who provide us with food, especially…
Father, we thank you for the example of Jesus.
He served others and did not turn them away. He welcomed women and men, old and young, the unwanted and the unloved.
We remember those who find time for chats, who visit the sick and lonely. We remember especially…
Father, we thank you for the example of Jesus.
He served the sick. He touched them and healed many.
We remember those who care for our health, especially…
Father, we thank you for the example of

Jesus.
He brought us wisdom from God. He taught us how to walk in God's ways.
We remember those who help us to know more of God, especially…

An alternative Prayer of meditative intercession (YearA.Proper21_1) is available from www.scriptureunion.org.uk/lightdownloads.

Ending the service

The leader could refer to a further parallel with *The Secret Millionaire*. In the programme, the millionaire themself returns to see how the people who have been gifted with money have managed their new wealth and adjusted to a different lifestyle. Some millionaires have continued to be involved. We too have been gifted by God. His involvement in our lives continues. We live out our lives under God's eye and we await the return of Jesus. How will he find us as stewards of his gifts?

Leave people with this challenge as the service comes to an end.

The Prayer of meditative intercession could be used here – see **Prayers of intercession**.

Helpful extras

Music and song ideas
Many hymns and songs are inspired by the idea of Jesus leaving heaven, becoming a human being, demonstrating service, and being given a place of honour. These include: 'You laid aside your majesty'; 'King of kings, majesty'; 'From heaven you came'; 'Jesus is the name we honour'. These could be sung or

one could be listened to if there is a soloist or a CD version to play.

If the name of Jesus is to be celebrated then 'King of Kings and Lord of Lords' could be sung as a round. 'May the mind of Christ my Saviour' could be appropriate to close the Prayer of meditative intercession. 'At the name of Jesus' or 'Jesus is the name we honour' could provide a sung **Statement of faith**.

Game

With: 10 pairs of opposite cards containing the following words: top/bottom; high/low; ascend/descend; king/servant; mountain summit/valley bottom; upper/lower; head/toe; attic/cellar; floor/ceiling; lift up/put down

To involve younger members and introduce the idea of Jesus coming down and lifting up, play 'Make the Pair'. Twenty individual cards need to be prepared, each containing one of the key words or phrases listed above.

The cards are given out randomly and each cardholder shows nearby people their card. They discuss what the opposite card would say. (This helps to include everyone.) The cardholders are then asked to find their opposite by asking around the congregation. When they have found their card pair they wait together.

Each pair is invited to say clearly the 'up' word as they look to the ceiling – then the 'down' word as they bend towards the floor.

Statement of faith

Paul quotes what was possibly a hymn used in the early church as a statement of faith.

It summarises the mission and exaltation of Jesus. One point of confession is verse 10 – that in honour of the name of Jesus all beings should bow and every tongue proclaim that Jesus Christ is Lord.

Verses 10 and 11 could be recited by the congregation. They can kneel and pause at the end of verse 10 and at the start of verse 11 stand up with hands lifted. These verses and the instruction can be put on an acetate or a PowerPoint, or they can be printed in a service sheet outline.

Alternatively, instead of a spoken statement of belief, a hymn could be sung, such as 'At the name of Jesus', which embodies the confession, or 'Jesus is the name we honour'.

Notes and comments

If there is a baptism as part of the service then the idea of going down in order to be raised up should be pointed out.

If Holy Communion is included, it might be appropriate to draw attention to how Jesus himself served others in an unexpected way during the Last Supper.

For a contemporary true life example of a secret millionaire, find out about King Abdullah II of Jordan; he went in disguise to visit a needy hospital. Use this in **Beginning the service** or **Ending the service**.

Alternative online options

Visit www.lightlive.org for additional activities for children, young people and adults.

DEDICATION FESTIVAL/CHURCH ANNIVERSARY

READINGS: **I Kings 8:22–30; Matthew 21:12–16**
Psalm 122:1–9; Hebrews 12:18–24

Bible foundations

Aim: to recognise that however important buildings are, we can worship God anywhere

King David had wanted to build a temple in Jerusalem to worship God. But because he had blood on his hands, God decreed that it was his son Solomon who was to be responsible for its design, construction and completion (I Kings 8:19). The temple was seen as an essential rallying point for the newly formed nation of Israel. (How ironic that Solomon was only the third and the last king to rule the united kingdom of Israel!) Building the temple involved a huge amount of manpower and raw materials, both of which included foreign imports. On completion, the sacred chest (the ark of the covenant) was moved inside, symbolic of the presence of God. It was quite fitting then that Solomon should lead the people in a prayer of gratitude for all that God is and all he has done.

Psalm 122 is one of the songs that the people of Israel sang when they went up to worship, possibly when they went to worship in Solomon's temple in Jerusalem and certainly when they went to the second temple, which was built after the people returned to Judah from exile in Babylon. Both this song and the words of Solomon will be used to enable the congregation to enter into worship.

The writer of the epistle to the Hebrews acknowledges that God's people need no longer worship God in a building but have the promise of the heavenly Jerusalem (Hebrews 12). In Matthew 21:12–16, Jesus himself pointed out the depths of abuse to which worship in the temple had sunk. He came to usher in a new age when people could worship God wherever they are – in a church building and anywhere else! An anniversary service provides an opportunity to celebrate God's goodness to you within your church building!

Beginning the service

If at all possible, begin the service with everyone outside the building coming in together in a procession. This could be accompanied by singing, a band, streamers and flags, dancing, fancy dress or whatever you can do to create a joyful procession. You may need to congregate in a hall beforehand rather than people sitting in church for the start of the service and then going outside for the service to begin.

As you come into the building, or as soon as people are inside, read Psalm 122 or another of the 'psalms of ascent' (Psalms 120–134), which people sang as they went up to worship in Jerusalem. It would be appropriate to give people time to greet each other before finally settling down for the service to continue.

If this is not possible, arrange for a few people to come into church joyfully, whatever that might mean for a robed choir who normally process into church!

Bible reading

The Old Testament reading from 1 Kings 8:22–30 could be read by a narrator and two voices as laid out in (YearA.Dedic_1) that is available from www.scriptureunion.org.uk/lightdownloads.

Explain that the Gospel reading, Matthew 21:12–16, shows what had happened to worship in the second temple by the time of Jesus.

Bible talk

With: pictures of a cairn in the countryside, the ark of the covenant and the inside of a grand cathedral or building (these pictures (YearA.Dedic_2) are available from www. scriptureunion.org.uk/lightdownloads)

The following script, presented by three people suitably dressed, will deliver the **Bible talk**. It is important to emphasise the words in bold so that the pictures can be displayed at those points.

1. Abraham – an old man, dressed in Middle Eastern robes, possibly carrying a stone to make an altar.
I am Abraham and I don't exactly know why God Almighty first spoke to me. I was living in the city of Haran and he appeared. He told me to leave the city, take my family and just go. We would live in tents and travel to the place he would show us. So I went. And every now and then he would appear to me again and remind me of his promise that he would make a great nation out of my descendants and he would give us a land. And every now and again I would build an altar, a pile of stones, which was a sacred place where I would worship God. **We did not worship God in a building but out in the open. We wanted to acknowledge and remember his greatness and our thankfulness to him.**

2. Moses – another old man but not so rich, possibly holding a stone tablet.
I am Moses. Around the Sinai Mountain, God met with his people, the people I was leading across the desert. We were travelling to the land that God had promised us all those

269

years ago when God spoke to Abraham. At the top of the mountain God gave me the rules to guide how we were to live our lives. After that, whenever we needed to hear from God, I would go into what we called a 'tent of meeting', which was far away from our campsite. Everyone would stand outside their tents and wait to see the thick cloud that dropped down in front of the 'tent of meeting' when God came to speak with me. But after a time, God told us to make a sacred chest, which we called the 'ark of the covenant'. In this we put the stone tablets on which God had written the rules to live by, a pot of manna (a sample of the special food that God had provided for us when we first went into the desert) and the rod of my brother, Aaron. **This sacred chest or ark was to come to symbolise the place where God was to be found. It helped us worship God. Wherever we travelled, we took it with us.** (*You could show some images of the ark of the covenant, if you think people would not be familiar with it. Images are available on the Internet or in good quality Bible reference books or on the PowerPoint available.*)

3. King Solomon – dressed as a king and holding a trowel or a piece of building equipment.
I am Solomon. By the time I became king of all Israel, God's people were settled in the land God had promised. Jerusalem was a great city and I had built a great palace. But we wanted to build a temple where we could worship God and where we could find a permanent home for the sacred chest or ark of the covenant. My father, King David, had wanted to build the temple but God said that he was not allowed to. **So at last we have**

completed this wonderful building. The sacred chest has been put in its special place. And now we can come here to worship and offer sacrifices.
I stood facing the altar with the people behind me. I wanted to say three important things to God:
• I told God what a great God he is and how he never breaks his promises.
• I told God that however grand the temple may be, nothing on earth can contain him. He's too big and great only to be found in a building. But we are privileged to belong to him. He is willing for us to worship him in this temple.
• I asked God to forgive us, if we looked towards the temple aware of our need for forgiveness.

Explain that the idea of worshipping God in a building has never been the whole picture. Look again at the three pictures displayed. These show three different places to worship. But each one is only part of the picture. In fact, even though he'd just had the temple built, King Solomon acknowledged that worshipping God in the temple was limited. And Jesus was furious at the way that people had turned the temple into a marketplace where people who sold animals and birds for sacrifice did so at a great profit. If you have used the Gospel reading refer to Matthew 21:12–13. In actual fact, however important buildings are (and talk about what you use your church building for), we can worship God anywhere. That is what the Holy Spirit has made possible.

If possible, add a personal testimony or examples about how we can worship God anywhere, for example when we see a sunset, a mountain, or a baby; some people do have special places where they met with God and going there reminds them of God's goodness (like Abraham).

Prayer activity

Go for a prayer walk around your church building. If this is not possible, create small groups of people (of all ages) who will act as representatives. Go to significant places in the building as a group and thank God for what happens in that part of the building, asking him to go on blessing you. Examples include the font or baptistry, the communion table, the cross, the entrance, the crèche, the place where the Bible is read, the place where refreshments are served or where the musicians are to be found. Remember also to thank God for all the people who are in the building for they are the real church. The bricks and mortar are only one way of understanding 'church'.

Prayer of confession

Everyone joins in the emboldened response, pausing after each initial statement.

Lord God, we have sometimes forgotten what a great God you are. We have tried to fit you into a box of our own making.
Lord God, forgive us.
Lord God, we have sometimes forgotten the promises that you have made to your people and have complained that you have not answered prayer as we would have wished.
Lord God, forgive us.
Lord God, we have sometimes worshipped you in a careless way, saying or singing things that we do not believe, or not taking you seriously.
Lord God, forgive us.
As we look to you, the one who promises to forgive all those who honestly seek forgiveness, help us to receive the forgiveness you offer.
Lord God, forgive us.
Amen.

Helpful extras

Music and song ideas
Songs could include: 'There is none like you'; 'Holy, holy, holy'; 'All heaven declares'; 'From the highest of heights to the depths of the sea'; 'For I'm building a people of power'.

Play joyful music when people come into church or some grand music to introduce the **Bible reading** from 1 Kings 8.

Game
Create a giant 12-piece jigsaw puzzle with the following words, each written on one piece: There's/ not enough/ room in/ all of heaven/ for you/ LORD God./ How could/ you possibly/ live in/ this temple/ I have/ built? (A template (YearA.Dedic_3), to be enlarged on a photocopier, is available from www.scriptureunion.org.uk/light.downloads.)

Hide these pieces around the building and ask members of the congregation to find all 12 pieces. Put the pieces together and explain that this was what Solomon said to God in 1 Kings 8:27. No one can contain God but places can go some way towards helping us to worship God together.

Ending the service

It would be good, especially if you did not begin the service outside, to process out of church to conclude the service by worshipping God in somewhere other than a building.

Whether or not you go outside, stand in a large circle where you can see each other. Sing at least one praise song and, holding hands if possible, conclude with the following words:

We are God's people in _____.
We thank you for meeting with us today in our building.
We thank you for meeting with us wherever we are.
We will go to worship and serve you wherever we are, in the name of Jesus Christ.
Amen.

Notes and comments

According to *Common Worship*, if the date is not known for a church anniversary or dedication festival, this outline could be used on the first Sunday in October. You may need to file this outline away to use at an appropriate time.

Anniversaries can be patronal festivals, the recognition of the date of the completion of a building or sometimes an acknowledgement of the anniversary when the leader of a church began their ministry. Whatever you do, ensure this is a joyful occasion, with something of a birthday flavour! This occasion gives scope for people to share their personal relevant memories and experiences, always directing any personal testimony to help people acknowledge who God is and what he has done.

You could create a giant birthday or dedication card, which everyone signs during the course of the service to show that they were present during this significant event.

If Holy Communion is part of this service, emphasise that this was a means that Jesus gave his followers to help remember the importance of his death and resurrection. Remembering is an important thing to do regularly, which is why we have anniversaries.

If a particular part of the building is being dedicated for a special purpose, incorporate that into the **Prayer activity**. Similarly, if a young child is being dedicated or someone is being dedicated for a special task of service, stress that God keeps his promises and that he will equip anyone for a new task, whether it is being a parent or being responsible for part of the church service or organisation.

Alternative online options

Visit www.lightlive.org for additional activities for children, young people and adults.

PROPER 22

READINGS: Isaiah 5:1–7; Matthew 21:33–46
Psalm 80:7–15; Philippians 3:4b–14

Bible foundations

Aim: to recognise the importance of accepting what God wants us to be

Much of Jesus' last week in Jerusalem is taken up with debates with Jewish leaders. The entry into Jerusalem and the cleansing of the temple are the backdrop for all the subsequent action. Both events were a threat to those in power. The parable of Matthew 21:33–46 is part of Jesus' reply to the challenge in verse 23, 'What is your authority?' It is highly charged and clearly pointed. In the Old Testament the vineyard is a symbol of Israel. The picture in Isaiah 5 tells its own story of a God who loves, cares for and protects his people, who obstinately go their own way. Jesus invites the 'chief priests and the elders' (verse 23) to see themselves as the successors of those who, centuries earlier, had disobeyed. They see Israel as theirs to rule and to control, assuming that, because they are leaders of God's chosen people, blessing will follow automatically. They are determined to hang on to power at all costs. They fail to see that they hold it on trust and are accountable.

By contrast, Paul gives up everything he might have valued in order to gain Christ. He will serve Jesus whatever the cost because he knows that what he will gain is far greater. Far from blessing being automatic, it comes only through the pain of identifying with the Crucified.

We face different challenges. For some, the lure of worldly power and reputation will prove too great, and the way of Jesus too hard. When we are young this is not much of an issue – although increasingly even young children face pressures to conform to the world's values. We have to make a decision whether we will run things our own way or give the control to God. This is not a once for all decision but one that is to be reviewed and renewed at different stages of life.

Beginning the service

With: some healthy looking fruit and some fruit that has gone off

Show the two different fruit. Talk about why the fruit may be bad (perhaps it has been around too long, or been infected while still on the tree). If a gardener is present, ask them to explain why fruit gets infected on a tree. It may not be too late in the year in the northern hemisphere to bring in windfall apples or a branch of a healthy apple tree.

Explain that you will be looking at the vineyard that is talked about in the Bible, which refers to God's special people. This vineyard did not produce all that God had hoped for – quite the reverse!

Bible reading

Isaiah 5:1–7 should be read in the middle of the **Bible talk** with one person reading verses 1–4 and a second person reading verses 5–7 a little later.

The Gospel reading from Matthew 21:33–46 lends itself to readers taking the following parts: a narrator, servants, Jesus and the chief priests or leaders.

Bible talk

With: a gardener who comes into church with boots, a spade and a wheelbarrow; a branch (that could be a mini-vine or tree); grapes (real, artificial or pictures of them) that can be attached to the branch

God as the gardener

God often uses the image of a gardener to describe himself – not for nothing were Adam and Eve found in the Garden of Eden. They were part of the garden God created and had a role in it. All through the Scriptures, God uses the image of vines and vineyards to talk about his people.

God had given Israel a job to do, and warned them what would happen if they failed. (*At this point, a gardener wearing boots, carrying a spade and even pushing a wheelbarrow comes into church. In the barrow is a large branch. He is asked to introduce himself as a gardener who has come to dig out some land to create a fruitful vineyard for growing grapes. He digs imaginary land, plants the branch, looks pleased with himself and then goes away.*)

The leader explains that you all have to wait for the tree to take root and grow fruit. It is October, which in the northern hemisphere is really too late for grapes to be growing. Ask people to imagine that you have waited for several years to pass. The vine has now grown strong and fruitful. The leader attaches pictures of some grapes (or artificial or real grapes) to the branch. (*The gardener comes back and is very pleased to see the branch. They take one of the pictures or some of the grapes off the branch and look pleased. They take a bite (real or imaginary) and screw up their face. These are not sweet-tasting grapes.*)

Israel as the vineyard

At this point read Isaiah 5:1–4. The image of the vineyard was used by the prophet Isaiah to warn Israel of what God would do. God had 'planted' Israel into the Promised Land. He had guided and guarded them. He had hedged them around with his protection. Isaiah says he expected 'sweet grapes' (CEV)

as the harvest. Sadly the harvest was 'bitter'. After years of investment into Israel, the harvest God was reaping did not reflect who he was, or his nature. Later the verses tell us that God had hoped for honesty and justice, but dishonesty and cries for mercy were all he found (verse 7, CEV). The Israelites had treated many people dishonestly – the poor and needy, strangers, and their neighbours.

So, God planned to deal with Israel. He had chosen them from all the nations. They were small and insignificant, but were offered the role of a lifetime – to represent God and his ways to the whole world. The picture they offered was distorted and inaccurate. By disciplining them, God hoped they would turn back to him and both become, and do, what he had intended them to be and do.

(*The gardener reappears and tears down the branch, does some imaginary digging and wheels the branch out of the church in disgust!*) Isaiah had the hard job of telling Israel that judgement was coming – and he did it through this story. Read Isaiah 5:5–7. God's people would be attacked, uprooted and eventually taken into exile to live hundreds of miles away in Babylon.

God as the landowner
By the time of Jesus, the religious authorities were still not being the people that God wanted them to be. Jesus told them what God his Father is like and how he wants all people to live. But the authorities hated Jesus and what he said because he threatened their authority and made them feel uncomfortable.

When Jesus told a story about a vineyard and a landowner, people listening would know

that Jesus was talking about God's people and God himself as the landowner. Refer back to the reading from Matthew 21:33–46. Ask if the congregation can remember the following points in the story:
• Where did the owner of the vineyard go?
• Whom did he send the first time and what happened?
• Whom did he send the second time and what happened?
• Whom did he send the third time and what happened?
• What did the chief priests and leaders say the landowner would then do?

The crowd were really involved in this story of the violent tenants. They suggested harsh judgements when the day of reckoning came. They could see how unjust it all was and how shameful was the servants' behaviour when they killed the son.

The chief priests and Pharisees certainly made the connection between themselves and the servants. They didn't like it – and immediately started plotting Jesus' death. It was just like God's people all those hundreds of years ago in the time of Isaiah.

In the same way, God invites us to welcome Jesus and all that he says about God and how God wants us to live. We can reject him and, in effect, produce sour, bad grapes, or we can welcome him, accepting how God wants us to live. Are we 'sweet' as God intends? Or, like Israel, are we 'bitter'? When we look at our own lives, what have we done that makes us feel proud? Is it fruit that makes God proud too? How is God challenging us?

In Philippians 3, the apostle Paul lists a whole

load of things that he had been proud about, in human terms, including his privileged birth and upbringing, and his skills and talents. He goes on to say that all these things are rubbish compared to knowing Jesus as his friend and saviour. Our cleverness cannot get us into heaven. Our creativity does not give us friendship with God. Our money cannot buy us security with God. Only knowing and loving God, through Jesus, can give us all those things.

Prayer activity

With: a large sheet of paper with a bare 'vine' outline; glue sticks; green or mauve grape-shaped pieces of paper; pens, pencils or felt-tip pens

In advance ask different people to lead each of these sections. Ensure everyone has some 'grapes' and something to write with and remind them that God is bothered about the world and wants to bring blessing to all of creation.

Think of situations that are 'bitter' – conflicts, illness, bereavements, unfair trade or politics. Write or draw something to symbolise those situations and stick the grape onto the vine to ask God to bring his healing, help or comfort.

Think of people whose lives are 'sweet', maybe in the way they are, or because of something they have done for others. Write their name or draw something that reminds you of them, and stick the grape on the vine to thank God for them and all the good things he has done through them.

Think about aspects of people's own lives where they are conscious that all is not as it should be. Write or draw something that they would like to change and stick the grape on the vine to show they are ready to welcome God to change them.

Prayer of confession

With: bunches of real seedless grapes, enough for everyone to have at least one

Pass around bunches of grapes and ask everyone to take one but not eat it! Ask people to think about things they have done, thought or said that were wrong and that they are sorry about. Ask them to think about things they could have done, thought or said that might have improved a situation or attitude.

When everyone has a grape or grapes and has had time to think, ask them to eat the grape(s) to show they want God to forgive them and to help them to live as God's people. Ask everyone to join in this prayer (YearA.Proper22_1) that is also available from www.scriptureunion.org.uk/light. downloads.

Loving Father,
We know you have good plans for us.
We know that we often think, say or do the wrong thing.
We are really sorry, and want to be more like you.
We know you can help us to change.
Help us to know better what you want
And help us to be brave or strong enough to do it. Amen.

Ending the service

Summarise the teaching that God wanted Israel to be sweet-tasting fruit, pleasing to him and reaching out to serve others. They failed and so were judged. God will judge us, like Israel, if we fail to welcome and respond to his invitation. However, we do not need to fear judgement, because God calls and equips us to be the people he wishes, if only we ask him.

One person could lead, or the congregation could bless each other using words like this:

Bless us, Lord, with your presence.
Bless us, Lord, with your equipping.
Bless us, Lord, with your wisdom.
Bless us, Lord, with your grace.
Lord we ask this, so we can bless others in your name.
Amen.

Helpful extras

Music and song ideas
Focus on the invitation to be a friend of God and to reflect him to others. For example: 'All I once held dear'; 'And can it be'; 'Be thou my vision'; 'Draw me close to you'; 'Give thanks to the Lord (our God and King)'; 'Hear these praises from a grateful heart'; 'Jesus be the centre'; 'There must be more than this'; 'In Christ alone'.

Statement of faith
This statement of faith (YearA.Proper22_2) is also available from www.scriptureunion.org.uk/light.downloads.

Lord God, you are loving and merciful.
Your people have rejected you.
But in Christ, you have made it possible for all people to belong to you.
You show us how to live.
You equip us to serve you.
We want to live as your people in this world.
Amen.

Notes and comments

This service outline could be adapted for a late harvest festival service since it includes material on gardeners and a harvest that did not produce all God had hoped for. Make sure that there is opportunity to thank God for harvest produce, which is the result of good farming and careful gardening; this could not be how one might describe God's people, Israel, as landowners or keepers of a vineyard.

Alternative online options
Visit www.lightlive.org for additional activities for children, young people and adults.

277

PROPER 23

READINGS: **Philippians 4:1–9; Matthew 22:1–14**
Isaiah 25:1–9; Psalm 23:1–6

Bible foundations

Aim: to explore what it means to have an attitude towards God that pleases him

In their search for power, the chief priest and elders put up fences around God's people. They assumed that they were inside and others outside. Like every good Jew in the first century they were looking forward to the coming of the kingdom, the time when God would be present with his people, ruling and protecting them in new ways. They believed that this was for them, as God's chosen people, and not for others. Jesus sees things rather differently. The kingdom is for all – those who were excluded are now welcomed, while those who believed that they were automatically insiders find that they have excluded themselves. God's choice is wider than they – and perhaps we – had imagined.

In Philippians Paul writes to one of the first congregations in Europe. Many of them would have been Gentiles, once outside but now included in the people of God. It is perhaps hardly surprising that Paul encourages them to rejoice. Once aliens, they are now citizens of heaven (Philippians 3:20). As those who belong to God they can experience relief from anxiety (4:6) – one of the great pressures of any age. But they, too, can slip into the trap of assuming that once they have entered into the new relationship with God they can relax. Not so – to serve the king is to have a new way of thinking (4:8), to live in harmony with one another (4:2) and to work hard at staying close to Jesus (4:1). Without these they will exclude themselves from the blessings of the kingdom. God is wonderfully, delightfully, amazingly inclusive. In response, we have to do our part by welcoming others and living in such a way that they can see God's values in us and be so impressed that they too want to live by them.

Beginning the service

With: food stuffs for a 'feast' that provoke reactions – marmite, olives, taramasalata, strong coffee, pork pie, cold porridge – and ones that 'everyone' loves – fruit, cheese sandwich, chocolate, crisps. (Be aware of food allergies!)

Welcome people in your usual way, and then explain that you are going to carry out an opinion poll. Invite twice as many people as you have food options to come in pairs to taste one option each. After each option has been tried by two people, invite them to say if they 'love it' or 'hate it'. Begin with one food option that is less likely to be liked and try to pick people who like most things or who are known to be fussy eaters, just to get some variety! Ask people to explain their response to the invitation to come to sample the food – how did they feel? Make sure you thank them for participating.

Explain that our reaction to a party depends on who is inviting us and whether we think we will 'fit' or like what we think will happen at the party. The same is true for God's invitation to his banquet. Our job is to prepare ourselves to be in God's company and belong to him, making sure we have the right attitude towards him.

Bible reading

Philippians 4:1–9 could be read at the end of the **Bible talk**.

Sing Psalm 23 in some form since it is probably the best known psalm but may not be so well-known for younger generations.

Read Matthew 22:1–14 with the following movement around the church; the reading (YearA.Proper23_1) is also available from www.scriptureunion.org.uk/lightdownloads. People of all ages can be involved but it will need practising! This needs to be read just before the **Bible talk**.

> Once again Jesus used stories to teach the people:
> The kingdom of heaven is like what happened when a king gave a wedding banquet for his son. (*The 'king' stands at the front with his arm around his 'son'.*)
> The king sent some servants to tell the invited guests to come to the banquet, but the guests refused. (*The king sends more than one 'servant' down the aisle to try to drag people to the front but they refuse.*)
> He sent other servants to say to the guests, "The banquet is ready! My cattle and prize calves have all been prepared. Everything is ready. Come to the banquet!" (*Other servants are sent down the aisle with no better success than previously.*)
> But the guests did not pay any attention. Some of them left for their farms, and some went to their places of business. (*These potential guests run to the back of the church.*)
> Others grabbed the servants, then beat them up and killed them. (*A bit of play-fighting.*)
> This made the king so furious that he sent an army to kill those murderers and burn down their city. (*More people are sent down the aisle, marching this time as an army would.*)
> Then he said to the servants, "It is time for the wedding banquet, and the invited guests don't deserve to come. Go out to the street corners and tell everyone you meet to come to the banquet." They

went out into the streets and brought in everyone they could find, good and bad alike. And the banquet room was filled with guests. (*Servants are sent to the sides of the church to bring people to the king at the front.*)
When the king went in to meet the guests, he found that one of them wasn't wearing the right kind of clothes for the wedding. (*The king stops before one 'guest', who is wearing dirty boots and clothes – dirty clothes are inappropriate for any special occasion whereas what some in the congregation might see as inappropriate styles of clothing might be acceptable with other groups!*)
The king asked, "Friend, why didn't you wear proper clothes for the wedding?" But the guest had no excuse. So the king gave orders for that person to be tied hand and foot and to be thrown outside into the dark. (*This 'guest' is tied up and led away.*)
That's where people will cry and grit their teeth in pain. Many are invited, but only a few are chosen.

Matthew 22:1–14 (CEV)

Bible talk

With: a giant party invitation

Invited to a party
Wave the invitation and act in an excited way. Ask if anyone has ever been to a great party. Welcome feedback from the congregation about how they were invited, why they were excited and what happened.

Ask if anyone has ever been to a party where they felt left out. Hear reasons why they felt excluded – no other friends there, wrong type of clothes, wrong type of music, wrong food, not in the right mood.

Explain that sometimes when we get invitations we feel obliged to accept them, although we don't want to. We can then feel awkward or out of place. Sometimes we get invitations we want to accept, because we know what to expect and we like the people or things that will be involved. At the party we will probably have a great time.

Sometimes we get invitations and we're not sure what to say – we don't know the person well, or we're not sure what will happen, or we don't know if we'll enjoy what is going to happen. God has said in Isaiah 25 and Psalm 23 that he is going to lay on a banquet. In the story Jesus told in Matthew 22, he shocked people with what he said about the banquet. Refer back to the Bible reading.

Invited to God's party
God's people automatically expected to be invited, but Jesus said these were the very people who were so distracted by their everyday lives that they ignored the invitation. When pressed, they reacted with rudeness and violence. Jesus warned that they would get the punishment they deserved from the king.

So, those who came to the banquet were any people whom the king's servants could round up – rich, poor, loved, unloved, good, bad, Jew, Gentile, men, women and children. And yet, although they were all called, they did not all get chosen. There was one person who was incorrectly dressed, who was unprepared, who had the wrong values and who had come with the wrong attitude – he ended up being thrown out. It cannot have been just what he was wearing that meant he was thrown out, for the poor and unloved would not have been splendidly dressed.

Accepting the invitation

Here is a warning – although God has invited us to the banquet, we need to respond in the right and appropriate way. We do this by taking on God's values, thinking the way he does, and acting as Jesus did (or would do in our place). Paul helps us to think about that in Philippians 4:1–9. If you have not done so already, read this passage and then summarise as follows:

- He reminds the Philippians to be faithful.
- He urges them to work for unity and agreement.
- He encourages them to rejoice in what God is doing.
- He outlines the attitude they should have towards each other.
- He suggests how they can keep their minds focused on God by concentrating on wholesome things.

Explore what this means for children – such as being kind towards others in their class, remembering to thank God every day for who he is and what he has done, filling their thoughts with what pleases God. This is not a list of things that 'good' children do to please their parents, but just an expression of the attitudes that anyone will hold who belongs to God and is at his party.

Prayers of intercession

Ask three or four people from all backgrounds and ages to prepare this in advance, 'personalising' the general prayers with topical events and incidents. Each should use the following introductory lines in turn:

Father, we want to thank you for…
Lord, we want to ask you…
Healer, we want to bring to you…
Conclude each prayer with the following, which could be projected or printed on the service sheet:
We ask you, our King, to answer our prayer.
We ask you in the name of Jesus your Son.

Prayer of confession

This uses the idea that 'repentance' means 'turning away'. Explain that repentance is a 'turning away' from something. Invite those who are able, and willing, to stand. Lead a prayer of confession using the following words and actions:

(Invite the congregation to think of specific attitudes they want to change; then encourage them to turn slowly in a circle on the spot to symbolise their sorrow.)
Loving Father, we thank you that you forgive us when we repent.
We come to you now to admit that our attitudes are not always right.
(Invite the congregation to think of specific things – gossip, sarcasm, swearing, answering back – that they want to change; encourage them to turn around again.)
We come to you now to admit that our words are not always helpful.
(Invite the congregation to think of real situations where they have let down God, others or themselves, and where they would like God to intervene; then turn around for a third time.)
We come to you now to admit that we don't always do what you would do.

Conclude with:

Hear us as we pray, Lord, and bring us freedom from our past. Help us to live in the future in your strength and might. Amen.

Helpful extras

Music and song ideas

Appropriate songs might include: 'Change my heart, O God'; 'There must be more than this'; 'O worship the King, all glorious above'; 'God is love, his the care'; 'Jesus, all for Jesus'.

There are many modern and not so modern versions of Psalm 23: 'The Lord's my shepherd, I'll not want' and 'The king of love, my shepherd is' (maybe to the ancient Irish melody, St Columba).

A suitable concluding blessing would be to play 'One thing I have asked of the Lord', which is based on the last verse of Psalm 23, on the album *Celtic Daily Prayer* produced by the Northumbria Community – see www. northumbriacommunity.org.for more details.

Statement of faith

This statement of faith (YearA.Proper23_2) is also available from www.scriptureunion.org. uk/lightdownloads.
We believe that God loves everyone.
We believe that Jesus died for everyone.
We believe that God invites everyone to his banquet.
We believe that he is working to prepare us for his banquet.
We believe that one day we will share the eternal banquet with him. Amen.

Ending the service

With: the foods from **Beginning the service**

Remind everyone that we all have different tastes and prefer different types of food, friends and parties. Show some of the 'love' and 'hate' foods. However, when God invites us to his banquet, he also invites us to change and become more like him. This means that when we get to the banquet, we will fit in – we will enjoy the food, the people and the party! What is even more amazing is that God asks us to invite all our friends, family and neighbours to come too. No one is a gatecrasher at God's party!

Bless the congregation before they go, either with a prayer from your regular liturgy, or from Numbers 6:24–26, or with words as follows:
Lord, thank you for your invitation.
Bless us with open minds to think your thoughts.
Bless us with open hearts to receive your love.
Bless us with open hands to show your love to others. Amen.

Notes and comments

Some people may be unable or unwilling to stand and turn around in the **Prayer of confession**, so offer an alternative symbolic action. This might be slowly to encircle their head or body with an open right hand, or to move one hand in a circle shape against the palm of the other, or on their lap.

Alternative online options

Visit www.lightlive.org for additional activities for children, young people and adults.

PROPER 24

_16/10?_

READINGS: I Thessalonians 1:1–10; Matthew 22:15–22
Isaiah 45:1–7; Psalm 96:1–9 [10–13]

Bible foundations

Aim: to understand that serving God is the most important thing even if it makes us unpopular

To follow Jesus is to be completely transformed. Paul reminds the Thessalonians that they had turned from one way of living to another – old objects of worship and devotion had gone (verse 9) to be replaced by a single-minded service of God motivated by faith, love and hope (verse 3). Their role model was Paul, who had modelled himself on Jesus. The Thessalonian Christians in turn became models for others.

The debate over taxes in Matthew 22:15–22 illustrates this transformation. Here is a politically charged situation. The alliance of the Pharisees, opposed to the incursions of Rome and concerned for spiritual purity and the Herodians, who colluded with Rome and compromised their religious principles, is an unlikely one, but it is no doubt deliberate. For different reasons both parties opposed Jesus and united to discredit him. For Jesus to argue for paying would arouse the anger of the Pharisees and damage his standing with the people. To argue for not paying would anger the Herodians and possibly lead to Roman action. The payment of the tax was greatly resented and in AD 6 a revolt over it had been put down with considerable force. Palestine was in continual ferment with those most opposed to Roman rule, and the Zealot groups, constantly stirring up activity. (There was at least one Zealot among the twelve disciples.)

Jesus avoids neat spiritual answers. He does not take the Zealot line to refuse to pay nor does he take the Roman line. The Emperor was increasingly being viewed as divine, so the coins would have born an inscription to this effect. To follow Jesus is to have a different set of attitudes. The Christian has ultimate responsibility to God, but is also required to live as a responsible citizen. This may involve cutting across normal standards of behaviour. Following Jesus brings some hard challenges.

Beginning the service

With: items distributed around the room, each labelled with the leader's name

Announce that you have lost some possessions. Ask everyone to look around to see if they can find anything with your name on to bring to the front. Show your name on each item to prove it's yours and express great gratitude to the 'finders'. Then explain that the service is exploring the idea of giving back to God what is his.

Bible reading

Matthew 22:15–22 can be read by four voices: the narrator, Jesus and two followers of the Pharisees. The followers should divide between them their words to Jesus.

As 1 Thessalonians 1:1–10 is read, ask people to listen out for all the good things Paul says about these Christians.

Bible talk

With: an assistant to play Mr Hugh Mann; gloves; a hat; a large paper speech bubble with lots of words scribbled on it; a football scarf or badge of loyalty; plus two questions on a screen or on a long strip of paper

Label each of Hugh's props with the phrase 'Belongs to God'. Hugh does not speak but performs exaggerated actions. A copy of the **Bible talk** with additional stage directions (YearA.Proper24_1) is available from www.scriptureunion.org.uk/lightdownloads. The following questions need to be seen either on a screen or on a long strip of paper: What belongs to God and what doesn't belong to

him? How does anyone give themselves back to God?

Introduce Mr Hugh Mann and explain that he has a question about today's Gospel reading. He heard Jesus say we should give back to God what belongs to God, and wants to know what belongs to God and what doesn't. (*Show the first question.*)

If you used the **Beginning the service** activity, point out that everyone knew to whom the lost property belonged because it had a name in it. Refer to Matthew 22 to check that everyone has followed the story and explain that people listening to Jesus would have known that the coin belonged to the Emperor Caesar because it had his picture on it. Everything in creation belongs to God because he made it and he keeps it going. That includes human beings. There is no picture of God on us but, when he created humans, he made us with some of his features such as the abilities to love, to create, to get to know people and to relate to God. Thus, we bear God's image. So, we belong to God and should give ourselves back to him.

Hugh has another question. How does he give himself back to God? (*Show the second question.*) Although it's pretty easy to give back lost property, or a coin, to someone you can see, it's harder to give ourselves back to God, whom we can't actually see. Explain that God wants us to give our whole lives back to him and that includes our actions, our words, our thoughts and our loyalty.

Actions

(*Give Hugh the pair of labelled gloves to put on.*)

Explain that Hugh does a lot of actions, such as eating food, using the computer, texting his friends, trying to find things he's lost, buying things, housework and watching television. All these activities could be given to God if he did them in such a way as to please God. The Pharisees tried hard to keep all God's laws but in their heart they were not living the way that Jesus said God wanted them to. If we do our best at whatever we do, and behave in the way Jesus would behave if he were at school, work, home, playing or resting, we are giving our actions back to God.

Words

(*Give Hugh the large speech bubble to hold over his mouth.*) Hugh says lots of things every day. He talks to his friends, his mum, his work mates, and through his online social networks. The Pharisees, who disliked what Jesus said and did, frequently tried to trick Jesus by what they said. When they said that they knew Jesus was honest and taught the truth, it was not what they really thought or believed. They used words to twist the truth. Our words can praise God and express God's love for people. If we say truthful, encouraging and respectful things, we are giving our words to him.

Thoughts

(*Give Hugh the labelled hat.*) Hugh thinks about lots of things every day, such as how to solve a problem, what to spend his money on, what he wants to be when he grows up, and how his mate is annoying him. He also has lots of not so nice thoughts, just like we all do. In Jesus' conversation with the Pharisees, it was clear that he knew their evil thoughts! We cannot hide from God what we are thinking. Last week in Philippians 4,

Paul urged the Christians in Philippi to fill their minds with what is pure and kind and of God. If we think about good things, and are thankful, we are giving our minds back to God.

Loyalty

Focus on Hugh's football scarf. Why does anyone wear a football scarf or wear a badge or logo of someone they admire? The Pharisees wanted to test where Jesus' loyalty lay – did he support God or the Emperor? Jesus was not going to be trapped into saying where his choice lay. It was important to be a good citizen! But ultimately, in his death he showed where his loyalty lay. Occasionally we need to give our loyalty to God, choosing to serve him rather than anyone else.

Make a link between Hugh and the people in the Thessalonian church, seeking to serve God in their actions, words, thoughts and loyalty.

Prayer activity

With: background music playing (see **Music and song ideas**); pictures of familiar individuals or groups displayed on the walls; copies of the prayer below, with the appropriate name inserted, placed next to each picture. (The prayer (YearA.Proper24_2) is also available from www.scriptureunion.org.uk/lightdownloads.)

This prayer activity uses 1 Thessalonians 1:1–10 to inspire prayer for believers (known to the congregation) who serve God in demanding situations. Include anyone who is serious about living out their faith to make a difference for God. If there is a special event coming, use this as a focus for prayer.

Father God, thank you for…
Be kind and bless them with your peace.
Help them when they are suffering.
Use them to spread your message everywhere.
In Jesus' name, Amen.

Invite everyone to move to different pictures around the room and use the printed prayer to pray. They can pray alone, as a group, silently or out loud. Take a picture to the less mobile.

Conclude by joining together to pray the Thessalonian prayer above for your whole church, replacing 'them' with 'us'.

Prayer of confession

With: a copy of the prayer below (Year A. Proper24_3) also available from www. scriptureunion.org.uk/lightdownloads

This prayer flows from the **Bible talk**. When the leader speaks, people point at an appropriate part of the body: 'actions' hands, 'words' mouth, 'thoughts' head, 'loyalty' heart. When people respond with the emboldened words, they hold up their hands as though offering a gift.

Heavenly Father, we have done things that have been selfish and uncaring. (*Pause*)
We are really sorry and offer our actions back to you.
We have said things that have been mean and careless. (*Pause*)
We are really sorry and offer our words back to you.
We have thought things that have been hateful and greedy. (*Pause*)

We are really sorry and offer our thoughts back to you.
We have not always given our wholehearted loyalty to you. (*Pause*)
We are really sorry and offer our loyalty back to you.
Thank you that you gave your Son, Jesus, so that we can be forgiven.
We offer our lives back to you. Amen.

Ending the service

With: one pipe cleaner for each person (be careful of any sharp ends); a large gift-wrapped box placed open at the front

Ask everyone to make the shape of the first letter of their name; then invite them to place their letter into the gift box during the final song, as a symbolic gesture of giving their whole life to God. (Some people might not be ready to make this commitment.)

Once the song is finished, close the box and lift it up as though offering a gift back to God. The whole congregation can say the following words of Paul from Ephesians 3:20,21 (TNIV). These words (Year A. Proper24_4) are also available from www. scriptureunion.org.uk/lightdownloads.

> Now to him who is able to do immeasurably more than all we ask or imagine, according to his power that is at work within us, to him be glory in the church and in Christ Jesus throughout all generations, for ever and ever! Amen.
> Ephesians 3:20,21 (TNIV)

Helpful extras

Music and song ideas

During the **Game** and **Prayer activity**, play recorded or live music. A repetitive and upbeat rhythm on the drums, piano or guitar would be a good accompaniment to the actions during the **Game**.

Songs and hymns might include: 'I will offer up my life in spirit and truth'; 'All of me, Jesus, you have all of me'; 'When I survey the wondrous cross'; 'Lord, you put a tongue in my mouth'; 'I reach up high, I touch the ground'; 'Father, let me dedicate (be glorified)'; 'In my life, Lord, be glorified' (ask for alternative words instead of 'life' and then include them – such as 'school', 'family', 'job', 'retirement'); 'Eyes fixed on Jesus' (*Bitesize Bible Songs* CD (SU), a Learn and remember verse based on Hebrews 12:1.

Game

With: people working in pairs; music playing (see **Music and song ideas**)

It's sometimes hard to know how to serve God and give him all of our life. Refer to 1 Thessalonians 1:1–10 in which Paul praises the people in Thessalonica for following the example of Jesus and other believers. This game provides an opportunity to follow someone else's example. It will help to first demonstrate the task with a volunteer.

Everyone should turn to face a partner – one is the leader and the other the follower. The follower copies everything the leader does, like a reflection in the mirror. The leader silently does a series of actions and facial expressions (see **Notes and comments** for suggestions). Initially the moves are

slow and simple becoming increasingly complicated. Do this for 60 seconds and then swap over.

It can be hard to follow someone's example, especially when things get complicated or you've been doing it for a while. However, following Jesus' example or the example of other believers is a good way of learning how to serve God.

Notes and comments

In the **Bible talk** a puppet could play the role of Mr Hugh Mann.

Examples of moves to do during the **Game** include: slowly waving a hand, nodding a head, reaching up with two hands, bending to the side. Gradually make the actions harder to follow by using more parts of the body simultaneously and moving faster, for example bending the knees while swinging the arms, or rubbing the stomach while patting the head. As an alternative to working in pairs during the game, the whole church could imitate the one leader, who will need to use larger, dramatic actions.

At **Ending the service**, the pipe cleaner letter could be placed in the collection plate. If you have an altar or cross in the church, consider placing the box in front of it. If Holy Communion is included with people walking to receive the elements, the letters could be brought to the front.

Alternative online options

Visit www.lightlive.org for additional activities for children, young people and adults.

PROPER 25 (BIBLE SUNDAY)

READINGS: **Psalm 1:1–6; Matthew 22:34–46**
Leviticus 19:1,2,15–18; 1 Thessalonians 2:1–8

Bible foundations

Aim: to see how God's Word (the Bible) affects the sort of people that we are

The writer of Psalm 1 and Jesus speak with one voice; they both want us to understand that the way we live should be shaped by what God says in the Bible. For the writer of the psalm, God's law is a source of joy and stability – and that is good news in a world that is short on joy and where there is so much to make our lives uncertain. As we take on board what God has said, we find that we have a firm base because of our relationship with him. 'Fruit' suggests that our lives will bring pleasure to God as we worship him and draw others to praise God as they see what he is doing in us. Those who base their lives on what God says will make a difference.

Jesus confirms it. The most important commandment in the Old Testament is to love God. If we take that to heart and put him first in all that we do, we will find that we grow closer to him and more like him. This has practical consequences. We cannot claim to love God unless we love others too (1 John 4:20). Loving God and caring for those around us go hand in hand. We are to put their interests on the same level as our own. If, every time we were considering how to treat others, we stopped to ask how we would want to be treated, the outcome might be very different.

If we want the Bible to shape our lives, we shall follow the example of the psalmist – spending time reading, thinking about and responding to what God has said. As we do this with the help of the Spirit we shall find that our lives take the shape that God wants.

Beginning the service

As today's theme is the Bible, explain that you are going to start the service with 'The Bible in 50 words'. This should be read thoughtfully by someone, or by several people, who are dramatic readers.
(Read column 1 first, followed by column 2 and then column 3.)

God made	People walked	Love talked
Adam bit	Sea divided	Anger crucified
Noah arked	Tablets guided	Hope died
Abraham split	Promise landed	Love rose
Jacob fooled	Saul freaked	Spirit flamed
Joseph ruled	David peeked	Word spread
Bush talked	Prophets warned	God remained
Moses balked	Jesus born	
Pharaoh plagued	God walked	

(by Rev Dana Livesay, Wanganui, New Zealand. Source: *Top of the Morning Book of Incredibly Short Stories*, selected by Brian Edwards, 1997, Tandem Press, Auckland, New Zealand, p41. The copyright source is unknown.)

Bible reading

On Bible Sunday it would be appropriate to include as much actual reading of the Bible as possible. If you are going to read all the set readings, make sure they are read well and explain why you are having so much reading of Scripture. The set readings are all examples of different types of Bible literature: Leviticus 19:1, 2 and 15–18 (laws and guidance for living), Matthew 22:34–46

(a story about a conversation that Jesus had, when he used the Old Testament) and 1 Thessalonians 2:1–8 (a letter that Paul wrote). The reading of other passages is also suggested in this outline and Psalm 1 is included in the **Bible talk**.

Bible talk

With: a flip chart and pen or a projector; a selection of books of different types; a preparation (see below) of Psalm 1 (YearA.Proper25_1) available from www.scriptureunion.org.uk/lightdownloads

Characteristics of the Bible

Write on a flip chart, or, using a projector, show the following and ask people to guess what it's all about:

3,566,480	L_____
783,137	W_____
31,101	V_____
1,189	C_____
66	B_____

Explain that we are talking about the Bible and that the numbers are the letters, words, verses, chapters and books it contains. Note that these figures relate to the Bible in English (not Hebrew, Aramaic or Greek) and come from the King James Version of the Bible.

Show two more numbers:

Over 1,500	Y_____
Around 40	A_____

The Bible was written over a period of over 1,500 years by around 40 different authors. All this makes the Bible a very unusual book.

Either, arrange beforehand for a number of different people to hold up a book that they have read and briefly describe it. Make sure each person brings a book of a different type: for example, romantic novel, crime mystery, biography, reference book, 'self help' book, information book, picture book, cookery book. Or, show your own selection of different books, commenting on what type of book each is and what it contains. In either case, make sure you include children's books.

Ask people to get into groups of mixed ages to list as many different kinds of writing that they can find in the Bible. When they have had time to do this, groups can call out their answers and record them in some way. The list might include: history, biography, adventure, love story, prophecy, songs, poems, letters.

Blessed by God and Sneerers at God
Show Psalm 1 on a screen using the PowerPoint. Alternatively, it should be read well. It could be accompanied by a background recording, or live selection, of relevant sound effects, such as harsh laughter, joyful giggling, bubbling streams and birds as signs of fruitfulness, wind, a gong for judgement day, and harsh and joyful laughter in competition.

A group of people, able to improvise drama, could work on Psalm 1 and present their ideas, which might include walking, standing and sitting in bad company, meditating on God's word, fruitful trees and useless chaff caught in the wind.

Draw attention to the two sorts of people in the psalm – those who are happy and blessed by God and those who sneer at God and will be judged by him. Invite two children to come to the front. Give one a basket of fruit or an evergreen branch (in the southern hemisphere branches could be coming into leaf) and to the other a scarf, gloves and hat to wrap around them because they are caught in the cold wind. Explain that these two people represent the 'Blessed by God' and the 'Sneerers at God'. Ask for words that describe what these two are like, such as – 'refuse evil advice, don't follow people who do wrong, love God, fruitful, happy, whole, full of life, protected, safe, love God's Word' and 'evil, sneer at God, lead people astray, judged, not going to last, not belong to God, ruined'.

Explain that what makes a difference is that the 'Blessed by God' engage with God's law or his Word, that is, the Bible. Give a Bible to the person holding the fruit or tree. The person wrapped up turns his back on everyone.

Invite one or two people of different ages (warned in advance) to briefly share a personal testimony of how the Bible has helped them to know God, either in a tricky situation or in everyday living. This could include knowing God's promise to be with them at all times, help in making decisions, using the words of the Bible to praise God, or leading someone to discover and then believe in Jesus. Encourage them to use phrases such as the Bible gives them life, and makes them fruitful. You could ask them about their favourite character in the Bible, or favourite story or Bible verse. They need to use language and concepts that are accessible to all ages.

Conclude by speaking briefly about the importance of reading the Bible regularly and using it to help us pray. Point out the Bible reading guide samples you've provided (see **Notes and comments**).

Prayer activity

With: a series of references written or printed on cards or slips of paper relating to prayers from the Psalms; Bibles for each group; pens and paper

Divide into groups of mixed ages. Give each group a slip of paper or card and ask someone to read out their group's prayer from their psalm. Each group decides what sort of prayer it is and then, as a group, writes their own version of the prayer applying it to their own situation. Involve everyone, even the youngest. Pray together, as one person in each group reads the prayer the group has written.

Prayers could include: Psalm 4:1 (a cry for protection); Psalm 9:1,2 (a shout of praise and gratitude); Psalm 10:1,2 (a cry of anger); Psalm 13:1 (a cry of loneliness); Psalm 19:1–4 (a cry of wonder); Psalm 23:1–3 (a shout of thankfulness); Psalm 51:1,2 (a cry of repentance); Psalm 67:1,2 (a request).

Prayer of confession

Use Psalm 51 as a prayer of confession. Alternate verses could be read antiphonally. The leader could read verses 9–11 at the end, replacing the words in the singular with 'our' and 'us'. Explain that King David is thought to have written this psalm after he realised his sin in committing adultery and arranging the death of Bathsheba's husband.

Ending the service

Ask the congregation to read aloud Psalm 19:7–14 as an affirmation of their commitment to reading the Bible and doing what it says. Follow this with the hymn 'O Jesus, I have promised', which is a prayer for God's help.

Helpful extras

Music and song ideas

If you know it (and has it ever been written in any hymnbook?) sing the children's song that sets all the books of the Bible to a simple tune. Someone who went to Sunday School 40 years ago is likely to remember it!

Put together a selection of songs that are composed of words directly from the Scriptures, such as 'Thy word is a lamp unto my feet' (Amy Grant and Michael W Smith).

Traditional hymns include: 'Break thou the bread of life'; 'Lord, thy word abideth'; 'Tell me the stories of Jesus'; 'Tell me the old, old story'; 'God has given us a book full of stories'; 'O Jesus, I have promised'; 'Jesus loves me, this I know, for the Bible tells me so'. (A church magazine article from Vancouver www3.telus.net/st_simons/cr9311.htm has some interesting stories about this hymn which you might like to tell if you use it.) The hymn 'Lord for the years' links thanks for God's Word with prayer for our country and our world. This song was specially commissioned for Scripture Union's centenary in 1967. Newer songs include: 'Create in me a clean heart, O God' and 'Everything' from *Bitesize Bible Songs* CD (SU), a Learn and remember verse for 2 Timothy 3:16.

Game

Divide the congregation into teams containing a mix of ages and challenge them with the 'Trees and the Bible' quiz (YearA. Proper25_2) that is available from www.scriptureunion.org.uk/lightdownloads. If anyone wants proof of the answers, a reference is supplied!

Notes and comments

Proper 25 is often the Sunday when Bible Sunday is celebrated, but other Sundays are also used. We can celebrate the Bible at any time of year.

Bible Sunday is a good time to launch or conclude a practical project that relates to Bible use or the distribution of the Bible. Bible Society, Wycliffe Bible Translators or your local Gideons could give ideas about what might be undertaken. Alternatively, perhaps you could create your own project, for example to present Bibles to a local school. Scripture Union has produced *Into the Bible*, a resource that contains 101 Bible extracts in a format suitable for use in the primary classroom along with a CD containing 24 lesson outlines; it is tied into the national RE guidelines, and provides everything a teacher needs for RE lessons on the Bible. For more details visit: www.scriptureunion.org.uk/intothebible.

Arrange to have available a selection of Bible reading guides and other helpful books. Your local Christian bookshop should be able to provide you with samplers or back issues of notes.

Alternative online options

Visit www.lightlive.org for additional activities for children, young people and adults.

Scripture Union has something for everyone!
Bible resources for all the family

ALL SAINTS' DAY

READINGS: **1 John 3:1–3; Matthew 5:1–12**
Psalm 34:1–10; Revelation 7:9–17

Bible foundations

Aim: to celebrate the way in which God is working to make his saints more like Jesus

We live in a world that emphasises the value of the individual, but in which many feel isolated and long for a sense of community. One of the places that they should find it is in the church. We are not intended to exist as detached individuals but as part of the wider people of God, the children of God as described in 1 John. We are one with those who have been true to God through the ages and throughout the world today. Being true to God means living as he wants. Jesus lays down some pretty tough standards in the Sermon on the Mount; however, today's verses are not demands but a description of how things are in the kingdom of God. God is with those who suffer and struggle, who have nothing by the standards of this age, who are oppressed and persecuted, and whose contribution to society is devalued. These beatitudes overturn the standards of the world, but that is the way it is with God.

The people of God are often not those who would gain recognition in this world. The world does not know them (1 John 3:1), but they are the people God loves and who, when they respond to the love of God, can look forward to the blessings of the kingdom that are experienced by the saints described in Revelation 7 and that we begin to enjoy now. We are being changed so that we will display the character of Jesus (1 John 3:3). As we celebrate being part of the wider people of God and recognise what God is doing, we can rejoice that he takes the poor and weak things of the world to show his power and glory through them. It is important for all ages to understand that God has a different set of values from the world.

Beginning the service

With: a set of 'Russian dolls' made from three cardboard boxes – the largest one has a sad face, the middle-sized box a blank face and the smallest one a happy face; a marker pen

As you welcome people to the service, explain that this is All Saints' Day (or the Sunday close to All Saints' Day) and you will be looking at the way God is working to make us more like Jesus. A 'saint' is someone in whom God is at work. It's not someone who has already arrived or who is extremely holy or devout. It's someone who is allowing God to transform them into the image and likeness of Christ. At the same time, we remember with gratitude those who have served God over the centuries.

Show the congregation your set of boxes as 'Russian dolls'. Slowly unpack them so that they can see how each box contains a smaller and slightly different box.

The largest box represents us as we would be if God were not working in us – proud and selfish. It's sad. Invite people to think of other characteristics that might show us when we are at our worst. Write or stick some of these suggestions on the outside of the box. Explain that, without Jesus shaping our lives, we are all broken and this box represents the worst that we can be.

The smallest box represents what we could be if we were truly perfected, which none of us is yet. This box is how we would be if we were truly the way God wanted us to be. Invite people to suggest characteristics that we might have if we were one hundred

per cent saints. Write some of these on the outside of the box.

The middle-sized box represents the place many of us find ourselves: somewhere in between. We are not perfect, but God is at work in us to help us become more like Jesus. We should rejoice and be glad that he is with us, even though we also need to admit our mistakes and keep on asking for his help. Invite people to think how God helps us to grow and be changed. Write these on the outside of the box.

Bible reading

Read the beatitudes in Matthew 5:1–12 antiphonally, either as two halves of the congregation or using two readers.

1 John 3:1–3 could be used as a **Statement of faith** (YearA.AllSaints_2) and it is available from www.scriptureunion.org. uk/lightdownloads. We can be certain of our identity as God's people – saints.

Bible talk

With: an empty wallet; a handkerchief; a photo of someone having their feet washed; a globe; a bottle containing just a little water; a box of plasters; crisp white tissue paper or cloth; a rainbow scarf or ribbon; chains or a cross; large jigsaw pieces with the following words and phrases written on them: 'poor in spirit'; 'mourn'; 'meek'; 'hunger and thirst for righteousness'; 'merciful'; 'pure in heart'; 'peacemakers' and 'persecuted' (TNIV)

If you are using the CEV, you will find the following phrases: 'depend only on God'; 'those who grieve'; 'the humble'; 'those who want to obey God'; 'the merciful'; 'those with pure hearts'; 'those who make peace'; 'those who are treated badly for doing right'. The TNIV wording of the phrases in the jigsaw (YearA.AllSaints_1) is available from www. scriptureunion.org.uk/lightdownloads.

Place the various items and jigsaw pieces around the room before the service.

Remind the congregation that you are thinking about the way God wants to transform us to make us more like Jesus. This is how the saints through the ages have known God at work in their lives. This part of Jesus' Sermon on the Mount, which is known as the beatitudes, contains a list of characteristics of those people who are being changed by God.

Explain that the symbols around the room represent these characteristics along with jigsaw pieces that name them. Invite people to hunt down the various symbols and try to connect them with a jigsaw piece. It may be better to ask a group of younger people to do the searching.

Once they have found all the symbols, ask people to say which one goes with which jigsaw piece. There are no right answers and there may be some wonderful alternative ideas, but these are some of the things you could say as the items are brought forward:

An empty wallet
If we have no money and no hope of getting any, we are literally poor. We know we need help to survive because there are essential things we can't afford to buy. If we are 'spiritually poor' we know that deep down

we need God's help; we are completely dependent upon him. Admitting that we are 'poor' in relation to God is the first step everyone must take before they can ask for God's help and also receive it.

A handkerchief
If we admit that we have worries, we can be encouraged and supported. If we see others in need or evil things happening in the world, then we can grieve or weep with those in need and take the action that God would want us to take, in his name. Blessed are those who mourn or grieve, for they will be comforted.

A globe or a photo of someone having their feet washed
Jesus showed what it meant to be meek and humble. This is so different from the priorities of the world around us – but then, what Jesus was saying here was really upside-down stuff! In God's kingdom, the first will be last, and the last first. Those who are humble and put others first are those to whom God can give responsibility.

A bottle containing just a little water
People who 'hunger and thirst for righteousness' or 'who want to obey God more than to eat or drink' are those who want everything to be done God's way. They're not satisfied with compromise or half measures – they want the bottle to be full. They won't rest until God's kingdom has been established. Their hunger and desire to obey God drives them to work, pray and campaign for change.

A box of plasters
Those who are willing to bandage the

wounds of others or are merciful will find that there are many people who are hurting whom they can help. Those who show mercy to others will inevitably receive mercy themselves.

Crisp white tissue paper or cloth
Purity is all to do with utter cleanliness and holiness – breathtakingly so. Those people whose very being (including their hearts) has been fixed on knowing, and indeed seeing, God and being like him, will have pure hearts. They will know God more and more and in that sense, they will see him.

A rainbow
The rainbow is a classic symbol of peace. It also represents diversity. Those who are willing to make peace with one another can be woven together in the wide variety of peoples who make up the family of God. Only those who make peace can truly know what it means to be one of God's children.

Chains or a cross
Jesus was willing to take up the cross and the suffering it represents, and yet his death made new life possible. In the same way, we need to be willing to face persecution or opposition, because the way we respond to persecution can often have a real impact on other people. The church grew in the face of terrible persecution and continues to grow in places where being a Christian is dangerous. We may not have to die for our faith in Jesus, but we can still show love to those who laugh at or mock our beliefs.

Put the pieces of jigsaw together with the symbols. God's people do not have everything sorted out, although we do fit together as a jigsaw. We are not perfect; rather we are people who are aware of our need for God, who are able to ask for help, who acknowledge our limitations, who are dissatisfied with the way things are, who are willing to reach out to others, and who are willing to face the challenges that come when we follow Jesus. We share all this with the saints who have gone before us. Nothing has changed!

Prayer of confession
With: the 'Russian dolls' introduced in **Beginning the service**

Remind people of the 'Russian dolls'. The largest of these represents all that can be bad about us. Read out some of the suggestions that the congregation made. Are these things true about us – even occasionally? Ask God for forgiveness.

Then read out some of the ideas that you wrote on the smallest box. Thank God that he is at work in us, turning us into the kind of people he wants us to be.

Ending the service
The second half of 1 John 3:2, which was the third set of statements in the **Statement of faith**, would make a good verse to Learn and remember to conclude this service.

Part 1: We do know that when Christ returns,
Part 2: We will be like him, because we will see him as he truly is.

Show the verse on a screen or whiteboard. Point out that right now we know that

Christ will return. But notice also that in the future we will be like him and we will see him as he truly is. We are being made holy, like Jesus, and that is a lifelong process. Half the congregation can read the first part, with the other half reading the second part. Repeat this several times and then conclude with a closing prayer.

Helpful extras

Music and song ideas
Relevant songs include: 'All I once held dear'; 'All over the world the Spirit is moving'; 'Amazing grace'; 'As the deer pants for the water'; 'Create in me a clean heart, O God'; 'For I'm building a people of power'; 'Give thanks with a grateful heart'; 'I am a new creation'; 'Jesus, you are changing me'; 'Love divine, all loves excelling'.

Statement of faith
The following declaration based on 1 John 3:1–3 (YearA.AllSaints_2) allows the congregation to declare publicly some of the certainties that make us saints, those who belong to God. It is available from www.scriptureunion.org.uk/lightdownloads.

Think how much the Father loves us.

> **He loves us so much that he lets us be called his children.**
> My dear friends, we are already God's children,

> **Though what we will be hasn't yet been seen.**
> We do know that when Christ returns,
> **We will be like him, because we will see him as he truly is.**
> We are indeed God's children, now and into eternity.
> **This hope makes us keep ourselves holy, just as Christ is holy.**
> based on 1 John 3:1–3

Notes and comments

The *Revised Common Lectionary and Common Worship* suggest that the readings for All Saints' Day could be used on Sundays between 30 October and 5 November. So this outline could be used on the fourth Sunday in Advent.

A simplified version of the **Bible talk** could be done without the jigsaw pieces or the searching. Present the symbols and explain them. This may be preferable for a less active congregation. Alternatively, you could develop the 'Russian dolls' idea from **Beginning the service**.

Alternative online options
Visit www.lightlive.org for additional activities for children, young people and adults.

FOURTH SUNDAY BEFORE ADVENT

READINGS: **Micah 3:5–12; I Thessalonians 2:9–13**
Psalm 43:1–5; Matthew 24:1–14

Bible foundations

Aim: to value the importance of discerning when God speaks, for he always speaks the truth

The *Revised Common Lectionary* diverges from *Common Worship* for the Gospel and reads Matthew 23:1–12, which describes Jesus in debate with the Pharisees. The common theme is that the kingdom of God, by which we mean the active rule of God in the world, must be our top priority. Matthew 24 is a difficult chapter, looking forward both to the fall of Jerusalem and to the return of Jesus with the two themes interwoven throughout. The broad sweep, however, is clear – the present age is coming to an end and a new age is coming; indeed it is already here. We live in a strange time when the kingdom is here, but we still wait for its full expression.

This means that many of the values of this age, which is on the way out anyway, are not ours. Many of the things that this age prizes – Herod's temple built specifically to impress the people, or the human wisdom and power of leaders like the Pharisees who confront Jesus in chapter 23 – have to be seen in the light of God's rule and God's standards. People will tell us that these things matter – they are the false prophets of Matthew 24:11 and Micah 3 who express that all is well when it is not. In time they, and the things they value, will be swept away. The buildings erected today, which are monuments to human achievement, such as prestigious business buildings, shopping malls, sports stadia, are passing. They may serve a purpose in this age, but have no permanent value. We can survive the pressures of this age – the wars, the famines, the tyrants – because we know that they too are passing and that our eyes are fixed on something better. As Paul reminds us in Thessalonians, God is at work in us and will help us see things from the perspective of God's rule.

Beginning the service

Welcome everyone by saying that you are genuinely delighted to see them. Give out the notices and news of the congregation. Then say again how pleased you are to see people. Ask how the musicians are and if they are ready and again say how genuinely pleased you are to see people.

By this time (unless you usually go over the top in your welcome) people will begin to think that there is something odd going on. Acknowledge that you are making a point. But you are pleased to see people and apart from the fact that you have gone on and on about it, how do people know that what you say is true? Expect comments such as: people know that you care for those in the congregation, you are not in the habit of telling lies, and they know that you enjoy worshipping with others. This service is about being genuinely truthful, and exploring how we know that what God says through other people is true and can be trusted.

Bible reading

Micah 3:5–12 is central to this outline. It should be read in a dramatic way with someone dressed up as a prophet, declaring God's words to his people. You could even create a small group of false prophets who turn away from God's words.

The verses from 1 Thessalonians 2:9–13 give an example of how Paul spoke the truth and was a reliable, trustworthy person. Read this with a kind, warm voice that inspires people to trust the writer.

Bible talk

With: two hats labelled 'Truth' and 'Lies' – inside each are two long strips of paper with the appropriate statements below written on them:

We can tell if someone tells the truth if they are trustworthy people.
We can tell if someone tells the truth if what they say ties in with the rest of Bible.
We can tell if someone is telling lies if they are not people to be trusted.
We can tell if someone is telling lies if what they say does not come true.

False prophets

The prophet Micah had a message from God for God's people, both those who lived in the northern kingdom of Israel and did not worship in Jerusalem (their capital was Samaria) and those who lived in the southern kingdom of Judah with the capital of Jerusalem. He was very aware that false prophets may sound very convincing, but what they say was not of God: it was not true and would not come to pass. Micah told these false prophets exactly what would happen to them (3:6,7).

If you have not done so already, play the 'True' or 'False' **Game** to introduce this **Bible talk**. Talk about how you know who is or is not telling the truth, bringing out that time will often tell if someone has told the truth but also that people with a record of telling the truth, those who can be trusted, are more reliable.

The false prophets at the time of Micah encouraged people to give them food and promised that anyone who gave them food and looked after them would be kept safe (and life was a bit dangerous in those days). The larger the gift the more favourable the prophecy! But they declared that people who refused to give them food would really suffer.

Give some parallel examples such as:
- Mrs X in church gives you, the leader, a box of chocolates and you say that tomorrow she will win a new car! She is really impressed until midnight tomorrow when the new car fails to turn up at the door. How disappointed she is!
- Mr Y gives you three boxes of chocolates, which result in the promise of two new cars. But neither car appears at his door.
- You ask Z, a boy in church, to give you a box of chocolates but he doesn't have any money and does not want to give you any chocolates. So you tell him that tomorrow he will be covered in spots! He will be really scared.

In all cases you are telling lies, and lies affect other people.

True prophets

Micah was different in what he had to say, different from the lies of the prophets. People may not have liked what he said but it was true because it came from God. He said that because the leaders of God's people were treating people badly and telling untruths and being greedy God would judge them. The people should have been scared because Micah had a reputation for telling the truth and what he said did indeed happen.

Jesus told the truth too, always. He said in Matthew 24:11 that many false prophets would interpret signs for the end of the world. Jesus said not to believe these people. Evil would happen all around but those who keep on doing right would be saved. When the good news about the kingdom of God has been preached all over the world, then and only then will the end come! We don't know when that will be. People need just to get on with living as God wants and not bothering about false prophets.

You may be using Matthew 23:1–12 as the Gospel reading. This criticises the Pharisees and teachers of the law for how they behave, for the burdens they place upon others, and because they say one thing and do another. It is all to do with being inconsistent and inauthentic. The truth of what we say matters! (Adapt the material accordingly.)

Discerning the truth

When someone whom we trust and who behaves in a way that puts God first tells us something about God, we need to listen very carefully. Paul, when writing to the Thessalonians in 1 Thessalonians 2:9–13, talked about how much he had set them a good example and had not wanted to burden them. He had spoken God's word. He had not made things up. We need, above all, to check that what anyone is saying to us ties in with what we know about God and his word in the Bible. We also need to check if the person speaking has a good reputation for telling the truth.

Show the two hats labelled 'Truth' and 'Lies'. How do we know when someone is speaking the truth?

Put the 'Truth' hat on a volunteer and then

ask them to pull out the following two statements:

We can tell if someone tells the truth if they are trustworthy people.

We can tell if someone tells the truth if what they say ties in with the rest of Bible.

Put the 'Lies' hat on another volunteer and then ask them to pull out the following:

We can tell if someone is telling lies if they are not people to be trusted.

We can tell if someone is telling lies if what they say does not come true, even though we may not live to see the effects of their lie.

We can be sure that God can be trusted and that he always speaks the truth. God is trustworthy. Everything he says happens. The Bible is full of times when God kept his promises.

Prayer of confession

There are times when everyone has told lies or has told untruths to manipulate people and lead them to do or say the wrong thing. So it is appropriate to hold a time of confession, asking God's forgiveness.

As a response between each of the following sentences, everyone says: **Lord, have mercy; Christ, have mercy; Lord, have mercy upon us.**

We have failed to speak your words of truth or have told half truths. (*Response*)
We have deliberately told lies to protect ourselves or get others into trouble. (*Response*)
We have not listened to you, Lord, or have not paid attention to all you say to us. (*Response*)

We have not tried to work out if someone is telling the truth or not. (*Response*)
Thank you that you always speak the truth and you want the best for us.
Amen.

Prayers of intercession

Leaders and those who speak with authority have a special responsibility to ensure that they always speak the truth and live authentic lives, consistent with what they say. It is important to pray for them.

Show pictures of leaders of the country, your local council, significant people in the community, like head teachers or football coaches, and church leaders, including children's and youth workers. You could call church leaders to the front to pray for them. Talk about how difficult it is sometimes to speak the truth.

Ending the service

With: a ball of wool for each group

The writer of Psalms 42 and 43 (today's psalm) wrote at a time of need. He wrote in verses 3 and 5: 'Send your light and your truth to guide me … I trust you.'

Divide people into groups of around ten, standing in a circle. Give one person in each group a ball of wool. This person throws the ball across the circle to another person, still holding tight to the end of the wool, and says an agreed version of the words from Psalm 43 such as:

… (name), may God send his truth and light to guide you.

The receiver responds by saying: I trust in God.

The receiver, not letting go of their piece of wool, throws the wool to someone else in the circle and repeats the above. At the end, everyone will have received a blessing and a 'blessing web' will have been made.

Helpful extras

Music and song ideas

Songs might include: 'Thy word is a lamp unto my feet'; 'Lord, thy word abideth'; 'Faithful one, so unchanging'; 'Give thanks to the Lord, our God and King'; 'May the mind of Christ my Saviour'.

Game

Ask people to vote on whether the following statements are 'True' or 'False'. At the end, ask how they knew which was true or not. Amend these statements as appropriate and check, using an Internet search, whether or not they are true.

The sun set yesterday in Edinburgh at 4.33 in the afternoon. (*Check if this is true or not.*)
It is the British Prime Minister's birthday next week. (*Check if this is true or not.*)
There are XX days to go to Christmas. (*Complete as appropriate.*)
The XX football team drew yesterday. (*Complete as appropriate.*)
You have to put a cake in the oven to bake it. (*True but does a microwave count as an oven and, if you are very clever, you can bake a cake over an open fire!*)
XX's favourite colour is blue. (*Complete as appropriate.*)

It is going to snow tomorrow. (*Don't know.*)
XX School is in XX Road. (*Complete as appropriate.*)

You can work out whether some statements are true or not; some just feel right or wrong; you just don't know about some statements, you may have to guess, or you may have to wait and see. For really serious matters though (which none of these statements is) it would depend on whether the person telling you could be trusted. If they had told lies before, you would be less inclined to believe them. If they had a record of telling the truth, then you would be more likely to believe them.

Notes and comments

The alternate Lectionary Gospel readings, Matthew 24:1–14 or Matthew 23:1–12 (not central to this outline) will affect this service.

Younger children are familiar with the implications of telling lies and being trustworthy. If there is time, talk with them before the service so that you include their perceptions. It matters that God does not tell lies and does not deceive, which is what the false prophets did. It affects a child's view of God.

Alternative online options

Visit www.lightlive.org for additional activities for children, young people and adults.

THIRD SUNDAY BEFORE ADVENT/
REMEMBRANCE SUNDAY

READINGS: I Thessalonians 4:13–18; Matthew 25:1–13
Amos 5:18–24; Psalm 70:1–5

Bible foundations

Aim: to prepare ourselves for the return of Jesus

Christians have their focus on the future. It is like waiting for an important visitor
to arrive. We have tidied the house, cleared away the rubbish and prepared the
meal. There is a sense of excitement as we wait. The Thessalonians felt just such a
sense of excitement. They were expecting Jesus to come back at any moment. But
they were puzzled, wondering about what would happen to those who had already
died. Paul reassures them that they too will have a place in God's future, but at the
same time encourages them to keep looking for Jesus. The best part of 2,000 years
later, we put the emphasis on Christians who die being with God, and find it hard to
remember that Jesus might come back at any moment.

The bridesmaids (TNIV, 'virgins') with no oil had forgotten that the bridegroom
might be delayed and were not prepared. Being ready starts with longing for Jesus
to come back, because that will be a time when all wrongs are put right. The writer
of Psalm 70 is troubled by the injustice around him and longs for God to act. We
may have the same feelings as we look around us. But being ready, as Amos 5 makes
clear, means more than spending lots of time in church services; it is about the
way that we live. We should encourage one another to look forward and to live
as Jesus wants (I Thessalonians 4:18). If this is difficult for adults – and it is – it is
even harder for children, especially younger ones for whom the concept of time
has limited meaning. But they can appreciate the idea of getting ready for significant
events, even when we are not entirely sure when they are happening.

Beginning the service

The theme of the service is being ready for when Jesus comes again. To stimulate ideas, the service leader needs to appear to be unprepared, while still maintaining the necessary reverence! Perhaps start the service a minute or two late, looking flustered. You have forgotten to set your alarm, so you've got on odd socks because you were in a rush. You have lost your glasses. As you start the service you discover that you've lost your notes and have to go to look for them. Then your microphone isn't on… After a suitable pause, explain what the theme of the service is, and begin properly!

You may begin the service with an Act of Remembrance, which is inevitably associated with the past. We need to prepare for the future, aware of what has happened in the past. This service is all about preparing for a significant event in the future.

Bible reading

For both of the set readings above, the CEV is very clear. The reading from 1 Thessalonians 4:13–18 should come first.

The story in Matthew lends itself to a dramatic reading, particularly if you have ten females willing to be either wise or silly! The narrator reads most of the Bible reading except where the girls, the messenger or the groom speak. It is largely done in mime with the narrator reading straight from the Bible. When the girls, messenger and groom do speak they use the words from Matthew. With plenty of rehearsal time there is lots of scope for miming and it would be especially effective if the foolish and wise girls can say their words in chorus!

Bible talk

With: the four pictures suggested below from (YearA.3Sunb4Advent_1) available from www.scriptureunion.org.uk/lightdownloads; four people to read the script, three of whom could wear a label A, B and C

Be prepared

Show four pictures of a guard dog, an athlete on the blocks about to start a race, a doctor, a Boy Scout. Ask what these pictures have in common. Give clues: the guard dog has to be on the alert (he wouldn't be much use asleep); the athlete needs to be 'set', ready to go as soon as the starter pistol sounds; doctors are sometimes 'on call' (ready to go if someone needs them urgently); the Boy Scouts' motto is 'Be prepared'.

In Matthew 25:1–13, Jesus was talking about being prepared – prepared for when he comes back. But the only One who knows when that moment will be, is God the Father. Jesus didn't know, and we certainly don't know. But he didn't want his disciples to be found napping when he returned, like the five foolish girls in the story. And he doesn't want us to be napping either. He wants us to be ready.

Imagine that you are away on holiday. What do you need to do beforehand? (Suggestions might include: cancel the papers and the milk, pack a suitcase, buy travel tickets, buy sun cream.) You could hide 'sun' or 'suitcase' shaped cards with those suggestions on around the room for children to find. When we go on holiday we prepare, often weeks or months in advance. The same is true for weddings, parties and even Christmas – how many of you have already started on Christmas preparations?

Be prepared even if you don't know the date

It's easier to prepare for something when we know exactly when it is due. We know Christmas is on 25 December. Hopefully, anyone getting married knows the date of the wedding some weeks in advance. But what about the time when Jesus comes back? We don't know when that will be. But he still urges us to be prepared, to be on the alert like the guard dog.

Jesus' return is like being told that an important test or exam is coming up. But your teacher hasn't told you when, just that some time you'll have a test. What do you do?

Here are three people to tell us what they'd do.

Person A: Hi. I'm Person A. I've just been told there's a test coming up. Now I reckon that it won't be tomorrow because there's too much to learn for tomorrow. And I don't expect it'll be next week because my teacher's away all week. Maybe it will be next month. Yup. It'll be next month. I'll prepare for next month then…

Person B: Hi. I'm Person B. I've just been told there's a test coming up. It'll probably be tomorrow or Tuesday. I'd better get on with revising. Then, at least if it's later in the week I won't look a complete idiot!

Person C: Hi. I'm Person C. I've made a list of all the things I have to learn. I'm going to do a bit each day. I've made a chart to help me so that I can tick off a bit each day.

SIX MONTHS LATER

Teacher: Today is the day for the test.

Person A: Test? What test? You never told us yesterday about a test!

Person B: A test? Bother. I did learn something a while ago, but I can't remember what, though!

Person C: Good thing I had that chart. I hope the test isn't too hard!

Be prepared for Jesus' return

One day Jesus will come back. We should be prepared and alert, like the doctor, the guard dog, the athlete or the scout. Jesus does not want us to be taken by surprise and frightened. Although the actual event of his return sounds frightening (trumpet blasts, shouts of command), Christians have nothing to fear. Otherwise why would Paul tell us to encourage each other about it? He wanted the Christians in Thessalonica to be sure of what they believed, and to know that it is all about having faith in Jesus. Jesus' return will be a wonderful event for us because then we will be with the Lord forever.

Be prepared for the wonderful event of Jesus' return.

Be prepared by trusting Jesus and by living godly lives.

Be prepared to be with the Lord forever.

Prayer activity

With: paper (possibly the back of a copy of one of the four pictures from the **Bible talk,** which could be used in **Ending the service**); pens or pencils

This activity can be done individually, in family groups or perhaps in regular small groups.

Leader: Lord Jesus, thank you that you are coming back to take us to be with you. Help us to be ready, looking forward to your coming.

Leader asks: If Jesus were to come back today, what would you want to thank him for? Write, draw, or think about what you might do, think or say. (*Give enough time for thought or brief discussion.*)

Leader asks: If Jesus came back today, who would he want you to be helping? Think about, write or draw your ideas.

Leader asks: If Jesus came back today, for what or for whom would he want you to be praying? It may be someone whom you pray for regularly or it may be a particular place in the world. On this Remembrance Sunday, we remember places in our world where there is conflict, unhappiness or unrest. (*Make or ask for suggestions.*) It may be a person or place you've seen in the news. Write, draw or think about whom or for what God wants you to pray.

Leader: Lord Jesus, we don't know when you are going to come back, so please help us to be ready by listening to you and doing your work in the world. Amen.

Encourage everyone to use their paper during the week as a reminder.

Prayer of confession

This is a responsive prayer reflecting the foolish and wise maidens so it would be best if it was used after the **Bible reading**. Introduce the two responses before each part.

Begin the prayer with a hand open as if to receive from God. Fold one finger (and your thumb) down for each of the five parts of the prayer. The response for the first part of the prayer is: **Father, forgive us for times when we are foolish.**

Father God, we don't always live in a way that pleases you.
(*Response*)
Sometimes the words we say hurt others and make them sad.
(*Response*)
Sometimes we don't think about what we do; we are selfish and we don't help others.
(*Response*)
Father God, sometimes the way we behave stops others from seeing you.
(*Response*)
Father God, sometimes we think that going our way is better than going yours.
(*Response*)

During the next five responses open one finger at a time so that you finish with an open hand again. The response for the second part is: **Lord, help us to be wise.**

When we aren't sure what to do...
(*Response*)
When we don't know what would be the right thing to say...
(*Response*)
When we don't feel like praying and reading your Word...
(*Response*)
When we would rather do nothing than help others...
(*Response*)
When we are tempted to waste our time doing things that don't honour you...
(*Response*)

This would be a good point at which to say the Lord's Prayer together, with open hands.

Ending the service

If possible, give everyone a small version of one of the pictures from the **Bible talk**. (This may have been used in the **Prayer activity**.) Encourage people to keep it in a prominent place to remind them about being prepared for Jesus' return.

Use this blessing:

May the blessing of God the Father, who sent his Son to be our Saviour,
The blessing of the Son, who will come back to take us to be with him,
And the blessing of the Holy Spirit, who helps us prepare for Jesus' return,
Be with us all, now and forever.
Amen.

As this is Remembrance Sunday you may end with an Act of Remembrance.

Helpful extras

Music and song ideas
Some relevant songs include: 'Soon and very soon we are going to see the King'; 'One more step along the world I go'; 'There's a sound on the wind like a victory song'; 'Reign in me'; 'Give me oil in my lamp'.

Hymns or songs suitable for this theme and Remembrance Sunday include: 'O Lord, the clouds are gathering'; 'O God, our help in ages past'.

Statement of faith
There is a simple creed that reflects the reading from I Thessalonians 4 and uses words directly from the CEV (YearA.3Sunb4Advent_2) that is available from www.scriptureunion.org.uk/ lightdownloads. It can be read antiphonally or as a whole congregation. Put some simple actions to it or, if children have practised, they could do the actions for all to see.

If you haven't done the final action of the **Statement of faith** all together, now would be a good time to share the Peace, but, instead of the traditional words of greeting, encourage one another by saying:

'We'll be with the Lord forever!'

Notes and comments

Instead of using the **Prayer activity** it might be more appropriate to use an Act of Remembrance (particularly if your service is timed at around 11.00am), or to include more prayers for places in the world where there is conflict. You could use the response:

Into the dark and painful places of your world
Come, Lord Jesus.

Alternative online options
Visit www.lightlive.org for additional activities for children, young people and adults.

SECOND SUNDAY BEFORE ADVENT

READINGS: **Psalm 90:1–8,12; Matthew 25:14–30**
Zephaniah 1:7,12–18; 1 Thessalonians 5:1–11

Bible foundations

Aim: to think about how we might live for Jesus while we wait for him to come back

We saw last Sunday how hard it can be to live in the light of Jesus' return. Paul knew that. A common thread runs through the readings from Thessalonians – 'encourage one another'. There is a constant need to be on our guard, making sure that, as we wait for Jesus to come back, we live as he wants. Paul expects us to avoid certain types of behaviour, wanting God's people to stand out from others. It is a tragedy when Christians think and behave in much the same way as anyone else. If we live to please God, rather than just doing what we want, we are less likely to find ourselves surprised when Jesus comes back.

The Parable of the 'Talents' is easy enough at one level, but is often misunderstood. It is too easy with the older translations to read the word 'talent' and take it to apply to natural skills or abilities. But the meaning is far wider than this. The key word is 'faithful' (Matthew 25:21, 23). God has given us a whole range of gifts, abilities, opportunities, resources, time and much else. The important thing is what we do with them. If we are faithful with all that God has given us, and use all these things for him rather than for ourselves, we will receive his thanks and congratulations. Do nothing with what he has given us and we will find ourselves with nothing.

Part of getting it right will be to pray with the psalmist (Psalm 90:12) that we might have a right view of our lives and have the wisdom to live as God wants. Different age groups will relate to this in different ways, but each will have something that they can use wisely and so they can begin to understand the difference between using things just for ourselves and using them for others and for God.

Beginning the service

With: three volunteers; flags and rattles to wave

Ask for three volunteers to do something not too difficult, such as spinning a plastic plate on the tip of a pencil, whistling a song, or playing a tune on an instrument. Choose your activities and volunteers carefully; make sure nothing will be too hard for them (see reference to this in the **Bible talk**). Whatever they do, and however well they do it, make sure you say, 'Well done' several times, quite clearly. This reflects the 'Well done' the master says to his faithful servants in the parable in Matthew 25.

Recall last week's theme – Be prepared. Then explain that today everyone needs to be prepared to hear the words 'Well done'. Encourage everyone to listen out for when they hear 'Well done' spoken in the service (and it will come in quite a lot!). Issue placards or flags to wave every time it's said, or get everyone to cheer.

Bible reading

The **Statement of faith** (YearA.2Sunb4Advent_1) is based on Psalm 90:1–8,12 (CEV) and is available from www.scriptureunion.org.uk/lightdownloads. Read it together, or antiphonally, two verses at a time. Finish with verse 12 all together.

Matthew 25:14–30 could be read by several voices: a narrator, a master and the three servants. Introduce the reading with the following words: Jesus told his followers another story…

If you are encouraging people to listen out for the words 'Well done' (see **Beginning the service**), don't use the CEV as it doesn't use those words, but the Good News or TNIV do. Remind the person reading the part of the 'master' that there will be cheers and flag waving whenever he says 'Well done'.

Bible talk

With: three people primed to take part as volunteers in a short sketch (at the start, the three remain in their seats to look as if you chose them at random); three parcels (two of which contain something useful, for example a trowel or a kettle); flags and rattles to wave when people hear 'Well done'. – see **Beginning the service**

Receiving a gift
Begin by saying: It looks like prize day here, or Christmas has come early. Hand the first parcel to your nominated volunteer, who says, opening their parcel excitedly, 'Wow, it's a… Hey, I know what I can do with this. I can use it to…' (They will need to have thought about what to say beforehand – a mixture of being creative, practical and amusing!)

The second person is handed their parcel and, on opening it, says something similar to the first person.

You offer a parcel to the third person, who replies, without even opening it, 'No thank you, I don't want it.'

You reply, 'But I've chosen it for you especially. I know you'll be able to make good use of it!' The third person says, 'I said, I don't want it. I'll just mess up and you'll be cross.

There's no point in my opening it. Keep it.'

Ask everybody how they think you feel after that! It's the same with God. If we reject the gifts he's given us, it makes him sad, because he knows what each of us can do. He knows exactly the right gifts to give us to help us to do his work. So not using those gifts is like handing the present back unopened.

Making use of a gift
In the reading from Matthew 25, the first man was given five talents because the master knew he would cope with five. He went off and used his five well and made five more. What did the master say when he came back? 'Well done, good and faithful servant.' (*There might be cheering or flag waving at this point!*)

The same happened to the man who had two talents. He made two more. And what did the master say to him? 'Well done, good and faithful servant.' (*Cheering again!*)

The master expected the man who was given one talent to use his one talent too. Refer back to **Beginning the service** where people tried to do things. Explain that you actually knew they probably could do it – you didn't ask a three-year-old to read from *War and Peace* or something impossible for them. You chose appropriately.

The master knew what the servant could do. God gives us gifts that are right for us. God doesn't call us to do things we can't do. He doesn't expect someone who's no good at maths to be an accountant!

This man could have done something with his talent. Was he lazy? Did he think his gift wasn't good enough? Was he jealous of what the others had? He said it was because he was afraid of his master, in which case he should have had the sense to do something with the talent so that his master wouldn't be angry! By avoiding doing the wrong thing with the talent he didn't do anything right either. If we don't use God's gifts, nothing good will come. But good did come from the others. What happened? Check that people can remember.

The man who had been given five talents made five more. He used his many gifts and talents to do what his master wanted. No wonder the master said, 'Well done.' (*If people are cheering try to say 'Well done' as many times as you can at this point!*) The man with two talents made two more. And the master said, 'Well done' to him, too. We don't know how they doubled their talents, but they were commended for it.

Using our gifts while we wait for Jesus
While we wait for Jesus to return, how can we live for him? We can say to God, 'I think I'm good at… how can I use it for you?' Maybe ask a friend to help you with this too. (*Make some suggestions.*) Maybe you're already using your gifts well for God. In which case, be on the lookout for he might trust you with more. But whatever you're like, do something good with what God has given. And be faithful with your gifts. Don't give up if things go wrong.

The master didn't get angry because the man tried and failed, but because he didn't try at all. As you wait for Jesus to return, use your gifts well and faithfully. When Jesus comes back, you want him to say to you, 'Well done, good and faithful servant.' It feels great when people say, 'Well done.' Imagine what it'll feel like to hear Jesus say it!

Prayer activity

In groups, think about the gifts that each person has. Encourage each person to see what their gifts are, rather than what they can't do! There are gifts of all sorts. Some people are very organised, some are good with children, and others clean the church well. Don't restrict ideas to what people do in church either. Their job may well be their gift. Be honest rather than 'spiritually modest', affirming each other and asking for God's help to use his gifts.

Help children to think beyond academic or sporting prowess to what else they are good at, for example being friendly, or helping at home. Ask questions such as, how can I use that gift to serve God?

If your congregation is comfortable to pray out loud, use the following prayer for the person on their left:

Thank you, God, for… (*Name.*)
Help them use their gift to serve you. (*The gift could be named.*)
If they know each other well, encourage them to use the time to help each other think about how to use their gifts.

Prayer of confession

This confession reflects the Gospel reading as well as using Psalm 90:8 as a response. The congregational response is: **And you know all of our sins, even the hidden ones.**

Heavenly Father, thank you for the gifts and talents you give us. We are sorry for the times when we don't use them to glorify you.
And you know all of our sins, even the hidden ones.
Sometimes we use our talents to hurt others, to put people down or to make ourselves feel important.
And you know all of our sins, even the hidden ones.
Sometimes we wish we didn't have the gifts you've given us and we're jealous of others.
And you know all of our sins, even the hidden ones.
Sometimes we bury our gifts because we think we know better than you.
And you know all of our sins, even the hidden ones.
Sometimes Lord, we don't do well. Instead we spoil what you have given us.
And you know all of our sins, even the hidden ones.
Sometimes, Lord, we aren't faithful to you. We follow others instead.
And you know all of our sins, even the hidden ones.
The Lord is merciful! He is kind and patient and his love never fails. He doesn't punish us as our sins deserve. As far as the east is from the west, so far has he taken our sins from us. Thank you, Lord. **Amen.**

Helpful extras

Music and song ideas
Relevant songs include: 'Jesus, take me as I am'; 'Take my life and let it be'; 'The wise may bring their learning'; 'We really want to thank you, Lord'; 'We wanna see Jesus lifted high'; 'The King is among us'.

Statement of faith

The words of Psalm 90:1–8,12 in the CEV can be used as a creed (YearA.2Sunb4Advent_1) available from www.scriptureunion.org.uk/lightdownloads. Read it together, or antiphonally (two verses at a time) or try this creative version.

Split into small groups and give each group art, craft and collage materials and two verses of the psalm: 1–2, 3–4, 5–6 and 7–8. Each group makes an artistic representation of their verses. Don't give people too long! Read the psalm together as a statement of faith, with the groups holding up their picture as their verses are read. Display the pictures afterwards. Finish by reading verse 12 all together.

Ending the service

Encourage the congregation to learn Psalm 90:12 (CEV): Teach us to use wisely all the time we have.

Learn it by saying it several times and then take away one word at a time. If you know anyone who does sign language, ask them to sign this verse so that everyone can learn actions and words. Alternatively, ask someone in advance to make up some actions for everyone to learn. Once you've learnt it, say this prayer, for which the response is the verse.

Heavenly Father, as we go out into your world
Teach us to use wisely all the time we have.
In our work, our play and our time at home
Teach us to use wisely all the time we have.
Whatever we do and wherever we go
Teach us to use wisely all the time we have.
Amen.

Challenge everyone to recite the verse and actions every day this week. You could begin the service with it next week!

Notes and comments

The 'talents' mentioned in the parable were actually large sums of money rather than actual 'gifts', but thinking about gifts and talents in our understanding of the word is not an invalid application of its meaning. So make something of the monetary collection in this service.

Alternative online options

Visit www.lightlive.org for additional activities for children, young people and adults.

SUNDAY BEFORE ADVENT

READINGS: **Ephesians 1:15–23; Matthew 25:31–46**
Ezekiel 34:11–16,20–24; Psalm 95:1–7

Bible foundations

Aim: to affirm the importance of loving others as Jesus did

Many of the kings and queens in our world do not have a great deal of real power, but are still people who command respect. Paul gives us a picture of the power and the majesty of Jesus, which is far greater than that of any human king. He is in charge of everything and everyone. He is worthy of our worship and our obedience. In Matthew 25:31–46, Jesus, still thinking of the time when he will come back, reminds us that each of us is accountable to him.

But there is something very surprising here. Where do we see the King today? Do we see him on a throne ruling in power? Well, yes, for Jesus is reigning now, but we also see him in his people who are often the weak, the lost, the powerless, the hungry and the imprisoned. The key to how we will be assessed when Jesus comes is the way in which we have treated others. By showing the sort of love that Jesus showed we demonstrate that he is our King. As King, Jesus is also Shepherd. Psalm 95 speaks of God in both ways and Ezekiel 34 of God as Shepherd. Jesus is a king who always loves and serves and protects.

Although Jesus is King now, not everyone can see this, but one day he will be universally acknowledged and recognised. We are called to make him our King now and live as he wants us to by following his example and showing love to others, especially those in need. He is present in the world now through his body, the Church (Ephesians 1:23). The challenge here is easy enough for all ages to see; the difficulty is not in seeing the point but in living by it!

Beginning the service

See if anyone can remember the phrase and actions that you finished with last Sunday. This will lead in to this week's theme: using our time wisely to love others as Jesus did.

Use Sydney Carter's hymn 'When I needed a neighbour' or 'With a prayer' to introduce the theme (see **Music and song ideas**). Ask different people or families in advance to look at one verse of the song each and to collect something that represents that verse that they can bring to the front during the singing of the hymn. They might, for instance, bring a bowl and drinking flask, a shawl or blanket, bandages, or a picture of a refugee. Encourage as much creativity as possible! As 'their' verse is being sung, each person or family brings their items to the front where they are placed to be seen by everyone. (If you are using the **Prayer activity** idea later, these groups could be responsible for one station each and could set them up during the hymn.)

Bible reading

Ephesians 1:15–23 should be read in a modern version.

Matthew 25:31–46 could be read by three people (one to be Jesus and two to be the people asking him the questions). Or ask a selection of people to walk through your worship space at the right moment saying:

'I was hungry and you fed me';
'I was thirsty and you gave me a drink', etc.

You could display the reading for all to see so that the congregation can read it to each other, one side being the righteous and the others the unrighteous(!), with one person reading the part of Jesus and the narrator.

Bible talk

With: Matthew 25:35,36 on display or Bibles for everyone to see; a flip chart and pens

This talk is designed to be interactive with people thinking together in groups about the different people mentioned in the parable in Matthew 25:31–46. Begin by talking about the many people today who need love and care. Jesus always pointed to those in society whom nobody else seemed to care for, like widows, orphans and people with skin diseases. God is always on the side of the weak and the poor. Jesus healed people whom no one else would touch. He ate with people no one else loved. He talked to people whom everyone else ignored. And he wants us to do the same: to care for people whom no one else wants to have anything to do with.

Looking at the people mentioned in the parable, we may not actually know people in prison or people who are hungry or naked. Get some ideas of what it might feel like to be like this, to help people to see those who need our love who might otherwise be overlooked. Display Matthew 25:35 and 36 on a screen or get people to look it up if you have church Bibles. Using a flip chart, or OHP acetate, make a list of people's suggestions. Ask:

- What does it feel like to be naked? You may get answers like: embarrassed, cold, etc.
- What does it feel like to be a stranger?

You may get answers like: lonely, unloved, etc.

- What does it feel like to be a prisoner? You may get answers like: desperate, confused, lonely, etc.

Using this list, ask people to think creatively of someone they know who might fit into one of those categories: for example, someone who's embarrassed because of the way they look; someone who is lonely; someone in the playground who doesn't have any friends; someone at work whom nobody talks to. Encourage everyone to think of someone, or think together as a family. Then think about how you might help that person. Is there something you can do individually, as a family, as a church?

Alternatively, do a more creative version of the above activity in small groups. Give each group one of the types of people above. Ask them to think together about how it would feel to be like that (again, give suggestions as above). Ask each group to produce a presentation about 'their' type of person. It could be a cartoon, a short sketch, a mime using words from the Bible, a song, or a collage – anything that will bring to life what it feels like to be that person. This will need careful timing. The idea is that each group presents their ideas to everyone else.

Finish by exploring how helping people and loving them, especially people who are different from us, isn't always easy, but is something that Jesus expects us to do. Loving others is part of being a Christian, part of our service to God. We may not always feel like helping others; this is one of the reasons why God sent his Holy Spirit to fill us with the love, compassion and care that Jesus had. If we ask him to give us this kind of love, he will. If people are hard to serve, remember that serving them is like serving Jesus. We need to imagine it's him whom we are helping when we help others.

Finish by singing 'From heaven you came, helpless babe'.

Prayer activity

With: five prayer stations with the necessary prayer prompts

Set up five prayer stations around your worship space reflecting the people in the parable: for instance, an empty bowl and spoon or an empty water container; a shawl or blanket; a Welcome sign; bandages or First Aid kit; a makeshift shelter or cardboard box to represent the homeless and refugees; a picture of prison bars.

Encourage people to use the prayer time to visit one or more of the stations to pray for people who are suffering from those situations, such as local people, people they've seen on the news, their local *Big Issue* seller. Put pictures or props at each station to help stimulate thought. Play quiet music in the background. A facilitator at each station could lead a group prayer, or you could put some key words in each place such as: 'Fear', 'Isolation', 'Lonely', 'Sad' and 'Cold'.

Provide simple prayers (easy enough for young children to read), such as:

Dear God, look after people who have no home.
Father God, please make sick people better.

Help me to be a friend to people who are lonely.
Dear Lord, please comfort people in prison and help their families.
Dear God, teach us to feed the hungry.

Be sensitive as to how long to let this time of prayer last.

Prayer of confession

Reading a parable like this can make people feel very inadequate! Use this confession (YearA.Sunb4Advent_1) to help people say sorry and ask for God's help rather than to make them feel even worse about themselves! The prayer is available from www.scriptureunion.org.uk/lightdownloads.

You can split the congregation into two parts or read it as leader and congregation.

Lord God, when I'm sad I like to be comforted.
Forgive me for when I ignore people who are sad.
Lord God, when I'm lonely I need a friend.
I'm sorry that sometimes I am not a good friend to lonely people.
Lord God, I have so much food. I can eat whenever I'm hungry and drink whenever I'm thirsty.
Forgive us all for failing to feed people in need.
Lord God, when I'm sick I like to be looked after.
Forgive me for times when I'm selfish and don't show people that I care.
Lord God, often I see people on the news who are desperate and sad.
Forgive me for the times when I turn off the TV or look the other way.

Lord God, forgive us for the times when it's easier to be selfish than to care for others. Fill us with the compassion and love that Jesus had, so that we are always looking for ways to help others. **Amen.**

Christ sacrificed his life's blood to set us free, which means that our sins are now forgiven. Christ did this because God was so kind to us. (Ephesians 1:7 CEV)

Ending the service

Use the words of this ancient benediction to encourage each other to serve others. It has been set to music by various people (including John Rutter) so, if you have a choir, they could sing it. Otherwise, say it all together or split it up into different parts to be said by ladies, men and children. As it's an old prayer, you may want to explain some of the language, or just let everyone absorb the words!

Go forth into the world in peace;
Be of good courage;
Hold fast to that which is good;
Render to no one evil for evil.
Strengthen the faint-hearted;
Support the weak;
Help the afflicted.
Honour all people;
Love and serve the Lord;
Rejoicing in the power of the Spirit.

Alternatively, read Ephesians 1:17–19b as a blessing.

Helpful extras

Music and song ideas
Songs that fit the theme include: 'When I needed a neighbour'; 'O God, my creator'

(Graham Kendrick); 'From heaven you came, helpless babe'; 'Lord, make us still in your presence' (Graham Kendrick); 'Brother, sister, let me serve you'; 'Beauty for brokenness'; 'With a prayer'.

Statement of faith

Ephesians 1:15−23 is a clear statement of faith. Read it all together or the leader could read each line with the congregation saying 'Amen. Come, Lord Jesus' after each line. (Explain that 'Amen' isn't just a word we say to close a prayer, but it means that we agree with what the person speaking has said.) This version (YearA.Sunb4Advent_2) is also available from www.scriptureunion.org.uk/lightdownloads. If you are not all reading this from a screen, everyone could face different ways as it is read.

(Begin by facing east, or wherever you have an empty cross on display.)
We believe that with great and mighty power God raised Jesus from the dead.
We believe that Jesus sits at the right hand of God.
We believe that Jesus rules over all beings in this world and will rule in the future world as well.
(Face each other.)
We believe that the Church is Christ's body and Jesus is its head.
We believe that God has chosen us to be his people.
(Face the doors or windows out onto 'the world'.)
We believe that God gives us his Spirit to make us wise and to help us to know God.
We believe that we should serve God and help others, as he commanded us to do. Amen.

based on Ephesians 1:15−23

Notes and comments

This parable in Matthew 25:31−46 speaks for itself. There is the challenge, too, at the end where the people who don't do good things are sent to eternal punishment! These ideas are intended to look at the positives: how we can help others close to us, without heaping guilt onto people or making them terrified that they might be sent to eternal punishment!

If you've used the **Prayer activity**, you could leave the stations up for a week or two, and if your church stays open, people could visit during the week to think or pray more deeply.

Do you have contacts with a local prison or do local churches provide support to the families of prisoners? Find out if you can send Christmas cards to any prisoners or help in some way this Christmas − this would be a real outworking of Jesus' words because it may be the only card some prisoners get.

For something completely different, ask a confident and well-known church member to come to this service in disguise! Choose as sensible a disguise as possible, but one that makes them look significantly different. See if they are welcomed, or treated differently because they are a stranger. Later in the service they could reveal their identity and talk about how it felt!

Alternative online options

Visit www.lightlive.org for additional activities for children, young people and adults.

LightLive

Quality, Bible-based resources for children's, youth and all-age ministry.

Faithful to the Bible

- **Plan** and manage your children's group like never before
- **Access** a bank of activities and ideas
- **Enrich** your programme with multimedia resources
- **Search**, save and print – all from one website

Over 650 activities are added every three months – that's in addition to the archive of over 10,000!

Help children in yo[ur] church engage with t[he] Bible. This FREE resou[rce] is available now, just v[isit] **www.lightlive.o[rg]** and register your group t[oday]

Scriptu[re] un[ion]

Using the Bible to inspire chil[dren,] young people and adults to know [God]

Registered Charity No. 213422